QUESTIONS & ANSWERS:
CIVIL PROCEDURE

QUESTIONS & ANSWERS: CIVIL PROCEDURE

Multiple-Choice and Short-Answer Questions and Answers

FOURTH EDITION

WILLIAM V. DORSANEO, III
Professor of Law and
Chief Justice John and Lena Hickman
Distinguished Faculty Fellow
SMU Dedman School of Law

ELIZABETH G. THORNBURG
Richard R. Lee Endowed Professor of Law
SMU Dedman School of Law

CAROLINA ACADEMIC PRESS
Durham, North Carolina

ISBN: 978–1–6328–2858–3
eBook ISBN: 978–1–6328–2859–0

This publication is designed to provide authoritative information in regard to the subject matter covered. It is sold with the understanding that the publisher is not engaged in rendering legal, accounting, or other professional services. If legal advice or other expert assistance is required, the services of a competent professional should be sought.

Carolina Academic Press, LLC
700 Kent Street
Durham, North Carolina 27701
Telephone (919) 489-7486
Fax (919) 493-5668
www.caplaw.com

Printed in the United States of America

ABOUT THE AUTHORS

William V. Dorsaneo, III, is Professor of Law and Chief Justice John and Lena Hickman Distinguished Faculty Fellow at Dedman School of Law, Southern Methodist University. Professor Dorsaneo was a litigation specialist in Dallas after graduation from law school. He is the principal author of the 26 volume TEXAS LITIGATION GUIDE and the co-author of the five-volume TEXAS CIVIL TRIAL GUIDE, as well as three casebooks entitled CASES AND MATERIALS ON CIVIL PROCEDURE, TEXAS PRE-TRIAL LITIGATION, and TEXAS TRIAL & APPELLATE PRACTICE, and several other volumes on Texas litigation. He has written numerous articles on civil procedure. He is Board certified by the Texas Board of Legal Specialization in Civil Appellate Law and maintains an active appellate practice. He is also a board member of the Appellate Judges' Education Institute and a member of the Institute's Education Committee, a member of the Advisory Committee to the Texas Supreme Court, and Chairman of the Committee's Appellate Rules Subcommittee and a member of the American Law Institute.

Elizabeth G. Thornburg is Richard R. Lee Endowed Professor of Law at Dedman School of Law, Southern Methodist University. After clerking for a federal judge, Professor Thornburg was a commercial litigator before she began teaching at SMU. She is a member of the American Law Institute, the American Bar Association, and the State Bar of Texas. She has served on the Executive Committee and the Complex Litigation Committee of the Civil Procedure section of the Association of American Law Schools, as well as on Texas Supreme Court task forces on procedure issues. Professor Thornburg specializes in the areas of civil procedure, alternative dispute resolution, conflict of laws, and comparative civil procedure. Her publications include numerous articles on civil procedure issues, as well as co-authorship of TEXAS PRE-TRIAL LITIGATION and TEXAS TRIAL & APPELLATE PRACTICE.

Together, Professors Dorsaneo and Thornburg have taught procedure for more than 50 years.

PREFACE TO THE FOURTH EDITION

Like its predecessors, the Fourth Edition of *Questions and Answers: Civil Procedure* is a supplementary text for use primarily by first-year Civil Procedure students to obtain a clear understanding of the subjects typically covered in either a four-hour first semester Civil Procedure class or a longer Civil Procedure class extending over subsequent semesters. The Fourth Edition builds on the foundation established in the first three editions, by revising and updating the topics covered in the Third Edition and by extending coverage to all of the subjects that are covered by the Civil Procedure sections of the Multistate Bar Examination. As a result, the Fourth Edition contains the following revisions and additions.

- Revisions to the coverage of personal jurisdiction based on the Supreme Court's two 2014 decisions in *Daimler AG v. Bauman* and *Walden v. Fiore.*
- Coverage of the Supreme Court's decision in *Atlantic Marine Const. Co. Inc. v. District Court* concerning venue transfer practice and forum selection clauses.
- Additional coverage of federal question jurisdiction applying *Grable & Sons Metal Products, Inc. v. Darue* in the context of patent suits under 28 U.S.C. § 1338(a) derived from the Supreme Court's opinion in *Gunn v. Minton.*
- Coverage of proposed revisions of the rules of civil procedure, especially rules on discovery relevance, discovery and other procedures and pretrial deadlines.
- Coverage of service of process and due process notice.
- Coverage of federal common law.
- Coverage of preliminary injunctions and temporary restraining orders.
- Coverage of jury practice, including jury selection, requests for and objections to jury instructions and jury verdicts.
- Revised and expanded coverage of challenges to jury findings and verdicts, judicial findings and conclusions, and challenges to the trial judge's findings of fact and conclusions of law in bench trials.
- Coverage of default judgments and involuntary dismissals.

As updated and expanded, this edition of the Q&A book allows professors and students to easily incorporate the topics covered in the Fourth Edition in a course syllabus that will cover subjects anticipated to be covered on the Multistate Bar Examination, whether or not the questions and answers on these subjects can actually be covered during class hours. As with each of the prior editions of the Q&A book, students will benefit by using the text to clarify, reinforce, and extend their comprehension of basic civil procedure course material.

We would like to thank our students, on whom many of the questions in the prior editions have been tested for years. Special thanks must also be extended to Katya Long, Juris Doctor Candidate (2016) for her dedicated and capable assistance in finalizing the preparation of this Fourth Edition.

PROFESSOR WILLIAM V. DORSANEO, III
PROFESSOR ELIZABETH THORNBURG
Dallas, Texas
January 2015

INFORMATION FOR STUDENTS: HOW TO USE THIS BOOK

Understanding Civil Procedure can unravel the mysteries of both the Civil Procedure course itself and the procedural context that shapes the cases you read in your other first-year courses. At its most basic, Civil Procedure covers a set of quite technical rules that litigators must master in order to guide their clients and their cases through the court system. Mastery at this technical level is important, but the fun of Civil Procedure comes when you begin to understand how the rules interact, and how they can be used to achieve legitimate goals. At a deeper level, a sophisticated knowledge of Civil Procedure is the key to thoughtful analysis of the policy issues involved: who do the rules benefit, and why? Who should they benefit? Should changes be made in order to better serve the interests of justice?

This book is designed to help you understand the nature and operation of the rules that govern procedure in the federal courts in the United States. The questions range from simple identification of the rules themselves to applying the rules to complex hypothetical fact patterns. Some questions invite you to begin to think about the strategic use of the rules, and about the policy implications of the choices the rules make. The individual topics address issues one at a time, while the Final Examination allows you to test your skill at recognizing the interplay of a number of issues in simulated cases.

The book begins by walking you through the steps of a typical lawsuit: the parties' pleadings, the proper joinder of claims and parties, the discovery process, summary judgment, trial, post-trial motions, the binding effect of judgments, state law in federal court, federal common law and appellate practice. It also covers questions about where suits can be brought. Finally, the book examines a specialized question of law application: when must the federal courts apply state rather than federal law (a topic often called the *Erie* doctrine). Civil Procedure teachers and texts introduce these topics in different orders. The topics are therefore treated independently, so you can use this book in the order in which you study procedure.

Questions & Answers: Civil Procedure is designed so that you can use the questions either to reinforce and clarify material as you move through the first-year course, or to test yourself in preparation for your final examination. As you read each question, try to identify the rule or rules involved, and then apply them to the facts presented. Think about the issues raised by both the correct and incorrect answers. This should help you to answer multiple choice format questions such as those found in this book. It should also help you to understand the rules in operation, and to recognize patterns of issues that will help you in answering questions on essay exams.

We hope that this book will help you enjoy Civil Procedure. Once the initial unfamiliarity begins to fade, it will in fact start to hang together. We would also like to thank our students over the years, who have given us ideas for both right and wrong answers.

PROFESSOR WILLIAM V. DORSANEO, III
PROFESSOR ELIZABETH THORNBURG
Dallas, Texas
January 2015

Table of Contents

Table of Contents

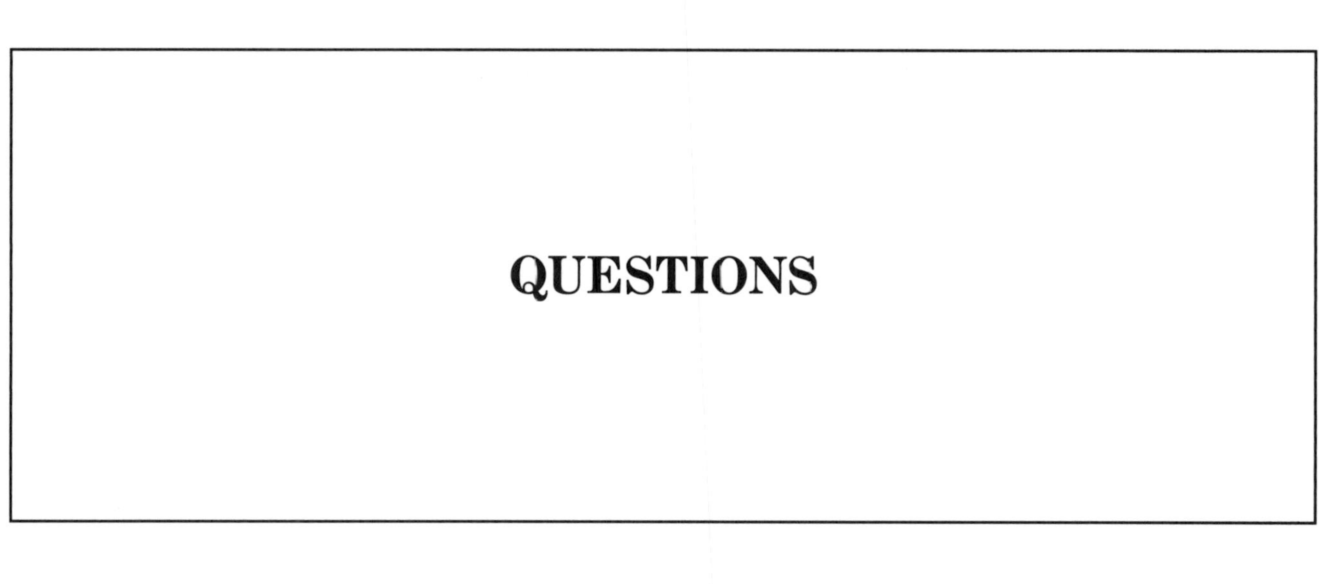

QUESTIONS

TOPIC 1: QUESTIONS
PLEADINGS: PLAINTIFF'S PLEADINGS

Bert was driving north on Hillcrest Road in Dallas when his car collided with Ernie's car, driving west on Mockingbird Lane. Both Bert and Ernie suffered serious personal injuries, and both cars were damaged. Bert wants to sue Ernie in federal court in Dallas.

1. To meet the requirements of the Federal Rules of Civil Procedure, Bert's complaint:

   (A) must state facts sufficient to form a cause of action.

   (B) must state a claim in ordinary and concise language without repetition.

   (C) must plead facts but not evidence.

   (D) must be a short and plain statement of the claim showing that Bert is entitled to relief.

2. What are the functions of pleadings in the federal court system?

ANSWER:

After the heading and the jurisdictional allegations, Bert's complaint describes his claim as follows:

> "On June 1, 2014, in the 2700 block of Mockingbird Lane, Ernie negligently drove his car into Bert's car. As a result, Bert suffered a broken pelvis and other physical injuries, suffered severe physical and mental pain and suffering and in all reasonable probability will continue to suffer physical and mental pain and suffering for a long time into the future, a loss of earnings in the past and in reasonable probability a loss of future earning capacity, and has also incurred medical and hospital expenses in the sum of twenty five thousand dollars.
>
> "Wherefore, plaintiff demands judgment against defendant in the sum of $90,000."

3. Is this complaint sufficient to meet the requirements of Rule 8?

ANSWER:

4. Bert's complaint alleges various types of injuries and damages. Which of them constitute special damages required to be alleged specifically within the meaning of Rule 9(g)?

   (A) All of them, including the allegation about Bert's pelvis, are special damages allegations.

(B) Allegations of past and future pain and suffering concern general damages, not special damages; the remainder are special damage allegations.

(C) Allegations of pain and suffering in the past are general damage allegations; the remainder are special damage allegations.

(D) Allegations about medical and hospital expenses are allegations claiming special damages; the rest are general damage allegations.

5. Ernie's vehicle actually held two persons at the time of the crash: Ernie and Travis. Both were thrown from the car by the collision. Bert believes that Ernie was the driver, but he is not certain. He therefore wants to sue both Travis and Ernie as the driver. May Bert do so?

(A) No. These allegations are inconsistent and so they both cannot be filed in good faith.

(B) No. The rules allow a party to plead in the alternative, but they do not allow factually inconsistent claims.

(C) Yes, but Bert will have to elect whether to proceed against Ernie or Travis before the case goes to the jury.

(D) Yes, under these circumstances the pleading is proper.

6. Bert noticed after the accident that Ernie's car had a bumper sticker proclaiming "Lawyers Do It In Their Briefs." Bert has always loathed bad puns, and he would like to add a cause of action for "annoyance," which he just made up. He can describe at length the bumper sticker and his reaction to it. The annoyance claim, if filed:

(A) is improper. The complaint must show that the pleader is entitled to relief.

(B) is proper. If a pleader has one good claim against an opposing party, claims of other types may be added.

(C) is improper. A plaintiff may not combine claims for negligent and intentional torts.

(D) is proper. Bert will be able to provide sufficient detail to meet the requirements of Rule 8.

7. Carl Customer finds it hard to believe that it is an accident that all mobile phone companies coincidentally and simultaneously raised the price of text messaging by the same amount, at the same time that the cost of providing that service decreased. Carl therefore files a nationwide antitrust class action against AllPhone, Horizon, and Race, the three biggest companies in the industry. Consistent with the language of the antitrust statute, Carl pleads that the companies "conspired" to fix prices. In support of this allegation, Carl alleges examples of parallel behaviors, details of industry structure, and industry practices that facilitate collusion. The complaint also alleges that in the face of steeply falling costs, the defendants increased their prices, all by the same amount, and argues that absent conspiracy this is not economically rational behavior. It does not allege any meetings at which the conspiracy was planned or any other instances of explicit agreement. All

defendants file a 12(b)(6) motion to dismiss the action. Should the court grant the motion?

ANSWER:

8. Lucy Lawstudent enrolled at Reynolds University Law School in the fall of 2013 and withdrew from school following exams in May 2014. Furious about the way she felt she was treated, Lucy filed a lawsuit against Reynolds, her professors, and Microsoft Corporation, alleging intentional infliction of emotional distress and invasion of privacy. Her *pro se* complaint alleged the following:

> "I don't know how they did it, but my professors sneaked into my apartment, spied on me, and moved my books to undermine my studying assignments. They followed me everywhere and must have reported all of my actions to the Dean. Then the school must have shared all of this private information with potential employers, because they all refused to hire me for a summer clerkship. Microsoft was in on it, too: it somehow configured Windows on my laptop to rewrite my class notes and outlines to make them wrong, attached a GPS tracking device to my car, and hid cameras in my apartment because Bill Gates was in love with me and Microsoft feared that Gates would lose his focus and bankrupt the company. Microsoft provided all of this information to the law school, and they used it against me."

All defendants filed a motion to dismiss the complaint under Rule 12(b)(6). Assume for purposes of this question that the facts alleged, if true, would support Lucy's legal theories. Should the court grant the motion?

(A) The court should dismiss Lucy's case. Even under *Conley v. Gibson* allegations of this kind did not have to be taken as true because they defy reality as we know it. The judge may dismiss the case with prejudice.

(B) The court may dismiss the case, but must give Lucy an opportunity to amend her complaint to cure its deficiencies. An initial dismissal may not be made with prejudice.

(C) These are facts, not conclusions, and Lucy must be given the opportunity to do discovery to support her allegations. While the court may limit discovery and ultimately grant summary judgment, dismissal on the pleadings would be improper.

(D) After *Twombly* and *Iqbal*, the court may dismiss Lucy's case, but prior to those decisions it would have been required to allow the case to proceed.

TOPIC 2:	QUESTIONS
PLEADINGS: DEFENDANT'S PLEADINGS	

Bert was driving north on Hillcrest Road in Dallas when his car collided with Ernie's car, driving west on Mockingbird Lane. Both Bert and Ernie suffered serious personal injuries, and both cars were damaged.

9. Assume that Bert sues only Ernie, and that the complaint includes both negligence claims arising out of the car wreck and the claim for annoyance described in question 6. Ernie wants to get rid of the annoyance claim. The best procedural vehicle for Ernie is:

   (A) a motion to dismiss for failure to state a claim upon which relief can be granted.

   (B) a motion for summary judgment.

   (C) a motion for more definite statement.

   (D) a general demurrer.

10. Ernie is annoyed about Bert's bogus annoyance claim. He believes that Bert personally is sincere but is nonetheless deluded about the claim; he spends a lot of time stuck in traffic jams around Dallas and is really tired of other people's irritating bumper stickers. Ernie has heard that Bert's lawyer is a nice guy and tries to do the right thing but got a D in Legal Research and prefers to avoid the library whenever possible. Ernie has a lot of friends who are lawyers (one of whom gave him the offending bumper sticker), and they have told him to investigate something called Rule 11. Does the annoyance claim violate Rule 11?

    (A) Yes, it violates Rule 11(b)(1).

    (B) Yes, it violates Rule 11(b)(2).

    (C) Yes, it violates Rule 11(b)(3).

    (D) No, Bert may get evidentiary support for the annoyance claim after a reasonable opportunity for further investigation or discovery.

11. Ernie has talked to his lawyer, who agrees that the annoyance claim may violate Rule 11. Ernie is pretty mad about this, and he wants to go to the court immediately. Is this a good idea?

ANSWER:

12. Some time has gone by, and the more Ernie thinks about this annoyance claim and what

it is costing him, the madder he gets. He wants to know if there is any way to make Bert compensate him for the attorney's fees he will have to pay defending against the annoyance claim, including filing the motion to get rid of that claim and including filing the motion asking for the fees. His lawyer sent Bert a demand to withdraw the annoyance claim a month ago, hoping that Bert would voluntarily withdraw it, but he got no response. Ernie's lawyer has therefore filed the Rule 11 motion with the court. Could the judge use Rule 11 to force Bert to pay Ernie?

(A) Because the annoyance claim is not warranted by existing law or a nonfrivolous argument for the modification of existing law, Ernie can recover all of his attorney's fees.

(B) Although the annoyance claim is not warranted by existing law or a nonfrivolous argument for the modification of existing law, all monetary penalties must be paid to the court and not to Ernie.

(C) Because the annoyance claim is not warranted by existing law or a nonfrivolous argument for the modification of existing law, Bert could be ordered to pay Ernie all or part of his attorney's fees if warranted for effective deterrence.

(D) Because the annoyance claim is not warranted by existing law or a nonfrivolous argument for the modification of existing law, Bert's lawyer could be ordered to pay Ernie all or part of his attorney's fees if warranted for effective deterrence.

13. Ernie has been served with Bert's lawsuit and must respond. Ernie is from New York and had never been to Texas prior to the day he ran into Bert. He would like to claim that he cannot be sued in Texas. His lawyer also informs him that the lawsuit papers were delivered to him incorrectly. Ernie files a motion to dismiss for insufficiency of service of process. The court denies the motion. Ernie then files an answer, complaining that Texas cannot properly assert personal jurisdiction over him, denying Bert's negligence allegations, and stating that he is without knowledge or information sufficient to form a belief as to the truth of the damages allegations. Under these circumstances:

(A) The court should dismiss the case for want of jurisdiction.

(B) The court should let Bert's case go forward.

(C) The court should retain the negligence claim and order Ernie to respond by admitting or denying the damages allegations.

(D) The court should dismiss Bert's claim because Ernie has denied negligence.

14. Assume that Bert filed his lawsuit on July 1 and that Ernie did not file a pre-answer motion, but that Ernie did file and serve his answer on July 30. A week later, Ernie realized to his horror that he had failed to include a claim that the case should be dismissed for lack of personal jurisdiction; therefore Ernie quickly amended his answer to include this defense. Ernie has:

(A) waived the personal jurisdiction defense by failing to file a pre-answer motion.

(B) waived the personal jurisdiction defense by failing to include it in his answer.

(C) preserved the personal jurisdiction defense by including it in his answer. Complaints about jurisdiction can be raised at any time.

(D) preserved the personal jurisdiction defense because the amended answer was one allowed as a matter of course.

15. Ernie has another issue he wants to raise. He maintains that even if he might have been driving slightly negligently, the accident was not his fault, or at least not all his fault. Bert was not driving safely either and that contributed to the cause of the accident, and so Ernie does not think he should have to pay for all of the damages. If Ernie wants to raise this at trial, does he have to include anything other than his denials?

ANSWER:

16. Ernie was himself injured in the accident, and his car required expensive repairs. Because Ernie believes the accident was Bert's fault, he thinks Bert should pay for these damages. What vehicle should Ernie use to make this claim?

ANSWER:

17. Ernie has another claim against Bert for damages arising out of Bert's breach of contract. Prior to the Hillcrest Road accident, Ernie agreed to sell Bert three antique flintlock long rifles for $80,000. Ernie promised that these rifles had been used at the failed defense of the Alamo. Bert and Ernie memorialized this agreement by reducing it to writing, which both parties signed. Bert refused to take delivery of the rifles because he determined that they were not used at the Alamo. If Ernie adds this claim in a separate part of his answer headed "Counterclaim," what, if anything, does Bert need to file in response?

(A) Bert does not need to file anything; the allegations in the answer, including the counterclaim, are taken as denied or avoided.

(B) Bert needs to file an answer to Ernie's counterclaim, including denial defenses, but not affirmative defenses.

(C) Bert needs to file an answer to Ernie's counterclaim, including denial defenses and affirmative defenses.

(D) Bert needs to file an answer to Ernie's entire answer, including the counterclaim, including denial and affirmative defenses.

18. What avoidance defenses should be made by Bert based on his determination that the long rifles are not authentic Alamo rifles?

ANSWER:

19. In his answer, Ernie also pleads the affirmative defense of release, alleging that Bert has signed a release settling all matters between them. Bert wants to claim that the release was procured by fraud. Does Bert need any additional pleading to be allowed to raise the fraud issue?

(A) Yes. Fraud is an affirmative defense that must be pleaded according to Rule 8(c).

(B) No. Rule 8(b)(6) provides that if "a responsive pleading is not required, an allegation is considered denied or avoided." The fraud claim avoids the affirmative defense of release.

(C) Yes. Responsive pleadings to answers are required under Rule 7, and so Rule 8(d) does not apply here.

(D) No. The pleading of issues in avoidance is always optional.

TOPIC 3: PLEADINGS: HEIGHTENED SPECIFICITY

QUESTIONS

20. The judge to whom *Bert v. Ernie* has been assigned thinks there is too much litigation clogging the federal courts. He is especially unenthusiastic about personal injury litigation and has adopted a practice of requiring that plaintiffs plead their claims with particularity, exceeding the normal requirements of Rule 8. He therefore orders Bert to plead in detail his factual theories of negligence (e.g., speeding, running a red light, etc.). This order:

    (A) is improper. Judges may not create heightened pleading requirements not found in Rule 9.

    (B) is proper. Pleading specificity requirements may be adjusted according to the needs of particular cases.

    (C) is improper, but the judge could order Bert to file a "Reply" under Rule 7, setting forth this information.

    (D) is proper. *Leatherman v. Tarrant County Narcotics & Intelligence Coordination Unit*, 507 U.S. 163 (1993), left an opening for judges to impose heightened pleading requirements.

21. Hotels, Inc. entered into a construction contract with Prime, Inc. to build a hospital facility in Houston, Texas. Prime, Inc. contracted with Planners Co., an architectural firm, and Dirt, Inc., an engineering firm hired to do soil testing. Because the completed facility has been sinking into the ground, Hotels, Inc. has sued Prime, Inc. for breach of contract and, in addition to alleging the facts contained in this question, has asserted the following fraud allegations in an amended complaint: "Prime, Inc. defrauded Hotels, Inc. by intentionally inflating the costs of the project and taking kickbacks from one or more of Prime, Inc.'s subcontractors." If Prime, Inc. moves to dismiss this fraud claim, what result?

    (A) The motion should be denied because the complaint contains enough factual detail for Prime, Inc. to fashion an answer and raise defenses.

    (B) The motion should be granted because the complaint does not allege knowledge specifically.

    (C) The motion should be granted because the complaint contains insufficient details of fraud.

    (D) The motion should be denied because it does not appear beyond doubt that Hotels, Inc. can prove no state of facts entitling it to recover for fraud.

22. Imagine that the Advisory Committee on the Rules of Civil Procedure changes Rule 8 to

require plaintiffs to plead "with particularity facts constituting a cause of action." In your opinion, would such a change tend to favor plaintiffs, defendants, or neither?

ANSWER:

TOPIC 4: AMENDED PLEADINGS

QUESTIONS

In January of 2009 Bitsy Boxer began a dog breeding operation with two small dogs; the business quickly grew to include over three hundred dogs. Initially, Boxer fed her dogs a dog food called K-9 and used a technique allowing them to eat their fill. Beginning in January of 2011, Boxer began feeding the dogs Broken Bone Dog Food. Boxer noticed no problems at first. On January 22, 2012, however, Boxer discontinued using the product because the dogs were not eating it.

On November 19, 2013, Boxer filed suit against BBD, Inc. in federal district court, serving process on its President, Martin Mastiff, and claiming that BBD manufactured Broken Bone Dog Food and that the food was low in calcium and therefore caused certain defects and abnormalities in the dogs. Asserting a claim for breach of warranty, Boxer asked for damages in the amount of $100,000. BBD filed and served its answer on December 1, 2013.

23. In the defendant's initial answer, it admitted that the dog food had a low calcium level. The defendant planned to rely on the testimony of its expert witness, Dr. Hund, who was expected to opine that the calcium could not have caused the symptoms of Boxer's dogs. When Dr. Hund's opinion turned out to be more equivocal, the defendant asked the court on January 15, 2014, for permission to amend its answer to deny that the dog food was low in calcium. Under these circumstances:

    (A) The judge should allow the amendment. This early in the litigation, the amendment could not prejudice Boxer.

    (B) The judge should allow the amendment because it could have been done as a matter of course.

    (C) The judge should deny the amendment because parties are not allowed to change their factual contentions.

    (D) The judge should allow the amendment because prejudice is unlikely, but the defendant should be sure its denial is warranted on the evidence.

24. Boxer also needs a pleading amendment. The original complaint identified "BBD, Inc." as the defendant. Shortly after filing, however, Boxer's lawyer discovered that the business had never been properly incorporated and no such corporation existed. Therefore, on February 1, 2014, Boxer filed a motion for leave to amend her complaint, changing the identity of the defendant to "Martin Mastiff, doing business as BBD Products." The proposed amended complaint also added a new claim for the recovery of consequential damages, which Boxer's lawyer had inadvertently omitted from the original complaint. Assume for purposes of this question only that there is no problem with the statute of limitations. Should the court allow the requested amendments?

ANSWER:

25. Assume that the court is favorably disposed toward allowing Boxer's proposed amendments. Boxer has an additional problem. The statute of limitations on any claim against Mastiff ran out on January 21, 2014. Therefore, Boxer's claims would be barred by the statute of limitations unless the amendment relates back to the filing of the original complaint. Should the amendment, if allowed, relate back?

(A) No, the consequential damages claim does not arise out of the same conduct, transaction, or occurrence as Boxer's original claim for damages.

(B) Yes, it arises out of the same transaction, Mastiff got timely notice, and he should have known that, but for a mistake, the suit would have been brought against him.

(C) No, the change to the defendant's name was not based on a mistake concerning the identity of the proper party.

(D) Yes, there would not likely be any prejudice to the defendant.

26. Boxer believes the flaw in the dog food is due to a chemical additive that Mastiff purchases from another company and adds to the mix. She has been unable to discover the name of the company that manufactured and sold it to Mastiff. Because the statute of limitations was about to bar her claim, Boxer sued "ABC Corporation." (Boxer knew this was not the correct name and was using ABC the way one would use "John Doe" for an unknown human party.) She later (but after limitations ran) learned through discovery that the manufacturer of the chemical was in fact PoroCal Company. Boxer filed a motion to amend her complaint to sue "PoroCal Company," and she asked that the change relate back to the filing of her original complaint. PoroCal got timely notice of the lawsuit, but argued that relation back should not be allowed because the misnomer was not based on a mistake. How should the court rule?

ANSWER:

27. Why do the rules allow pleadings to be amended? Given this purpose, why do the rules put limits on amendments?

ANSWER:

TOPIC 5: JOINDER OF CLAIMS

QUESTIONS

28. Athena sued Aphrodite for slander, following a nasty dispute about the results of a beauty contest. Since Aphrodite also owes Athena money (she breached a contract to buy 1,000 copies of Athena's book, "It's Better to Be Smart"), Athena combined both claims in a single federal lawsuit. Are the claims properly joined?

    (A) No. These claims do not arise out of the same transaction or occurrence.

    (B) Yes. Since there is only one party on each side, Rule 18 allows free joinder of claims and Rule 20's requirements do not apply.

    (C) No. The rules do not allow tort and contract claims to be joined in the same lawsuit.

    (D) Yes. Since both claims involve disagreements between the same two people, they automatically are considered to share a common question of law or fact.

29. Paris and Hector, who own adjacent farms, got into a boundary dispute that ultimately involved who was responsible for fence maintenance and crop damage caused by trespassing livestock. When Paris impounded one of Hector's cows, Hector filed a criminal complaint for cattle theft against Paris. After the criminal case was dismissed, Paris confronted Hector who retaliated by breaking Paris' nose and blackening both of his eyes. Paris (who is actually a citizen of a neighboring state) has brought suit against Hector in federal court for malicious prosecution and battery. Claiming misjoinder of claims, Hector has filed a motion for dismissal and an alternative motion for severance of the claims. How should the court rule?

    (A) The motion must be denied because in a case involving only one plaintiff and one defendant, there can be no misjoinder of claims. Neither dismissal nor severance is permitted in the absence of misjoinder.

    (B) The motion should be denied, but only because the claims arise from the same transaction or occurrence or series of transactions or occurrences and, hence, are properly joined.

    (C) The motion to dismiss must be denied, but the motion to sever must be granted because the claims are unrelated and misjoinder is a basis for severance of unrelated claims.

    (D) The trial judge has discretion to sever the claims or to dispose of them in the same proceeding.

TOPIC 6: PERMISSIVE JOINDER OF PARTIES — QUESTIONS

30. Morris has a claim for malicious prosecution against Boris resulting from Boris' complaint to the police. Morris also has a separate and unrelated claim against Doris for assault and battery. Morris wants to sue them in the same case to save time. May he?

    (A) Morris' attempt to sue Boris and Doris in the same case should not survive a motion to dismiss for misjoinder of parties.

    (B) Morris' attempt to sue Boris and Doris in the same case should not survive a motion for severance or for a separate trial.

    (C) Morris can join both claims in the same action to avoid a multiplicity of suits.

    (D) The trial judge has discretion to allow or to disallow joinder of the claims against Doris and Boris.

31. Donald wants to bring a lawsuit against Rhona and Robin, his former assistants, for breach of a contract that both Rhona and Robin signed. In addition, he wants to sue Robin for libel because one year ago Robin called Donald "an unscrupulous con artist with no morals and bad hair." In this situation, if Rhona filed a motion for dismissal or, in the alternative, separate trial of the libel claim based on misjoinder, how should the court rule on the motion?

    (A) The motion to dismiss should be granted because Rhona is not concerned with the libel claim against Robin and joinder is improper for this reason.

    (B) The motion to dismiss should be denied because Rhona and Robin are properly joined on the contract claim, and Rule 18 does not require the libel claim to be related to the contract claim against them.

    (C) Rhona's motion for dismissal based on misjoinder should be denied. However, to avoid any prejudice resulting from the joinder of the unrelated libel claim, the trial court has the discretion to try the libel claim and the contract claims separately.

    (D) (B) and (C) are both correct.

TOPIC 7: COMPULSORY JOINDER OF PARTIES — QUESTIONS

32. Albert, Barbara, Clarence, and David each have a claim against Edward for labor and material separately supplied by each of them to Edward in connection with the construction of Edward's summer home in the country. Foxworth has a deed of trust to the house and lot executed by Edward to finance the construction of the summer house. Assuming no subject matter jurisdiction problems exist, may Albert, Barbara, Clarence, and David join together as plaintiffs in the same action to foreclose their respective mechanics' and materialmen's liens on Edward's property, without joining Foxworth as a party?

    (A) No, the joinder of the claims of Albert, Barbara, Clarence, and David is improper because each one separately furnished labor and material.

    (B) Yes, the joinder of Albert, Barbara, Clarence, and David as co-plaintiffs is proper and Foxworth is not a person who should be joined if feasible under Rule 19.

    (C) No, although the claims of Albert, Barbara, Clarence, and David satisfy Rule 20, Foxworth is a person to be joined if feasible under Rule 19, assuming that Edward files a Rule 12(b)(7) motion complaining about Foxworth's nonjoinder.

    (D) No, although the claims of Albert, Barbara, Clarence, and David satisfy Rule 20, Foxworth is jurisdictionally indispensable to the adjudication of any claim concerning Edward's summer house.

33. If Foxworth is not joined as a party and his absence is not raised in the trial court by Edward or by any of the other parties, and if Edward loses in the trial court because judgment is rendered judicially foreclosing the plaintiffs' mechanics' and materialmen's liens, can Edward challenge the judgment on appeal because of Foxworth's nonjoinder?

    (A) Yes, Foxworth's deed of trust lien represents a substantive right that makes him indispensable to the trial court's exercise of jurisdiction.

    (B) Yes, Foxworth's interests are such that the court should have dismissed the action after considering the factors listed in Rule 19(b) given the nature of his lien interest in the summer home.

    (C) No, insofar as the judgment affects Edward, Edward's failure to raise Foxworth's nonjoinder in the trial court forecloses Edward's ability to attack the judgment foreclosing the mechanics' and materialmen's liens on Edward's property.

    (D) No, Edward cannot challenge the judgment because of Foxworth's nonjoinder because Foxworth's deed of trust lien is inferior to the plaintiffs' liens.

34. If Foxworth is not joined as a party, can Foxworth judicially foreclose his deed of trust lien on the property described in his deed of trust? Who may or must be added as parties in such an action?

ANSWER:

TOPIC 8: INTERPLEADER — QUESTIONS

Albert Riggs of Odessa, Texas, had a full life that came to a peaceful end when he did not awaken on a cold November morning in 2010. For the last 15 years of his life, Albert worked as a petroleum engineer for Rough Rider Exploration Co. Part of his compensation included coverage under a Group Life Insurance Policy purchased by Rough Rider Exploration Co. for the benefit of certain highly paid employees. The policy was issued by Confederation Life, a Connecticut corporation having its principal office in Hartford, Connecticut. The policy provided a death benefit in the sum of $125,000 to Albert's spouse or another designated beneficiary. When Albert began work for the company, he designated his wife, Cookie Riggs, as his beneficiary. Some few years later Cookie and Albert divorced and Albert remarried Dorothy Riggs, but without changing beneficiaries. This was the status-quo when Albert died. Both Cookie and Dorothy are Texas domiciliaries and both have made conflicting claims to the policy proceeds. Dorothy is aided by a Texas statute that de-designates ex-spouses as beneficiaries unless a de-designation would be contrary to the insured's intent.

35. In view of the conflicting claims, can Confederation Life bring suit against Cookie and Dorothy in federal court in a judicial district in Texas to determine who is entitled to the policy proceeds?

    (A) No, Confederation Life cannot interplead Cookie and Dorothy because there is no diversity of citizenship between Dorothy and Cookie.

    (B) Yes, Rule 22 allows the interpleader of conflicting claimants, who do not need to be of diverse citizenship as between themselves.

    (C) Yes, Rule 22 has liberalized the requirements for interpleading conflicting claimants and Confederation Life may use interpleader to avoid double vexation and double liability.

    (D) (B) and (C) are both correct.

36. If the death benefit does not exceed $75,000 and if Cookie is actually domiciled in New Mexico when suit is filed, must Confederation Life restrict its efforts to interplead Cookie and Dorothy to state court?

    (A) No, statutory interpleader is available under 28 U.S.C. § 1335 if the value of the group policy amounts to $500 or more.

    (B) No, statutory interpleader under 28 U.S.C. § 1335 is available because Dorothy and Cookie do not reside in the same state.

(C) No, 28 U.S.C. §§ 1397 and 2361 solve potential problems of personal jurisdiction and venue.

(D) (A), (B), and (C) are correct.

37. If Cookie sues Confederation Life in Connecticut before Confederation Life brings suit in Texas or New Mexico, what, if anything, can Confederation Life do to protect itself?

ANSWER:

TOPIC 9: INTERVENTION

QUESTIONS

Albert places a deed in Ben's hands with instructions to Ben to deliver the deed to Clarence on payment by Clarence of $5,000. Ben notifies Clarence of this escrow arrangement, but before Clarence acts, Albert instructs Ben to hold the deed in escrow pending further instructions. At the same time, Clarence tenders $5,000 to Ben and demands the deed. Ben seeks further instructions from Albert, who instructs Ben to deliver the deed to Albert's legal counsel.

38. If Clarence does bring an action against Ben for delivery of the deed and Ben does not attempt to interplead Albert, may Albert intervene in the action to protect his interest?

    (A) Albert may not intervene in the action, unless a statute confers the right to intervene.

    (B) Albert may have the permissive right to intervene because his claim and the main action have common questions of law or fact.

    (C) Albert probably must be permitted to intervene because he claims an interest in the property or transaction and the disposition of the action in his absence may impair or impede Albert's ability to protect his interest.

    (D) The trial judge has broad discretion to grant or to deny Albert's motion to intervene.

TOPIC 10:	**QUESTIONS**
JOINDER OF ADDITIONAL PARTIES	

Duds Laundry Co.'s driver Juan Rios had an intersectional collision in San Antonio, Texas, with Hubert Nelson. Duds is a Nevada corporation with its principal place of business in San Antonio, Texas. Rios is a citizen of New Mexico. Nelson lives and works in Chicago, Illinois. As a result of the accident, Duds' truck was totaled and both Rios and Nelson suffered severe personal injuries.

At the time of the accident, Nelson was driving a passenger car manufactured by Big Motors, a Delaware corporation, having its principal place of business in Detroit, Michigan.

Under the applicable substantive law, negligence claims are available against parties whose negligence proximately caused personal injuries or property damage. The law also provides for strict tort liability claims against sellers of defective products that cause injuries and damages. In addition, contribution statutes authorize jointly and severally liable defendants to sue other tortfeasors for contribution to the extent of any "overpayment of the defendants' contribution shares."

39. After settlement negotiations failed, Duds brought a property damage claim in federal district court in San Antonio, Texas, against Nelson for damages to its laundry truck in the amount of $100,000. Nelson brought a third-party action impleading Rios to recover for Nelson's personal injury damages in the amount of $500,000. Was the third-party action an appropriate method for joining Rios in the action?

    (A) Yes, Rios' potential liability to Nelson for personal injury damages could be the basis for a third-party action.

    (B) No, third-party actions are available for derivative claims like contribution and indemnity claims, not as a basis for the defendant's individual tort claims against nonparties.

    (C) Yes, impleader must be permitted to avoid a multiplicity of suits.

    (D) Both (A) and (C) are correct.

40. Assuming that Nelson made a claim for contribution against Rios in Nelson's third-party complaint, can Nelson also assert his personal injury claims against Rios in the same third-party complaint?

    (A) Yes, because Rios is properly joined in the contribution claim, Nelson can assert any claims of his against Rios.

    (B) No, although the tort damages claims can probably be added later after Rios is impleaded for contribution, they cannot be included in the third-party complaint.

    (C) No, third-party practice is not a basis for direct damage claims.

(D) (B) and (C) are both correct.

TOPIC 11: COUNTERCLAIMS & CROSS-CLAIMS

QUESTIONS

Duds Laundry Co.'s driver Juan Rios had an intersectional collision in San Antonio, Texas, with Hubert Nelson. Duds is a Nevada corporation with its principal place of business in San Antonio, Texas. Rios is a citizen of New Mexico. Nelson lives and works in Chicago, Illinois. As a result of the accident, Duds' truck was totaled and both Rios and Nelson suffered severe personal injuries.

At the time of the accident, Nelson was driving a passenger car manufactured by Big Motors, a Delaware corporation, having its principal place of business in Detroit, Michigan. Under the applicable substantive law, negligence claims are available against parties whose negligence proximately caused personal injuries or property damage. The law also provides for strict tort liability claims against sellers of defective products that cause injuries and damages. In addition, contribution statutes authorize jointly and severally liable defendants to sue other tortfeasors for contribution to the extent of any "overpayment of the defendants' contribution shares." These claims do not mature, however, until a defendant pays more than its contribution share.

41. After settlement negotiations failed, Nelson brought a diversity action against Duds and Rios, seeking personal injury damages in excess of $75,000. Duds and Rios would prefer to wait and see what happens in the federal case and file suit in Texas state court against Nelson for damages. Are there any problems presented by such a choice?

    (A) Yes, because Duds' and Rios' damages claims arise from the same occurrence as the claim made by Nelson, their counterclaims are compulsory, which could ultimately preclude prosecution of the claims in state court.

    (B) Yes, because Nelson is an "opposing party" as provided in Rule 13(a).

    (C) Yes, because when Nelson sued, Duds and Rios hadn't already asserted their claims in another action.

    (D) (A), (B), and (C) are all correct.

42. Assume further that Nelson files an amended complaint in federal court and joins Big Motors as a co-defendant with Duds and Rios, claiming that the car was defectively designed and that the defect caused Nelson to be more seriously injured than he would have been if his car had been properly designed. Must Duds and Rios file their negligence and contribution claims against Big Motors in the same action?

    (A) No, cross-claims between co-parties are permissive, not compulsory.

    (B) Yes, Duds and Rios' claims are compulsory because they arise from the same occurrence as Nelson's claims against them.

(C) No, Nelson's claims against Big Motors are about his own injuries and so do not arise out of the same transaction or occurrence as Duds' and Rios' claims.

(D) (A) and (C) are both correct.

43. If Duds and Rios do file cross-claims against Big Motors for damage to Duds' truck and for Rios' personal injury damages, may Big Motors assert a claim against Duds and Rios for contribution?

(A) No, because Big Motors' contribution claim is not mature under state law until Big Motors pays Nelson more than Big Motors' contribution share, a cross-claim is also not available to Big Motors for contribution under Rule 13(g).

(B) No, any contribution claim by Big Motors against Duds and Rios would be a counterclaim, which would be premature until Nelson obtains payment from Big Motors because counterclaims should not be filed until they mature under Rule 13(e).

(C) Yes. Although Big Motors is not permitted to make a premature *counter* claim for contribution in the federal action, Big Motors is expressly permitted to file a *cross*-claim under Rule 13(g).

(D) No, premature contribution claims must be made the subject of a separate action under federal joinder rules; they may not be brought either as counterclaims or cross-claims.

TOPIC 12: CLASS ACTIONS	QUESTIONS

44. Andie, a purchaser of a sewing machine manufactured by Panos, Ltd., has filed an antitrust class action in federal district court on behalf of a nationwide class of approximately 1,000 sewing machine purchasers, each of whom is alleged to have suffered an economic loss based on alleged price fixing by Panos and its supposed business competitors. Andie purchased her sewing machine directly from Panos, but all other purchasers bought them from the regional distributors (wholesalers) used by Panos to market its products. Assume that Andie's claim is much easier to prove because she dealt directly with Panos, but that the class claimants could prevail in an action for money damages on proof that a direct pass-through of prices from the wholesalers to them had occurred. Andie is prepared to aggressively litigate all claims through well-qualified and well-heeled class action counsel. Panos has filed an answer denying liability and an objection to class certification on multiple grounds. Andie has filed a motion to certify her case as a class action. What threshold requirement(s) of Rule 23 will be the most difficult to prove at the certification hearing?

    (A) The claims or defenses of the representative parties are typical of the claims or defenses of the class.

    (B) The class is so numerous that joinder of all members is impracticable.

    (C) The representative parties will fairly and adequately protect the interests of the class.

    (D) There are questions of law or fact common to the class.

45. If Andie satisfied all requirements under Rule 23(a), under which provision of Rule 23(b) would her class claim most likely be certified?

    (A) Individual actions by class members would lead to inconsistent adjudications that would prejudice the party opposing the class.

    (B) The questions of law or fact that are common to class members predominate over individual questions and a class action is a superior method to resolve the dispute.

    (C) The party opposing the class has acted on grounds generally applicable to the class, thereby making injunctive relief appropriate for the class.

    (D) Individual actions by class members would prejudice the interests of members who are not parties to those individual actions.

46. Absent a settlement, if notice to the class is required, the costs of sending required notices

to class members must be paid by:

(A) Defendant Panos because it is more able to bear the costs and it is likely to lose on the merits because it lost to the government on a similar claim.

(B) Andie, the named representative, because she has brought the action and is responsible for prosecution of the class action.

(C) The members of the class who will substantially benefit if Andie wins the case and they recover damages, and who will be responsible for costs of suit if the class loses on the merits.

(D) Andie and Panos, with costs divided based on an allocation determined by the court in a probable merit hearing prior to certification.

TOPIC 13: QUESTIONS
DISCOVERY: AUTOMATIC INITIAL DISCLOSURES

After an unpleasant dispute with local authorities gave her an interest in the law, Hester Prynne went to law school. While in school she married Holgrave, a fellow student, who also adopted Hester's daughter Pearl. After graduation, both began practice in Massachusetts. Both parents doted on Pearl, and both reduced their billable hours in order to spend more time with her. Concerned about quality child care, Prynne contacted Nanny Nation, a respected national agency that trains and recruits child care providers from throughout the United States and the world, with its main office in New York. Through Nanny Nation, Prynne and Holgrave hired Hibbins, a 22-year-old British citizen, to live in their home, do light housework and cooking, and care for Pearl while they were at work.

About a month later, tragedy struck. Hibbins picked up Pearl from piano lessons and was driving her home. Unfortunately, Hibbins had succumbed to homesickness for the local pub and had three beers before getting Pearl. On the way home they were involved in a serious traffic accident. Hibbins suffered only superficial injuries, but Pearl received significant head and neck injuries. Prynne fired Hibbins, and she returned home to England.

Pearl has recovered from most of her injuries, although the doctors continue to watch for signs of permanent brain damage. Prynne and Holgrave have paid substantial medical bills for her treatment and have lost income while tending to her psychological and medical needs. They have suffered mental anguish from watching Pearl struggle with her injuries. Prynne and Holgrave no longer feel comfortable leaving Pearl with anyone other than a family member, and so Holgrave has retired from practice and takes care of Pearl full time.

Prynne and Holgrave sued Nanny Nation for damages in federal district court in Massachusetts. Their theories of recovery are negligence (in hiring and training Hibbins), gross negligence (for a pattern of ignoring serious psychological and behavioral problems of potential nannies), and fraud (for representing that their nannies are highly responsible and well qualified to care for young children), and they seek both actual and punitive damages.

47. Which of the following types of information does Nanny Nation need to disclose to the plaintiffs even without a formal discovery request?

    (A) The names of disgruntled former clients.

    (B) The e-mail addresses of persons likely to have discoverable information that Nanny Nation may use to support its defense.

    (C) A copy or a description by category and location of Nanny Nation's entire file on Hibbins, including a troublesome evaluation from Hibbins' former employer mentioning a possible drinking problem.

    (D) The names and contact information for persons that Nanny Nation may use as supportive witnesses at trial.

48. Prynne and Holgrave have claimed $5 million in damages. What further information do they have to provide to Nanny Nation at the outset of the litigation?

(A) A computation only of economic damages such as medical bills and lost income.

(B) A computation of each type of damages, including the underlying documents showing the nature and extent of their injuries.

(C) Correspondence with their attorney concerning the best way to compute their damages.

(D) A computation of any out-of-pocket expenses that they will claim as damages.

49. Assume that the Rule 16(b) scheduling order in this case is due on August 30. If each required conference takes place on the last possible day, and the court has not entered an order changing the deadlines, when are the parties' automatic initial disclosures due?

ANSWER:

50. Both Prynne/Holgrave and Nanny Nation will be hiring expert witnesses to testify in support of their claims and defenses. In the absence of a court order to the contrary, the following disclosures will be required regarding these experts:

(A) Prynne/Holgrave must identify their expert witnesses. For each expert they must provide a report describing the expert's opinions and the basis for the opinions, the information considered by the expert in forming the opinions, any exhibits to be used while testifying, the expert's qualifications, the compensation to be paid the expert, and a list of other cases in which the witness has testified as an expert at trial or by deposition within the preceding four years. This must be done at least 90 days before the trial date. Nanny Nation must do the same within 30 days after Prynne/Holgrave's disclosure.

(B) Prynne/Holgrave must identify their expert witnesses. For each expert they must provide a report describing the expert's opinions and the basis for the opinions, the information considered by the expert in forming the opinions, any exhibits to be used while testifying, the expert's qualifications, the compensation to be paid the expert, and a list of other cases in which the witness has testified as an expert at trial or by deposition within the preceding four years. This must be done at least 90 days before the trial date. Nanny Nation must do the same thing simultaneously with Prynne/Holgrave's disclosure.

(C) The parties only need to make these disclosures about expert witnesses if specifically so ordered by the court.

(D) The parties need to make the disclosures described in Rule 26(a)(2) only with respect to one expert each.

51. Nanny Nation has disclosed that it will use Mary Bobbins, an employee from its Human

Resources department, to testify and give an opinion on industry standards for nanny recruitment and training. Bobbins is a bit nervous about this, as she has never testified before. Does she have to prepare a report prior to being deposed?

(A) Yes. Rule 26(a)(2) requires reports for all testifying experts, and the need for the report to make the deposition efficient is the same for employees as for retained experts.

(B) Yes. Rule 26(a)(2) requires reports of testifying experts over whom the litigant has control, whether by regular employment or by specially retaining them to testify in the case.

(C) No. Bobbins' duties do not regularly involve giving expert testimony.

(D) No. As an employee, Bobbins is a fact witness, not an expert.

52. Rule 26(f) says that in the initial discovery conference you should discuss "any issues about claims of privilege or of protection as trial-preparation materials, including — if the parties agree on a procedure to assert these claims after production — whether to ask the court to include their agreement in an order." What kind of agreement might the parties want to make?

(A) That production of a privileged document automatically waives the privilege.

(B) That if the producing party inadvertently produces a privileged document, production does not waive the privilege and it may claim privilege and request the return of the document after it has been produced.

(C) That a judge will personally supervise all document production as it occurs in order to rule on any privilege claims.

(D) That production of privileged documents may or may not waive privilege, depending on a number of factors such as the efforts made to screen for privilege, the volume of documents produced, and the centrality of the documents to the subject matter of the litigation.

53. Additional automatic disclosures must be made shortly before trial. Unless the court orders otherwise, which of the following is true?

(A) At least 30 days before trial, parties must disclose the name of each witness it expects to call at trial (except solely for impeachment).

(B) At least 14 days before trial, parties must disclose the name of each witness it expects to call, including anticipated impeachment witnesses.

(C) At least 30 days before trial, parties must identify each document or other exhibit that the party expects to offer at trial.

(D) Both (A) and (C) are correct.

54. With respect to the list of expected exhibits disclosed under Rule 26(a)(3), which of the following is true:

(A) Disclosure is for the court's convenience and is unrelated to the admissibility of those exhibits at trial.

(B) The opposing party has 14 days in which to object to the admissibility of documents on the list. Any objection (except about relevance under Rules 402 and 403 of the Federal Rules of Evidence) not made at this time cannot be made at trial unless the party convinces the court that there was good cause not to object on time.

(C) Additional documents can be offered into evidence at trial despite not being on the list; the rule only aims to give notice of the most crucial exhibits in an effort to encourage settlement.

(D) The documents and exhibits must be introduced at trial in the order in which they appear on the party's pretrial disclosure list.

TOPIC 14: QUESTIONS
DISCOVERY: SCOPE OF DISCOVERY & DISCOVERY RELEVANCE

55. The discovery rules in effect in 2014 provide that parties may obtain discovery regarding:

(A) any nonprivileged matter that is relevant to the subject matter of the litigation.

(B) any nonprivileged matter that is relevant to any party's claim or defense and is admissible in evidence.

(C) any nonprivileged matter that is relevant to any party's claim or defense, including relevant information that would be inadmissible but that appears reasonably calculated to lead to the discovery of admissible evidence.

(D) any nonprivileged matter that is relevant to any party's claim or defense and for which the discovering party can show good cause.

After an unpleasant dispute with local authorities gave her an interest in the law, Hester Prynne went to law school. While in school she married Holgrave, a fellow student, who also adopted Hester's daughter Pearl. After graduation, both began practice in Massachusetts. Both parents doted on Pearl, and both reduced their billable hours in order to spend more time with her. Concerned about quality child care, Prynne contacted Nanny Nation, a respected national agency that trains and recruits child care providers from throughout the United States and the world, with its main office in New York. Through Nanny Nation, Prynne and Holgrave hired Hibbins, a 22-year-old British citizen, to live in their home, do light housework and cooking, and care for Pearl while they were at work.

About a month later, tragedy struck. Hibbins picked up Pearl from piano lessons and was driving her home. Unfortunately, Hibbins had succumbed to homesickness for the local pub and had three beers before getting Pearl. On the way home they were involved in a serious traffic accident. Hibbins suffered only superficial injuries, but Pearl received significant head and neck injuries. Prynne fired Hibbins, and she returned home to England.

Pearl has recovered from most of her injuries, although the doctors continue to watch for signs of permanent brain damage. Prynne and Holgrave have paid substantial medical bills for her treatment and have lost income while tending to her psychological and medical needs. They have suffered mental anguish from watching Pearl struggle with her injuries. Prynne and Holgrave no longer feel comfortable leaving Pearl with anyone other than a family member, and so Holgrave has retired from practice and takes care of Pearl full time.

Prynne and Holgrave sued Nanny Nation for damages in federal district court in Massachusetts. Their theories of recovery are negligence (in hiring and training Hibbins), gross negligence (for a pattern of ignoring serious psychological and behavioral problems of potential nannies), and fraud (for representing that their nannies are highly responsible and well qualified to care for young children), and they seek both actual and punitive damages.

56. Nanny Nation has heard rumors about Prynne's pre-law school exploits. They have asked her to describe in detail her sexual history. Is this discoverable?

    (A) Yes. Prynne's sexual conduct gives insight into her character and is therefore relevant.

    (B) Yes. Prynne has waived any privacy rights she might have by bringing this lawsuit.

    (C) No. Prynne's sex life is not relevant to the claims against Nanny Nation.

    (D) Yes. The truthfulness or falsity of Prynne's answer to this question will help to show whether she is a truthful person, and that might be admissible to impeach her testimony generally.

57. Nanny Nation will defend itself, in part, by asserting that Hibbins' driving did not cause the accident in which Pearl was injured. It therefore sends an interrogatory asking for the names, addresses, and phone numbers of all persons who witnessed the accident. Is this information relevant?

    (A) No. The relevant issue is Hibbins' intoxication, and these people will not have knowledge of that.

    (B) No. These names will not be admissible in evidence.

    (C) Yes. These people have knowledge of the circumstances surrounding the accident, which may, in turn, be relevant to the issue of causation.

    (D) Yes. Nanny Nation may discover the identity of anyone to whom Prynne's lawyers talked while investigating the case.

58. Why would Nanny Nation want to send the interrogatory discussed above when it will already have learned, through automatic initial disclosures, the identity of people who Prynne knows have information about the case?

ANSWER:

59. Nanny Nation is skeptical of the lost income amounts claimed by Holgrave. The company doubts that his practice was ever as successful as he claims, and therefore doubts that Holgrave's lost future income is as great as he claims. Nanny Nation has sent a request for production of documents to Holgrave, asking for all documents relevant to his income from law practice. The request asks for every piece of paper related to Holgrave's practice. Are these documents relevant?

    (A) Yes, they are relevant to the amount of Holgrave's claim for damages and must be produced.

    (B) While some of the documents will be relevant, Holgrave should object to the request as drafted because many of the documents clearly will not be relevant.

(C) No. Information relevant only to damages is not discoverable beyond that required in the automatic initial disclosure rules.

(D) All of them are relevant, but some should be withheld because they will be protected by the attorney-client privilege.

60. Discuss how the definition of discovery relevance interacts with the rules on pleadings, including how the pleading/discovery process fits into the overall philosophy of the FRCP.

ANSWER:

TOPIC 15: DISCOVERY: WORK PRODUCT

QUESTIONS

61. When is material protected from discovery by work product protection?

    (A) When it is confidential material prepared by a party's representative.

    (B) When it is prepared in anticipation of litigation or for trial by a party or by or for that party's representative.

    (C) When it is a confidential communication between a party and that party's attorney.

    (D) When it is prepared in anticipation of litigation or for trial by any person.

After an unpleasant dispute with local authorities gave her an interest in the law, Hester Prynne went to law school. While in school she married Holgrave, a fellow student, who also adopted Hester's daughter Pearl. After graduation, both began practice in Massachusetts. Both parents doted on Pearl, and both reduced their billable hours in order to spend more time with her. Concerned about quality child care, Prynne contacted Nanny Nation, a respected national agency that trains and recruits child care providers from throughout the United States and the world, with its main office in New York. Through Nanny Nation, Prynne and Holgrave hired Hibbins, a 22-year-old British citizen, to live in their home, do light housework and cooking, and care for Pearl while they were at work.

About a month later, tragedy struck. Hibbins picked up Pearl from piano lessons and was driving her home. Unfortunately, Hibbins had succumbed to homesickness for the local pub and had three beers before getting Pearl. On the way home they were involved in a serious traffic accident. Hibbins suffered only superficial injuries, but Pearl received significant head and neck injuries. Prynne fired Hibbins, and she returned home to England.

Pearl has recovered from most of her injuries, although the doctors continue to watch for signs of permanent brain damage. Prynne and Holgrave have paid substantial medical bills for her treatment and have lost income while tending to her psychological and medical needs. They have suffered from mental anguish from watching Pearl struggle with her injuries. Prynne and Holgrave no longer feel comfortable leaving Pearl with anyone other than a family member, and so Holgrave has retired from practice and takes care of Pearl full time.

Prynne and Holgrave sued Nanny Nation for damages in federal district court in Massachusetts. Their theories of recovery are negligence (in hiring and training Hibbins), gross negligence (for a pattern of ignoring serious psychological and behavioral problems of potential nannies), and fraud (for representing that their nannies are highly responsible and well-qualified to care for young children), and they seek both actual and punitive damages.

62. Prynne's lawyer hired a private investigator to look into Hibbins' background. This investigator interviewed Prynne's neighbors about Hibbins' habits and took notes on those interviews. Nanny Nation wants to discover those notes. Are they discoverable?

(A) Yes. Only notes created by the lawyer are work product.

(B) No. They are opinion work product.

(C) No. They are ordinary work product and Nanny Nation could easily discover the substantial equivalent of this information.

(D) Yes. The information in the notes concerns pre-lawsuit behavior and so they are not made in anticipation of litigation.

63. Prynne sends Nanny Nation an interrogatory asking about Hibbins' behavior during the nanny training program. Nanny Nation's management team knows some of this information only because they learned it from the investigations brought on by the lawsuit. Do they have to disclose this part of the information to Prynne?

ANSWER:

64. A year before Prynne came to Nanny Nation, the company did an internal review of its recruiting policies. The reviewer looked at two years' worth of files and wrote a report to the CEO that suggested improvements that could be made to the recruiting practices in order to weed out undesirable potential nannies. Prynne has sent Nanny Nation a request for production of documents that covers this report. Must Nanny Nation produce it?

(A) Yes. It is relevant to Prynne's claim of a pattern of misconduct and it is not protected by work product.

(B) No. It is relevant to Prynne's claim of a pattern of misconduct and it is protected by work product.

(C) Yes. It is relevant to Prynne's claim of a pattern of misconduct and it is protected by work product, but Prynne could show substantial need of the report and undue hardship if the report is not produced.

(D) No. Searching for this report would be too burdensome.

65. Nanny Nation has hired a private investigator to help with this lawsuit. The investigator has gone to Hibbins' village in England to learn more about her background. The investigator interviewed Phoebe Pyncheon, a childhood friend of Hibbins, and taped the interview. The tape concerns Hibbins' habits as a teenager, including her drinking habits and her proficiency at driving. Pyncheon has since left England for an extended stay in Afghanistan, where she is helping to set up schools for women. Prynne would like to hear the tape, but Nanny Nation does not want to produce it. Is the tape discoverable?

(A) No. It is protected as ordinary work product.

(B) No. It is protected as opinion work product.

(C) Yes. It is protected as ordinary work product, but Prynne can show substantial need of the report and that she is unable without undue hardship to obtain the substantial equivalent of this information by other means.

(D) Yes. Relevant information is always discoverable.

66. Nanny Nation's lawyer has interviewed Holgrave's former boss in order to help get information about Holgrave's lost income claim. The lawyer took notes on the interview, including evaluative comments about the kind of witness the boss would make and the impact that information might have on Nanny Nation's case. Prynne wants to discover the lawyer's notes. Are they discoverable?

(A) No. They are protected as ordinary work product.

(B) No. They are protected as opinion work product.

(C) Yes. They are protected as ordinary work product but Prynne could meet the substantial need/undue hardship requirement.

(D) Yes. They are not protected because Holgrave's boss is not the client of the lawyer who did the interview.

67. Why do the rules protect work product from discovery? What is being protected? What are its costs?

ANSWER:

TOPIC 16: QUESTIONS
DISCOVERY: ATTORNEY-CLIENT PRIVILEGE

68. Which of the following is NOT required for a communication to be protected by the attorney-client privilege?

    (A) The communication was made in confidence.

    (B) The communication was for the purpose of securing legal advice.

    (C) The communication was made in anticipation of litigation or for trial.

    (D) The communication was not voluntarily revealed.

After an unpleasant dispute with local authorities gave her an interest in the law, Hester Prynne went to law school. While in school she married Holgrave, a fellow student, who also adopted Hester's daughter Pearl. After graduation, both began practice in Massachusetts. Both parents doted on Pearl, and both reduced their billable hours in order to spend more time with her. Concerned about quality child care, Prynne contacted Nanny Nation, a respected national agency that trains and recruits child care providers from throughout the United States and the world, with its main office in New York. Through Nanny Nation, Prynne and Holgrave hired Hibbins, a 22-year-old British citizen, to live in their home, do light housework and cooking, and care for Pearl while they were at work.

About a month later, tragedy struck. Hibbins picked up Pearl from piano lessons and was driving her home. Unfortunately, Hibbins had succumbed to homesickness for the local pub and had three beers before getting Pearl. On the way home they were involved in a serious traffic accident. Hibbins suffered only superficial injuries, but Pearl received significant head and neck injuries. Prynne fired Hibbins, and she returned home to England.

Pearl has recovered from most of her injuries, although the doctors continue to watch for signs of permanent brain damage. Prynne and Holgrave have paid substantial medical bills for her treatment and have lost income while tending to her psychological and medical needs. They have suffered mental anguish from watching Pearl struggle with her injuries. Prynne and Holgrave no longer feel comfortable leaving Pearl with anyone other than a family member, and so Holgrave has retired from practice and takes care of Pearl full time.

Prynne and Holgrave sued Nanny Nation for damages in federal district court in Massachusetts. Their theories of recovery are negligence (in hiring and training Hibbins), gross negligence (for a pattern of ignoring serious psychological and behavioral problems of potential nannies), and fraud (for representing that their nannies are highly responsible and well-qualified to care for young children), and they seek both actual and punitive damages.

69. Nanny Nation's lawyer has organized an internal investigation into the hiring of Hibbins. He sent a questionnaire to all of the employees who might have been part of that process, and he has now received the employees' responses. One completed questionnaire comes

from Matthew Maule, Vice President for Human Resources. This questionnaire is:

(A) protected by attorney-client privilege only in a "subject matter test" jurisdiction.

(B) protected by attorney-client privilege only in a "control group test" jurisdiction.

(C) protected by attorney-client privilege in either type of jurisdiction.

(D) not protected by the attorney-client privilege.

70. Another completed questionnaire comes from Roger Chillingworth, a disgruntled former vice president with a reputation for finding fault. This questionnaire is:

(A) protected by attorney-client privilege only in a "subject matter test" jurisdiction.

(B) protected by attorney-client privilege only in a "control group test" jurisdiction.

(C) protected by attorney-client privilege in either type of jurisdiction.

(D) not protected by the attorney-client privilege.

71. Prynne has sent an interrogatory to Nanny Nation that reads, "What did Nanny Nation's CEO tell the company's attorney about the circumstances surrounding the hiring of Hibbins?" Nanny Nation has objected to this interrogatory on the basis of work product and attorney-client privilege. The judge has sustained the objection. What alternative method(s) might Prynne use to get information about Nanny Nation's hiring of Hibbins?

ANSWER:

TOPIC 17: QUESTIONS

DISCOVERY: EXPERT WITNESSES

After an unpleasant dispute with local authorities gave her an interest in the law, Hester Prynne went to law school. While in school she married Holgrave, a fellow student, who also adopted Hester's daughter Pearl. After graduation, both began practice in Massachusetts. Both parents doted on Pearl, and both reduced their billable hours in order to spend more time with her. Concerned about quality child care, Prynne contacted Nanny Nation, a respected national agency that trains and recruits child care providers from throughout the United States and the world, with its main office in New York. Through Nanny Nation, Prynne and Holgrave hired Hibbins, a 22-year-old British citizen, to live in their home, do light housework and cooking, and care for Pearl while they were at work.

About a month later, tragedy struck. Hibbins picked up Pearl from piano lessons and was driving her home. Unfortunately, Hibbins had succumbed to homesickness for the local pub and had three beers before getting Pearl. On the way home they were involved in a serious traffic accident. Hibbins suffered only superficial injuries, but Pearl received significant head and neck injuries. Prynne fired Hibbins, and she returned home to England.

Pearl has recovered from most of her injuries, although the doctors continue to watch for signs of permanent brain damage. Prynne and Holgrave have paid substantial medical bills for her treatment and have lost income while tending to her psychological and medical needs. They have suffered mental anguish from watching Pearl struggle with her injuries. Prynne and Holgrave no longer feel comfortable leaving Pearl with anyone other than a family member, and so Holgrave has retired from practice and takes care of Pearl full time.

Prynne and Holgrave sued Nanny Nation for damages in federal district court in Massachusetts. Their theories of recovery are negligence (in hiring and training Hibbins), gross negligence (for a pattern of ignoring serious psychological and behavioral problems of potential nannies), and fraud (for representing that their nannies are highly responsible and well-qualified to care for young children), and they seek both actual and punitive damages.

72. Prynne has hired a child care expert, Nate Hawthorne, to consult in the preparation of her case against Nanny Nation. Hawthorne will not be testifying when the case goes to trial. Nanny Nation wants to learn Hawthorne's identity and take his deposition. Will this be allowed?

ANSWER:

73. Nanny Nation employs Richard Bellingham, who has a Ph.D. in early childhood education, to design and evaluate its training program. He has worked for Nanny Nation for the last 10 years. Prynne would like to take Bellingham's deposition and ask about Nanny Nation's program, but Nanny Nation says he is a protected consulting expert witness. Under these circumstances:

(A) Bellingham may be deposed. He was not retained as an expert in anticipation of litigation, so the consulting expert privilege does not apply to him.

(B) Bellingham may be deposed. He is not an expert.

(C) Bellingham may not be deposed. He is a non-testifying expert, and so he is protected by Rule 26(b)(4).

(D) Bellingham may not be deposed. Employees may always be designated as protected consulting experts.

74. If Nanny Nation's counsel shares privileged information with Mary Bobbins to prepare her for giving testimony as an expert witness, can Prynne/Holgrave obtain discovery of the information?

ANSWER:

75. Discuss the reasons expert witnesses are used by parties to litigation and how those reasons are reflected in the discovery rules concerning experts.

ANSWER:

TOPIC 18: DISCOVERY DEVICES

QUESTIONS

After an unpleasant dispute with local authorities gave her an interest in the law, Hester Prynne went to law school. While in school she married Holgrave, a fellow student, who also adopted Hester's daughter Pearl. After graduation, both began practice in Massachusetts. Both parents doted on Pearl, and both reduced their billable hours in order to spend more time with her. Concerned about quality child care, Prynne contacted Nanny Nation, a respected national agency that trains and recruits child care providers from throughout the United States and the world, with its main office in New York. Through Nanny Nation, Prynne and Holgrave hired Hibbins, a 22-year-old British citizen, to live in their home, do light housework and cooking, and care for Pearl while they were at work.

About a month later, tragedy struck. Hibbins picked up Pearl from piano lessons and was driving her home. Unfortunately, Hibbins had succumbed to homesickness for the local pub and had three beers before getting Pearl. On the way home they were involved in a serious traffic accident. Hibbins suffered only superficial injuries, but Pearl received significant head and neck injuries. Prynne fired Hibbins, and she returned home to England.

Pearl has recovered from most of her injuries, although the doctors continue to watch for signs of permanent brain damage. Prynne and Holgrave have paid substantial medical bills for her treatment and have lost income while tending to her psychological and medical needs. They have suffered mental anguish from watching Pearl struggle with her injuries. Prynne and Holgrave no longer feel comfortable leaving Pearl with anyone other than a family member, and so Holgrave has retired from practice and takes care of Pearl full time.

Prynne and Holgrave sued Nanny Nation for damages in federal district court in Massachusetts. Their theories of recovery are negligence (in hiring and training Hibbins), gross negligence (for a pattern of ignoring serious psychological and behavioral problems of potential nannies), and fraud (for representing that their nannies are highly responsible and well-qualified to care for young children), and they seek both actual and punitive damages.

76. Prynne wants to make sure her lawsuit has correctly identified Nanny Nation and its corporate structure. She would also like to know precisely who is in charge of what. What would be the best discovery device to use to get this information?

    (A) Request for admissions confirming Prynne's beliefs about these facts.

    (B) Request for production of articles of incorporation and corporate organizational charts.

    (C) Interrogatories asking for this information.

    (D) Deposition of Nanny Nation's Director of Human Resources (DHR) asking these questions.

77. Nanny Nation wants reliable information about Pearl's current medical condition. The company thinks her treating physician is exaggerating the possibilities of future complications. What would be the best discovery device to use to get this information?

    (A) Request for admissions admitting that Pearl has recovered fully.

    (B) Request for production of Pearl's medical records.

    (C) Interrogatories asking for this information.

    (D) Motion for physical examination of Pearl.

78. Nanny Nation is skeptical of Holgrave's lost income claims. It has requested copies of his financial records from two years prior to Pearl's accident to the present. Holgrave has refused to produce them, saying he does not keep copies of such records and so Nanny Nation will have to get them from his accountant. Is Holgrave correct?

ANSWER:

79. Prynne wants to know everything about the circumstances that led to Hibbins' hiring, and everything about Hibbins' training, but she does not know who within the Nanny Nation hierarchy would have this information. What can she do to depose the knowledgeable employees?

    (A) She can notice the deposition, by name, of all Nanny Nation employees she knows about who might possibly have information about Hibbins.

    (B) She can notice the deposition of Nanny Nation and describe with reasonable particularity the matters on which she wants to examine the company.

    (C) She can notice the deposition of Nanny Nation's DHR and force him to find out the answers to her questions.

    (D) She can depose Hibbins and ask her who knows about her hiring and training.

80. Prynne has learned that Nanny Nation subcontracts some of its headhunting activities to Poppins, Ltd., and that Poppins may have been the first to recruit Hibbins. Prynne wants to depose Poppins' DHR and see any documents relating to Hibbins. What discovery device should Prynne use?

    (A) Prynne can notice the deposition of Poppins' DHR and send Poppins a request for production of documents.

    (B) Prynne can subpoena Poppins' DHR for deposition and include in the subpoena a command to produce designated documents.

    (C) Prynne can force Nanny Nation to produce Poppins' DHR for deposition.

(D) Prynne will have to wait until trial of the case to compel answers from Poppins. There is no pretrial device to get information from non-parties.

81. Nanny Nation wants to take Prynne's deposition. It believes she has a lot of information relevant to its defense on both liability and damage claims. Absent agreement or court order, for how long can Nanny Nation depose Prynne?

ANSWER:

82. Prynne is trying to minimize litigation costs, and she has heard that interrogatories are the least expensive way to get information. How many interrogatories may Prynne use in this case without needing permission from the court?

ANSWER:

83. How might Prynne combine the various discovery devices into a coherent discovery plan for this case?

ANSWER:

TOPIC 19: QUESTIONS
DISCOVERY: ELECTRONICALLY STORED INFORMATION

Thomas Eliot is a serious cat lover. He was devoted to his favorite tabby cat, Jennyanydots. Jenny (her nickname) was a lovely, loving feline, but a picky eater. Eliot, therefore, carefully bought her only Special Kitty Select Cuts, sold by Kliban Foods. Kliban sells only on the Internet, through its website. Its customers go to the company website, place an order, provide a credit card number, and the food is delivered to their homes. Kliban's elite clientele spreads the news of the wonders of its cat food by word of mouth — the company has never advertised except by paying Google for sponsored links that appear when anyone searches for "gourmet cat food."

Kliban, in December, decided it could increase its profits by purchasing inexpensive wheat gluten from China to use in its cat food. Unfortunately, it turned out that the gluten contained an industrial chemical called melamine, used to falsely increase the apparent protein content of the wheat gluten. Melamine is helpful in making fertilizer, but can be toxic when ingested in large quantities.

Eliot, as was his habit, bought Special Kitty Select Cuts for Jenny throughout the early spring. In late March, Jenny became very lethargic and suffered from a loss of appetite and vomiting, and so Eliot took her to a veterinarian. The vet diagnosed Jenny as suffering from kidney failure, and eventually Jenny had to be euthanized to relieve her suffering.

Eliot is beside himself with grief. He has filed suit against Kliban in federal district court, seeking damages in excess of $100,000. (The courts in his state allow pet owners to recover damages for emotional distress arising from the loss of a pet.) The complaint alleges that Kliban is liable for breach of warranty, for negligently inspecting the cat food, and for delaying its recall of tainted food until early April even though it knew of the problems much sooner. He believes that Kliban may have known about the problem as early as January, and the press has reported that its Chief Financial Officer sold half of his shares in the company in late February. Consider the following issues that may arise concerning discovery in *Eliot v. Kliban.*

84. Defendant Kliban has been served with process and answered. It is time for counsel to confer regarding discovery. Under Rule 26(f), they will have to discuss "any issues about disclosure or discovery of electronically stored information ("ESI"), including the form or forms in which it should be produced." If you represented Eliot, what would you need to know before going into this conference? What would you want to find out at the conference? What would you want Kliban to agree to with regard to format?

ANSWER:

85. A dispute has arisen about the proper format for the production of ESI. Kliban maintains that when it is the producing party, it gets to designate the format and that it has an absolute right to choose to produce the information in.pdf format or to print it out in hard copy. Is Kliban correct?

(A) Yes. Rule 34 provides that the responding party may indicate the form it intends to use for production.

(B) No. Absent agreement or court order, Kliban must produce ESI in the form in which it is normally maintained or which is reasonably usable.

(C) No. Rule 34 allows the requesting party to specify the format in which ESI should be produced.

(D) Yes and No. Kliban has a right to convert data to.pdf files as it can be searched, but hard copy is not searchable and therefore not reasonably usable.

86. Eliot sent a discovery request to Kliban seeking "all documents concerning Pound's February sale of his Kliban stock." Kliban had agreed at the discovery conference to put a "litigation hold" on the destruction of documents relevant to the litigation. Its tech support people interpreted this to include only desktop computers kept on company property. Kliban, however, supplies all of its management-level employees with laptops and with smartphones that allow the employees to bring work home and on the road. So while work done on the desktop computers was retained, many employees continued to routinely delete documents from their mobile devices, including documents relevant to claims about cats with kidney failure. In particular, in early May, Ezra Pound (Kliban's CFO) deleted all e-mail files by using his mobile devices for the period January–April, in what he called a "routine spring cleaning." In many instances, therefore, there is no easy way to get at relevant e-mails and text messages. Kliban has produced only a few pieces of paper in response to the request for information about Pound's stock sale. Eliot believes the missing data is relevant, but can't afford to employ computer forensic experts to try to reconstruct the lost data. Should the court order Kliban to pay for it?

(A) No. Rule 37 provides that there should be no sanctions for the routine, good faith deletion of data.

(B) Yes. The producing party is responsible for paying the costs of production.

(C) No. Kliban will point out that the deleted communications are not reasonably accessible because of undue burden or cost.

(D) Yes. The information requested is relevant to Kliban's knowledge of the tainted cat food, Eliot's request is sufficiently specific, and the deletion of the data was not routine or in good faith.

TOPIC 20: DISCOVERY SANCTIONS

QUESTIONS

After an unpleasant dispute with local authorities gave her an interest in the law, Hester Prynne went to law school. While in school she married Holgrave, a fellow student, who also adopted Hester's daughter Pearl. After graduation, both began practice in Massachusetts. Both parents doted on Pearl, and both reduced their billable hours in order to spend more time with her. Concerned about quality child care, Prynne contacted Nanny Nation, a respected national agency that trains and recruits child care providers from throughout the United States and the world, with its main office in New York. Through Nanny Nation, Prynne and Holgrave hired Hibbins, a 22-year-old British citizen, to live in their home, do light housework and cooking, and care for Pearl while they were at work.

About a month later, tragedy struck. Hibbins picked up Pearl from piano lessons and was driving her home. Unfortunately, Hibbins had succumbed to homesickness for the local pub and had three beers before getting Pearl. On the way home they were involved in a serious traffic accident. Hibbins suffered only superficial injuries, but Pearl received significant head and neck injuries. Prynne fired Hibbins, and she returned home to England.

Pearl has recovered from most of her injuries, although the doctors continue to watch for signs of permanent brain damage. Prynne and Holgrave have paid substantial medical bills for her treatment and have lost income while tending to her psychological and medical needs. They have suffered from mental anguish, watching Pearl struggle with her injuries. Prynne and Holgrave no longer feel comfortable leaving Pearl with anyone other than a family member, and so Holgrave has retired from practice and takes care of Pearl full time.

Prynne and Holgrave sued Nanny Nation for damages in federal district court in Massachusetts. Their theories of recovery are negligence (in hiring and training Hibbins), gross negligence (for a pattern of ignoring serious psychological and behavioral problems of potential nannies), and fraud (for representing that their nannies are highly responsible and well-qualified to care for young children), and they seek both actual and punitive damages.

87. Prynne sent a request for production of documents to Nanny Nation. Nanny Nation produced a handful of documents, objecting that the remaining requests called for material that was not relevant to the claims and defenses in the lawsuit. Prynne disagrees. She believes that the requested documents are discoverable. What should she do next?

    (A) Confer or attempt to confer in good faith with Nanny Nation in an effort to secure the material. Absent agreement, move for an order compelling production of the documents and reimbursement of Prynne's expenses incurred in making the motion, including attorney's fees.

    (B) Move for an order compelling production of the documents and reimbursement of Prynne's expenses incurred in making the motion, including attorney's fees.

(C) Confer or attempt to confer in good faith with Nanny Nation in an effort to secure the material. Absent agreement, move for an order striking Nanny Nation's answer as a sanction for its noncompliance with a proper discovery request.

(D) Move for an order striking Nanny Nation's answer as a sanction for its noncompliance with a proper discovery request.

88. Imagine that *Prynne & Holgrave v. Nanny Nation* is in trial. Nanny Nation is attempting to call a very important witness on its behalf, and this witness was not disclosed in the initial disclosures or any amendment thereof, and the witness also has not been disclosed in response to any discovery device. What are the most severe sanctions available?

ANSWER:

89. In response to Prynne's request for production of documents, Nanny Nation has produced some documents, but has also objected to Request No. 4, claiming that it calls for documents that are not relevant within the meaning of Rule 26(b)(1). Yet Prynne is not sure whether Nanny Nation is actually withholding anything. Is it proper not to tell?

ANSWER:

TOPIC 21: QUESTIONS
INVOLUNTARY DISMISSALS AND DEFAULT JUDGMENTS

90. Paul Kimball filed a personal injury action in federal district court in Houston, Texas, against Reliable Energy Corporation. Uncharacteristically, the case stayed on the trial court's docket for several years, partly because the plaintiff's lawyers sought extensions of time to perform various required pretrial acts and continuances of scheduled trial dates. Ultimately, the federal judge scheduled a Rule 16 pretrial conference, which Kimball's lawyer failed to attend because the attorney needed to complete work on a brief that was due in the Texas Supreme Court. Although Kimball's lawyer called the court clerk to explain himself and to inform the court that he could not attend the pretrial conference until two days later, the district judge dismissed Kimball's case with prejudice for want of prosecution under the authority of Federal Rule of Civil Procedure 41(b). On appeal of the dismissal order to the Fifth Circuit Court of Appeals:

   (A) The court of appeals probably will reverse the judgment of dismissal as an abuse of discretion because the trial court did not give Kimball and his lawyer advance notice of the court's intent to dismiss the action and an opportunity to make counter-arguments at a hearing.

   (B) The court of appeals will probably reverse the judgment of dismissal because dismissal of Kimball's claim with prejudice based on his counsel's unexcused conduct imposed an unjust penalty on Kimball.

   (C) The court of appeals will probably conclude that the federal judge had authority to dismiss Kimball's case *sua sponte* under the circumstances presented.

   (D) (A) and (B) are both correct.

91. Margie Morgan, a citizen of Pennsylvania, sustained serious bodily injuries while attempting to ride a mechanical bull at the Jim Bob Club located in Dallas, Texas, during the Christmas holidays. As a result, Margie brought suit against Jim Bob Wright, who owned and operated the Jim Bob Club, in federal district court in Dallas, seeking unliquidated damages of $150,000 based on Jim Bob's negligence in the maintenance of his premises. After Jim Bob was served with the summons and complaint in compliance with Texas law, he retained a Dallas lawyer named Rance Tabor to file an answer. If Jim Bob fails to appear and answer or otherwise defend, what should Margie do and when should she do it?

   (A) Margie should file a motion requesting the federal district clerk to enter a default judgment with the clerk as soon as possible and serve the motion on Jim Bob together with a notice of hearing.

   (B) Margie should contact the court clerk as soon as possible on the expiration of 21 days after the date Jim Bob was served with the summons and complaint, show "by affidavit or otherwise" that Jim Bob has defaulted, and request the clerk to enter a default judgment for the damages sought in the complaint.

(C) Margie need not do anything because the court will enter a default judgment, without further action on her part if Jim Bob has not answered in the time required by law.

(D) Margie should show the court clerk that Jim Bob has failed to plead or otherwise defend, within the time required by law, by the process server's affidavit and request entry of default by the clerk and then apply to the court for a default judgment for the damages sought in the compliant.

92. Although Jim Bob's lawyer, Rance Tabor, actually prepared a Rule 12 motion in response to Margie Morgan's complaint and even served it on Margie's lawyer by mail, for some reason the Rule 12 motion was never received by the federal district clerk. Under these circumstances, what is the likely outcome at the default judgment hearing before the trial judge?

(A) On proof of the amount of unliquidated damages by Margie, the trial court must grant a default judgment in that amount.

(B) If the court learns about the circumstances that led to Jim Bob's failure to defend, and believes that Jim Bob was acting in good faith in hiring and relying on Rance Tabor, the trial judge probably will set aside the entry of default and refuse to enter a default judgment.

(C) Unless Jim Bob was given written notice of Margie Morgan's application before the hearing, the trial judge probably will refuse to enter judgment on due process grounds.

(D) (B) and (C) are correct.

93. What procedures must Margie follow if the damages sought in her complaint are based on Jim Bob's failure to pay Margie liquidated damages evidenced by the terms of a promissory note?

ANSWER:

TOPIC 22: QUESTIONS
SUMMARY JUDGMENT: SUMMARY JUDGMENT BURDENS

94. The primary difference between a motion for summary judgment and a motion for judgment as a matter of law at the close of all the evidence is:

    (A) The standard the movant must meet.

    (B) The non-movant's burden to avoid summary judgment.

    (C) The record on which the court will base its decision.

    (D) The nature of the court's review of the record.

95. Prior to the U.S. Supreme Court's decision in *Celotex Corp. v. Catrett*, 477 U.S. 317 (1986), a defendant moving for summary judgment based on the weakness in the plaintiff's case had to meet which of the following burdens before the plaintiff was required to respond?

    (A) Demonstrate the existence of a fact issue regarding all elements of the plaintiff's cause of action.

    (B) Negate some element of the plaintiff's cause of action.

    (C) Negate each element of the plaintiff's cause of action.

    (D) Claim that some element of the plaintiff's cause of action would lack evidentiary support.

96. In the Supreme Court's 1970 decision, *Adickes v. S.H. Kress & Co.*, 398 U.S. 144 (1970), the plaintiff Sandra Adickes needed to prove the existence of a conspiracy between defendant Kress and the police. The trial court granted summary judgment, and the court of appeals affirmed, finding that the record contained no evidence from which a reasonably minded person could draw an inference of conspiracy. The Supreme Court reversed. Justice Harlan's opinion explained that Kress had failed to meet its burden as a summary judgment movant because:

    (A) Kress failed to foreclose the possibility that there was a policeman in the Kress store while Adickes was awaiting service, and that this policeman reached an understanding with some Kress employee that Adickes was not to be served.

    (B) Kress was not specific enough in pointing out to the trial court the weaknesses in Adickes' claim.

    (C) Adickes had not been given sufficient time for discovery in order to acquire evidence to use in opposing summary judgment.

(D) Adickes could defeat summary judgment by referring to the allegations of her complaint.

97. In *Celotex*, Justice Rehnquist's plurality opinion requires the summary judgment movant to:

(A) negate some element of the non-moving party's claim.

(B) point out the absence of evidence to support some element of the non-moving party's case.

(C) produce some evidence to show there is a fact issue regarding the non-moving party's case.

(D) wait until the end of the discovery period before filing a motion for summary judgment.

98. Justice White's concurring opinion in *Celotex* provides the crucial fifth vote. His opinion requires:

(A) more than a conclusory allegation that the plaintiff has no evidence to prove her case.

(B) the movant to disprove the claimed basis for the suit.

(C) the plaintiff to depose the witnesses whose testimony she wants to use in opposition to summary judgment.

(D) simply that the defendant move for summary judgment; this obligates the plaintiff to reveal enough evidence to support her claim.

99. Once a defendant has met its initial burden of moving for summary judgment, the plaintiff must:

(A) produce evidence in admissible form showing the existence of a genuine issue of material fact.

(B) point to the parts of the plaintiff's pleadings that allege the matters in issue.

(C) point out to the court supporting evidence already in the record that would support a reasonable inference in the plaintiff's favor.

(D) point out to the court evidence already in the record, or provided in response to the motion for summary judgment, reducible to admissible evidence, that would support a reasonable inference in the plaintiff's favor.

100. In considering the summary judgment record, what attitude should the court adopt in evaluating the materials offered?

(A) The court should draw all reasonable inferences in favor of the party moving for summary judgment.

(B) The court should draw all reasonable inferences in favor of the non-movant.

(C) The court should weigh the evidence and decide whether there is a genuine issue of material fact.

(D) The court should deny summary judgment if there is any doubt as to the facts.

101. What are the consequences of the shifts in the Supreme Court's attitude toward summary judgment?

ANSWER:

TOPIC 23: QUESTIONS
SUMMARY JUDGMENT: THE BURDENS APPLIED

Brandon and Sarah were young, in love, and in search of a house to buy in celebration of Brandon's law school graduation. They were thrilled to be selected to participate in the popular reality television show, "Home Hunters" (HH). The show paired them with Rhea Max, a local realtor, who showed them three places: one nice but boring, one way out of their price range, and one a "fixer upper" with real potential. Encouraged by the HH producers, they chose the fixer upper after HH promised to install a fabulous chandelier in the bedroom. (It was large and heavy, but HH assured the couple that they would attach it firmly.) Unfortunately, two weeks after Brandon and Sarah moved in and the HH staff installed the chandelier, it crashed onto the bed in the middle of the night, breaking Brandon's leg and injuring Sarah's pretty face.

Brandon and Sarah have sued the company that produces the show, alleging negligence in the selection and installation of the chandelier. HH has denied their claims, alleging that the chandelier fell because of hidden flaws in the ceiling. HH also relies on a contract that Brandon and Sarah signed, absolving the show of liability for any damages related to the purchase of the house or its redecoration by HH.

102. About two months after being sued, HH took Sarah's deposition. They asked her, "What makes you think it was the show's fault that the chandelier fell?" She answered, "Well I don't really know yet, but it's certainly not my fault." Based on this answer, HH filed a motion for summary judgment. The motion, which is extremely brief, states that the plaintiffs have no evidence to support the necessary elements of breach of duty and causation. It points to Sarah's deposition testimony in support of its motion. The plaintiffs, in fact, have no evidence right now, but they know that chandeliers are not supposed to fall on you. How should the plaintiffs respond?

    (A) The plaintiffs can ignore the motion. They have not had enough time for discovery.

    (B) In the interest of caution, the plaintiffs should respond to the motion. While it is not clear whether this motion meets the movant's burden, it would be safer to formally ask the court for more time to respond under Rule 56(d).

    (C) They should assemble evidence, including drafting affidavits, all of which must be in admissible form, and file them with the court in opposition to the motion.

    (D) The plaintiffs can ignore the motion. HH has not disproved either breach or causation.

103. Assume that the court denies the original HH motion for the time being, with leave to refile it after more time for discovery. HH files a second motion for summary judgment, this one based on the release. It includes an affidavit proving that Brandon and Sarah signed the release. Under applicable substantive law, however, such releases are not enforceable when

they purport to release a party from its own negligence. The plaintiffs respond to the motion, briefing this legal issue, but they do not come forward with any evidence in opposition to summary judgment. Under these circumstances:

(A) The court should grant the motion because the plaintiffs have not demonstrated the existence of a genuine dispute as to any material fact as to whether they signed the release.

(B) The court should deny the motion because successive motions for summary judgment are improper.

(C) The court should deny the motion because, as a matter of law, this release is not enforceable. The issue of the genuineness of the signatures is not material.

(D) The court should grant the motion because the plaintiffs did not produce evidence of the cases about releases.

104. After about a year, HH renews its original motion for summary judgment. It supports its motion with an affidavit from an expert structural engineer. The engineer opines, based on his examination of the post-accident chandelier and the plaintiffs' bedroom, that the chandelier was appropriate for the location and correctly installed. He further swears that the ceiling material was weakened by invisible wood rot that caused the chandelier to fall. The plaintiffs do not respond. How should the court rule?

(A) The court should deny the motion for summary judgment. HH has not gone through the whole record and shown that the plaintiffs have no evidence to oppose the expert.

(B) The court should deny the motion for summary judgment. Such motions cannot be based on expert testimony.

(C) The court should grant the motion. The motion was adequately supported and the plaintiffs failed to respond in a way that demonstrates that a fact issue exists.

(D) The court should grant the motion and must do so whenever the non-movant fails to respond.

105. Assume that HH files the same motion as in the previous question, but this time the plaintiffs respond with an affidavit from their own expert and their own motion for summary judgment. The plaintiffs' expert swears that he has examined the wood of the ceiling and there is no wood rot. He further notes that if there were wood rot any competent carpenter would have seen it, and so it would have been negligent to proceed with the plan to install a heavy chandelier. The plaintiffs' expert opines that the 50-pound chandelier was negligently attached only to sheet rock rather than to a sturdier ceiling joist, and that the weight of the chandelier plus its inadequate anchoring caused it to fall. How should the court rule?

(A) The court should grant the plaintiffs' motion. Their expert is more believable.

(B) The court should grant the defendant's motion. Its expert is more believable.

(C) The court should deny both motions. Neither one was adequately supported.

(D) The court should deny both motions. The conflicting expert affidavits demonstrate that there is a genuine issue of material fact.

106. Imagine a different combination of motion and response. HH files a motion for summary judgment. The motion argues that the plaintiffs have had a year to do discovery and still lack evidence of breach and causation. It supports its motion by pointing to the plaintiffs' automatic initial disclosures, which contain no evidence of negligence, and their answer to Defendant's Interrogatory No. 3. The interrogatory stated: "Please identify all evidence that you intend to use to prove that the negligence of defendant caused the occurrence in question." The plaintiffs' answer was: "Unknown at this time. Will supplement after further discovery." Plaintiffs have not supplemented their response, and the discovery period has just ended.

The plaintiffs respond to the motion by filing the following: (1) a copy of a letter from their insurance adjuster stating that he has inspected the chandelier and ceiling and believes that the chandelier was both too heavy and improperly installed; and (2) the deposition of Rhea Max (now deceased) from a different lawsuit, brought against her by a different HH contestant, in which Max blames the HH in-house carpenter (no longer so employed) for consistently poor work. The plaintiffs also state that they intend to call the carpenter as a witness at trial, but they have so far been unable to locate him to depose or subpoena him.

How should the court rule on the defendant's motion, and why?

ANSWER:

TOPIC 24: RIGHT TO JURY TRIAL — QUESTIONS

107. Martha and Fred own adjoining tracts of land in Starr County, Texas. Fred claims that Martha has interfered with Fred's use and enjoyment of the property. Fred brings suit on this claim in federal district court in the Southern District of Texas, the requirements of diversity jurisdiction being satisfied. Which of the following propositions is most accurate?

    (A) If Fred seeks an injunction, Martha will be entitled to a jury trial of all fact issues.

    (B) If Fred seeks a money judgment, Martha will not be entitled to a jury trial of all fact issues.

    (C) If Fred seeks both an injunction and incidental money damages, Fred will not be entitled to a jury trial of all fact issues.

    (D) If Fred seeks both money damages and an injunction, he will be entitled to a jury trial of all fact issues.

108. Down-South Corporation filed suit in federal district court in New Orleans, Louisiana, seeking damages and an award of declaratory and injunctive relief against Peppy Cola Corporation and four of its officers. Down-South alleged that the defendants had violated Sections 1 and 2 of the Sherman Act and Section 2 of the Robinson Patman Act. If Down-South made a jury demand by endorsing it on the Complaint filed and served on Peppy Cola Corporation, is Down-South entitled to a jury trial?

    (A) Down-South is not entitled to a jury trial of any fact questions because the gist of the action is equitable.

    (B) Down-South is not entitled to a jury trial because there were no antitrust statutes in 1791.

    (C) Down-South is entitled to a jury trial of all fact issues under the Seventh Amendment.

    (D) Down-South is entitled to a jury trial on the claims for declaratory and injunctive relief.

109. After extensive pretrial discovery it is apparent that the factual issues in the case are very complex and arguably beyond the practical abilities of the jurors to resolve. As a result, Peppy Cola Corporation has filed a motion to strike the jury demand made by Down-South Corporation on the basis that the complexity of the case has made it necessary to regard the antitrust claims as equitable rather than legal or call for the application of a complexity exception to the Seventh Amendment. How should the trial judge rule on the motion?

ANSWER:

TOPIC 25: SELECTION AND COMPOSITION OF JURIES

QUESTIONS

110. How many members must a civil jury have in federal court?

   (A) twelve.

   (B) no less than six and no more than twelve.

   (C) eight.

   (D) the number is entirely within the discretion of the trial court.

111. Unless the parties stipulate otherwise, what level of agreement is required of a civil jury in federal court?

   (A) whatever the number of jurors, their verdict must be unanimous.

   (B) with a jury of twelve, at least ten of the jurors must agree on the answers to all of the questions.

   (C) with a jury of twelve, the same ten jurors must agree on the answers to all of the questions.

   (D) more than half of the jurors must agree on the verdict.

112. In choosing the actual jury from the larger pool of potential jurors,

   (A) only the judge may question the jury panel.

   (B) each party may exercise only six challenges for cause.

   (C) the parties alternate choosing jurors until the full number is chosen.

   (D) each party may exercise three peremptory challenges (although the court may group multiple parties as a "party" for this purpose).

113. John Prentice has sued Drayton Industries for tortious interference with his contract with Ryan Corporation. During voir dire, Drayton's lawyer used his three peremptory challenges to eliminate the only three African-Americans in the pool of potential jurors, and Prentice suspects that Drayton was deliberately striking black jurors. Prentice would prefer a more diverse jury. What recourse, if any, does he have?

   (A) None. Peremptory challenges can be exercised for any reason or no reason, and the lawyer making them cannot be required to explain his or her choices.

(B) Prentice should provide the judge with sufficient information to draw an inference that discrimination has occurred.

(C) Drayton's lawyer would then have a chance to provide a race-neutral explanation for those strikes. If successful, Prentice could respond by trying to show that the explanation is a pretext. To be entitled to relief, Prentice must demonstrate that Drayton's lawyers purposefully discriminated on the basis of race in exercising the peremptory strikes.

(D) Both (B) and (C) are correct.

TITLE 26: JURY INSTRUCTIONS: FORM AND OBJECTIONS — QUESTIONS

US District Judge Chamberlain Haller has been presiding over litigation arising out of damage to a car. Plaintiff Mona Vito is suing defendant Billy's Carwash for negligently damaging her vintage Buick Skylark with gold-dipped steering wheel and crocodile-skin upholstery. While Mona herself was uninjured in the disastrous drive through the swirling brushes, her once pristine car is one big mess, and she seeks compensation for her losses. Billy wishes he could blame this on Mona's own negligence, but his only defense is that he was not negligent and that Mona is overestimating her damages.

114. Your represent Mona, trial is approaching, and you doubt that the case is going to settle. You think that the way in which Mona's claims are presented to the jury in this case will be extremely important. What jury instruction formats might Judge Haller choose to use to get the jury's decision on Mona's negligence and damage claims?

    (A) A general verdict allowing the jury to make its own decisions about the meaning of negligence and allowable components of Mona's damages.

    (B) A general verdict, providing the jury with definitions of relevant legal terms and asking whether Billy's Carwash was negligent and what amount of money (if any) would properly compensate Mona.

    (C) A special verdict asking only a few questions on facts about which Judge Haller feels uncertain.

    (D) A general verdict asking about negligence accompanied by written questions, but only if the questions cover every single disputed issue of fact so Judge Haller has a check on the jury's thought processes.

115. You'd like the opportunity to actually try to influence Judge Haller's instructions by suggesting both format and wording. There's no local rule about this, and Judge Haller has not entered a relevant case-specific order. When should you make your request for instructions in order for that request to be timely?

    (A) The request should be made at the final pretrial conference provided for in Rule 16(e).

    (B) The request should be made before voir dire.

    (C) The request should be made before the plaintiff calls her first witness.

    (D) The request should be made no later than the close of the evidence.

116. Judge Haller believes that the legal issues in this case are simple and has decided on a

general verdict instruction format. When will he read his instructions to the jury?

(A) He must read them before the lawyers make their closing arguments.

(B) He must read them after the lawyers make their closing arguments.

(C) He has discretion to read them before or after the arguments.

(D) Is this a trick question? No judge today wants to waste time reading some long document while the jury zones out. The judge will give each juror a written copy of the instructions in the jury room.

117. Judge Haller has informed the parties of his proposed charge before instructing the jury and before closing arguments, as required by Rule 51(b). You think part of the instruction is legally incorrect (although you kind of think Mona might win anyway). What should you do?

(A) Do nothing for now. Maybe Mona will win, and if she loses then you can object to the language of the instruction for the first time on appeal. It's nice to have a probable error to rely on for reversal.

(B) Make a general objection to the instruction — that will keep your options open to craft your argument on appeal if Mona loses.

(C) Object now. This is your chance to preserve error under Rule 51, and if you don't do it you're absolutely out of luck.

(D) Object now. This is the time to preserve error under Rule 51, unless you can show that the problem with the instruction was plain error that affects substantial rights.

118. Imagine that Judge Haller decided to submit the case to the jury using a special verdict under Rule 49(a). He therefore informed the parties that he would ask the jury this question:

Do you find from a preponderance of the evidence that Billy's Carwash was negligent in its handling of Mona Vito's car? (Billy's Carwash was "negligent" if it failed to act the way a reasonable, prudent carwash would act under the same or similar circumstances).

ANSWER: ____Yes ____No

What amount of money, if paid now in cash, would reasonably compensate Mona Vito for the damage to her car during its handling by Billy's Carwash? Answer in dollars and cents, if any.

ANSWER: ________

Neither party objected to these questions or requested the submission of additional questions before the jury retired to consider its verdict. After several hours of deliberation, the jury answered Question 1 "Yes," and Question 2 "$100,000." Neither party objected to the jury's response, and the jury was discharged. Several weeks later, the court entered judgment for Mona on the jury's verdict. Billy's Carwash hired a new lawyer on appeal, and the lawyer realized that the jury was asked no question about proximate cause. Assuming that there are no other issues on appeal, the court of appeals:

(A) Must reverse and remand the case for a new trial because an essential element was omitted from the special verdict questions.

(B) Must vacate and remand the case to the trial court for the judge to make a specific finding on the issue of proximate cause.

(C) Must affirm the trial court's judgment because Billy's Carwash waived the right to have the causation issue submitted to the jury.

(D) Must reverse and remand the case for new trial because the jury's answers contain a fatal conflict.

TOPIC 27: QUESTIONS

BURDENS OF PROOF AT TRIAL; PRIMA FACIE CASE AND PRESUMPTIONS

Kate sues Dave, alleging that his negligence caused her personal injuries. Dave denied these allegations and also pleaded the affirmative defense of contributory negligence. Assume that in this jurisdiction contributory negligence must be pleaded and proved by the defendant and is a complete bar to any recovery by the plaintiff.

119. At a trial of *Kate v. Dave*, as to the elements of Kate's claim,

    (A) Kate would have the burden of production and the burden of persuasion on all elements of her cause of action.

    (B) Kate would have the burden of production initially, but after Kate puts on legally sufficient evidence of each element of her claim, the burden of production shifts to Dave to raise one or more fact issues. The burden of persuasion remains on Kate for her cause of action and on Dave for his defense of contributory negligence.

    (C) Kate would have the burdens of production and persuasion for her cause of action initially, but both shift to Dave after Kate puts on her case in chief.

    (D) Because he has raised the affirmative defense of contributory negligence, Dave has the burdens of production and persuasion throughout the case to show that Kate was negligent and that he was not.

120. At a trial of *Kate v. Dave*,

    (A) Kate's failure to prove the elements of her claim by a preponderance of the evidence could result in the judge entering judgment as a matter of law for Dave before the case goes to the jury.

    (B) Kate's failure to produce evidence on which a reasonable jury could find for Kate could result in the judge entering judgment as a matter of law for Dave before the case goes to the jury.

    (C) Kate's right to jury trial under the Seventh Amendment means that her case must be permitted to go to the jury even if she fails to meet her burden of production.

    (D) If Kate produces evidence in her case in chief demonstrating that no reasonable jury could fail to find for Kate, it is irrelevant what evidence Dave might have; the judge could grant judgment as a matter of law for Kate before the case goes to the jury.

121. At a trial of *Kate v. Dave*,

(A) Dave would have the burden of production and the burden of persuasion on all elements of his affirmative defense.

(B) Dave would have the burden of persuasion but not the burden of production on all elements of his affirmative defense.

(C) Dave would have the burden of persuasion and the burden of production on at least one element of his affirmative defense.

(D) Dave would have the burden of production but not the burden of persuasion on all elements of his affirmative defense.

122. Ruben and Noel Salmon are the owners and operators of a fertilizer company in Rio Grande City known as Red Barn Chemical Company. One evening at about 10:00 p.m., their employee, Tomás Vasquez used a company truck to travel to Camargo, Mexico on a personal errand. Tomás was allowed to use the truck for the purpose of going to and from work at the fertilizer plant, but not allowed to cross the border in the truck for any reason.

Because Tomás did not leave Camargo until 5:30 a.m. the next day, he did not return to the ranch, but proceeded directly to the fertilizer plant. Before he arrived, however, while operating the truck on Main Street in Rio Grande City, he lost control of the truck and crashed into another vehicle severely injuring Jose Hinojosa.

Jose sued Ruben and Noel Salmon for damages resulting from Tomás' negligent operation of the partnership's truck in the course and scope of employment.

At the trial of *Hinojosa v. Salmon and Vasquez*, as to the course and scope of employment element of Jose's negligence claim against the Salmons:

(A) The course and scope of employment element is established conclusively under the law by the evidence that Tomás was operating the Salmon's truck when the accident occurred.

(B) The course and scope of employment element is established conclusively by the presumption that an employee operating a truck owned by his employers was acting within the course and scope of employment on the occasion in question.

(C) The course and scope of employment element will not be established by a presumption if evidence is introduced that Tomás was merely on his way to work when the accident occurred, which evidence destroys the presumption.

(D) The course and scope of employment element is supported by the reasonable inference that Tomás was acting within the scope of his employment, independently of any presumption.

123. Melissa, a sixty-five year old "food prep" specialist employed by Tommy's Taco Warehouse at an hourly wage rate of $10 per hour had her work hours reduced by one-third after twenty years of service. Melissa believes that she was the subject of discrimination in violation of employment discrimination laws, because during her twenty years of service at Tommy's Taco Warehouse, she always received favorable employment reviews. At the time

she had her hours cut, Melissa's supervisor, George, who had recently been hired to head the food preparation operations, told Melissa that her hours were being reduced because of economic reasons.

Melissa sues Tommy's Taco Warehouse for employment discrimination based on her age, claiming that she was qualified for the position of "food prep" specialist, that her reduction in hours was an adverse employment action, and that her hours were assumed by younger employees.

Assume that Tommy's Taco Warehouse filed an answer denying Melissa's claims that her reduced hours were assigned to younger employees or that she was otherwise discriminated against because of her age. Assume further that Tommy's moves for summary judgment and supports its motion with an affidavit signed by Melissa's supervisor, George, averring that Melissa's age was not a motivating factor in the reduction of her hours, and that her hours were not assigned to younger employees. How can Melissa defeat Tommy's Taco Warehouse's motion?

(A) Melissa has the burden of production of a prima facie case of age discrimination.

(B) If Melissa meets her burden of production of a prima facie case of age discrimination, the burden of production shifts to Tommy's Taco Warehouse to produce legally sufficient evidence of a legitimate nondiscriminatory reason for its actions.

(C) If Tommy's Taco Warehouse asserts that a reduction in force due to economic conditions is a legitimate nondiscriminatory reason for Melissa's reduction in hours, Melissa should be able to avoid summary judgment by offering contrary evidence, but will have the burden of proving purposeful discrimination as a matter of fact (or law) at trial.

(D) (A), (B), and (C) are all correct.

TOPIC 28: QUESTIONS

MOTIONS FOR JUDGMENT AS A MATTER OF LAW; STANDARD AND SCOPE OF REVIEW

124. Margaret McPherson engaged Dr. House to diagnose and treat her mysterious abdominal symptoms. After Dr. House performed an appendectomy, McPherson continued to experience pain in her abdomen and reported her problems to Dr. House who told McPherson that an infection had developed and that a second operation would be necessary. Both before and after the second operation, performed by Dr. House, McPherson experienced severe abdominal pain and could not work or engage in normal physical activities for several months. Ultimately, after being billed more than $20,000 for the second operation, McPherson sued Dr. House for medical negligence. At trial, which was before a six-person jury in the federal district court in New Jersey, McPherson testified to the foregoing matters and also testified that, in her opinion, Dr. House was extremely sloppy and negligent in not correctly diagnosing and treating her medical condition. After presenting other evidence concerning her injuries and loss of income due to her inability to work, McPherson rested her case. Dr. House has moved for judgment as a matter of law. How should the federal judge rule on Dr. House's motion?

ANSWER:

125. Maurice, who is clearly not a public figure, brought a libel suit against News Ltd. alleging that News Ltd.'s publication of a news story defamed Maurice by casting him as a *de facto* member of Creedlove, a phony charity actually involved in the distribution of illegal drugs for private gain. After removing the action to federal court, and asserting the defense of truth, News Ltd. defended the case at a jury trial by obtaining admissions from Maurice that Maurice had regularly attended Creedlove's public meetings and made cash contributions for the last 10 years. At trial, Maurice testified that his reputation had been ruined by News Ltd., causing him humiliation and economic harm. With respect to the issue of his *de facto* membership in Creedlove, Maurice testified that, although he had attended some meetings and made annual contributions, Creedlove's membership rolls did not include his name and that over the same period he had published several magazine articles showing opposition to Creedlove's practices. After Maurice rested, News Ltd. moved for judgment as a matter of law based on its affirmative defense of truth on the issue of Maurice's *de facto* membership in Creedlove. How should the trial judge rule on the motion?

(A) The trial judge should grant the motion because Maurice's testimony is unbelievable.

(B) The trial judge should overrule the motion because there is a factual controversy about the pivotal fact of Maurice's membership based on the totality of the direct and circumstantial evidence.

(C) The trial court should deny the motion because Maurice's direct evidence negates any reasonable inference that could be drawn from the circumstantial evidence about meetings and contributions.

(D) The trial court should grant the motion if the trial judge concludes that Maurice's testimony is unconvincing.

126. Assume the same facts as in the preceding question, but assume further that the case is tried to the court in a bench trial rather than to a jury. How may the court rule?

ANSWER:

127. Rule 50(b) provides that a motion for judgment as a matter of law made before submission of the case to the jury may be renewed after verdict by filing a motion no later than 28 days after entry of judgment, with an alternative motion for new trial under Rule 59. But if no motion is made before submission of the case to the jury, a Rule 50(b) motion cannot properly be sustained after entry of judgment. What is the reason for this approach?

ANSWER:

128. In *Maurice v. News Ltd.*, what if News Ltd.'s pre-verdict motion is denied and News Ltd. does not renew the motion after judgment?

(A) Unless the Rule 50(b) renewal motion is made and ruled on by the trial judge, News Ltd. cannot complain about the overruling of the Rule 50(a) motion on appeal.

(B) News Ltd. is not required to renew the Rule 50(a) motion after judgment to complain about the overruling of the Rule 50(a) motion on appeal.

(C) News Ltd. can probably complain about the legal insufficiency of the evidence on appeal, if News Ltd. made a post-verdict motion for new trial complaining about the legal insufficiency of the evidence; appellate relief will be limited to a remand under these circumstances.

(D) (A) and (C) are both correct.

129. In *Maurice v. News Ltd.*, if News Ltd. moved for summary judgment contending that it was entitled to judgment as a matter of law on the issue of Maurice's *de facto* membership in Creedlove, can the denial of this motion for judgment as a matter of law be a basis for appellate complaint after full trial on the merits?

ANSWER:

TOPIC 29: QUESTIONS
BENCH TRIALS; FINDINGS OF FACT AND CONCLUSIONS OF LAW

Professor Xavier Goodnight sued Mainland University in federal court for gender discrimination in violation of federal and state discrimination statutes. His complaint is based on a claim that Mainland University gave preferential treatment to his female colleagues in matters concerning their compensation. In its answer, Mainland University admitted that Goodnight was a member of protected class and that he was qualified for his academic position but denied that he was treated less favorably than his female colleagues. After completion of discovery and the denial of Mainland University's motion for summary judgment, a bench trial was conducted. After Professor Goodnight rested his case, Mainland University moved for judgment and the trial judge granted the motion by ruling on the record in open court that Professor Goodnight's discrimination claim should be denied and by signing a written judgment in favor of Mainland University. The judge also adopted findings of fact and conclusions of law corresponding almost exactly with findings of fact and conclusions prepared by Mainland University's lawyers.

130. Is the trial court's judgment vulnerable to challenge on appeal to the court of appeals on the basis that the trial judge adopted Mainland University's proposed findings and conclusions verbatim?

ANSWER:

131. What, if anything, must Professor Goodnight do in the trial court to preserve complaints about the sufficiency of the evidence to support the trial court's findings and the legal validity of the trial court's conclusions, and what standard of appellate review applies to the trial court's findings, conclusions, and judgment?

    (A) Findings of fact are subject to a clearly erroneous standard of review on appeal under which the reviewing court must give due regard to the trial court's opportunity to judge the witness' credibility.

    (B) In order to preserve his complaints about the sufficiency of the evidence to support the findings, Professor Goodnight must challenge the findings in the trial court by objecting to the findings or requesting different ones.

    (C) Challenges to the trial court's legal conclusions are subject to a non-deferential de novo standard of review on appeal.

    (D) (A) and (C) are both correct.

132. Was the trial court at liberty to grant Mainland University's motion for judgment after Professor Goodnight had rested his case?

ANSWER:

TOPIC 30: QUESTIONS
MOTIONS FOR NEW TRIAL & RULE 60(B) MOTIONS

133. Clark brings an action against Sunderland for copyright infringement concerning a book about Civil Procedure. The case is tried to a jury. Assume that Clark offered and the trial court admitted evidence, over Sunderland's objection, that Sunderland had committed other copyright violations involving stories about lawyers. Assume further that the trial judge instructed the jury erroneously that Clark had to prove that Sunderland knowingly violated the copyright laws by clear and convincing evidence. Nonetheless, the jury returned a verdict for Clark.

    Which of the following statements is most accurate?

    (A) Sunderland should request the judge to make findings of fact and conclusions of law.

    (B) Sunderland may move for and probably has the right to obtain a new trial as a result of the erroneous jury instructions.

    (C) Sunderland may move for and probably has the right to a new trial based on the admission of the evidence of other copyright violations.

    (D) Sunderland may challenge the factual sufficiency of the evidence for the first time in a motion for new trial.

134. If Sunderland attempted to raise the factual sufficiency of the evidence for the first time in the court of appeals, what result?

ANSWER:

135. Under the same facts as in question 133, assume that the jury returns a defense verdict for Sunderland. Which of the following statements is most accurate?

    (A) Clark may move for a new trial, but cannot move for judgment as a matter of law because he had the burden of proof on the whole case.

    (B) Clark can move for a judgment on the basis that the jury's verdict is against the great weight and preponderance of the credible evidence and is clearly wrong.

    (C) Clark may combine a motion for new trial with a motion for judgment as a matter of law even though these remedies are inconsistent with each other.

    (D) None of the above.

136. What if the verdict loser has not made a proper motion for judgment as a matter of law

"before the case is submitted to the jury," but does make a proper challenge to the verdict (based on answers to special interrogatories) by filing a motion for new trial challenging the sufficiency of the evidence to support the jury's $1,000,000 damages award, no later than 28 days after entry of judgment? What can a reviewing court do on appeal if the trial judge overrules the motion for new trial?

ANSWER:

137. Ace Pickles (Ace) brought suit against Duke Power Co. (Duke) for damages based on a complaint that Duke had failed to promote Ace in violation of Ace's rights to equal employment opportunity under the Civil Rights Act of 1964. After Duke was served with the summons and complaint, it failed to answer and Ace obtained a default judgment against it for $100,000 based on Ace's damages allegations concerning lost income and his false affidavit concerning the differential between his current wages and the wages that he would have earned, if he had been promoted. The clerk entered the $100,000 judgment. With respect to the default judgment:

(A) If Duke learns of the entry of judgment within 28 days, Duke should move for a new trial because it was improper for the clerk to enter the default judgment.

(B) If Duke learns of the judgment more than 28 days after its entry, Duke should move to have the default set aside in accordance with Rule 60(b) on the basis of its excusable neglect.

(C) Regardless of when Duke learns of the judgment, the trial court should set it aside because a judgment based on false testimony is absolutely void.

(D) (A) and (B) are both correct.

138. If less than one year has elapsed from the date that the $100,000 default judgment was entered against Duke, under what circumstances can Duke attack the judgment in the trial court?

ANSWER:

139. Four years after a take-nothing judgment became final in a diversity case, Molly obtains very clear proof that Mike deliberately withheld documents that would have defeated Mike's affirmative defense, which was the basis of the trial court's summary judgment against Molly. The documents were definitively covered by a request for production sent by Molly to Mike. Under these circumstances what would be Molly's most likely avenue for setting aside the judgment?

ANSWER:

TOPIC 31: QUESTIONS
SUBJECT MATTER JURISDICTION: DIVERSITY OF CITIZENSHIP

140. Tom, from Texas, wants to sue Mark, from Mississippi, and Acme Corp., an Alabama corporation with its principal place of business in Texas, for $100,000 alleging breach of contract. Can Tom properly file his suit in federal court?

    (A) Yes. There is diversity of citizenship because Tom and Mark are citizens of different states.

    (B) Yes. There is diversity of citizenship because Mark and Acme are citizens of different states.

    (C) Yes. There is diversity of citizenship because Tom is a citizen of a different state from Mark and Acme.

    (D) No. Tom and Acme are both citizens of Texas and the diversity statute requires that no plaintiff be a citizen of the same state as any defendant.

141. Clara and Carl, from California, want to sue Ida and Irene, both of whom are citizens of Illinois, for a $500,000 personal injury claim. Can they properly file their suit in federal court?

ANSWER:

142. Pam was born and grew up in Pennsylvania. She went away to college in Massachusetts (her parents paid her tuition), but she always returned home to work in the summers. During her senior year, her parents moved to Virginia, and she lived there between college and law school. She is now a law student at a law school in Texas. She really likes it there and has decided to take the Texas bar exam and look for a job there after graduation. Where is Pam domiciled?

    (A) Pennsylvania. This is her domicile of origin and she keeps it until she is no longer a student.

    (B) Massachusetts. She changed her domicile when she went to live there to attend college.

    (C) Virginia. Her domicile changed when her parents moved there and she went to join them.

    (D) Texas. By being present there and having the intention to stay indefinitely, she has made the state her domicile.

143. Karen has always lived in Kansas. She wants to try new experiences, and so she has decided to move to New York City. She has started getting home delivery of The New York Times and is looking for a job and an apartment. Karen loads up her Audi and begins the move to New York. While on the road, she is involved in a serious automobile accident and is hospitalized in Ohio. Where is Karen domiciled at this point?

(A) Kansas. This is her domicile of origin.

(B) Ohio. Given the extent of her injuries, she will be there indefinitely.

(C) New York. She has made the decision to make New York her home.

(D) Karen is in transit — at the moment she has no domicile.

144. Mike, from Maine, enters into a contract with Monster Motors, Inc. (also from Maine) to buy a rare and extremely valuable tricked-out sports car for $100,000. Monster Motors breaches the contract, as it has decided that Mike is not cool enough to drive such a car. Mike, in the meantime, has moved to New Hampshire, bought a house, gotten a job, and considers New Hampshire his home. Mike then sues Monster Motors in federal court in Maine. Does the court have subject matter jurisdiction?

(A) No. Mike is still a citizen of Maine for purposes of diversity jurisdiction because he lived there when the cause of action arose.

(B) Yes. Mike has changed his citizenship by moving to New Hampshire with the intent to make it his home. Diversity jurisdiction is determined as of the time the suit is filed.

(C) No. Mike has changed his citizenship for other purposes, but he cannot do so in order to confer jurisdiction on the federal courts.

(D) Yes. As long as Mike owns property in New Hampshire he is a citizen there for purposes of diversity jurisdiction.

145. Greg, from Georgia, wants to sue Frank, from Florida, for personal injuries totaling $250,000. Must he file the suit in federal court?

(A) Yes. The complete diversity requirement has been met.

(B) Yes. This is necessary to protect Frank from local prejudice.

(C) No. While federal jurisdiction would be proper, it is not exclusive.

(D) No. Only federal question jurisdiction is exclusive in the federal courts.

146. Marilyn, from Minnesota, wants to sue Brotherhood of Bison in federal court. The Brotherhood is an unincorporated association with its headquarters in Wisconsin. More than half of its members are from Wisconsin, another quarter is from Illinois, and the rest are from a smattering of states, including Minnesota. If Marilyn were to file her suit in federal court, would the diversity requirement be met?

(A) Yes. The Brotherhood is a citizen of Wisconsin because its headquarters are there.

(B) Yes. The Brotherhood is a citizen of Wisconsin because a majority of its members are domiciled there.

(C) No. The citizenship of an unincorporated association can never form the basis of diversity jurisdiction.

(D) No. Diversity of citizenship is lacking.

147. Terry, from Tennessee, wants to file a class action on behalf of all purchasers of Cheap Computers notebook computer model A1. She alleges, as named plaintiff, that this model has a design flaw that causes the hard disk to crash without warning, losing in the process all of the owner's data. In Terry's case, this happened just before her first-year law school finals and she lost all of her notes and outlines. Her proposed class would include all U.S. purchasers in the last two years. Cheap Computers, a Montana corporation with its principal place of business in Montana, sold its notebook model A1 in college bookstores in every state in the U.S. Assuming there is no problem with the amount in controversy requirement, for purposes of diversity jurisdiction, does Terry's class meet the requirements of 28 U.S.C. § 1332(a)?

(A) Yes. Terry's citizenship is diverse from Cheap Computers' citizenship.

(B) No. At least some members of the class will be citizens of Montana, thus destroying complete diversity.

(C) Yes. The diversity of citizenship requirement does not apply to class actions.

(D) Yes, but only if Terry defines the class to exclude citizens of Montana.

148. An Upside Airlines (UA) jet tragically crashed in a snowstorm while flying over Idaho, killing all 86 passengers. Upside is a Delaware corporation with its principal place of business in Utah. The passengers were citizens of Utah, Idaho, and Wyoming. Larry Lawyer represents the families of several of the passengers, including some from each state. He wants to file suit against UA in federal court. Each plaintiff has damages far in excess of $75,000. Would federal jurisdiction be proper?

(A) No. Since some of the plaintiffs are from Utah, and UA is a citizen of Utah, complete diversity of citizenship is lacking.

(B) Yes. UA is a citizen of Delaware, and so it is diverse from all of the plaintiffs.

(C) Yes. There is diversity between at least some of the plaintiffs and UA, more than 75 people died in the same location, and the accident took place in a state different from UA's residence.

(D) No. There is only minimal diversity, and substantial parts of the accident did not take place in different states.

149. Northeast Airlines, Inc., a Delaware corporation, was founded in the 1970s as a local

carrier, specializing in short business flights between New England cities. It has since expanded dramatically across the country, absorbing other airlines, and now its most extensive business is elsewhere. While the company's executive offices remain in Boston, it has more employees, more flights, and owns more property in Texas than in any other state. For purposes of diversity jurisdiction, Northeast is a citizen of Delaware and:

(A) Texas, because Texas is the Northeast's locus of operations.

(B) Texas, because Texas is Northeast's center of gravity.

(C) Massachusetts, as well as all other states in which Northeast is subject to personal jurisdiction.

(D) Massachusetts, because it is the company's nerve center.

150. Mark, from Iowa, purchased a motor scooter from Big Star Cycle Corporation, which is incorporated in Nevada and has its corporate headquarters in Dallas, Texas. The motor scooter was manufactured in Germany by Rhine Ludwig AG, a German corporation with its principal place of business in Frankfurt, Germany. Unfortunately, the scooter was defective and unreasonably dangerous as designed, and this defect caused an accident and severe personal injuries to Mark. Mark wants to sue both Big Star Cycle Corporation and Rhine Ludwig AG in federal court. Assuming no problem with the amount in controversy, would federal jurisdiction be proper?

(A) No, although there is diversity of citizenship between Mark and Big Star Cycle Corporation, the joinder of Rhine Ludwig AG would destroy diversity because Rhine Ludwig AG is a corporation rather than an individual citizen of an American State or a foreign state.

(B) Yes, not only is there a diversity jurisdiction over Mark's claim against Big Star Cycle Corporation, there is an alienage jurisdiction over Mark's claim against Rhine Ludwig AG.

(C) Yes, not only is there diversity jurisdiction, there is also jurisdiction if Rhine Ludwig AG is joined as a party by Mark because it is an additional party that is a citizen of a foreign state.

(D) Answers (B) and (C) are both correct.

151. Jason Toranto and his mother, Barbara, want to file a federal lawsuit against Pacific American Airlines as a result of personal injuries they suffered on a flight from Austin to Los Angeles. Jason, a citizen of Canada, was lawfully admitted for permanent residence (given a "green card") in 2012. He is domiciled in California. Barbara is a Canadian citizen. Pacific American Airlines is a California corporation with its corporate headquarters in Austin, Texas. Assuming no federal question and no problem with the amount in controversy, would federal jurisdiction be proper?

(A) No, by virtue of his status as a permanent resident, Jason cannot bring a diversity action against Pacific American Airlines even though he is a Canadian citizen.

(B) Yes, because there is diversity jurisdiction between Barbara Toranto and Pacific American Airlines, Jason probably can be joined as an additional party, despite his green card.

(C) Yes, there is alienage jurisdiction between Jason and Barbara, citizens of Canada, and Pacific American Airlines, a citizen of California (State of incorporation) and of Texas (principal place of business).

(D) Answers (B) and (C) are both correct.

TOPIC 32: QUESTIONS
SUBJECT MATTER JURISDICTION: AMOUNT IN CONTROVERSY

152. Nick, from North Carolina, wants to sue Carol, from Connecticut. Nick has two claims against Carol. One claim, for $50,000, is for breach of a contract to buy Duke basketball souvenirs. The other, for $30,000, is for breach of a separate contract to buy University of Connecticut women's basketball t-shirts. Carol took delivery of the items but has failed to pay for them. If Nick filed his suit in federal court, what would be the amount in controversy?

    (A) $50,000

    (B) $30,000

    (C) $80,000

    (D) $80,000 plus interest

153. Martha and Maude, from Maryland, want to sue David and Don, from Delaware, for personal injuries. They each claim $50,000 in damages. Would their suit satisfy the federal amount in controversy requirement?

ANSWER:

154. Tom and Ted, from Texas, jointly own an obligation against Olivia, from Oklahoma, by virtue of a promissory note signed by Olivia payable to "Tom and Ted" in the amount of $100,000. Between themselves, Tom and Ted each own a one-half interest in the $100,000 note. If Tom and Ted file suit on the obligation in federal court, what is the amount in controversy?

    (A) $100,000 for Ted and Tom.

    (B) $50,000 for Tom.

    (C) $50,000 for Ted.

    (D) $50,000 each for Ted and Tom.

155. Alice, an artist from Alabama, wants to sue Truman and Theodora, from Tennessee, on two breach of contract claims. When visiting Alice's gallery in Tuscaloosa, Truman and Theodora each bought one of Alice's large oil paintings of Alabama landscapes and paid by check. The painting purchased by Truman cost $45,000 and the painting purchased by Theodora, being somewhat smaller, cost $35,000. Sadly for Alice, both of the checks

bounced. If Alice brings a single suit against Ted and Theodora in federal court seeking to recover the purchase prices of the paintings from Truman and Theodora, is there federal jurisdiction over the claims made in the action?

(A) Yes, $80,000 is the amount in controversy because separate claims against multiple defendants are aggregated and there is complete diversity of citizenship.

(B) No, the $45,000 (Truman) and $35,000 (Theodora) breach claims are not aggregated; separate claims against codefendants are not aggregated.

(C) No, because Truman and Theodora are from the same state, there is no diversity jurisdiction, regardless of the amount in controversy.

(D) Both (B) and (C) are correct.

156. Calvin, from California, is the owner of a private lake in a remote part of Alaska. Unfortunately, the lake has been polluted by two separate exploration companies, Drill Deep, Inc. and Well Bore Co., Delaware corporations having their principal places of business in Texas, that have completed oil and gas wells and separate pipelines on acreage adjacent to Calvin's lake. Calvin believes that under applicable law, each defendant could be held jointly and severally liable for the entire loss although the amount of each polluter's individual harm is approximately $50,000, based on evidence concerning the amount of pollution each company added to the lake. If Calvin sues both Drill Deep, Inc. and Well Bore Co. in federal court, what is the amount in controversy?

(A) $50,000, because the claims cannot be aggregated.

(B) $100,000 if Calvin claims that Drill Deep, Inc. and Well Bore Co. are jointly and severally liable and applicable law could support joint and several liability against both defendants.

(C) $50,000, even if it ultimately is determined that the defendants are jointly and severally liable. Each will end up paying $50,000 unless one is insolvent.

(D) $100,000, but only if it is established at trial that both defendants are jointly and severally liable.

157. Susan, from South Carolina, wants to sue Nate, from North Carolina. Susan owns a beachfront lot which, but for Nate's erection of an unsightly shack on the beach, would be worth $250,000. With the shack (and its associated squatters) the land is worth only $150,000. It would cost Nate about $300 to have the shack torn down and hauled away. Susan wants to sue for an injunction ordering Nate to remove the shack. What would be the amount in controversy?

(A) $250,000.

(B) $100,000.

(C) $300.

(D) There is no amount in controversy in injunction cases.

158. Laurel, from Louisiana, sues Olivia, from Oklahoma, for $40,000 for damages from a car wreck. Olivia files a counterclaim for $55,000 for her own damages in the same wreck. Is the amount in controversy requirement satisfied?

(A) No. The counterclaim is not counted in determining the amount in controversy.

(B) Yes. This is a compulsory counterclaim and so it is counted in determining the amount in controversy.

(C) No. The amount in controversy would be $15,000, the difference in value between the two claims.

(D) Yes. Counterclaims are always counted in determining the amount in controversy.

159. Naomi, from North Dakota, sues Sherry, from South Dakota, for breach of a $15,000 contract. Naomi is extremely annoyed by the breach, which she thinks was spiteful, and so she also includes a claim for $100,000 in punitive damages. Under the applicable state law, punitive damages cannot be recovered in cases based on contract. Is the amount in controversy requirement satisfied?

(A) No. Damage claims that are invalid on their face cannot be included in computing the amount in controversy, leaving only the $15,000 claim.

(B) No. It is extremely unlikely that a jury would award Naomi punitive damages of that size, leaving the total probable damages less than $75,000.

(C) Yes. Damages based on contract and tort theories against a single defendant should be combined in computing the amount in controversy.

(D) Yes. Because the $100,000 claim is sufficient by itself, it does not matter whether you can also add the $15,000.

160. Romeo and Juliet were married for 10 years, and their marital domicile was New Jersey. Sadly, their marriage missed that spark of excitement that came from the family feud, and so they decided to divorce. Romeo moved to Rhode Island, where he had better job prospects. The marital estate is worth more than $100,000. Romeo wants to file suit for divorce in federal court. Would that be proper?

(A) No. Romeo and Juliet are both domiciled in New Jersey so there is no diversity of citizenship.

(B) Yes. The size of their marital estate satisfies the amount in controversy requirement.

(C) No. The size of the marital estate, when halved, does not satisfy the amount in controversy requirement, making each spouse's claim too small.

(D) No. This case does not fall within federal jurisdiction.

161. Heather started a new business selling Miracle Jeans. These jeans utilized a scientific breakthrough and guaranteed every wearer would look 10 pounds thinner. BlueCloth Ltd. contracted to supply Heather with all her denim needs. Unfortunately, BlueCloth breached its contract and so Heather was unable to fill her orders on time, and many customers cancelled. The delay also decreased the value of Heather's big media campaign launching her new business. Heather sued BlueCloth in federal court, seeking $500,000 in lost profits. BlueCloth filed a motion to dismiss for lack of subject matter jurisdiction, arguing that a new business such as Heather's will not be able to prove lost profits with sufficient certainty. How should the court rule on BlueCloth's motion?

ANSWER:

TOPIC 33: QUESTIONS
SUBJECT MATTER JURISDICTION: FEDERAL QUESTIONS

162. When Officer Krupke arrested Tony, a scuffle ensued. Tony believes that Krupke used excessive force in making the arrest. He wants to sue Krupke for violating his federal constitutional rights, but his injuries amount to only about $2,000 worth of medical bills and a sore jaw. Both Tony and Krupke are citizens of New York. Can Tony file his case in federal court?

    (A) No. The amount in controversy is insufficient.

    (B) No. There is no diversity of citizenship.

    (C) No. The suit lacks both diversity and a sufficient amount in controversy.

    (D) Yes. The suit would be proper under federal question jurisdiction.

163. Tony has a low opinion of federal courts. Could he file his case in state court instead?

    (A) No. The federal courts have exclusive jurisdiction over federal questions.

    (B) No. The federal courts have exclusive jurisdiction over federal questions based on constitutional rights.

    (C) Yes. State and federal courts have concurrent jurisdiction over most federal questions, including this one.

    (D) Yes, but only if Tony also joins a state law claim for battery.

164. News parody journal "The Potatoe" ran a story about a former Secretary of Defense, still a prominent national figure, suggesting that he had a personal financial stake in companies that repair infrastructure in the aftermath of U.S. wars. The Secretary wants to sue "The Potatoe" for libel under state tort law. He is aware that "The Potatoe," in its defense, will assert its constitutional free press rights under the First Amendment in order to force proof of malice. Because the Constitution will play a key role in the case, the Secretary would like to file the case in federal court. Will the federal court have subject matter jurisdiction?

    (A) Yes. The federal courts have a clear interest in consistent interpretation of the Constitution.

    (B) Yes. An issue of federal law will inevitably be determined in the case.

    (C) No. The First Amendment issue is merely a defense and therefore does not create federal question jurisdiction.

(D) No, unless the Secretary anticipates the constitutional defense by including it in his complaint.

165. Polly, from Paris, Texas, purchased some diet pills from her pharmacy because she wanted to lose a few pounds. Instead, the pills increased her blood pressure and caused her to suffer a cerebral stroke. Polly has sued the manufacturer, Megadrugs, Inc., for damages in a products liability action based on a common law negligence *per se* claim. Federal law is invoked in her complaint which rests in part on her claim that the pills were sold in violation of the Federal Food, Drug, and Cosmetic Act (FDCA). Specifically, the Federal Act is one of the bases for negligence *per se* liability under Polly's pleading. Is there a basis for federal question jurisdiction under these circumstances?

(A) No, the claim is a state law products liability claim, not one created by federal law. The FDCA does not provide consumers an express or implied federal right of action. Allowing federal jurisdiction over negligence *per se* claims premised in federal statutes would greatly expand federal question jurisdiction, upsetting the allocation of cases between state and federal courts.

(B) Yes, the FDCA violation is alleged, and thereby has been made an ingredient or element of the plaintiff's claim which rests in part on federal law.

(C) No, federal question jurisdiction requires the claim to be created by a federal statute or based on a recognized federal law claim grounded on a violation of Constitutional rights.

(D) Yes, federal law is a central issue in the case.

166. Henry Gale purchased a home in Dallas, Texas, using the proceeds of a loan insured by the Federal Housing Administration (FHA), a loan that he obtained from Cyclone Bank (Cyclone). To secure the loan, Gale signed a deed of trust that explicitly provided that if Gale is late with a mortgage payment, Cyclone may demand immediate payment in full, but *only* if it has complied with applicable federal regulations of the Department of Housing and Urban Development (HUD). These provisions requiring compliance with HUD regulations are included in all FHA-insured loans. Gale lost his job and, after exhausting his savings, missed several mortgage payments. Cyclone informed him that his loan had been accelerated (the total balance was due immediately) and that his home would be foreclosed on. It followed up by actually foreclosing.

Gale filed suit against Cyclone in Texas state court in Dallas, claiming wrongful foreclosure under state law. Cyclone then removed the case to the U.S. District Court for the Northern District of Texas. Gale's complaint alleges that Cyclone breached the contract by failing to comply with HUD regulations referred to in the deed of trust. Under HUD rules, Gale alleges, before accelerating his loan and posting his home for foreclosure, Cyclone was required to make reasonable efforts to conduct a face-to-face interview with him. "Reasonable efforts" includes at least one letter and one trip to the property. Since Cyclone didn't do that, says Gale, Cyclone's foreclosure was wrongful.

Both Gale and Cyclone agree about what was done — they just disagree about whether those regulations apply to loans like Gale's. They also agree: (1) that there is no private right of action to directly enforce the HUD rules; and (2) that currently there are at least 555,000 FHA-insured homes whose mortgage payments are in default and headed toward foreclosure.

Gale has filed a timely motion to remand his case to state court. How should Judge Elmira Gulch rule?

(A) Judge Gulch should remand the case. Gale's claim is basically just a state law breach of contract claim and not a federal question, and there is no private right of action under the HUD regulations.

(B) Judge Gulch should keep the case. The claim that Cyclone's breach of contract was the result of violating HUD regulations is an embedded federal issue that is necessary, actually disputed, and substantial, making this a federal question under *Grable & Sons Metal Products, Inc. v. Darue Engineering & Manufacturing.*

(C) Judge Gulch should keep the case — with thousands of mortgages in default, it is important that federal judges interpret the HUD rules consistently.

(D) Judge Gulch should remand the case. Even though there is a federal issue, necessary to the resolution of Gale's claim, actually disputed and substantial, Congress has provided no welcome mat for this type of claim, and allowing the thousands of defaulting homeowners with FHA-insured loans to bring wrongful foreclosure claims in federal court would disturb the balance of state and federal judicial responsibilities.

167. Hamlet sues Ivy University for breach of contract. He claims that the university wrongfully discontinued a program in Paranormal Studies before he could graduate with his P.S. degree. Hamlet has also included a claim for breach by Ivy of his right to an A average, which Hamlet believes arises out of the Privileges and Immunities Clause of the U.S. Constitution. Based on the latter claim, Hamlet has filed his case in federal court. Does the court have jurisdiction?

(A) Yes. Although his federal claim may be somewhat sketchy, Hamlet has pleaded it in good faith.

(B) Yes. Decisions about subject matter jurisdiction must be based on the issues pleaded and not on the merits.

(C) No. A claim such as Hamlet's is wholly insubstantial and frivolous and therefore cannot confer jurisdiction on the federal courts.

(D) No. When parties lose their federal claims, as Hamlet will lose this one, it ousts the court of jurisdiction.

TOPIC 34: QUESTIONS
SUBJECT MATTER JURISDICTION: SUPPLEMENTAL JURISDICTION

Dorothy Woodman, a Texas resident, was treated by Dr. Kate Houston, a Texas cardiologist. Dr. Houston referred Dorothy to the National Clinic, which is located in Rochester, Minnesota, for heart bypass surgery by Dr. Jeffrey Heart. Dr. Heart is an employee of the National Clinic. Following surgery, Dorothy spent 10 days at the National Clinic before being discharged to return to Texas. During this post-operative time, Dorothy noticed that the fairly large incision on her chest kept getting redder and more tender to the touch. Dr. Heart assured her that it was nothing. Following Dorothy's return to Texas, the incision remained very red and Dorothy developed a slight fever. She immediately contacted Dr. Houston, who examined her and assured her that it was just a slight infection at the incision site, prescribed a mild antibiotic, and sent Dorothy home. The redness continued to get worse, Dorothy's fever increased, and she began experiencing terrible chest pain. She returned to Dr. Houston, who ran some tests and determined that Dorothy was suffering from a fairly advanced infection of the sternum (a large bone in the chest which must be cut through in order to reach the heart). Dorothy was confined to bed for eight weeks and was administered massive doses of IV antibiotics. Dorothy believes that had the infection been prevented or caught earlier, either by Dr. Heart or Dr. Houston, this treatment would not have been necessary and Dorothy would have been spared significant pain and suffering and the possibility of permanent impairment.

168. Dorothy sued the National Clinic in federal court. She alleges that the Clinic and its agent, Dr. Heart, were negligent in treating Dorothy and that this negligence caused her harm in the amount of $5 million. (You may assume that National Clinic would be liable for Heart's negligence, if any.) National Clinic is a Minnesota corporation with its principal place of business in Minnesota. The Clinic takes the position that it was Dr. Houston's fault that Dorothy Woodman suffered serious consequences from her infection of the sternum. The Clinic therefore added Dr. Houston to the lawsuit. The Clinic says that if it is found liable then Dr. Houston should have to pay the judgment. Does the federal court have jurisdiction over these claims?

    (A) The court has jurisdiction over Dorothy's claim against the Clinic because there is complete diversity and a sufficient amount in controversy. It does not have jurisdiction over the Clinic's claim against Houston, because Houston and Dorothy are both Texas citizens.

    (B) The court has jurisdiction over Dorothy's claim against the Clinic based on diversity and amount in controversy. It also has jurisdiction over the Clinic's claim against Houston, because it arises out of a common nucleus of operative fact with Dorothy's claim against the Clinic.

    (C) The court has lost whatever jurisdiction it might have had over these claims because of the lack of diversity of citizenship between Dorothy and Houston.

(D) The court has jurisdiction over both claims, because in both cases there is diversity of citizenship between the parties and a sufficient amount in controversy.

169. The Clinic learned that Woodman has also taken extra-legal steps in her unhappiness. She has taken a computer class and learned to create a website of her own. Using that knowledge, she launched Stop the Clinic, at www.heartattack.com. This website contains allegations of various acts of malpractice by Clinic doctors (including Dorothy's experience), provides a chat room for people to share bad Clinic experiences, and has an e-mail based newsletter that sends direct mailings to doctors, discouraging them from referring cases to the Clinic. The Clinic is not thrilled about these activities. Although the Clinic's reputation is secure enough to survive Woodman's attack, her claims have cost the Clinic at least two patients. The Clinic has therefore filed a counterclaim against Woodman for commercial disparagement (a corporate version of libel) in the amount of $50,000. Does the court have jurisdiction over this claim?

(A) Yes, because the court always has jurisdiction over counterclaims.

(B) No, because the amount in controversy is insufficient.

(C) Yes, because the Clinic's claim is not a claim made by a plaintiff.

(D) No, because the Clinic's claim is not part of the same case or controversy as Woodman's claim against the clinic.

170. Woodman's husband Cyrus, a law professor at SMU in Dallas, Texas, also has a legally cognizable claim against National Clinic for loss of society and companionship under either Texas or Minnesota law. Because Cyrus and Dorothy don't live together and don't spend much time together, there is a real question whether Cyrus' claim exceeds $75,000, exclusive of interest and costs. Does the federal court have supplemental jurisdiction over Cyrus' claim?

(A) Yes, but only if Cyrus joins Dorothy as an original plaintiff under Rule 20.

(B) Yes, even if Cyrus intervenes in the action brought by Dorothy against National Clinic.

(C) Yes, Cyrus is a person needed for just adjudication under Rule 19.

(D) No, Cyrus' claim is not part of the same constitutional case as Dorothy's claim.

171. Consider the same facts as the preceding question, except that Cyrus had established a new domicile in Minnesota by taking a permanent job at one of the four Minnesota law schools before becoming a plaintiff in the lawsuit brought by Dorothy against National Clinic. Would the federal court have supplemental jurisdiction over Cyrus' claim?

ANSWER:

172. National Clinic is considering a third-party claim against Dr. Heart for contribution. There is no amount in controversy problem in either case, but Dr. Heart's citizenship in

Minnesota appears to be inconsistent with the jurisdictional requirements of § 1332. Does supplemental jurisdiction exist with respect to the potential contribution claim against Dr. Heart?

(A) No, although the contribution claim is so related to the Woodman claim that both claims are part of the same constitutional case, § 1367(b)'s first exception prohibits the cross-action.

(B) No, the contribution claim is a different case or controversy from the Woodman claim.

(C) Yes, § 1367(a) permits the claim and § 1367(b) does not prohibit it, even though the Clinic and Dr. Heart are citizens of Minnesota.

(D) No, the contamination theory created by the majority opinion in *Exxon* prohibits supplemental jurisdiction under these circumstances.

173. Cyrus also wants to know whether he can join Dr. Kate Houston (the Texas Cardiologist) in the same action that he plans to institute against National Clinic. Assuming that there is no amount in controversy problem with this claim, would the federal court have supplemental jurisdiction over Cyrus's claim against Dr. Houston?

(A) Yes, because the claims derive from a common nucleus of operative facts, there is supplemental jurisdiction under § 1367(a).

(B) Yes, the last sentence of § 1367(a) establishes the existence of supplemental jurisdiction over Dr. Houston.

(C) No, § 1367(b) precludes the exercise of supplemental jurisdiction over Dr. Houston because Cyrus and Dr. Houston are not of diverse citizenship.

(D) Yes, the permissive joinder provisions of Rule 20 allow for joinder of National Clinic and Dr. Houston in the same action.

174. Woodman never paid Dr. Houston's bill, because she believed that Houston committed malpractice and deserved no payment. Dr. Houston has therefore added a claim against Woodman for her unpaid medical bill for this treatment. That claim is for $10,000. Does the court have jurisdiction over Houston's claim against Woodman?

(A) Yes, because Rule 14 allows third-party defendants to bring claims against plaintiffs.

(B) No, because Houston and Woodman are both from Texas and the claim is too small.

(C) Yes, because Houston's claim is not a claim made by a plaintiff.

(D) No, because Houston's claim is not part of the same case or controversy as Woodman's claim against the Clinic.

175. Assume that the court has decided to allow Houston's claim against Woodman. Woodman has filed a motion for leave to amend her complaint to add a claim. She was not going to sue Dr. Houston originally, since she kind of likes the doctor's bedside manner, but now

that Houston is in the lawsuit, Dorothy has gone ahead and asked to amend the complaint to include a malpractice claim against Houston. She seeks the same $5 million as in the original lawsuit. If the court wanted to grant leave to amend, would it have subject matter jurisdiction over Woodman's claim?

ANSWER:

TOPIC 35: QUESTIONS

SUBJECT MATTER JURISDICTION: COMPARING SUPPLEMENTAL JURISDICTION & THE CLASS ACTION FAIRNESS ACT

One spring, *Today in America* ("TA") did a show about sheets — more specifically, a show about thread count. The National Textile Association defines thread count as the number of threads running both horizontally and vertically in a square inch of fabric. For example, a sheet with a thread count of 400 would have 200 threads running vertically and 200 threads running horizontally. The higher the thread count, the more expensive the sheets, because the higher thread count sheets are softer and more comfortable for sleeping. The report on TA disclosed that a number of national retailers were knowingly selling sheets with much lower thread counts than the packages listed.

The following persons and entities have claims they would like to bring:

- Sleep Hotels, Inc. (a Texas corporation with its principal place of business in Texas) has a claim against Mall Mart (an Arkansas corporation with its principal place of business in Arkansas), claiming fraud, breach of warranty, and violations of the Texas Deceptive Trade Practices Act. Sleep Hotels has for years bought all of the sheets for its national chain of hotels from Mall Mart, paying extra so that it could advertise itself as providing a superior night's sleep to its customers. It seeks damages in the amount of $80,000.
- Alice, a resident of Texas, bought four sets of sheets labeled 1,000 thread count when in fact they were only 500 thread count. She seeks $200 in damages.
- Barbara, a resident of Arkansas, bought about 10 sets of sheets during the past three years, labeled as 600 thread count when they were actually 300 (she always buys sheets as wedding presents) and seeks $500 in damages.

176. Suppose Sleep Hotels and Alice join as plaintiffs to sue Mall Mart. Would the federal court have jurisdiction over the case?

    (A) Yes. Sleep Hotels (a Texas citizen) is diverse from Mall Mart (an Arkansas citizen) and has a sufficient amount in controversy, and there is supplemental jurisdiction over Alice's claim even though on its own it would be too small.

    (B) No. Alice's claim is much too small, and so it is a claim by a plaintiff inconsistent with the requirements of § 1332.

    (C) No. Alice's claim is precluded by § 1367(b).

    (D) Yes. The aggregated claims of Sleep Hotels and Alice exceed $75,000.

177. Suppose Sleep Hotels and Barbara join as plaintiffs to sue Mall Mart. Would the federal court have jurisdiction over the case?

(A) Yes. Sleep Hotels is diverse from Mall Mart and has a sufficient amount in controversy, and there is supplemental jurisdiction over Barbara's claim even though on its own it would lack diversity of citizenship.

(B) No. Barbara and Mall Mart are both Arkansas citizens, and so it contaminates Sleep Hotels' claim and eliminates jurisdiction.

(C) No. Sleep Hotels' claim and Barbara's claim are part of the same constitutional case or controversy, but § 1367(b) removes jurisdiction over Barbara's claim.

(D) Yes. Minimal diversity is all that Article III requires.

178. Suppose Sleep Hotels and Alice sue Mall Mart and SheetSheet Company, Mall Mart's supplier (an Arizona corporation with its principal place of business in Tennessee). Can they file their lawsuit in federal court?

ANSWER:

179. Claire, another purchaser of mislabeled sheets, filed a class action against Bed Bath & Barrels ("BBB") (a New York corporation with its principal place of business in New York) in federal court in New Jersey, Claire's home state. Claire's complaint describes the class as "all New York and New Jersey citizens who have purchased mislabeled sheets from one of BBB's New York stores." Her complaint estimates that there are about 10,000 class members (7,000 from New York), each of whom overpaid about $55 for sheets. Under applicable state law, Claire would be entitled to recover both her $55 in damages and reasonable attorney's fees. Assume that, given the complexity of the case, the complaint's request for $150,000 in attorney's fees is a reasonable one. Does the federal court have jurisdiction over this class action?

(A) No. Claire's claim is OK, but the class members' claims are too small for federal court.

(B) No. Claire's claim is OK, but some of the class members are from the same state as the defendant and so the lack of complete diversity eliminates jurisdiction.

(C) Yes. The federal court would have jurisdiction over this case under the Class Action Fairness Act, and so complete diversity is not required.

(D) Yes. Claire is diverse from BBB and her claim is large enough. The court has supplemental jurisdiction over the class members' smaller claims.

180. Dana bought mislabeled sheets from Cotton and Things ("CT"), a Connecticut corporation with its principal place of business in Connecticut. She filed a class action against CT in federal court in Connecticut, Dana's home state. Dana's complaint describes the class as "all Connecticut, Massachusetts, Rhode Island, Vermont, New Hampshire, and Maine citizens who have purchased mislabeled sheets from one of CT's New England stores." Her complaint estimates that there are about 100,000 class members (75,000 from Connecticut, with others scattered throughout Massachusetts, Rhode Island, Vermont, New Hampshire,

and Maine). Each class member overpaid about $55 for her sheets, as did Dana. Under applicable state law, Dana would be entitled to recover only her actual damages of $55. Does the federal court have jurisdiction over this class action?

(A) No. Dana is the class representative, and she is from the same state as the defendant.

(B) Yes. There is sufficient minimal diversity, there are more than one hundred class members, and the amount in controversy exceeds $5 million.

(C) Yes. The court has supplemental jurisdiction over the class members' claims because they share a common nucleus of operative fact with Dana's claim.

(D) No. More than two thirds of the class members and the primary defendant are from Connecticut, and the damages were incurred in Connecticut. Connecticut law is also very likely to apply.

TOPIC 36: SUBJECT MATTER JURISDICTION: REMOVAL

QUESTIONS

181. Martin, from Michigan, sued his employer, Blue Hat Computers, a Delaware corporation with its principal place of business in Oregon, for wrongful discharge. He filed suit in state court in Detroit, Michigan, asking for damages of $85,000. He had his lawyer draw up the lawsuit papers on May 1, but he continued to negotiate with Blue Hat. Negotiations finally broke down on July 1. As a last ditch effort at settlement, Martin's lawyer faxed a copy of Martin's potential complaint to Blue Hat on July 2. After receiving no response, Martin had his lawyer file the case and serve Blue Hat with the summons and complaint on July 15. Blue Hat would like to remove the case to federal court. When is/was its deadline for removal?

(A) May 31.

(B) August 1.

(C) August 14.

(D) This is a trick question. There is no deadline for removal.

182. Assume the same facts as in the question above, except that Martin files suit in state court in Oregon. Is the case removable?

(A) Yes, it can be removed at any time.

(B) Yes, it can be removed because the diversity of citizenship and amount in controversy make it a case that could have been brought in federal court.

(C) Yes, if Blue Hat files the proper papers by the removal deadline.

(D) No. This case is not removable.

183. Assume the same controversy between Martin and Blue Hat with the following changes: Blue Hat is a Michigan corporation with its principal place of business in Oregon, and Martin adds a claim that he was discriminated against based on his age in violation of the federal Age Discrimination in Employment Act (ADEA). The case is filed in state court in Michigan. Is the case removable?

(A) No. Resident defendants cannot remove cases to federal court.

(B) No. Blue Hat is a citizen of both Michigan and Oregon, and since Martin is a citizen of Michigan, complete diversity is lacking.

(C) Yes. This case contains a federal question.

(D) Yes. The state of incorporation is not considered in deciding whether a corporate defendant is a citizen of the state where the action is brought.

184. Assume that the original state court action brought by Martin against Blue Hat included an employment discrimination claim under federal law and a worker's compensation claim under Michigan law. May this action be removed to federal court?

(A) No, state workers compensation claims are not removable.

(B) Yes, the inclusion of a federal claim makes the entire action removable and subject to federal jurisdiction.

(C) No, the inclusion of the state workers compensation claim precludes removal of the entire civil action.

(D) Yes, the entire action is removable, but the state workers compensation claim will be severed and remanded back to state court for adjudication.

185. Assume that *Martin v. Blue Hat* is pending in state court in Detroit, and that Blue Hat is a citizen of Delaware and Oregon. To what federal district court can the case be removed?

(A) The Eastern District of Michigan (in which Detroit is located).

(B) Any judicial district in Michigan.

(C) Oregon.

(D) Blue Hat can choose any of these districts.

186. *Martin v. Blue Hat* has been pending in state court in Oregon for over a year and contains only Martin's state law breach of contract claim. Eighteen months after filing suit, Martin amends his complaint to add the ADEA claim. Can Blue Hat remove the case to federal court?

(A) No. His 30 days to remove ran out a long time ago.

(B) No. Removability is based on the status of the lawsuit when it is first filed.

(C) Yes, if Blue Hat files the proper removal papers within 30 days after it receives a copy of the amended complaint.

(D) No. Federal question cases must be removed within one year of commencement of the action.

187. Assume that Martin sued Blue Hat, a Delaware corporation with its principal place of business in Oregon, for $85,000 for breach of contract in state court in Michigan. Martin also sued Marty, the former boss who fired him, for intentional infliction of emotional distress. Marty is a citizen of Michigan. Eighteen months after the suit was filed, Martin amended his complaint to drop the claim against Marty. Can Blue Hat remove the case to federal court now?

(A) Yes. With Marty removed, there is complete diversity, sufficient amount in controversy, and no in-state defendant.

(B) Yes, if Blue Hat files the proper removal papers within 30 days after it receives a copy of the amended complaint.

(C) No. Removability is based on the status of the lawsuit when it is first filed.

(D) No. Diversity jurisdiction cases must be removed within one year of commencement of the action unless the district court finds that Martin acted in bad faith in order to prevent Blue Hat from removing the action.

188. Martin sued Blue Hat in state court in Michigan, and Blue Hat timely removed the case to federal court. Martin has noticed, however, that Blue Hat failed to sign its notice of removal and failed to attach the required pleadings. Can Martin get the case sent back to state court?

(A) Yes, if he files the motion to remand within 30 days of the filing of the notice of removal.

(B) Yes, if he files the motion to remand within 30 days of when he received the notice of removal.

(C) Yes. Because subject matter jurisdiction cannot be waived, Martin can file a motion to remand at any time.

(D) No. Unless there is a jurisdictional flaw in the removal process, the case will stay in federal court.

189. Martin sued Blue Hat in state court in Michigan, and Blue Hat properly removed the case to federal court. Martin would far rather be in state court, so he forms a plan to destroy complete diversity by adding his former boss, Marty, as an additional defendant. Marty is a citizen of Michigan. Martin files a motion for leave to amend his complaint to add Marty as an additional defendant. What are the court's options in ruling on Martin's motion?

ANSWER:

TOPIC 37: TERRITORIAL JURISDICTION: VOCABULARY

QUESTIONS

190. *In personam* jurisdiction:

(A) requires the presence of the defendant's property in the forum state.

(B) gives the court the power to impose personal liability on the defendant in favor of the plaintiff.

(C) requires the presence of the defendant in the forum state.

(D) gives the court the power to enter a judgment involving only the property that is the subject of the dispute.

191. *In rem* jurisdiction:

(A) allows the court to resolve the interest of all the world in the property that is the subject of the dispute.

(B) permits the court to enter judgment to the full extent of the wrong done to the plaintiff.

(C) allows only a judgment involving the parties' interest in the property that is the subject of the dispute.

(D) requires jurisdiction over the people claiming an interest in the property in order to bind them to the outcome of the litigation.

192. *Quasi in rem* jurisdiction:

(A) may allow a state to take jurisdiction to enforce a foreign judgment against the defendant's property, present in the state, that is unrelated to the claim that led to the foreign judgment.

(B) must also meet the due process requirements of *in personam* jurisdiction.

(C) allows the court to resolve the interest of all the world in the property that is the subject of the dispute.

(D) (A) and (B) are both correct.

TOPIC 38: QUESTIONS
CONSENT, STATUS, DOMICILE & TRANSIENT JURISDICTION

193. Goneril and Regan enter into a contract to purchase a year's supply of heating oil from Lear Energy. The contract provides, in paragraph 25: "Any suit to collect overdue payments under this contract may be filed in any state or federal court in the State of New York." Goneril and Regan reside in Michigan, and Lear is a New York corporation with its principal place of business in New York, but it does business in a number of states and negotiated the contract with Goneril and Regan and delivered their oil from Lear's Michigan office. Goneril and Regan, who are not particularly honest, take the oil but fail to pay. Lear wants to sue them in New York. Are Goneril and Regan subject to personal jurisdiction on this claim in a New York court?

    (A) No. Goneril and Regan are not domiciled in New York.

    (B) Yes. This suit is about the "status" of the contract, and so jurisdiction over Lear is sufficient.

    (C) Yes. Goneril and Regan have consented to jurisdiction in New York, which has some connection to the underlying dispute.

    (D) No. Goneril and Regan lack sufficient contacts with New York to be sued there.

194. Goneril and her husband Albany are unhappily married and totally broke. Albany moves out of the family home and moves to Idaho to start a new life. About five years later, things are looking up for Goneril, and she wants a divorce. As the couple have no children and no assets, the divorce itself is all she needs. Can she get an enforceable divorce by filing in her home state of Michigan?

    (A) Yes. Cases involving personal status are a traditional exception to the requirement that a court have personal jurisdiction over the defendant.

    (B) Yes. Because Michigan was once Albany's home, it will always have personal jurisdiction over him.

    (C) No. Albany has been gone too long for Michigan still to have sufficient minimum contacts with him to justify personal jurisdiction.

    (D) No. Albany has not consented to jurisdiction in Michigan.

195. Cordelia, disinherited by her family, has moved to Iowa and bought a farm. She is very happy in her new home. Unfortunately, she has a difficult former business partner, Edmund, who believes that Cordelia owes him money from a failed venture in Dover, Delaware. Edmund has sued Cordelia in Iowa. At the time, Cordelia was out of state

attempting a family reconciliation back in Michigan, and so Edmund arranged for Cordelia to be served with process while she was there. Assuming this is permitted under Iowa's long-arm statute, may Iowa constitutionally assert jurisdiction over Cordelia?

(A) No. Defendants must be served with process in the forum state to be subject to personal jurisdiction.

(B) No. The transaction that is the subject of Edmund's suit has nothing to do with Iowa.

(C) Yes. Cordelia has enough contacts with Iowa to allow specific jurisdiction.

(D) Yes. Courts of human defendants' home states traditionally have personal jurisdiction over them in all cases.

196. Kent makes his home in Kansas, but he and his family have for years spent two weeks of each summer in a cabin in Estes Park, Colorado. Kent purchased gardening supplies for his Kansas home from A Thousand Acres, a mail order company headquartered in Phoenix, Arizona. Kent has refused to pay the bill, and the company has sued him in Colorado, as that is far more convenient. Knowing that Kent would be in Colorado on vacation, the company had its process server hand the lawsuit papers to Kent at the summer cabin. Does Colorado have personal jurisdiction over Kent in this case?

(A) Yes. Coming to Colorado every summer creates sufficient contacts to justify jurisdiction.

(B) Yes. Service within the state under these facts makes jurisdiction proper.

(C) No. Kent's contacts with Colorado are not related to the company's claim.

(D) No. Transient jurisdiction is no longer constitutional.

TOPIC 39: QUESTIONS

IN PERSONAM JURISDICTION: OVERVIEW

197. Under personal jurisdiction doctrine as applied in the nineteenth century, a state could assert personal jurisdiction over an individual defendant who had not consented to jurisdiction:

    (A) when the defendant was a domiciliary of the state.

    (B) when the defendant owned property located in the state.

    (C) when the defendant was served with process while physically present in the state.

    (D) (A), (B) and (C).

198. Which of the following developments helped to erode the mechanical application of the "presence" test?

    (A) The difficulty in determining where a corporation was "present."

    (B) The enactment of state statutes creating presumed consent to be sued in the state.

    (C) Changes in the national economy involving an ever greater volume of interstate commerce.

    (D) All of the above.

199. Specific jurisdiction gives the court the power to adjudicate:

    (A) causes of action arising out of or related to the defendant's contacts with the forum state.

    (B) all disputes between the plaintiff and the defendant, even if they are not related to the defendant's contacts with the forum state.

    (C) all disputes described with sufficient particularity in the plaintiff's complaint.

    (D) any cause of action between the plaintiff and the defendant, as long as one of the plaintiff's claims arises out of or relates to the defendant's contacts with the forum state.

200. Which of the following best describes the constitutional test for specific jurisdiction?

    (A) The defendant must be a resident of the forum state.

(B) The defendant must purposefully establish a sufficient level of contacts with the forum state, and the forum's taking jurisdiction must not offend traditional notions of fair play and substantial justice.

(C) The defendant's contacts with the forum state must be extensive, continuous, and systematic.

(D) The defendant must be present in the forum state.

201. A court has general jurisdiction over a defendant when:

(A) the defendant does business in the forum state.

(B) the defendant has sufficient purposeful contacts with the forum state so as not to offend traditional notions of fair play and substantial justice.

(C) the defendant's contacts with the forum state are so substantial that the forum can be regarded as the defendant's home.

(D) the plaintiff is a resident of the forum state.

202. General jurisdiction over a defendant gives the court the power to adjudicate:

(A) only causes of action arising out of or related to the defendant's contacts with the forum state.

(B) all claims against the defendant, even if they are not related to the defendant's contacts with the forum state.

(C) only causes of action involving the defendant's use of the forum as a substitute headquarters when some crisis prevents doing business in its normal location.

(D) all claims against all the defendants properly joined in the case.

TOPIC 40:	**QUESTIONS**
SPECIFIC JURISDICTION	

For all of the following questions, assume that the forum state has a long-arm statute that would authorize jurisdiction over the defendant.

203. Sydney Carton traveled to Paris, Texas, on vacation. While shopping at a local department store there (a "mom and pop" establishment that has never advertised outside of Texas), he was wrongfully detained and searched. Back home in Virginia, Carton filed suit against the store. Can a Virginia court constitutionally assert jurisdiction over Carton's claim against the Texas store?

(A) Yes. The store intentionally injured a resident of Virginia.

(B) Yes. Plaintiffs can always file suit in their home states.

(C) No. The store's contacts with Virginia are insufficient to permit the assertion of jurisdiction.

(D) Yes. The store profited from selling its products to a Virginian.

204. Carton learned that the store, on several occasions in the past, sold copies of some book about the French Revolution and shipped them to residents of Virginia who had called the store and ordered the books. Now can a Virginia court constitutionally assert jurisdiction over the store in Carton's case?

(A) Yes. The store intentionally injured a resident of Virginia.

(B) Yes. The store now has sufficient contacts with Virginia to permit the assertion of jurisdiction.

(C) No. The store's contacts with Virginia are unrelated to Carton's claim.

(D) Yes. The store profited from selling its products to a Virginian.

205. DeFarge, Inc. sells knitting needles in every state in the United States. It has sold 5,000 pairs of needles to customers in California over the past three years. At least one pair was defective, and it broke and injured Lucie Manette while she was knitting. Lucie, a resident of California, would like to sue DeFarge there, even though its headquarters is in Paris, Texas. Can California constitutionally assert jurisdiction over DeFarge?

(A) Yes. DeFarge has purposefully done business in California and should have anticipated being haled into court there.

(B) Yes. By selling its products in California, DeFarge has consented to jurisdiction there.

(C) No. DeFarge does not have continuous and systematic contacts with California.

(D) No. If the customers initiated the orders, the mere sale of goods in the forum state will not be sufficient to make the assertion of jurisdiction constitutional.

206. DeFarge also sells another product, the Super Chopper. This is a large, expensive machine used in manufacturing plants. It advertised the Super Chopper in the January issue of a nationally-circulated trade publication. After a DeFarge-employed salesman made a persuasive presentation on a swing through Maine, DeFarge sold one Super Chopper to a customer there. Because of a flaw in the chopper's safety system, it cut off the hand of Jarvis Lorry, an employee of the customer. Lorry wants to sue DeFarge in Maine for his personal injuries. Can a Maine court constitutionally assert jurisdiction over Lorry's claim against DeFarge?

(A) No. This isolated transaction is not enough to be the basis for personal jurisdiction.

(B) Yes. DeFarge reached out to Maine because national advertising is sent there.

(C) No. DeFarge's customer could sue in Maine, but Lorry cannot.

(D) Yes. Lorry's cause of action arises directly out of DeFarge's contacts with Maine, which were purposeful and from which DeFarge earned profits.

207. Catherine grew up in Kentucky, where she lived for some time. While there, Catherine purchased a stepladder from Hindley's Hardware, a local store. Fleeing an unhappy love life, Catherine moved to Tennessee. After the move, she went back to Kentucky for a visit, chatted with the owner of Hindley's about her new life in Tennessee, and bought a chain saw. Back in Tennessee, Catherine was injured while standing on the ladder attempting to trim a tree with the chain saw. The stepladder collapsed and the saw cut her badly. Catherine would like to sue Hindley's in Tennessee. Could Tennessee constitutionally assert jurisdiction over Hindley's?

(A) Yes. Hindley's could foresee that its customer might take the stepladder to another state, including Tennessee.

(B) Yes. Hindley's knowingly sold the saw to a resident of Tennessee.

(C) No. Hindley's did not seek to serve residents of Tennessee.

(D) No. There is not enough profit in a saw and a stepladder to justify jurisdiction over Hindley's.

208. Catherine was quite a public figure in her day, and her injuries and litigation have caught the attention of the media. The *Atlanta Journal* printed a story about Catherine, dredging up all the old scandals with Heathcliff, and claiming that Catherine has become an alcoholic and that's why she is hiding out in Tennessee and that's why she fell. The Journal sells 95% of its papers within the state of Georgia, but it has about a dozen subscribers in each state

in the southeast, including Tennessee. Catherine wants to sue the *Journal*, but even more she wants to sue Nelly Dean, the author of the story, for writing a story full of intentional lies. Nelly has never been to Tennessee herself, but she talked to Tennessee sources on the phone when researching the story and sent a photographer there to try to get a picture of the no-longer-glamorous Catherine. As Catherine is still somewhat immobilized by her injuries, she wants to sue Nelly in Tennessee rather than going all the way to Atlanta. Can Tennessee constitutionally assert jurisdiction over Nelly?

ANSWER:

209. Online publication "TheDirt.com" picked up the story about Catherine from the Atlanta paper, added some gossip of its own about Catherine's life in Tennessee, and published the story online. "TheDirt.com" does not really have an office *per se*, nor does it print or distribute any physical newspapers. Its content is supplied by a handful of freelance reporters from around the country. The stories are uploaded to the Internet from the personal computer of Emily Haworth, a resident of South Dakota, at which point it becomes accessible to anyone in the world with internet access. Emily has had the publication incorporated so it does exist as a legal entity. Catherine wants to sue "TheDirt.com" for intentional libel. How will the court decide whether she may constitutionally do so in Tennessee?

ANSWER:

210. Goggles.com is a successful e-commerce business. It sold a computer program to Winkle; sadly, the program did not quite meet the expectations created by the website, and Winkle wants his money back. Winkle had been at home in Massachusetts when he discovered Goggles.com's business while surfing the net, he was in Massachusetts when he downloaded the program, and he used his credit card with a Massachusetts billing address to pay for the program. Assume that Goggles.com's website contained no choice of forum clause, and that other than whatever sales it might make from its website (and it has made many to Massachusetts residents), Goggles.com has no contacts with Massachusetts. Can a court in Massachusetts constitutionally assert jurisdiction over Winkle's claim against Goggles.com?

(A) Even if Goggles.com's website had been purely passive (just pictures of its products), that website makes it present in Massachusetts and Winkle can sue it there.

(B) Because Goggles.com's website is extremely interactive, allowing customers to learn about merchandise and to purchase it online, Massachusetts can assert jurisdiction over Goggles.com.

(C) Because Goggles.com's website is constantly available in the state of Massachusetts, it constitutes continuous and systematic contact and justifies general jurisdiction over Goggles.com, even if it never makes a sale to a resident of Massachusetts.

(D) No, internet contacts take place only in virtual space and cannot provide the basis for contact-based jurisdiction.

211. HairCo, a small Montana corporation, manufactures tiny blonde wigs that are used in the manufacture of Peppy, a doll that looks like a cheerleader. The dolls, in turn, are manufactured by ToyCo, a Missouri corporation, which distributes them in the southeastern United States. HairCo has no control whatsoever over where ToyCo chooses to sell the Peppy dolls, but it knows from payments it has received over the last 10 years that ToyCo has been selling 1,000 dolls a year in South Carolina. HairCo's contract with ToyCo calls for it to be paid based on the number of dolls sold. In South Carolina, a toddler chews on the wig of a Peppy doll and suffers personal injuries. Does HairCo have enough contacts with South Carolina to constitutionally be sued there?

(A) Under Justice Kennedy's opinion in *J. McIntyre Machinery, Ltd. v. Nicastro*, HairCo's knowledge of its profits from the sale of the dolls (with wigs) would be sufficient evidence of purposeful availment.

(B) Under Justice Kennedy's opinion in *Nicastro*, HairCo would have had to take some additional action that specifically targets South Carolina. For example, it might reach out directly to South Carolina buyers ("*Trouble with styling Peppy's hair? Call HairCo's helpline at 1-800-555-HAIR.*").

(C) *Nicastro*, like *Asahi* before it, is irrelevant to this issue because it involved a non-U.S. defendant.

(D) Justice Breyer's concurring opinion indicates that the small size of HairCo and the distance between Montana and South Carolina should not be a factor in due process analysis.

212. In specific jurisdiction cases, the Court has sometimes articulated another step in the analysis in which the interests of the parties, the forum state, and other states are balanced and utilized these factors as part of the *International Shoe* inquiry into "traditional notions of fair play and substantial justice." Which of the following factors has been considered in doing the due process fairness analysis?

(A) whether the forum state's procedural rules resemble the Federal Rules of Civil Procedure.

(B) whether the forum state has good judges.

(C) how sincere the plaintiff seems in explaining his desire to sue there.

(D) the burden on the defendant of defending itself in the forum state.

TOPIC 41: GENERAL JURISDICTION

QUESTIONS

213. Massive Mining Corporation (MMC) was located in West Virginia and did all of its business there. Unfortunately, after a major mine collapse, MMC had to suspend its mining operations. Due to local hostility, the company's management decided to move the company headquarters to Vermont. The CFO opened a bank account in Vermont and paid all the bills there. Dan Blankenboat, the CEO, bought a house in the mountains of Vermont, and any board meetings and management team conferences that happened after the collapse occurred there. It is unknown at this time when MMC will be able to re-open the mine and move back to West Virginia. Morgan, a miner who worked for MMC, was killed when the mine collapsed. His widow has moved to New Hampshire, so the possibility of suing MMC in Vermont is very appealing. Could Vermont constitutionally assert jurisdiction over MMC for a claim arising out of the collapse of the mine?

    (A) Yes. MMC has a level of contacts with Vermont that would satisfy the Supreme Court's test for specific personal jurisdiction.

    (B) Yes. MMC now has continuous and systematic contacts with Vermont.

    (C) No. MMC's contacts with Vermont do not involve mining.

    (D) No. Morgan's injuries did not arise out of MMC's contacts with Vermont.

214. Coaster Country is an amusement park in North Dakota. Word of mouth among coaster enthusiasts is that Coaster Country has the biggest, fastest, most amazing roller coasters of any theme park in the world. For years, Coaster Country has purchased all of the food sold in the park from Acme Packing, a Texas company. Dave, a resident of New Mexico, loves roller coasters, and so he goes to Coaster Country on vacation. While there, he is injured when a coaster goes faster than planned and flies off the track. Recuperating back home in New Mexico, Dave would like to sue Coaster Country in Texas, as that is closer than North Dakota. Can a Texas court constitutionally assert jurisdiction over Coaster Country?

    (A) Yes. Coaster Country has created continuous and systematic contacts with Texas by purchasing food there over a long period of time.

    (B) Yes. Dave's cause of action is related to Coaster Country's contacts with Texas.

    (C) No. Coaster Country's contacts with Texas are insufficient to justify general jurisdiction.

    (D) No. Dave must sue either in New Mexico or in North Dakota.

215. Really Big Eggs (RBE) is a multinational corporation that owns fast food outlets throughout the United States and the world. The company believes in concentrating its management structure in a single location, however, and so despite the far flung nature of its business all company officers work in the company's Illinois headquarters. The company is also incorporated in Illinois, and Illinois has more outlets per capita than any other state in the nation. Little, a resident of Nebraska, gets salmonella while on vacation in San Diego, and she thinks she got it from undercooked eggs at an RBE outlet. Little has heard that juries in Illinois are really sympathetic. Can Illinois courts constitutionally assert jurisdiction over RBE on Little's claim that they caused her food poisoning in California?

(A) No. RBE's contacts with Illinois are not related to Little's cause of action.

(B) No. There is no such thing as general jurisdiction over corporations.

(C) Yes. Although there is some question about the extent of contacts that justifies a finding of general jurisdiction over a corporation, the contacts here are enough.

(D) Yes. Because RBE is a huge corporation it can be sued anywhere.

TOPIC 42: QUESTIONS
PERSONAL JURISDICTION: PROCEDURAL ISSUES

216. Peter sues Dan in federal court in Arizona. Dan believes that he has insufficient contacts to be sued there, and he immediately files a motion to dismiss for lack of personal jurisdiction. Assuming the court agrees with Dan, what action should it take?

    (A) The court should ask Peter where he would like the case transferred.

    (B) The court should dismiss the case. Peter may refile it where personal jurisdiction over Dan would be proper.

    (C) The court should dismiss the case with prejudice. Peter may not refile it.

    (D) The court should keep the case. By appearing, Dan has waived any objection he may have had to personal jurisdiction.

217. Paul sues Dick in federal court in Wyoming. Dick answers the complaint, and 90 days later he realizes that he may have insufficient contacts to be sued in Wyoming and files a motion to dismiss for lack of personal jurisdiction. Assuming the court agrees with Dick, what action should it take?

    (A) The court should ask Paul where he would like the case transferred.

    (B) The court should dismiss the case. Paul may refile it where personal jurisdiction over Dick would be proper.

    (C) The court should dismiss the case with prejudice. Paul may not refile it.

    (D) The court should keep the case. By filing an answer that omits the personal jurisdiction defense and failing to amend the answer to include it within 21 days, Dick has waived any objection he may have had to personal jurisdiction.

218. Pam sues Donna in federal court in Wisconsin. Donna is from Pennsylvania, and she does not think the Wisconsin court has the power to make her defend herself there, so she does not respond. Pam takes a default judgment against Donna. Because Donna has no assets in Wisconsin, Pam brings her Wisconsin judgment to Pennsylvania to try to collect from Donna. What defenses can Donna raise?

    (A) None. When Donna failed to respond to the lawsuit she lost the right to complain about jurisdiction or defend on the merits.

    (B) Donna can still complain about the Wisconsin court's lack of jurisdiction over her. If she is right, the judgment is not enforceable.

(C) Donna can still complain about the Wisconsin court's lack of jurisdiction over her. If she is wrong, then she can still assert her defense on the merits.

(D) Donna can assert her defenses on the merits, but she has lost the right to complain about personal jurisdiction by failing to make a special appearance.

TOPIC 43: SERVICE OF PROCESS — QUESTIONS

219. RobCo, a New York corporation, hired Texas lawyer, Sally Smart, to represent RobCo in a Texas lawsuit. Although RobCo contracted to pay Sally (at her office address in Austin, TX), it later refused to pay. Sally sues RobCo in the federal court of the Austin Division of the Western District of Texas. Because RobCo refused to waive service of summons, Sally decided to serve RobCo by using the Texas General Long Arm statute, which authorizes service on the Texas Secretary of State if a nonresident defendant contracts with a Texas resident and the defendant fails to "perform the contract in whole or in part in this State . . . provided that the secretary of state immediately mails the process to the defendant by certified mail, return receipt requested." Will this procedure satisfy federal law?

   (A) No, no federal statute or rule of civil procedure authorizes service of process under state law procedures.

   (B) No, service on a domestic or foreign corporation is made by delivering a copy of the summons and of the complaint to a corporate officer or another agent authorized by appointment or by law to receive service of process.

   (C) Yes, this method is authorized by Rule 4 of the Federal Rules of Civil Procedure.

   (D) No, RobCo probably is not subject to personal jurisdiction in Texas on Sally's contract claim.

220. Paulette has filed a complaint in federal court in Houston, Texas alleging that her employer, National Development Company (NDC) discriminated against her on account of her race. Paulette served NDC, a foreign corporation, with its principal place of business in Arkansas, by having the registered agent served by delivery of the summons and complaint to the registered agent in person by an Arkansas Sheriff who prepared a return of service and sent the return, which showed the person served, the manner of service, and the date of service, back to the clerk of the trial court. If NDC moves to dismiss the action because of insufficient service of process, what result?

   (A) The action should be dismissed because the Arkansas Sheriff was not authorized to serve the summons and complaint by federal law.

   (B) The motion to dismiss should be denied because the case is pending in a federal court in Texas as long as Texas law allows service of process in Arkansas by an Arkansas sheriff.

   (C) The motion to dismiss should be denied if Arkansas law authorizes service of process by an Arkansas sheriff on a domestic corporation's registered agent.

(D) (B) and (C) are both correct.

221. Under what circumstances is publication a proper way to effect service of process on a defendant?

ANSWER:

TOPIC 44: VENUE GENERALLY

QUESTIONS

222. Woolf, who resides in the Northern District of Texas (N.D. Tex.), wants to sue Austen, who resides in the Western District of Louisiana (W.D. La.), for negligence resulting in an automobile accident. The accident occurred in Oklahoma (E.D. Okla.). Where would venue be proper?

   (A) N.D. Tex.

   (B) W.D. La.

   (C) E.D. Okla.

   (D) W.D. La. or E.D. Okla.

223. Woolf (N.D. Tex.) wants to sue Austen (W.D. La.) and Bronte (E.D. La.) for violating her federal civil rights in an incident that took place in Oklahoma (E.D. Okla.). Where would venue be proper?

   (A) W.D. La., E.D. La., or M.D. La.

   (B) E.D. Okla.

   (C) W.D. La., E.D. La., M.D. La., or E.D. Okla.

   (D) W.D. La., E.D. La., or E.D. Okla.

224. Woolf (N.D. Tex.) wants to sue Austen (W.D. La.) and Bronte (E.D. La.) for theft of trade secrets. The alleged theft arose out of a series of events: (1) Austen approached Woolf in New York City (S.D.N.Y.) while Woolf was there to see a Broadway play and got access to the secret; and (2) Bronte wrongfully used the secret in her business in Hartford (D. Conn.). Aside from Louisiana, where would venue be proper?

   (A) D. Conn.

   (B) S.D.N.Y.

   (C) N.D. Tex.

   (D) D. Conn. or S.D.N.Y.

225. Dickinson (D. Mass.) wants to sue Alcott (D.N.H.) and Montgomery (D. Me.) for trespassing on Dickinson's property in Massachusetts. Where would venue be proper?

(A) D.N.H.

(B) D. Me.

(C) D.N.H. or D. Me.

(D) D. Mass.

226. Fast Ride Co. is a Delaware corporation with its principal place of business in King of Prussia, Pennsylvania. It is in the business of selling motor scooters throughout the United States and has contracted with independent regional distributors, which have separate contracts with independent retailers in many markets, including all districts in California. Lance Racer purchased a scooter in Los Angeles (C.D. Cal.) and wants to sue Fast Ride Co. for breach of warranty. Because Lance lives in San Francisco (N.D. Cal.), he would like to sue Fast Ride Co. there, if possible. What are Lance's options?

(A) Lance can sue Fast Ride Co. in San Francisco because Fast Ride Co. is a corporation and it is subject to general personal jurisdiction in the state of California.

(B) Lance can sue Fast Ride Co. in San Francisco because Lance resides there, even though the events giving rise to his cause of action occurred elsewhere.

(C) Regardless of where Lance resides, Fast Ride can be sued in N.D. Cal. because the sales of its scooters there, through independent distributors and retailers, are sufficient to subject it to jurisdiction as if that district were a separate state, even for sales that are unrelated to the N.D. Cal. sales.

(D) Lance must sue in Los Angeles.

227. Wow Chemicals is a Delaware corporation with its headquarters in Houston, Texas (S.D. Tex.). All of Wow's management team works out of the Houston office. Wow also has a manufacturing plant in Amarillo, Texas (N.D. Tex.), that manufactures the company's entire line of its best-selling chemical, Titanic Chloride. It otherwise does no business in Texas. Jack Dawson (S.D. Cal.) wants to sue Wow for personal injuries he believes were caused by the company's Titanic Chloride. He has heard that the federal courts in Texas are good, so he wants to file suit there. Where would venue be proper?

ANSWER:

228. Kathy (D. Kan.) goes to England where she is involved in a three-car accident with Otis, a resident of the Northern District of Oklahoma, and Nancy, a resident of Nebraska (all of them were confused about driving on the left). Kathy would like to sue Otis and Nancy in federal court in the U.S. Which part of § 1391 will determine where venue is proper?

(A) § 1391(b)(1)

(B) § 1391(b)(2)

(C) § 1391(b)(3)

(D) Answers (A) and (C) are both correct.

TOPIC 45: CHANGE OF VENUE

QUESTIONS

229. Bloomer sued Pankhurst (D. Utah) for breach of a contract to deliver 100 widgets to Bloomer's business in Boulder (D. Colo.). Bloomer's summer home is in Cheyenne, Wyoming, and she filed her suit in the federal court in the District of Wyoming. Pankhurst knows that she is subject to personal jurisdiction in Wyoming, but she does not think this particular lawsuit should be there. What can Pankhurst do, and do you expect it to succeed?

ANSWER:

230. Wendy's husband, Peter, was killed in the crash of a private plane in Iowa. The plane was manufactured by Pepper Corp., which is headquartered in St. Louis, Missouri, where the planes are manufactured (E.D. Mo.). Wendy (who lives in southern Minnesota), as Peter's surviving spouse, filed a wrongful death lawsuit against Pepper in federal court in Iowa. Pepper knows that it is subject to personal jurisdiction in Iowa, but it would rather defend at home in Missouri. What motion could Pepper file to achieve this objective, and what law will be applied if Pepper's motion is granted?

(A) Pepper should file a motion to dismiss the case under 28 U.S.C. § 1406 because venue is not proper in Iowa.

(B) Pepper should file a motion to transfer the case to Missouri for the convenience of witnesses and parties; if granted, the federal court in Missouri will apply Missouri law, including Missouri's choice of law rules.

(C) Pepper should file a motion to transfer the case to Missouri for the convenience of witnesses and parties; if granted, the federal court in Missouri will apply the law that would have been applied by the federal court in Iowa if the case had not been transferred, including Iowa's choice of law rules.

(D) Pepper should file an alternative motion to dismiss the case or to transfer the case to Missouri for the convenience of witnesses and parties; if the case is transferred to Missouri, the federal court in Missouri will have the discretion to apply Missouri law or Iowa law.

231. Edison (D. Nevada), a notable scientist, brought a patent infringement action against Franklin (N.D. Texas) in the Northern District of Texas, claiming that Franklin infringed several of Edison's patents there. Somewhat surprisingly, Franklin moves to transfer the case to the federal court in the District of Nevada, where Edison resides. If Edison objects to the transfer, do the venue statutes authorize it anyway?

ANSWER:

TOPIC 46: QUESTIONS
VENUE, FORUM NON CONVENIENS, AND PROCEDURAL ISSUES

Rhett Butler Construction Company ("Butler"), a Georgia corporation with its principal place of business in Georgia entered into a contract to build a hospital for the State of Texas in Austin, Texas. Butler entered into a subcontract with Travis Enterprises, Inc. ("Travis"), a Texas corporation with its principal place of business in Texas for the performance of architectural and engineering services at the construction site.

The construction contract between Butler and Travis contained a forum selection clause which provides that all disputes between the parties must be litigated in "the United States District Court for the Middle District of Georgia."

Six months after the contract was executed, a dispute arose between the parties about their respective obligations to one another. As a result, Travis sued Butler in the Western District of Texas, Austin Division for nonpayment of its fees.

Butler believes that Austin is an unfavorable forum and wants to have the action dismissed or transferred to federal court in the Middle District of Georgia.

232. What motion or motions should Butler file to enforce the forum selection clause?

(A) Butler should file a 12(b)(3) motion for dismissal of the action because the forum selection clause makes venue improper in Austin.

(B) Butler should file a motion to dismiss or transfer under 28 U.S.C. § 1406 because the clause makes venue improper in Austin.

(C) Butler should file a motion to transfer the case from the Western District of Texas in Austin to the Middle District of Georgia under 28 U.S.C. § 1404(a).

(D) Butler should file a motion under Federal Rule of Civil Procedure 7(b) invoking the common law doctrine of forum non conveniens seeking dismissal of the case.

Wow Chemicals is a Delaware corporation with its principal place of business in Delaware. All of Wow's pesticide development team works out of the company's Houston office. During the 1980s, Wow manufactured, in New Jersey, a chemical designed to enhance the productivity of banana growing by eradicating a worm that otherwise destroys a sizeable portion of the banana crop. The chemical is very effective because it sterilizes the worms, making them unable to reproduce. Unfortunately, the chemical has the same effect on banana workers — they were also rendered sterile, unable to have children. Use of the chemical was banned in the United States. Wow, however, had already produced large quantities of the chemical and sold it to banana growers outside the United States, including some in Costa Rica.

Juan Alfaro was a worker on a Costa Rican banana plantation. He was 25 years old, newly married, and wanted to have many children. However, he was exposed to the chemical at work and is now medically sterile. He and a number of his coworkers filed suit against Wow in state court in Harris

County, Texas. Wow removed the case to the federal district court for that area, the Southern District of Texas. Wow admits that it is subject to personal jurisdiction in Texas, but it has filed a motion to dismiss the case based on the doctrine of forum non conveniens, saying that the case would be far better handled in Costa Rica where the plaintiffs live and where they were exposed to the chemical. Alfaro opposes this motion.

233. What test should the court apply in deciding whether to dismiss Alfaro's case?

(A) Whether the defendant resides in the Southern District of Texas.

(B) Whether Alfaro's claim accrued in the Southern District of Texas.

(C) Whether considerations of party and forum convenience override Alfaro's choice of forum.

(D) Whether Costa Rica uses U.S.-style discovery in civil cases.

234. How will the judge in *Alfaro v. Wow Chemicals* probably rule on the motion to dismiss, and why?

ANSWER:

TOPIC 47: CLAIM PRECLUSION

QUESTIONS

Paul and Doug are in a car wreck. Paul sues Doug for negligence, seeking $100,000 in damages for his personal injuries. The case goes to trial, the jury finds that Doug was not negligent, and the court enters a final judgment that Paul take nothing. Assume that the jurisdiction in which the court sits follows the Restatement (Second) of Judgments.

235. Paul thinks he'd do better a second time around — practice makes perfect — and so he sues Doug again for negligence in the car crash. Paul's second suit is:

   (A) barred by claim preclusion.

   (B) merged into the first judgment.

   (C) permissible only if Paul hires a new lawyer.

   (D) permissible as long as the statute of limitations hasn't run on Paul's negligence claim.

236. Paul knows he can't sue again for negligence, but on reflection he believes that Doug actually rammed him with his car on purpose. Paul therefore files a second suit, but this time his legal theory against Doug is battery. Paul's second suit is:

   (A) permissible. Negligence and battery are not the same claim.

   (B) permissible. Paul has not yet litigated the battery claim.

   (C) barred by the judgment for Doug in the first suit.

   (D) Both (A) and (B) are correct.

237. Suppose that instead of losing the first suit, Paul wins and gets a final judgment in his favor for $50,000. But then Paul realizes that his Bentley was totaled in the wreck, and he forgot to include a claim for those damages in the first suit. He files a new suit against Doug seeking only damages for the costs of replacing his car. Paul's second suit is:

   (A) barred by claim preclusion.

   (B) merged into the first judgment.

   (C) permitted because it asserts a different right from the personal injury claim.

   (D) permitted because property damages and personal injury damages are not the same remedy.

238. Doug was also injured in the wreck, but he asserted no claim in Paul's suit. Now that he's won that one, he'd like to file his own case against Paul, seeking to recover for his injuries caused by Paul's negligence. Can he properly do so?

(A) No. Claim preclusion makes it improper.

(B) Yes. *Doug v. Paul* is not the same claim as *Paul v. Doug*, because if more than one party has a right to relief arising out of a single transaction, each such party has a separate "claim" for purposes of merger and bar.

(C) No. While Doug's claim is probably not barred by claim preclusion, it was a compulsory counterclaim in *Paul v. Doug*, and Doug's failure to assert it there means that he has lost it.

(D) Answers (B) and (C) are both correct.

TOPIC 48: ISSUE PRECLUSION

QUESTIONS

Brandon and Sarah were young, in love, and in search of a house to buy in celebration of Brandon's law school graduation. They were thrilled to be selected to participate in the popular reality television show, "Home Hunters" (HH). The show paired them with Rhea Max, a local realtor, who showed them three places: one nice but boring, one way out of their price range, and one a "fixer upper" with real potential. Encouraged by the HH producers, they chose the fixer upper after HH promised to renovate the kitchen and install a fabulous chandelier in the bedroom. (The chandelier was large and heavy, but HH assured the couple that they would attach it firmly.) Andy Handy, a carpenter working on HH's behalf, installed the chandelier and put in new kitchen cabinets — all in one day! Unfortunately, two weeks after Brandon and Sarah moved in, the chandelier crashed onto the bed in the middle of the night, breaking Brandon's leg and injuring Sarah's pretty face.

Brandon and Sarah sued the company that produces the show, alleging that HH's carpenter was negligent in the installation of the chandelier. HH denied their claims, alleging that the chandelier fell because of hidden flaws in the ceiling. It claimed that Andy Handy was an independent contractor rather than an employee, so that HH would not be liable for his negligence, if any. HH also asserted an affirmative defense: Brandon and Sarah signed a contract, absolving the show of liability for any damages related to the purchase of the house or its redecoration by HH.

239. Suppose that *Brandon & Sarah v. HH* went to trial. The jury found that the carpenter was negligent, that he was acting as HH's employee in his work on their house, and awarded Brandon damages of $50,000 and Sarah damages of $100,000. The judge ruled as a matter of law that the contract Brandon and Sarah signed was legally unenforceable to absolve HH of its own negligence. HH did not appeal, and the court's judgment based on this verdict became final. Later, Brandon files a second suit against HH, this time seeking damages (cost of repair) for the HH carpenter's faulty installation of new kitchen cabinets. HH answers, denying negligence and also claiming Andy Handy was an independent contractor. Brandon files a motion for partial summary judgment, properly proving up the judgment in the first case, and arguing that HH is estopped from denying that Handy was acting as its employee on the renovation project. Should the court grant Brandon's motion?

    (A) No, the problems with the kitchen cabinets are not the same claim as the installation of the chandelier.

    (B) No, the question of whether Handy was HH's employee was not necessary to the result in Brandon and Sarah's first lawsuit.

    (C) No, Handy was not a party to the first suit.

    (D) Yes, this is the same issue, and it was actually litigated, actually decided, necessary to the first judgment, and both Brandon and HH were parties.

240. Suppose instead that this is what happened in the first case: (1) in response to Brandon and

Sarah's motion for summary judgment, the judge rules that the contract they signed does not protect HH if it is found to be negligent; (2) at trial, the jury finds that Handy was acting as HH's employee, but that Handy was not negligent in installing the chandelier. The court entered judgment in HH's favor, which is now final. This time, in the second case, Brandon sues HH for Handy's negligence in installing the kitchen cabinets. HH asserts a defense based on the exculpatory contract, but Brandon argues that issue preclusion means that HH is bound by the judge's decision in the first case that the contract is not enforceable. Is Brandon right?

(A) Yes. It's the same issue, same parties, and was actually litigated and decided.

(B) No. Because the jury found that Handy was not negligent, the court's ruling that the exculpatory contract was unenforceable was not necessary to the first judgment.

(C) No. Only decisions made by a jury can form the basis for issue preclusion.

(D) Yes. Alternative grounds for the same result are always a valid basis for issue preclusion.

241. Suppose that Brandon and Sarah successfully sued HH for their injuries resulting from the fall of the chandelier, as described in question 211. Although they did not sue Andy Handy because they assumed he was judgment proof, it turns out that Handy is actually quite wealthy but does carpentry for HH because he's hoping to break into show business. Brandon and Sarah therefore file a second lawsuit, this one against Handy. They also file a motion for summary judgment, arguing that Handy's negligence, proximate cause, and their damages were all determined in the first suit, and that Handy was bound by that decision. Should the judge grant the motion?

(A) Yes. The issue of Handy's negligence was fully litigated in the first suit.

(B) No. The issue of Handy's negligence was not necessary to the judgment against HH.

(C) Yes. The jury actually decided the issue of Handy's negligence and it would be inefficient to relitigate that fact.

(D) No. Handy was not a party to the first suit.

TOPIC 49: NON-MUTUAL ISSUE PRECLUSION

QUESTIONS

242. Kelly, a professional wrestler, was under the care of Dr. MacMahon for heart trouble. Dr. MacMahon advised Kelly that he could resume his strenuous occupation on a full duty, full contact, no-holds-barred basis. During Kelly's first match, in the second period, he experienced chest pains and is convinced that he suffered a heart attack. He therefore believes that he is no longer able to pursue his profession and filed a claim for disability benefits against his insurer, Worldwide Fund (WWF). When they denied his claim, Kelly sued. In that case, the jury found (in answer to Special Interrogatory #1) that Kelly did not suffer a heart attack. Based on this answer, the judge entered a judgment for WWF. Kelly next sued Dr. MacMahon for medical malpractice, claiming that Dr. MacMahon's negligence in advising him to resume wrestling proximately caused Kelly to have a heart attack. Dr. MacMahon's lawyer has invoked the affirmative defense of issue preclusion. (You can assume for purposes of this question that Kelly needed to prove that he had a heart attack to win both his first suit and his malpractice suit against the doctor.) Assume that the jurisdiction in which these cases are litigated follows the Restatement (Second) approach to issue preclusion. Will his attempt to rely on that defense be successful?

    (A) No. Dr. MacMahon was not a party to the first suit, and so mutuality of estoppel is lacking.

    (B) Yes. The heart attack question was actually litigated, actually decided, the judgment in the first case rests on the jury's finding, and Kelly had a full and fair opportunity to litigate the issue.

    (C) No. WWF and Dr. MacMahon are not in privity with each other.

    (D) Answers (A) and (C) are both correct.

243. Henrietta brought a wrongful death action in state court in New York against Wings-Are-Up, the manufacturer of a single engine airplane, claiming that a design defect caused the plane to crash — and that the crash caused the untimely death of Henrietta's husband, Harry. The action was tried to a jury that found that the airplane was defective as designed, unreasonably dangerous, and that the defect proximately caused the crash and Harry's death. The trial judge rendered judgment on the verdict for Henrietta for $6,300,000. Thereafter, another death action, also in New York, was filed against Wings-Are-Up by the parents of Harry's dead co-pilot, Larry, who also died in the crash. What effect, if any, will the judgment in Henrietta's case have on the second action brought by Larry's parents? (Assume that New York follows the Restatement (Second) of Judgments.)

    (A) The judgment in Henrietta's case will have no effect on Wings-Are-Up's liability in the federal action.

(B) Larry's parents will probably not be able to use the liability findings in the first action against Wings-Are-Up because they were not parties in the first action.

(C) Larry's parents may be able to use the liability findings obtained in the first action against Wings-Are-Up to estop it from contesting liability in their case.

(D) Larry's parents will be barred from bringing their suit because it involves the same claim (a strict liability claim against Wings-Are-Up based on the crash of its plane) that was the basis for Henrietta's judgment. If Larry's parents knew about the action they should have intervened, but instead purposely bypassed the proceeding, and so they lost their chance to bring a claim through claim preclusion.

TOPIC 50: THE LAW OF THE CASE DOCTRINE

QUESTIONS

244. Williams and Spencer brought a class action against the City of Akron claiming that allegedly discriminatory policies violated their civil rights and the rights of black police officers and black applicants for employment in the Akron Police Department (APD). After the class was certified, white, Hispanic, and female members sought to intervene. Shortly before trial, Williams and Spencer announced a settlement with Akron and the APD and submitted a comprehensive consent decree to the district judge for approval. The district court approved the consent decree but denied the intervention. The court subsequently granted partial intervenor status to other members of the department for the limited purpose of challenging the consent decree. Both the consent decree and the order denying full intervenor status were appealed to the court of appeals, which affirmed the order denying full intervenor status and remanded the case to the trial court for further action. On remand, intervention was again attempted and again denied. On further appeal, the court of appeals probably will:

(A) deny relief to the intervenors under the law of the case doctrine because all subsequent proceedings in a case must follow prior appellate rulings.

(B) consider the intervenors' request for relief under a *de novo* standard of review.

(C) deny relief unless the appellate record shows substantially different evidence, a change in controlling legal authority, or that the earlier appellate decision was clearly erroneous and would work a manifest injustice.

(D) dismiss the appeal for want of jurisdiction.

TOPIC 51: QUESTIONS
STATE LAW IN FEDERAL COURT: OVERVIEW

245. A statute called the Rules of Decision Act (RDA) has been part of federal law since 1789. It instructs federal courts to apply:

   (A) "the laws of the several states," except where federal law otherwise requires or provides.

   (B) "the common law of each state," except where federal law otherwise requires or provides.

   (C) "federal law, both statutory and common law," in all cases in federal court.

   (D) "the laws of the several states" to every issue in cases where jurisdiction is based on diversity of citizenship.

246. In 1934, Congress passed the Rules Enabling Act (REA), which authorizes the Supreme Court to adopt rules of practice and procedure for the federal courts. In order for rules adopted pursuant to the REA to be valid:

   (A) they must be "general rules of practice and procedure" or "rules of evidence."

   (B) they must not "abridge, enlarge or modify any substantive right."

   (C) both (A) and (B) are required.

   (D) they only need to be adopted following the proper procedure, because that means they have already been approved by both the Supreme Court and Congress.

247. The Supreme Court case of *Swift v. Tyson*, 41 U.S. 1 (1842), interpreted the RDA in a way that limited the circumstances under which federal courts were required to apply state law. *Swift* held that the phrase "laws of the several states" meant only:

   (A) state statutes, and state law regarding rights and titles to things "having a permanent locality."

   (B) state statutes, and cases decided by the state's highest court.

   (C) state statutes, and state common law consistent with the national majority rule.

   (D) state laws based on the law of England in 1789.

248. Under *Swift v. Tyson*, what law did the federal courts apply to tort claims in diversity cases?

ANSWER:

249. In 1938, the Supreme Court changed its mind. In *Erie R.R. Co. v. Tompkins*, 304 U.S. 64 (1938), the Court held:

   (A) The Rules of Decision Act was unconstitutional.

   (B) *Swift*'s interpretation of the Rules of Decision Act, and the ensuing creation of federal general common law, was unconstitutional because it invaded rights reserved by the Constitution to the states.

   (C) *Swift*'s interpretation of the Rules of Decision Act was unconstitutional because it discriminated and therefore violated the Equal Protection Clause of the Fourteenth Amendment.

   (D) The federal common law of premises liability to trespassers is the same as the law of Pennsylvania — land owners' only duty is to refrain from willful or wanton injury.

TOPIC 52: QUESTIONS
STATE LAW IN FEDERAL COURT (THE *ERIE* DOCTRINE)

250. Bush filed a diversity action against Gore in a federal court in Kansas, but did not serve the complaint until after the Kansas two-year statute of limitations had expired. Because the pertinent Kansas statute clearly and expressly states that a civil action is not deemed to have been commenced until service is accomplished under Kansas law, the action would have been barred if filed in a Kansas state court. Federal Civil Procedure Rule 3, however, provides: "A civil action is commenced by filing a complaint." Under this approach, the action would have been commenced in time. Which approach is the proper one?

(A) Federal law should be followed because the action is pending in federal court and the Federal Rules of Civil Procedure adopted in conformity with the Rules Enabling Act (28 U.S.C. § 2072) govern the proceeding.

(B) Kansas law must be applied under the Rules of Decision Act (28 U.S.C. § 1652) and the Constitution because the Kansas approach is "outcome determinative."

(C) Kansas law must be applied because no countervailing federal policies outweigh the *Erie* policy of avoiding different outcomes in state and federal courts.

(D) (B) and (C) are both correct.

251. Paul Payne sued Harris County Hospital (HCH) and Dr. Mel Practer in federal court in Houston, Texas, for providing Payne with negligent medical care after he suffered a cerebral stroke. Payne's federal complaint was prepared and filed in accordance with the federal rules. Similarly, Payne has complied with all federal procedural requirements in prosecuting his claims in federal court. Under Texas law, if a plaintiff fails to serve an expert report on each physician or health care provider not later than the 120th day after the claim was filed, the trial court must, on motion of the affected physician or health care provider, "enter an order of dismissal" with prejudice to the refiling of the claim. Expert report means a written report that provides a fair summary of the expert's opinions regarding applicable standards of care, how those standards were violated, and the causal relationship between the violation and the injury, harm, or damages claimed. Tex. Civ. Prac. & Rem. Code § 74.301. Because Payne did not file any reports, both HCH and Dr. Practer have moved to dismiss Payne's claims with prejudice. The judge is trying to figure out how the Supreme Court's recent decision in *Shady Grove Orthopedic Associates, P.A. v. Allstate Insurance Co.*, 130 S. Ct. 1431 (2010), might affect the question of whether the Texas law requiring expert reports applies in federal court. Which of the following is true?

(A) The correct result will turn on whether a majority of Supreme Court Justices would conclude that Rule 8's pleading requirements determine the issue of whether additional expert reports can be required.

(B) Some Justices will analyze that question based primarily on the language of the federal rule, and will then inquire whether Rule 8 "really regulates procedure." For them, the purpose of the state rule or its partially substantive purpose is not a relevant question.

(C) Some Justices will decide whether Rule 8 governs by construing it in a way that avoids conflicts with important state regulatory interests, and since the Texas law is designed to protect defendants (and their insurers) from the expense of defending non-meritorious medical malpractice suits, that may lead those Justices to interpret the Texas and federal rules as compatible rather than conflicting.

(D) All of the above are correct (and a lot will turn on Justice Kagan's approach to this kind of *Erie* issue).

Sleep Hotels, a citizen of Texoma, has sued Mall Mart (MM) (a Delaware corporation with its principal place of business in New Jersey) in federal district court for the Southern District of Texoma. Sleep Hotels purchased thousands of dollars' worth of sheets from MM, which were labeled as 1,000 thread count but were actually only 200 thread count, resulting in an overcharge that Sleep Hotels estimates at approximately $150,000. Two weeks prior to trial, Sleep Hotels (which was outraged but wanted to continue to do business with MM) had offered to settle the case for $50,000 but MM rejected the offer. The settlement offer was in the form of a formal "offer of judgment." (See below.) The case went to trial, and the jury returned a verdict in favor of Sleep Hotel for $100,000.

Rule 68 of the Federal Rules of Civil Procedure provides that if a defendant makes a settlement offer in the form of a formal "offer of judgment," and the plaintiff rejects the offer, there can be serious consequences: even if the plaintiff wins the case, if its judgment is for less than the settlement offer, the plaintiff must pay the defendant its post-offer costs. This rule applies only to offers by defendants (not plaintiffs) and allows the award of costs but not attorney's fees.

Rule 68 of the Texoma Rules of Civil Procedure states that "at any time more than ten days before trial, any party may serve an offer in writing to allow judgment to be taken in accordance with its terms and conditions, and any offeree who rejects an offer and fails to obtain a more favorable judgment . . . shall pay the offeror's post-offer costs plus reasonable attorney's fees actually incurred by the offeror from the time of the offer." The Texoma rule thus allows both plaintiffs and defendants to make offers of judgment and allows the recovery of both costs and attorney fees. Texoma considers this rule to be procedural and applies it where applicable regardless of whose substantive law applies to other issues in the case.

Absent an offer of judgment, the applicable state law does not allow for recovery of attorney's fees in cases such as this. However, Sleep Hotel has filed a motion for entry of judgment that includes $50,000 for attorney's fees incurred after its offer was made. MM does not dispute that that sum represents a reasonable attorney's fee for the work done, but claims that the federal offer of judgment rule applies so that plaintiff may not use the offer of judgment device, and that even if they could, attorney's fees would not be recoverable.

252. What argument should MM make that Federal Rule 68 is broad enough to cover the issue of whether Sleep Hotels can recover the $50,000 in attorney fees? What opposing argument will it need to counter?

ANSWER:

253. Suppose that the judge indicates that she does not believe that Federal Rule 68 is broad enough to cover the issue. What is Sleep Hotel's best argument that the Texoma rule is outcome determinative?

ANSWER:

TOPIC 53: FEDERAL COMMON LAW

QUESTIONS

254. The *Erie* decision states that there is no "general federal common law" under a proper interpretation of the Rules of Decision Act, but is there any specialized federal common law?

ANSWER:

TOPIC 54: APPELLATE JURISDICTION

QUESTIONS

Paul Payne sued Harris County Hospital (HCH) and Dr. Mel Practer in federal district court in Houston, Texas, for providing Payne with negligent medical care after he suffered a heart attack. Payne did not file expert reports with the district court or serve them on the defendants in compliance with Texas Civil Practice and Remedies Code Section 74.351, which requires claimants to serve an expert report on each affected physician or health care provider or suffer a dismissal with prejudice to the refiling of the claim.

255. Because Payne did not file any reports, the district judge dismissed Payne's complaint with prejudice by signed written order on Monday, June 11, 2014. Payne timely filed his notice of appeal. Which of the following statements is correct with respect to the appealability of the dismissal order?

(A) The order is appealable as a final judgment under 28 U.S.C. § 1291.

(B) The order is appealable as a final judgment under 28 U.S.C. § 1291 and Fed. R. Civ. P. 54(b).

(C) The order is not appealable because it is not a final judgment on the merits of Payne's malpractice claim.

(D) The order is appealable under the collateral order doctrine.

256. Now assume that Payne filed a sufficient report concerning Dr. Practer in compliance with Texas law, but that Payne's separate report for HCH was deficient. Thus, on the defendants' motions to dismiss, the district judge ordered Payne's case dismissed as to HCH and in a separate order denied Dr. Practer's motion to dismiss. If Payne files a notice of appeal complaining of the dismissal of HCH, does the court of appeals have jurisdiction of the appeal?

(A) Yes, the dismissal of HCH is a final order that is appealable under 28 U.S.C. § 1291.

(B) No, because Federal Rule 54(b)'s requirements were not satisfied and no severance order was entered, the dismissal order is not final and appealable under 28 U.S.C. § 1291.

(C) No, the order is not appealable because it is not a final judgment on the merits of Payne's malpractice claim.

(D) Yes, the order is appealable under the collateral order doctrine.

257. Paula Prisoner sues Sergeant Ducote and Officer Mary Jane in federal court in the Northern District of Texas, Dallas Division, claiming that Paula's constitutional rights were

violated after she was arrested and incarcerated in the city jail on the day of the Texas/Oklahoma football game. Paula claims that she was denied medical treatment as a result of the deliberate indifference of Ducote and Jane to Paula's serious medical needs, which were obvious. Paula's summary judgment evidence shows that she requested medical treatment from the police, who told her that because she wasn't concerned about the safety of the public the police weren't concerned about her medical needs. The defendants do not dispute Paula's version of the facts. If a motion for summary judgment made by the defendants is denied by the district judge, which of the following statements is correct?

(A) The order is not appealable before final judgment on the merits.

(B) The order is appealable under the collateral order doctrine if the motion is based on the officers' defense of qualified immunity.

(C) The order is immediately appealable if the judge issues a written order for interlocutory appeal under 28 U.S.C. § 1292(b), unless the court of appeals refuses permission to appeal.

(D) (B) or (C), alternatively.

TOPIC 55: APPELLATE PROCEDURE

QUESTIONS

Paul Payne sued Harris County Hospital (HCH) and Dr. Mel Practer in federal district court in Houston, Texas, for providing Payne with negligent medical care after he suffered a heart attack. Payne did not file expert reports with the district court or serve them on the defendants in compliance with Texas Civil Practice and Remedies Code Section 74.351, which requires claimants to serve an expert report within 120 days after commencement of suit on each affected physician or health care provider or suffer a dismissal with prejudice. Because Payne did not file any reports, the district judge dismissed Payne's complaint. Assume that the first order concerning HCH was signed and entered on Monday, June 11, 2014, and that the second order concerning Dr. Practer was signed and entered on Wednesday, June 13, 2014. Assume further that neither the district judge nor the court clerk prepared a separate judgment embodying both dismissal orders.

258. What must Payne do to commence an appeal?

  (A) Payne must file a notice of appeal in the trial court within 30 days after June 11, 2014.

  (B) Payne must file a notice of appeal in the trial court within 30 days after June 13, 2014.

  (C) Payne must file notices of appeal in the trial court within 30 days after June 11 and within 30 days after June 13, 2014.

  (D) Payne must file a notice of appeal within 30 days after 150 days have run from entry of the last dismissal order (June 13) in the civil docket.

259. If Payne filed a motion for new trial on Friday, June 15, 2014, and the motion was overruled by a signed written order entered in the civil docket on Friday, June 22, 2014, what must Payne do to commence an appeal?

  (A) Payne must file a notice of appeal within 30 days after June 11, 2014.

  (B) Payne must file a notice of appeal within 30 days after June 13, 2014.

  (C) Payne must file a notice of appeal within 30 days after June 22, 2014.

  (D) Payne must file a notice of appeal within 60 days after June 22, 2014.

260. Under the same facts as the preceding question, if Payne does not receive notice of the entry of the trial court's order overruling Payne's motion for new trial until July 23, 2014, because the court clerk did not mail notice of the entry of the order to Payne's counsel, what, if anything, can Payne do to prosecute an appeal to the court of appeals?

  (A) Payne can do nothing; the time to commence an appeal has expired.

(B) Payne can file a motion for extension of time to commence the appeal within 60 days after entry of the order denying Payne a new trial.

(C) Payne can move the trial court to reopen the appeal if the motion is filed within 180 days after the judgment or order is signed.

(D) Payne can use Rule 60(b) to ask the trial court to vacate the order denying the new trial so that the same order can be entered again to restart the appellate timetable.

261. Once Payne has properly given notice of appeal, what must Payne do to prosecute the appeal to judgment in the court of the appeals?

ANSWER:

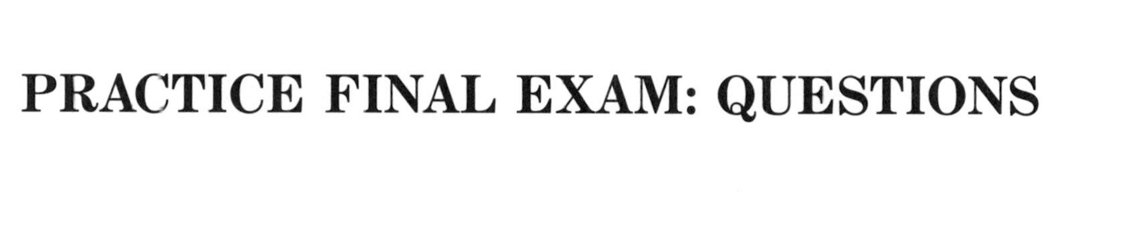

PRACTICE FINAL EXAM: QUESTIONS

QUESTIONS

PRACTICE FINAL EXAM

Instructions: This exam consists of 68 multiple-choice and short-answer questions. It will take 3–4 hours to answer these questions, depending on the length of your short-answer responses. You might also choose to separately take on a series of questions based on the same fact pattern as a sort of mini-exam.

Charley, Donald, and Mark met to try to finalize the formation of a joint venture to obtain a Mini Cooper dealership for New Britain, Connecticut. Unfortunately, the meeting went from bad to worse, with all of the parties blaming the others for the collapse of the deal. Donald and Mark stormed out immediately, heading for their cars while still fuming about the meeting. Charley followed several minutes later, still preoccupied over what he saw as the lack of vision of his business partners. No one is quite sure what happened next, but the result was a serious accident in the parking lot in which Charley, while walking to his car, was caught between Mark and Donald's cars as they collided. Charley was seriously injured. Donald and Mark escaped without physical injury, but both suffered significant damage to their cars.

Because of a longstanding business relationship, Charley does not want to sue Donald for breach of contract, and Donald does not want to sue Charley for breach of contract. Charley does, however, sue Donald for his injuries, claiming that Donald was driving negligently, causing the accident. The suit is filed in federal court based on diversity jurisdiction (Charley is from Connecticut, Donald is from Delaware, and Mark is from Maine).

For questions 262–266, consider only issues arising under the federal joinder rules. For questions 267–269, consider whether the federal court would have subject matter jurisdiction over the claims in question.

262. Donald wants to bring Mark into this lawsuit. What procedural vehicles could he use?

ANSWER:

263. Donald decided to use Rule 14 to bring Mark into the lawsuit, alleging that Mark drove negligently and requesting contribution and indemnity. Can Donald also add a claim against Mark for negligence to seek damages for the damage to Donald's car?

(A) Yes, he can do that under Rule 13.

(B) Yes, he can do that under Rule 18.

(C) No, that is not a derivative claim.

(D) Yes, but only if it arises out of the same transaction or occurrence as the Rule 14 claim.

264. Assume that Donald used Rule 14 to bring Mark into the lawsuit. Can he add a claim for

breach of contract?

(A) Yes, he can do that under Rule 20.

(B) Yes, he can do that under Rule 18.

(C) No, that is not a derivative claim.

(D) Yes, but only if it arises out of the same transaction or occurrence as the Rule 14 claim.

265. Assume that Donald used Rule 14 to bring Mark into the lawsuit. Mark in turn has filed a claim against Charley for negligence. Can Mark bring a claim against Charley for breach of contract?

(A) Yes, he can do that under Rule 18.

(B) No, it does not arise out of the same transaction or occurrence as Charley's claim against Donald.

(C) Yes, Rule 14 permits the third-party defendant to bring any and all claims against the original plaintiff.

(D) No, not unless he also brings a claim against Charley alleging that his negligence caused the accident and the damage to Mark's car.

266. Assume that Donald filed a counterclaim against Charley for negligence, claiming that Charley dashed out from between parked cars and caused the accident. Can he use that counterclaim to bring a breach of contract claim against Mark?

(A) Yes, but only if he also brings a negligence claim against Mark.

(B) Yes, Rule 13(h) provides complete authorization for the contract claim alone.

(C) No, defendants can only bring in new parties through impleader.

(D) No, the contract claim is not part of the same transaction or occurrence as Charley's claim against Donald.

267. Assume that Charley has sued Donald for negligence for $500,000. Donald has filed a counterclaim for damages to his car for $10,000. Does the court have jurisdiction over the counterclaim?

(A) Yes, Charley and Donald are from different states.

(B) No, the amount in controversy is less than $75,000.

(C) No, this would be inconsistent with the requirements of 28 U.S.C. § 1332.

(D) Yes, the counterclaim is part of the same constitutional case as Charley's claim, and Donald is not a plaintiff.

268. Assume that Charley sued Donald for negligence for $500,000, and that Donald impleaded Mark for contribution and indemnity. Donald also added a negligence claim against Mark for his own damages ($10,000) and a breach of contract claim for $50,000. Over which of Donald's claims does the federal court have jurisdiction?

   (A) Only the contribution and indemnity claim.

   (B) The contribution and indemnity claim and the negligence claim.

   (C) The contribution and indemnity claim, the negligence claim, and the breach of contract claim.

   (D) None of the claims; two are clearly too small, and Mark's percentage of causation might make the indemnity claim too small as well, so the amount in controversy requirement is not satisfied for any of the claims.

269. Assume that Charley sued Donald for negligence for $500,000, and that Donald impleaded Mark for contribution and indemnity and added a negligence claim for $10,000. Mark wants to file a breach of contract claim against Charley for $100,000. Does the federal court have jurisdiction over this claim?

   (A) Yes, it meets the requirements of the diversity statute.

   (B) No, it does not share a common nucleus of operative fact with Charley's claim against Donald.

   (C) No, it is a claim by a person made a party under Rule 14.

   (D) Yes, because Mark is not a plaintiff within the meaning of 28 U.S.C. § 1367.

Charley v. Donald v. Mark went to trial including the following claims:

Charley v. Donald for negligence (personal injuries)

Donald v. Charley for negligence (damage to car) (counterclaim)

Donald v. Mark for negligence (damage to car) and breach of contract (additional party to counterclaim)

Mark v. Donald for negligence (damage to car) and breach of contract (counterclaim)

The court entered a judgment for Donald on his negligence claim against Mark, based on jury findings that the accident was caused 100% by Mark's negligence. It entered a take-nothing judgment on Charley's and Donald's negligence claims against each other. It also entered a take-nothing judgment on Mark's and Donald's claims against each other for breach of contract, based on jury findings that neither Mark nor Donald breached the contract. No one appealed.

270. One year later, the trial has taken a toll on the parties' remaining relationships, and no one feels a reluctance to sue anyone. Assume that no statute of limitations bars any potential claims. Donald got a judgment for damage to his car, but he has decided that his persistent backaches must also be a result of the accident. He wants to sue Mark for personal injury damages resulting from the accident. May he?

(A) Yes. This issue was not actually litigated in the first case.

(B) No. That claim is barred by the judgment in the first case.

(C) No. That claim is merged into the judgment in the first case.

(D) Yes. That claim is not the same cause of action as the property damage claim.

271. Donald is also feeling peevish about losing the Mini Cooper dealership, and he no longer cares whether he offends Charley. Can he now sue Charley for breach of contract?

(A) Yes. The contract claim was not the same cause of action as Donald's negligence claim against Charley.

(B) No. The contract claim against Charley was a compulsory counterclaim in the first case.

(C) No. It is barred by the results of Donald's claim against Mark.

(D) Yes. The judgment in the first case was not final because there was no appellate court decision.

272. Although Charley, Donald, and Mark were too wrapped up in themselves to notice at the time, a fourth person also suffered injuries due to the parking lot accident. Donald ricocheted backward after hitting Charley and ran his car into a parked car belonging to Ed. Now Ed sues Donald for the damages. There is no claim that Ed was negligent in any way. Donald claims that his lack of negligence was established in the first case, and asks the court to dismiss Ed's case. Should the court dismiss the case?

(A) No. The finding of Donald's lack of negligence was not necessary in the first case.

(B) Yes. The issue of negligence was actually decided and Donald was found not to be liable.

(C) It depends on whether the jurisdiction allows non-mutual collateral estoppel.

(D) No. Ed was not a party to the first case.

Steven Stress was a first year law student at Elite University School of Law (EUSL). During the fall semester, he purchased a book called "The Ultimate Study Guide," a 200-page text that promised that it contained the secret to law school success. The book's publisher, DTPA Press, went so far as to guarantee that those who purchased and studied the book would be guaranteed a spot on law review. Steven bought the book, studied it religiously, took his exams, and ended up with a very respectable B average but no spot on law review. (At EUSL the only road to law review is grades.) He sued DTPA Press for fraud and breach of warranty, seeking actual and punitive damages for himself individually and for a class composed of all law students in the United States who purchased DTPA's book but failed to make law review. His suit is now pending in federal court, based on diversity of citizenship. (Steven is a citizen of California, and DTPA Press is a Nevada corporation with its principal place of business in Nevada, and Steven seeks damages in excess of $75,000 for himself and each class member.)

273. Steven's complaint, with regard to the fraud claim, reads as follows: "DTPA Press guaranteed law review membership, and DTPA knew this promise was false. Plaintiff Stress relied on this promise, and carefully read the book, but did not make law review. He has suffered severe mental anguish and lost significant future income due to this reliance." Does this pleading satisfy the federal pleading rules?

ANSWER:

274. Steven's case is moving forward, and the parties have begun to engage in discovery. Steven has sent an interrogatory to the Elite University campus bookstore, asking for the names of all persons who purchased The Ultimate Study Guide from 1990 to the present. The bookstore has objected to answering it. Should the court order an answer?

(A) No. This question is too burdensome.

(B) Yes. These names, while not themselves admissible, might lead to the discovery of admissible evidence, because they too may have failed to make law review.

(C) No. The bookstore is not a party to the lawsuit.

(D) Yes. But the court should narrow the question to only require information since 2000.

275. Steven has also sent a request for production of documents to DTPA Press. One request asks for "all documents constituting or referring to research done by DTPA Press to substantiate the claim that all readers of The Ultimate Study Guide would make law review." DTPA Press has objected that this information is a trade secret and need not be disclosed to anyone. Should the court order production of these documents?

(A) No. The company's research is not relevant to the reason Steven failed to make law review.

(B) Yes. It is unlikely that this information is a trade secret. Even if it is, it is highly relevant to Steven's fraud claim.

(C) No. The trade secret privilege is absolute.

(D) Yes. Trade secrets, if relevant, are not protected in litigation.

276. DTPA Press has retained William Blackstone as a non-testifying expert to help it prepare for trial. Steven thinks that Blackstone has a lot of helpful information about the proper use by law students of study guides and wants to take his deposition. Can he do so?

(A) Yes. Blackstone's information is relevant to both the warranty claim and the fraud claim.

(B) No. Consulting experts can never be deposed by opposing parties.

(C) No. Blackstone is a consulting expert, and there are many such experts available.

(D) Yes. Blackstone is really famous, so Steven can show exceptional circumstances allowing the deposition.

277. Steven has retained Oliver Holmes as a testifying expert. Holmes makes his living as an educational expert witness, working primarily for plaintiffs, and Steven would prefer not to disclose Holmes' list of prior cases. He says this is confidential information and has refused to reveal it. Will DTPA Press be successful in its motion to compel Steven to comply with the automatic disclosure provisions by revealing all the cases on which Holmes has worked?

(A) Yes. The automatic disclosure rules require parties to reveal all of the cases that a testifying expert worked on.

(B) Yes and no. Steven will have to reveal all the cases in which Holmes testified as an expert at trial or deposition, but only for the last four years.

(C) Yes and no. Steven will have to reveal only the cases in which Holmes testified at trial during the last four years.

(D) No. Information about Holmes' other cases is not relevant to his opinion in Steven's case.

278. DTPA Press has taken Steven's deposition. Steven refused to answer questions regarding the names of his friends, the extent of his law school social life, his health (physical and mental), and the names of his health care providers. He believes that this information is private and therefore protected from discovery. DTPA has moved to compel answers to these questions. How should the court rule on DTPA's motion?

(A) The court should order answers. This information is relevant to issues of causation and damages, and Steven has waived his privacy interest by bringing suit.

(B) The court should not order answers. Disclosure of this information would violate Steven's privacy rights and possibly even lead to an invasion of doctor-patient privilege.

(C) The court should order answers. Privacy interests are not listed in Rule 26 and are therefore not protected in discovery.

(D) The court should not order answers. Steven's friends should have an opportunity to object to information about them being revealed.

279. Steven has had a number of conversations with fellow law students regarding his case. DTPA Press asked Steven at his deposition to describe these conversations. He objected. Should the court order him to answer?

(A) No. These conversations were in anticipation of litigation and are therefore protected as work product.

(B) No. Steven reported these conversations to his attorney, and those communications are protected by the attorney-client privilege.

(C) Yes. Informal venting with friends does not become work product simply because the speaker is a party to a lawsuit.

(D) Yes. DTPA Press will be able to show substantial need and undue hardship if this question is not answered, because Steven's friends will not be as honest with them as they would be with Steven.

280. DTPA Press employs Charles Clark as general counsel. DTPA's President had a conversation with Clark back when they were beginning to market The Ultimate Study Guide. It went like this:

President: "Charley, we need a big seller in the law student market. How can we get students to buy this new study guide?"

Clark: "Tell them it will guarantee they make law review. That will make them buy it."

This conversation is:

(A) protected by the attorney-client privilege. The President would be the "client" under either a control group or subject matter test.

(B) protected by attorney-client privilege. The President was asking his lawyer for advice, and he gave it.

(C) not protected by attorney-client privilege. The conversation was not made in anticipation of litigation.

(D) not protected by attorney-client privilege. The President was not seeking legal advice.

281. Steven has filed a motion to certify his lawsuit as a class action. Which of the following will he *not* have to demonstrate to achieve class certification?

(A) The class is so numerous that joinder is impracticable.

(B) The class action would be superior.

(C) DTPA Press acted or refused to act on grounds generally applicable to the class.

(D) Steven's claim is typical of those of class members.

282. The court has held a hearing on class certification. Steven has established that 2,500 copies of The Ultimate Study Guide have been sold to U.S. law students since August 1, 2009. He also introduced evidence regarding the qualifications of his lawyers, his own serious devotion to the case, and the adoption by 49 U.S. states of the Uniform Commercial Code provisions regarding breach of warranty. Steven stated that, because he and the class members all relied on written representations on the back of the book, the class meets the commonality requirements and his claim is typical of those of class members. He also alleges that the common and identical misrepresentation makes the class manageable. DTPA Press introduced evidence of differing legal standards regarding warranty and,

especially, fraud in the 50 states. They also argued that class members (who cannot easily be individually identified) must each prove that they relied on DTPA Press' representations, and must individually prove their damages from failure to make law review and that this failure was caused by the defendant. Should the judge certify this class?

ANSWER:

283. The court also needs to rule on another issue in the case. Assume that under the law of California, the state in which this case is pending in federal court, plaintiffs claiming punitive damages must swear to their complaints. This rule is intended to make litigants think hard before bringing claims for punitive damages. The federal pleading rules contain no such requirement. DTPA Press moved to dismiss Steven's complaint (which is not sworn to), arguing that the federal court must apply the state procedure here. The court, in ruling on this motion, should first consider:

    (A) whether Federal Rule 11 is broad enough to cover this issue.

    (B) whether the state rule is outcome determinative.

    (C) whether the state rule is judge-made.

    (D) whether the federal rule is outcome determinative.

284. If the court determines that the relevant federal rules cover the issue of whether pleadings must be sworn to, it should next ask:

    (A) whether the federal rule is valid under the Rules Enabling Act.

    (B) whether the difference between the rules is outcome determinative.

    (C) whether there is a strong federal interest.

    (D) whether the federal rule is proper under the Rules of Decision Act.

Maria Rodriguez is a 66-year-old woman living in Houston, Texas. She has a modest income, and her first language is Spanish. Rodriguez shops regularly at Alpha Omega, a grocery store in her neighborhood. One day she had a serious fall there — Rodriguez went to pull out a grocery cart, but the carts stuck together, the whole line of carts came toward her and pushed her down, and she fell on her right wrist, causing severe pain and permanent incapacity. Rodriguez has sued Alpha Omega in federal court on a theory of premises liability. This will require her to prove that the grocery store was negligent and, more specifically, that: (1) the stuck grocery carts constituted a dangerous condition; (2) Alpha Omega knew or should have known of the condition; (3) the condition caused her fall; and (4) she suffered damages as a result.

285. One month after Rodriguez filed her lawsuit, Alpha Omega filed a motion for summary judgment. The motion read: "Plaintiff will not have any evidence that Alpha Omega knew or should have known that the carts were stuck together. It would be wasteful to force Alpha Omega to spend time and money defending this case. Alpha Omega is entitled to judgment as a matter of law." This motion:

(A) satisfied Alpha Omega's burden as movant because it identified the issue on which Rodriguez was said to lack evidence.

(B) failed to satisfy Alpha Omega's burden as movant because in the summary judgment context it must disprove its state of knowledge.

(C) was filed too soon under Rule 56.

(D) failed to satisfy Alpha Omega's burden because it did not point to the record or otherwise demonstrate Rodriguez's lack of evidence.

286. Assume that the court denied Alpha Omega's initial motion for summary judgment. Alpha Omega then deposed Rodriguez about her accident. After she described the circumstances of her fall, the following exchange occurred:

Q: Tell me what happened on the occasion in question.

A: I walked in the store, and I was going to get my basket. And they were all stuck together. And I pulled with my right hand and they were all, at the beginning —

Q: In other words, they were inside each other, as store employees customarily stack baskets?

A: Yes.

Q: Do you know what caused the baskets to adhere to each other?

A: No.

Q: And every week when you patronize the store, the baskets are stacked in an identical manner?

A: Yes, sir.

Q: You don't have any particularized knowledge regarding the reason the two or three or four of them stayed together?

A: No, sir.

Q: Did you ever make a close inspection of the baskets?

A: No, sir.

Q: Do you have any reason to believe that any employee was knowledgeable with regard to any defect in these particular baskets?

A: No.

Alpha Omega re-filed its motion for summary judgment, arguing that Rodriguez admitted that she did not look at the baskets, did not know why they stuck together, and did not have any reason to believe that Alpha Omega employees knew of a problem with the baskets. Rodriguez responded with an affidavit that states: "I had a hard time understanding the questions I was asked at my deposition. I want to make it clear that I did not carefully examine the baskets on the day that I fell, but I did look at them generally, the way anyone looks at baskets when shopping. I have shopped in that store for five years and I know that the baskets are often bent and in bad condition. The wheels don't roll straight. The neighborhood kids crash the carts into each other in the parking lot. I think the store people must be aware of the bad condition of their carts." How should the court rule on the motion?

(A) The court should grant the motion. Rodriguez admitted in her deposition that she had no knowledge of the condition of the baskets or the defendant's knowledge, and she cannot take back that admission.

(B) The court should grant the motion. Rodriguez has no direct evidence that the baskets that caused her fall were dangerous.

(C) The court should deny the motion. The circumstances here make Rodriguez's clarification of her deposition testimony permissible. Her affidavit provides some evidence of the dangerous condition and Alpha Omega's knowledge.

(D) The court should deny the motion because Rodriguez's affidavit constitutes a scintilla of evidence on her behalf.

287. Assume that the court denies the motion for summary judgment and the case goes to trial. During the plaintiff's case in chief, she testifies as follows:

Q: Did you look at the baskets?

A: I looked at them just like that, that is all, when I went to get one.

Q: What was the condition of the baskets on the day you fell?

A: I didn't see the baskets then, but I know they were pretty old in that store. They don't seem to fix up the store in our neighborhood very often.

Q: How long have you shopped at this particular Alpha Omega store?

A: About five years.

Q: Did you ever see the grocery carts taken outside onto the parking lot?

A: Yes. Some of the kids take them outside and play with them and crash them together.

Q: Did you ever see anyone abandon a cart out there and leave it out in the parking lot?

A: Yes.

Q: Did you ever notice carts at this store that were bent?

A: Yes. I've seen other people have trouble getting carts out of the line. Sometimes I have to ask my granddaughter for help with the carts when they stick together.

At the close of the evidence for Rodriguez, Alpha Omega moved for judgment as a matter of law, arguing that Rodriguez presented no evidence that it knew or should have known of a dangerous condition. In considering this motion, the court should canvass the entire record and then:

(A) only give credence to direct evidence in favor of Rodriguez.

(B) refuse to rule. This motion is premature.

(C) only give credence to evidence and reasonable inferences in favor of Rodriguez.

(D) weigh the evidence and decide whether a reasonable jury could find for Rodriguez.

288. Assume that the judge denied Alpha Omega's motion for judgment as a matter of law at the close of Rodriguez's evidence. Alpha Omega therefore presented its own case. Former store manager Hugh Cumber testified that he inspected the grocery carts 30 minutes after Rodriguez fell, and there was nothing wrong with any of the carts that would cause them to stick together. On cross-examination, Cumber testified that he has worked for Alpha Omega for 10 years and that just after his deposition in this case he was assigned to manage a bigger store in a wealthier neighborhood at a big increase in salary. He also testified that he is on probation at this new assignment. Alpha Omega also called Kay Rett,

who testified that she works for Alpha Omega and is the supervisor in charge of repairing baskets in all Houston area stores. During the year that Rodriguez fell, each store was visited for basket repairs every 90 days. About 25 damaged baskets would be repaired or replaced on each visit. On cross-examination, she testified that the store where Rodriguez fell was a "high loss" store, meaning that there was a high rate of basket damage and disappearance. High loss stores are not visited for repairs as often as other stores because the damage is seen as inevitable. She further testified that basket frames become bent when hit by cars or damaged by children, and that this could cause a row of baskets to stick together.

At the close of all the evidence, Alpha Omega once again moved for judgment as a matter of law. What evidence and what inferences may the court consider in ruling on the motion?

ANSWER:

289. Assume that the court denied the motion and sent the case to the jury. The jury found that the baskets were a dangerous condition, that Alpha Omega knew or should have known of the condition, that the condition caused Rodriguez to fall, and that she was damaged in the amount of $125,000. Alpha Omega filed a timely motion for new trial arguing only that the jury verdict was not supported by the evidence. In ruling on the motion:

(A) the judge should decide whether he thinks the verdict was correct. If not, he should grant a new trial.

(B) the judge should decide whether a reasonable jury could have found for Rodriguez. If so, he should deny the motion for new trial.

(C) the judge should question the jurors as to the basis for their verdict.

(D) the judge should decide whether the jury verdict was clearly contrary to the weight of the evidence. If not, he should enter judgment on the verdict.

Robert Builder runs a construction company in West Virginia, although Builder lives in Ohio. Builder is currently involved in a large road construction job in West Virginia. Pilchard Supplies is a Pennsylvania company (incorporated and with its principal place of business there) that sells construction materials. Builder called Pilchard, and after negotiations involving more than a dozen phone calls between Builder in Ohio and Pilchard in Pennsylvania, Pilchard accepted Builder's offer and they entered into a contract. The contract obligated Pilchard to deliver $1 million worth of materials to Builder's job site in West Virginia. Pilchard defaulted on the contract, failing to deliver any materials. This caused Builder to lose a $500,000 early-completion bonus and to incur $1 million in missed deadline penalties.

Under the law of Ohio, Pilchard would be liable to Builder for both the lost bonus and the penalties. Under the law of West Virginia, Pilchard would be liable to Builder for the penalties but not the lost bonus. Under the law of Pennsylvania, Pilchard would be liable only for any higher price that Builder had to pay for replacement materials, in this case only $100,000.

Builder wants to sue Pilchard and is trying to decide where to file suit. *Assume that any of the three states would apply its own law to Builder's claim against Pilchard if it is the original forum.* Help Builder think through the consequences of choosing where to sue.

290. Builder likes the law of Ohio best and would love to sue at home. Suppose Builder sues Pilchard in federal court in Ohio. The Ohio long-arm statute provides for service on anyone who enters into a contract with an Ohio resident. Under these circumstances:

(A) Builder's claim is proper under the Ohio statute, but he has a weak claim for personal jurisdiction over Pilchard there and venue is incorrect.

(B) Builder's claim is proper under the Ohio statute, and he has a strong claim for personal jurisdiction over Pilchard but venue is incorrect.

(C) Builder's claim is proper under the Ohio statute, he has a strong claim for personal jurisdiction over Pilchard, and venue is correct.

(D) Builder's claim exceeds the scope of the Ohio statute, and he has a weak claim for personal jurisdiction over Pilchard, although venue is correct.

291. Suppose Builder files in Ohio. Pilchard files a motion to dismiss or, in the alternative, to transfer the case to the Eastern District of Pennsylvania under 28 U.S.C. § 1406. The court decides that both venue and personal jurisdiction are improper in Ohio. What could the court do that would make Builder especially unhappy?

(A) Dismiss the case.

(B) Transfer the case to E.D. Pa.

(C) Remand the case to state court.

(D) Transfer the case to N.D.W. Va.

292. Would a federal court in Pennsylvania have jurisdiction over Pilchard and proper venue in Builder's case? Why?

ANSWER:

293. Builder really does not want his claim to end up in Pennsylvania. What would happen if he filed his suit in federal court in West Virginia (N.D.W. Va.) and Pilchard filed a motion to transfer to Pennsylvania, alleging that venue is improper?

(A) The court would probably grant the motion. Pilchard does not reside in West Virginia.

(B) The court would probably deny the motion. Pilchard does reside in West Virginia for venue purposes.

(C) The court would probably deny the motion. A substantial amount of the acts or omissions giving rise to Builder's claim took place in West Virginia.

(D) Both (B) and (C) are correct.

294. If you represented Builder (who is a very risk-averse client), what would you advise him

about the advantages and disadvantages of his potential choices of forum?

ANSWER:

Imagine that Builder has filed his claim against Pilchard in state court in Ohio. Pilchard, who was served with process a week ago, believes that Ohio lacks personal jurisdiction over him. He is trying to decide whether to file a motion to dismiss in state court or whether to remove the case to federal court and *then* file an immediate motion to transfer the case to Pennsylvania. The statute of limitations is not even close to running out. Help Pilchard consider the consequences of these options.

295. If Pilchard were to file a motion to dismiss in state court in Ohio, what would be the probable result?

(A) The court would dismiss the case and Builder would refile in West Virginia.

(B) The court would dismiss the case and Builder would be precluded from refiling it.

(C) The court would transfer the case to a state court in Pennsylvania.

(D) The court would keep the case.

296. If Pilchard wanted to remove the case from state court to federal court in Ohio, would this be permissible under the federal removal statutes?

ANSWER:

297. If Pilchard first removed the case, and then filed a motion to transfer the case to Pennsylvania because of lack of personal jurisdiction, improper venue under 28 U.S.C. § 1406, and also in the interests of justice under 28 U.S.C. § 1404, what would be the probable result?

(A) The court would keep the case. Pilchard has waived his complaints about personal jurisdiction and venue by filing the removal notice first.

(B) The court would transfer the case because both personal jurisdiction and venue are improper.

(C) The court would transfer the case because it lacks personal jurisdiction and because most of the witnesses and most of the evidence is in Pennsylvania rather than Ohio.

(D) The court would keep the case because venue is correct in a removed case in the district that includes the location of the state court.

298. In addition to Pilchard's complaint that Ohio lacks personal jurisdiction over him with regard to Builder's claim, what other argument could Pilchard make to try to get the case dismissed from state court?

ANSWER:

299. If you represented Pilchard, and he was sued in state court in Ohio, what action would you recommend?

ANSWER:

300. Builder has just learned that five years ago, Pilchard was sued in Ohio state court by another customer. In that case, Pilchard was accused of delivering substandard materials to an Ohio building site. Pilchard challenged Ohio's personal jurisdiction in that case, but the court found that Pilchard had sufficient purposeful contacts with Ohio and that it was fair to subject Pilchard to suit there. Builder wants to argue that Pilchard is now bound by this finding of personal jurisdiction and cannot contest the Ohio court's jurisdiction over *Builder v. Pilchard Corp.* Is Builder correct?

(A) No. This would be offensive non-mutual collateral estoppel and that is not allowed in any court in the United States.

(B) Yes. Pilchard had a chance to litigate this issue and lost.

(C) No. Personal jurisdiction in one specific jurisdiction case is not generally the same issue as specific jurisdiction in another case.

(D) Yes. The issue of Pilchard's contacts with Ohio was necessarily decided in the first case.

301. What limits exist on the plaintiff's ability to choose a forum?

ANSWER:

302. Amy, a purchaser of "DietAid" diet drink, filed a class action in federal court in California, Amy's home state, against Smith Pharmaceuticals (a California corporation with its principal place of business in California), the manufacturer of DietAid. Amy's complaint alleges that DietAid actually has no weight loss benefits and alleges breach of implied warranty claims against Smith Pharmaceuticals. The complaint seeks recovery of the amount that Amy and each class member paid for the pills. The complaint describes the class as "all citizens and legal residents of the United States who have purchased Dietaid from Smith Pharmaceuticals from January 1, 2007, to December 31, 2010." Approximately 60,000 class members each paid $100 for DietAid, which was sold in California, Texas, New York, and Florida. There are about 15,000 class members in each of the four states. Amy's individual claim is for $225 in out-of-pocket expenses. Does the federal court have jurisdiction over this class action?

(A) No. Amy is the class representative and she is from the same state as the defendant.

(B) Yes. The court has supplemental jurisdiction over the class members' claims because they share a common nucleus of operative fact with Amy's claim.

(C) Yes. There is sufficient minimal diversity, there are more than one hundred class members, and the amount in controversy exceeds $5 million.

(D) Both (B) and (C) are correct.

303. Lance, a resident of Louisiana, has filed suit against Legalstuff, a New York corporation with its principal place of business in New York, seeking $200,000 in damages resulting from inaccurate legal advice he obtained from the company's website, legalstuff.com. A search of the Better Business Bureau website revealed that previous customers have complained about the inaccurate legal information on legalstuff.com. Lance believes the company was aware of the problem, but failed to correct it. He has requested discovery of the e-mails and computer files of all management-level employees since January 2010. The parties do not agree on the proper format for the production of electronically stored information ("ESI"). Legalstuff maintains that, as the producing party, it gets to designate the format and has the right to choose to produce the information printed out in hard copy. Is Legalstuff correct?

(A) Yes. Rule 34 provides that the responding party may indicate the form it intends to use for production.

(B) No. Rule 34 allows the requesting party to specify the format in which ESI should be produced.

(C) No. Legalstuff must produce the information both in the desired format of the requesting party and the format indicated by the responding party.

(D) No. Absent agreement or court order, Legalstuff must produce ESI in the form in which it is normally maintained or which is reasonably usable.

304. Oliver Smith filed suit against Hayden Corp., his former employer, based on federal discrimination law. Smith has requested discovery of all of Hayden Corp.'s e-mails concerning Smith's treatment by his supervisors sent between January 1, 2010, and May 1, 2011, contending that various e-mails exchanged among Hayden Corp. employees contain evidence of gender discrimination. Hayden Corp. stores old e-mails on backup tapes with other computer files that are difficult and expensive to access and search. In contrast, the e-mail messages from January 1, 2011, through May 1, 2011, are currently stored on the company's computers and are easily accessible. Hayden Corp. has asked the court to shift the cost of production of the e-mails from January 1, 2010, through December 31, 2010, to Smith, as production would be unduly burdensome because Hayden Corp. would have to search 392 backup tapes to locate the requested e-mails at an estimated cost of $175,000. What will the court likely order?

(A) The court will probably shift the cost of production of all e-mails from January 1, 2010, through May 1, 2011, to Smith because the requesting party should bear the cost of production.

(B) The court may not shift the cost of production of any of the requested information to Smith, because the producing party should bear the cost of production.

(C) The court may shift some of the cost to Smith, but Hayden Corp. will bear the cost of producing the e-mails currently stored on the company's computers.

(D) The court will not order Hayden Corp. to produce the 2010 e-mails because production would place an undue burden on Hayden Corp.

305. Robin Roberts brought suit in federal district court in Philadelphia against Harry Anderson and Ashburn Sports Products, Inc. ("Ashburn Sports") for damages based on fraud claims against Anderson and Ashburn Sports, coupled with a breach of contract claim against Ashburn Sports. Roberts claimed that Anderson made false representations concerning the future profits that Roberts would probably receive as a franchisee of Ashburn Sports to induce Roberts to enter into a franchise agreement with Ashburn Sports to operate a sporting goods store in Montgomery County, Pennsylvania. Unfortunately, instead of making a profit, Roberts' store operated at a loss and had to be closed. Roberts' breach of contract claim alleged that Ashburn Sports violated the terms of the franchise agreement in a number of ways. (Anderson was not sued for breach of contract because he was not a party to the contract.)

Anderson and Ashburn Sports filed motions for summary judgment based on the defense that the representations alleged by Roberts could not be fraudulent because they were statements of opinion or predictions that could not be a basis for fraud claims. Ashburn Sports also moved for summary judgment on Roberts' contract claim against it based on the defense of failure of consideration. The trial court granted Anderson's motion, but denied Ashburn Sports' motion concerning the breach of contract claim against it. If Roberts chooses to appeal the summary judgment, does the court of appeals have jurisdiction of the appeal?

(A) Yes, the order is appealable under the collateral order doctrine.

(B) No, the order is not appealable because it is not a final judgment disposing of all claims.

(C) No. Because Federal Rule 54(b)'s requirements were not satisfied and no severance order was entered, the summary judgment is not final and appealable under 28 U.S.C. § 1291.

(D) Answers (B) and (C) are correct.

306. Assume the same facts as in the preceding question, except this time the court granted summary judgment in favor of both defendants on all claims. Summary judgment in favor of Anderson was signed and entered on July 24, 2011, and summary judgment in favor of Ashburn Sports was signed and entered on July 26, 2011. Assume that neither the district judge nor the court clerk prepared a separate judgment indicating the successful disposition of both summary judgment motions. What may or must Roberts do to commence an appeal?

(A) Roberts must file a notice of appeal in the trial court within 30 days after July 26, 2011.

(B) Roberts must file a notice of appeal in the trial court within 30 days after July 24, 2011.

(C) Roberts may file a notice of appeal within 30 days after 150 days have run from entry of the last dismissal order (July 26) in the civil docket.

(D) Roberts must file notices of appeal in the trial court within 30 days after July 24 and within 30 days after July 26, 2011.

307. Marsha Kent sued Dr. Lane for medical malpractice in a federal district court in Texas. Kent failed to serve an expert report regarding Dr. Lane's actions, as required by Texas law. The district judge, therefore, dismissed Kent's complaint with prejudice. Kent filed a motion for new trial on June 5, 2011, but the district judge overruled Kent's motion in a signed order entered in the civil docket on June 12, 2011. Kent, however, did not receive notice of the district court's entry of the order denying her motion for new trial until July 24, 2011, because the court clerk did not mail notice of the entry of the order to Kent's attorney. What, if anything, can Kent do to prosecute an appeal to the court of appeals?

(A) Because the time to commence an appeal has expired, Kent cannot do anything.

(B) Kent can file a motion for extension of time to commence the appeal within 90 days after entry of the order denying Kent's motion for new trial.

(C) Under Rule 60(b), Kent can ask the trial court to vacate the order denying the new trial so that the same order can be entered again to restart the appellate timetable.

(D) Kent can move the trial court to reopen the appeal if the motion is filed within 180 days after the judgment or order is signed.

308. Builder, Pilchard, and Wendy each have a claim against Pickles for work each separately performed in connection with the construction of Pickles' new farm house. Travis Bank supplied the financing for the construction of the new farm house and now holds a deed of trust, executed by Pickles, to the farm and farm house. Builder, Pilchard, and Wendy join together as plaintiffs under Rule 20, seeking a judgment to foreclose their mechanics' and materialmen's liens. If Travis Bank is not joined as a party and its absence is not raised in the trial court by Pickles or by any other party, and judgment is rendered for the plaintiffs, can Pickles challenge the judgment on appeal on the basis of Travis Bank's nonjoinder?

(A) Yes, the nature of Travis Bank's lien interest in the farm house makes it a person that "should be joined if feasible" under Rule 19(b).

(B) Yes, Travis Bank's deed of trust lien represents a substantive right that makes it indispensable to the trial court's exercise of jurisdiction.

(C) No, Travis Bank's deed of trust lien is inferior to the plaintiffs' liens; therefore, Pickles cannot challenge the judgment based on Travis Bank's nonjoinder.

(D) No, Pickles' failure to raise Travis Bank's nonjoinder in the trial court eliminates Pickles' ability to attack the judgment foreclosing the plaintiffs' liens on Pickles' property.

309. ASAP Delivery's driver, Rick, was killed when his delivery vehicle collided with Paula's car. Paula has filed a diversity action against ASAP in federal district court in Wyoming, seeking personal injury damages in the amount of $150,000. Paula also joined Hybrid Cars, the manufacturer of Paula's car, under a manufacturing defect theory, because Paula's brakes failed during the collision. ASAP's truck was badly damaged in the accident, so ASAP filed a cross-claim against Hybrid Cars. May Hybrid Cars make a claim for contribution against ASAP in the same action?

   (A) No. Contribution claims are premature until judgment in the underlying action. Thus, Hybrid Cars cannot make a cross-claim against ASAP for contribution under Rule 13(g).

   (B) Yes. ASAP became an "opposing party" by claiming against Hybrid Cars, making Hybrid Cars' contribution claim against ASAP a compulsory counterclaim.

   (C) Yes. Although Hybrid Cars cannot make a counterclaim for contribution because its contribution claim is premature until judgment in the underlying action, Rule 13(g) expressly permits Hybrid Cars to file a cross-claim against ASAP.

   (D) Yes. Hybrid Cars can file a contribution claim against ASAP either as a counterclaim or a cross-claim because Hybrid Cars' contribution claim is mature.

In the summer of 2007, Brad Smith and his wife Angelina visited the Americana Resort in Bogota, Montana, where they enjoyed hiking, fishing, and marksmanship classes. After their return to their home in Dallas, Texas, the Smiths realized that they had been added to the Americana's e-mail marketing list. They received an e-mail newsletter once a month from the Americana, touting its championship golf, state-of-the-art spa, and lovely scenery. The e-mailed newsletters contained links to the hotel website, which also extolled the beauties of Montana and the luxurious amenities of the Americana, and provided a toll-free number for reservations. There are over 500 Texans on the Americana's targeted e-mail list, and since 2007 approximately 50 Texans have visited the small and exclusive resort.

After a particularly stressful time at work, the Smiths decided to make a return trip to the Americana in the summer of 2010 and booked a five-night stay. They also scheduled a series of spa treatments. While at the Americana Brad enjoyed his first massage, but disaster soon followed. Vince, the masseuse, instructed Brad to step into the shower. Unfortunately, Brad's feet were still slick with massage oils, and there were no mats on the shower's wet floor. As Brad stepped into the shower, he slipped, fell, and tore his rotator cuff, a painful injury that required surgery. The temporary disability that ensued also injured Brad's business, as he was not able to make a scheduled trip to Morocco.

In early 2011, Brad brought suit in the United States District Court for the Northern District of Texas against the Americana Hotel (a Delaware corporation with its principal place of business in Montana) and Vince (a citizen of Montana). Brad alleged that both defendants were negligent under applicable state law. He sought damages of $500,000 for his medical expenses, pain and suffering, and lost income.

The Americana filed an Answer denying negligence, subject to a motion to dismiss for lack of personal jurisdiction and, in the alternative, a motion to transfer venue under § 1404. Vince filed an answer denying negligence.

310. Consider the Americana's motion to dismiss for lack of personal jurisdiction. Brad has responded, relying on the Americana's solicitation of him and other Texas residents, including the solicitation to book spa treatments, as the basis for Texas jurisdiction over the Americana. Should the court consider Brad's claim for jurisdiction based on principles of specific jurisdiction or general jurisdiction?

ANSWER:

311. Now consider the Americana's motion to transfer venue. What private factors will the Americana stress in its argument to the court?

(A) Montana law will probably govern Brad's negligence claim.

(B) Montana courts have less crowded dockets and can more easily hear the case.

(C) The witnesses with information about the operation of the spa and Brad's fall are all in Montana.

(D) Montana is not as hot in the summer as Dallas is.

312. Still subject to its motions to dismiss, the Americana filed a counterclaim against Brad for $10,000. It seems that Brad and Angelina were so angry about his injury that they left without paying their hotel bill, continue to refuse to pay the bill, and the counterclaim represents the unpaid balance. Does the court have subject matter jurisdiction over this counterclaim?

(A) No. A claim for only $10,000 does not meet the amount in controversy requirement for federal jurisdiction.

(B) Yes. Both Brad's claim against the Americana and this counterclaim arise out of the same transaction or occurrence, because they are logically related and will involve overlapping evidence, and so this is a compulsory counterclaim.

(C) No. This claim is inconsistent with the requirements of § 1332.

(D) Yes. Although there is no independent basis for subject matter jurisdiction over this claim, it meets the requirements for supplemental jurisdiction under § 1367.

313. Brad brought Angelina into the case as a third-party defendant under Rule 14, alleging that if he has to pay the Americana for the bill, she has to pay half of it. (Although they are still married, their relationship has suffered since the injury and he doesn't mind suing her.) Assuming that applicable law gives Brad this claim for reimbursement and that spouses may sue each other, is this claim properly included in the *Brad v. Americana* lawsuit?

(A) No. Although it is a proper impleader claim, the court lacks subject matter jurisdiction.

(B) No. Plaintiffs may not use Rule 14 to add new parties, even though there would be subject matter jurisdiction over the claim.

(C) No. This is not a proper impleader claim, nor is there subject matter jurisdiction.

(D) Yes. Both joinder and subject matter jurisdiction are proper.

314. Once added to the lawsuit, Angelina asserted a claim against the Americana for her own injuries, primarily her emotional distress from seeing Brad's terrible fall and her subsequent loss of consortium. She requested $50,000 in damages. What kind of claim is this?

(A) Angelina is a co-plaintiff with Brad.

(B) Angelina is a third-party defendant, added by Brad acting as a defendant to the Americana's counterclaim, and this is a claim against the Americana, authorized by Rule 14.

(C) This is a cross-claim against the Americana.

(D) This is a third-party claim.

315. Does the court have subject matter jurisdiction over this claim?

(A) No. Although Angelina and the Americana are diverse, the amount in controversy is too small.

(B) Yes. Rule 14 allows third-party defendants to assert claims against the original plaintiff as long as they arise out of the same transaction or occurrence as the original claim. Here, Angelina's claim is sufficiently related to the Americana's claim against Brad to meet that requirement.

(C) Yes. There is supplemental jurisdiction over the claim.

(D) Both (B) and (C) are correct answers.

Vince (who chose not to challenge the jurisdiction of the Texas court) filed a cross claim against the Americana. Vince's claim, brought under Montana tort law, accuses the Americana of wrongful termination in violation of public policy. He claims that he was fired (six months after Brad's mishap) because he complained about the spa's violation of federal workplace safety requirements. He says that the spa improperly stored toxic substances, exposing its workers to serious medical risks. While the federal law in question (the Occupational Safety and Health Act — OSHA) does not provide employees with a private right of action to sue their employers, Montana law provides a cause of action for employees fired in violation of state or federal public policy. Vince seeks $35,000 in lost wages and $1 million in punitive damages. The Americana denies that it violated OSHA rules and that its firing of Brad had anything to do with his complaints. Rather, it claims that Vince was fired for getting in a fight with a guest at the spa's juice bar.

316. Is Vince's claim against the Americana a proper cross-claim?

(A) Yes. They are both defendants to Brad's claims, and claims between co-parties are proper under Rule 13.

(B) Yes. Vince's claims, like Brad's claims, are about things that happened at the spa at the Americana and so they arise out of the same transaction or occurrence.

(C) No. Cross-claims are only allowed for claims that a "coparty is or may be liable to the crossclaimant for all or part of a claim asserted in the action."

(D) No. Vince's claims about storage of toxic substances (and the Americana's defense about a fight at the juice bar) are factually separate from Brad's claims arising from his fall, and so this does not meet the requirements of Rule 13(g).

317. Suppose that the Americana asserted a contribution claim against Vince arising out of Brad's claims against the Americana, and Vince has asserted his OSHA-based Montana tort law claim as a counterclaim against the Americana. Does the federal court have jurisdiction over Vince's claim under § 1332?

(A) No. Vince and the Americana are both citizens of Montana, so there is no diversity of citizenship.

(B) Yes. Although there is no independent basis for diversity jurisdiction, there is supplemental jurisdiction over this cross-claim because Vince is not a plaintiff.

(C) No. Vince's claims and Brad's claims do not share a common nucleus of operative fact.

(D) (A) and (C) are both correct.

318. Suppose that the Americana asserted a contribution claim against Vince arising out of Brad's claims against the Americana, and Vince has asserted his OSHA-based Montana tort law claim as a counterclaim against the Americana. Does the federal court have federal question jurisdiction over Vince's claim?

(A) No. Vince's claim is based on state tort law, not federal law.

(B) Yes. The OSHA issue is embedded in the state law claim, it is actually disputed, it is substantial, and recognizing federal question jurisdiction over OSHA claims will not disturb the balance between state and federal courts.

(C) No. While there is an embedded federal issue, many of the requirements for federal question jurisdiction are not present here.

(D) Yes. Vince's claim is essentially a federal claim, despite its state law shell.

319. Assume that the court has transferred this case to the District of Montana, where discovery is about to get under way. When the Americana initially filed its motion to dismiss and answer, it neglected to allege that Brad's contributory negligence, rather than the slippery floor, was the cause of his injuries. Now, two months into the lawsuit, the Americana has filed a motion for leave to amend its answer to allege contributory negligence. Should the court grant the motion?

(A) No. It's too late to amend, because it's more than 21 days since the Americana served its answer.

(B) Yes. Amendments are favored, and there is no indication that Brad will be prejudiced by this amendment.

(C) No. Defeating a contributory negligence defense makes Brad's position more difficult, and so this amendment would prejudice him.

(D) It should only grant the motion if the statute of limitations has not yet run.

On July 1, 2013, Jeremy Flax was driving his Grand Canyon minivan home from his daughter Charlotte's swim meet in Bantam, Connecticut. Jeremy's wife Rachel Flax was in the front passenger seat. Charlotte was in the left rear passenger seat, and her eight-month-old brother Joshua was in his car seat immediately behind Rachel. While the minivan was stopped at a red light, Susan Sprint, the driver of another car, slammed into the back of the minivan at 50 mph. When the minivan was hit from the rear, the front passenger seat collapsed, propelling Rachel and her seat backward. Rachel was not injured, but her seat collided with Joshua's skull, fracturing it and causing Joshua to die the following day.

Jeremy and Rachel Flax have filed suit in federal district court against Car Company ("CC"), the manufacturer of the minivan, and against Sprint, the driver of the car that rear-ended them. The Flaxes allege that CC is liable for actual and punitive damages, based on ordinary and gross negligence and strict product liability. They claim that CC was aware of the defect in the seat but failed to repair the problem or warn buyers. The Flaxes allege that Sprint was negligent in driving.

You are the law clerk for Judge Prius, in whose court this case is pending. Please give the judge your best advice as to the issues discussed below.

320. The Flax lawsuit was filed on May 1, 2014. (This type of cause of action has a one-year statute of limitations.) On May 15th, defendant CC filed a motion to dismiss for improper venue. The court denied this motion on June 1st. On June 5th, CC filed an "amended motion to dismiss," this time including an allegation that it was improperly served with process in the case. Assuming that CC is right about the method of service, how should Judge Prius rule?

(A) Judge Prius should grant the motion. While the defense should have been included in the original motion, this amended motion was filed less than 21 days after the original was served, so the motion to dismiss for insufficient service of process will be treated as if it had been filed on May 15th.

(B) Judge Prius should deny the motion. Rule 12(g) & (h) say nothing about amended motions, and even if the judge has discretion to allow an amended motion, it was too late to amend CC's motion because the original has already been ruled on. Filing the original motion to dismiss (improper venue) while omitting the allegations about service of process waived it.

(C) Judge Prius should deny the motion, but CC could re-urge the problem with service of process by including it in its answer.

(D) Judge Prius should grant the motion. Proper service is a component of due process, and the Flaxes have not been prejudiced by the delay in raising the service issue.

321. On August 1, 2014, the Flaxes filed a motion for leave to amend their complaint. Their original complaint alleges that Susan Sprint was speeding, and that her negligence was a proximate cause of Joshua's injury and death. The proposed amended complaint adds another count, alleging that Sprint was negligent per se in that she was talking on her cell phone while driving, in violation of a recent Bantam city ordinance prohibiting drivers from talking on cell phones while the vehicle is in motion. Should Judge Prius grant the motion for leave to amend?

(A) No. The amendment would be pointless because it is barred by the statute of limitations.

(B) Yes. The case has only been pending for three months, and allowing the amendment will not prejudice Sprint.

(C) Yes. The cell phone claim asserts a claim that arose out of the same conduct, transaction, or occurrence as the Flaxes' speeding claim.

(D) Both (B) and (C) are correct.

322. Assume that Judge Prius grants the Flaxes' motion for leave to amend. Sprint then files a motion to sever the claim against her from the claim against CC because they are misjoined. How should Judge Prius rule?

(A) The motion should be granted. The claim against CC is about the design of the minivan, and the claim against Sprint is about the way she was driving. That's not the same transaction or occurrence.

(B) The motion should be granted. Either the van design caused the injuries or Sprint did, and the Flaxes should have to make up their minds.

(C) The motion should be denied. The claims against CC and Sprint are logically related, and both will involve evidence about the nature of the crash, the van's response, and the Flaxes' injuries.

(D) The motion should be denied. Sprint had to include her complaint about misjoinder in her first motion, and since she didn't it's waived.

The parties have had a number of discovery disputes during this lawsuit, some of which grow out of the role of former CC engineer Paul Sheridan. In 2010, Sheridan was appointed by CC's President to chair CC's "Minivan Safety Leadership Team" to investigate minivan concerns. (The President decided to assemble the team after learning of three injuries and threatened lawsuits.) This team studied CC's rear impact safety tests and learned that minivan seats collapsed in each of them. While this is helpful for the front seat passengers, it can be lethal for those in the back seat, particularly for infants in car seats. In addition to looking at pre-existing documents, the team commissioned certain studies for its own use. Within the CC organization, the team interviewed employees from the most senior engineers down to the technical employees who carried out the crash tests. The Leadership Team, which was composed of a number of CC engineers, in-house lawyers, and outside lawyers, concluded that the collapsing seatbacks needed to be redesigned. CC received the report, disbanded the team, and destroyed both the report and the minutes of its meetings. About a month later, after Sheridan threatened to go to federal regulators with the Leadership Team findings, Sheridan was fired.

This resulted in a different lawsuit, back in 2011. Sheridan sued CC for wrongful termination, and CC filed a counterclaim against Sheridan for improper disclosure of trade secrets and other proprietary information. That lawsuit was settled, with an undisclosed sum being paid to Sheridan. Sheridan agreed to the entry of a judgment against him finding that the CC crash test data were protected trade secrets, that some of the Leadership Team information was protected by the attorney-client privilege, and ordering Sheridan never to testify against CC.

323. The Flaxes would like to take Sheridan's deposition, and so they have served him with a subpoena. Sheridan is willing to cooperate, and the Flaxes would like to ask him about the investigation and deliberations of the Leadership Team. CC files a motion to quash the subpoena and prevent Sheridan from testifying. CC argues that the judgment in the lawsuit between CC and Sheridan prevents the Flaxes from seeking Sheridan's testimony and conclusively establishes that the Leadership Team's work involved trade secrets and attorney-client privilege. Is CC right?

  (A) Yes. Claim preclusion prevents the Flaxes from challenging the judgment against Sheridan, and issue preclusion establishes that the material is privileged.

  (B) Partly. Sheridan's right to testify is part of the same claim as the one in the first suit, but since the judgment was the result of a settlement nothing was actually litigated and so issue preclusion won't apply.

  (C) Partly. The Flaxes can't be bound by the result of the first suit as claim preclusion, but it did establish that the Leadership Team material is privileged and issue preclusion doesn't require mutuality of estoppel.

  (D) No. While Sheridan might be held in contempt for violating the injunction contained in his agreed judgment with CC, the Flaxes were not a party to that case and so are not bound by that judgment. In addition, no issue preclusion arises because nothing was actually litigated.

324. The Flaxes would also like to see any documents in CC's possession that were examined by, created for, or created by the Leadership Team. As noted above, the official reports and minutes were destroyed before Joshua Flax was even injured, but the Flaxes suspect that copies of certain documents (including e-mails between team members) may still exist on archival backup tapes. CC maintains that the Leadership Team data is inextricably mixed with other company information, and that extracting it would cost hundreds of thousands of dollars. Should Judge Prius order production, and if so should she attach any conditions?

  (A) The information on the backup tapes is not reasonably accessible, and so CC should not be required to produce it.

  (B) Because CC destroyed the more easily-accessible versions of the information after they were aware that people had been injured and that their design was flawed, and because of the centrality of the information to the litigation, the Flaxes can show good cause to compel CC to produce the information from the backup tapes.

(C) Judge Prius could begin by ordering that a sample of designated backup tapes be searched for designated terms, as a way to gauge the burden of production and the materiality of the information that can be found.

(D) Answers (B) and (C) are both correct.

325. The Flaxes hear rumors that there have been a number of similar incidents involving Grand Canyon minivans and infants in car seats. They further believe that CC has been settling these cases to keep the seat safety problem out of the public eye. The Flaxes have therefore sent a document production request to CC asking for copies of settlement agreements in all similar lawsuits. CC objects, arguing that other settlements are not relevant. The Flaxes, after unsuccessfully conferring with CC, have filed a motion to compel production. How should Judge Prius rule?

(A) Judge Prius should grant the motion. The settlements in other cases are reasonably calculated to lead to the discovery of admissible evidence because they might help substantiate the existence of the design flaw and failure to warn, identify people with knowledge of the seat collapse problem, and show CC's knowledge of the design problem with the Grand Canyon, which is relevant to the punitive damages claim.

(B) Judge Prius should deny the motion. These settlement agreements will merely list names and amounts of money, and so they will not make any fact of consequence to the Flaxes' suit more likely or less likely than it would be without the settlement agreements.

(C) Judge Prius should deny the motion. The settlement agreements will not be admissible in the *Flax* case.

(D) Judge Prius should grant the motion. Settlement agreements are public records and CC should make them freely available.

326. Sprint denies that she was talking on her cell phone at the time of the crash. The Flaxes have requested that she produce her cell phone billing record from the month of the crash, and she has objected, claiming that to do so would invade her right of privacy, and filed a motion for protective order. How should Judge Prius rule?

(A) Judge Prius should grant the motion. It's none of anyone's business who Sprint talks to, and just because she's been sued she doesn't lose her right to privacy.

(B) Judge Prius should deny the motion. Sprint's cell phone habits are relevant to this lawsuit.

(C) Judge Prius should grant the motion in part and deny it in part. The records are relevant to show whether Sprint was talking on the phone at the time of the crash, but only the parts of the billing records for that time period should be discoverable.

(D) Judge Prius should grant the motion. Although there is an issue about whether Sprint was using her phone while driving, she can be asked that question directly and the cell phone billing records would only be used for impeachment. Impeachment materials like these cell phone records are not relevant to any party's "claim or defense" because they're not about what happened in the crash.

327. CC has designated Edwin Engineer as its testifying expert witness for this case, and has produced a report in accordance with Rule 26(a)(2). The Flaxes' attorney suspects that CC's attorney has been heavily involved in drafting the report, and that if only he could see those earlier drafts it would provide a great basis for cross-examining Engineer. Therefore, the Flaxes request that CC produce all earlier drafts of the report, including any notations made by counsel for CC. Does CC have to produce them?

(A) Yes. Those drafts constitute "facts or data considered" by Engineer in forming his opinions.

(B) No. Rule 26(b)(4) protects drafts from discovery by defining them as work product.

(C) Yes. If Engineer's opinions have been heavily influenced by the lawyers' directions, the Flaxes should be allowed to discover that.

(D) No. Drafts of the report are not relevant in the discovery sense.

328. The Flaxes' lawyer is going to depose Edwin Engineer, and intends to ask him about all of his communications with CC's attorney. He'd especially like to know whether the attorney told Engineer to make any assumptions about what happened in the accident in forming his opinion, and on which Engineer based his opinion. Is that information discoverable?

(A) No. All communications between the expert witness and the party's attorney are protected as work product.

(B) No. All communications between the expert witness and the party's attorney are protected by attorney-client privilege, because the expert is the agent of the attorney.

(C) Yes. While most communications between testifying expert and the party's attorney are protected, communications that identify assumptions that the party's attorney provided and that the expert relied on in forming the opinions to be expressed are discoverable.

(D) Both (A) and (B) are correct.

329. Early in the litigation, the Flaxes sent an interrogatory to CC asking it to identify all persons who were involved in the design and testing of the Grand Canyon minivan. CC answered it, but it did not identify Dave Disgruntled, nor did they ever supplement their answer to include Dave. Dave has even more information about poor design decisions than Sheridan does, and CC just didn't want the Flaxes to know about him. However, the Flaxes' private investigator has found out about Dave and while they're happy to be able to speak with Dave, they're really irritated that they had to spend time and money locating a person that CC should have identified. After unsuccessfully conferring with CC about this situation, the Flaxes have filed a motion for sanctions. CC claims that the only sanction for

failing to identify a witness is the exclusion of that witness from testifying (and they're happy to agree that Dave could not testify at trial). The Flaxes, on the other hand, intend to call Dave at trial but think there should be some other sanctions for CC's misbehavior. What are Judge Prius's options?

(A) CC is right — Judge Prius's only option under Rule 37(c) is to prohibit CC from using Dave as a witness.

(B) Judge Prius may not only allow the Flaxes to call Dave to testify, he may also inform the jury that CC should have, but did not, identify Dave in answer to the Flaxes' interrogatory.

(C) Judge Prius may strike CC's answer and order a default judgment against it.

(D) Judge Prius may not award any sanction against CC. Since Dave's testimony would be harmful to CC, their failure to disclose his identity was substantially justified.

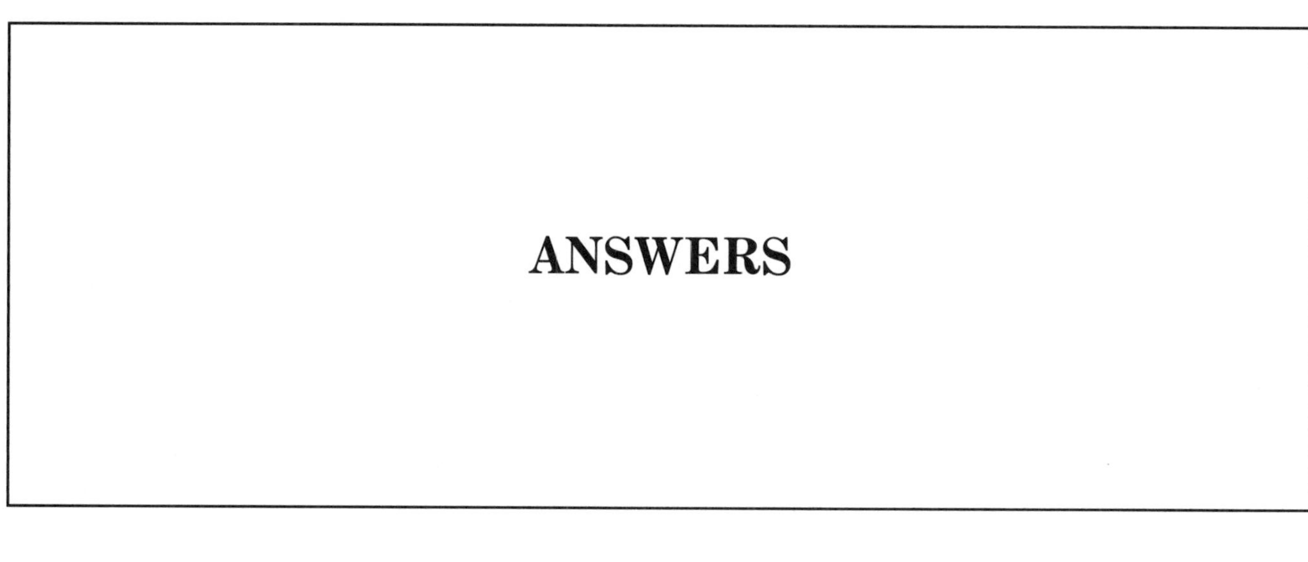

ANSWERS

TOPIC 1: PLEADINGS: PLAINTIFF'S PLEADINGS — ANSWERS

1. **Answer (D) is the best answer.** This is the language of Rule 8 of the Federal Rules of Civil Procedure, and the language is significant because it was deliberately chosen by the drafters to eliminate some of the technicalities and disputes about pleadings that occurred under pre-FRCP practice.

   Answer (A) is incorrect. This is the rule that was applied under the rules of "code pleading," which predated the FRCP. This rule led to a very technical approach to analyzing pleadings that the FRCP drafters wanted to avoid.

   Answer (B) is incorrect. It is not a correct statement of the test in federal court. Its language is also a part of the requirements of the old "code pleading" standards.

   Answer (C) is incorrect. Under pre-FRCP pleading practice, it was difficult to determine the difference between facts, which a pleader was supposed to allege, and evidence, which a pleader was not supposed to allege. The language of Rule 8 was intended to avoid this kind of dispute.

2. In the federal court system, pleadings are designed to accomplish three purposes. First, the complaint gives notice to the defendant of what the plaintiff is complaining about, at least in a general way, and allows the defendant to prepare a response. Second, pleadings are designed to provide an outline for the court that will guide the development of the case as it goes along. For example, the scope of discovery will be largely determined by the issues set forth in the pleadings. Third, in some cases the pleadings may be used to determine the merits of the case, as when the face of the complaint shows that the plaintiff has no right to relief, even if the plaintiff's version of the facts is taken as true. Until recently, early merits decisions based on the pleadings alone were rare because they are generally inconsistent with the philosophy of the FRCP that disputes should usually be decided based on evidence presented at a trial on the merits rather than on the pleadings. In two recent Supreme Court cases, however, the Court expanded pleadings' role in dismissal based on concerns about the cost of litigation. *See Bell Atlantic Corp. v. Twombly*, 550 U.S. 544 (2007); *Ashcroft v. Iqbal*, 129 S. Ct. 1937 (2009). The ultimate impact of these cases is still evolving.

3. This complaint should satisfy the requirements of Rule 8. In fact, it is very similar to the complaint included in Federal Form 11. The Forms were included by the framers of the FRCP to demonstrate for the bench and bar the meaning of their new system of pleading, and they are attached as an Appendix to the FRCP. By providing information about the general nature of the plaintiff's complaint, the complaint should meet the requirement of being a "short and plain statement of the claim," without requiring the plaintiff to plead the specific factual basis for his negligence claims. In some state systems, Bert would likely have to plead that Ernie "was negligent due to speeding" or "was negligent in that he followed too closely" or the like, but federal courts have traditionally not used the pleadings as the vehicle

to supply this type of information.

The answer to this question is not so clear as it once was. In 2007, the Supreme Court began to endorse the use of pleadings as a vehicle for dismissal. In *Twombly*, the majority held that an antitrust conspiracy claim had to plead specific facts showing that illegal conspiracy, and not legal parallel conduct, was a plausible inference. Further, the majority limited the reach of *Conley v. Gibson*, 355 U.S. 41 (1957), the Court's classic pleading case. In *Conley* the Court stated: "a complaint should not be dismissed for failure to state a claim unless it appears beyond doubt that the plaintiff can prove no set of facts in support of his claim which would entitle him to relief." 355 U.S. at 45–46. The *Twombly* majority characterized this as merely "an incomplete, negative gloss on an accepted pleading standard: once a claim has been stated adequately, it may be supported by showing any set of facts consistent with the allegations in the complaint. *Conley* described the breadth of opportunity to prove what an adequate complaint claims, not the minimum standard of adequate pleading to govern a complaint's survival." In *Iqbal* the Court went further. Justice Kennedy's majority opinion appears to require a two-step process for analyzing the sufficiency of pleadings: (1) Identify allegations that are merely "conclusions of law" or "conclusory." Ignore them; (2) Take any remaining allegations as true, but if they are circumstantial — as they often will be, especially when "conclusory" statements are disregarded — look to see if they support a "plausible" inference that the plaintiff might be able to prevail. To be "plausible" in this sense, it must be at least as likely as other competing inferences, decided based on the judge's own experience and common sense. If the pleaded circumstantial evidence is not sufficient, *Iqbal* instructs the trial judge to dismiss the case without allowing discovery. Lower courts are still struggling to determine the range of situations in which this method should be employed to dismiss cases, but some commentators have noted that many of the complaints included in the official Forms, including the allegation in Form 11 that the defendant "drove negligently," would be considered conclusory under *Iqbal*. The *Twombly* majority, however, cited Form 11 (then Form 9) as clearly alleging that "the defendant struck the plaintiff with his car while plaintiff was crossing a particular highway at a specified date and time," and contrasted that with the insufficient allegation of antitrust conspiracy involved in *Twombly* itself.

Effective December 1, 2015, however, the FRCP will be amended to delete Rule 84 and the Forms. Partly because of concern that the Forms were in "tension" with *Iqbal*, the Advisory Committee claimed that although the Forms were designed to demonstrate "the simplicity and brevity of the statement which the rules contemplate," today that purpose "has been fulfilled."

4. **Answer (C) is the correct answer.** General damages follow "naturally" and "necessarily" from the occurrence made the basis of the action. Because the only damage that would meet this test "necessarily" is past physical pain and mental suffering resulting from a serious injury, it is the only general damage allegation, i.e., the only one that did not need to be "specifically stated." Of course, it is routine for plaintiffs to claim both past and future pain and suffering with specificity.

Answer (A) is not correct because pain and suffering "naturally" and "necessarily" will result from a serious injury, such as a broken hip suffered in an automobile accident. The others might "naturally" occur, but that is not "necessarily" true. For example, Bert might not have suffered any loss of earnings or earning capacity or incurred medical and hospital expenses.

Answer (B) is not correct because future pain and suffering will not "necessarily" be suffered by Bert. By the time of trial, when the fact finder will decide whether to award damages for future pain and suffering, Bert might have completely recovered.

Answer (D) is not correct because future pain and suffering and lost earnings or earning capacity are considered to be special damages.

5. **Answer (D) is correct.** Rule 8(d)(2) provides that a "party may set out 2 or more statements of a claim or defense alternatively or hypothetically" and 8(d)(3) states that a "party may state as many separate claims or defenses as it has, regardless of consistency." The claims that Ernie was the driver and that Travis was the driver, although factually inconsistent, are therefore allowed.

   Answer (A) is incorrect because inconsistent claims can be proper. It is true that Bert's ability to plead inconsistently is subject to the requirement of Rule 11 that the allegations be made in good faith. If Bert knew who was driving the car, the alternative pleading would not be proper. Because Bert does not know, the alternative pleading is allowed.

   Answer (B) is incorrect because, as noted, Rule 8 allows the pleading of inconsistent claims.

   Answer (C) is incorrect. Although it may be strategically difficult or unwise to maintain the alternative pleading through trial, the rules do not require an election before going to the jury. Imagine, for example, that at trial of this case Ernie claimed that Travis was the driver and Travis claimed that Ernie was the driver. Bert will be allowed to leave the decision to the jury.

6. **Answer (A) is correct.** Although generally speaking the federal pleading rules are quite forgiving, a plaintiff must sue for a cause of action that is recognized under the applicable substantive law. Your neighbor, for example, could not sue you for being a law student and adding to some kind of perceived national oversupply. Similarly, Bert cannot invent a cause of action for "annoyance" and pursue it against Ernie based on his bad taste in bumper stickers. Rule 8 does provide that the complaint must show "that the pleader is entitled to relief."

   Answer (B) is incorrect. Although, as you will learn when you study subject matter jurisdiction, there are situations in which jurisdiction over one claim will justify jurisdiction over others, stating one legally valid claim does not give a party the right to add into the same lawsuit claims that have no legal basis.

   Answer (C) is also incorrect. Rule 8 allows a plaintiff to combine "as many separate claims . . . as it has." There is no longer a rule in federal court requiring separate suits for different types of claims, even claims that in earlier times would have been brought in different types of courts.

   Answer (D) is incorrect. A "short and plain statement" of a nonexistent claim is not salvaged by providing the required amount of detail.

7. This question illustrates the difficulty in applying the reasoning of *Twombly* and *Iqbal*. This problem is very much like *Twombly* itself — an antitrust case with an allegation of conspiracy. In this case, Carl lacks even a somewhat-incriminating statement made by a

CEO to the media, and his other allegations amount to circumstantial evidence regarding market structure. So it is possible that a court could dismiss the complaint, finding that Carl's allegations are merely conclusory and the inference of conspiracy implausible. On the other hand, in *In re Text Messaging Antitrust Litigation*, 630 F.3d 622 (7th Cir. 2010), the Seventh Circuit affirmed a decision by the district court that a complaint very similar to this one was sufficient. The court distinguished *Twombly*, and found that "complex and historically unprecedented changes in pricing structure made at the very same time by multiple competitors, and made for no other discernible reason" supports a plausible inference of conspiracy.

8. **Answer (A) is the best answer.** The facts of this problem are reminiscent of *Richards v. Duke University*, 480 F. Supp. 2d 222 (D.C. Cir. 2007), which dismissed the plaintiff's claims for a variety of reasons, including their "fanciful nature." As Justice Souter (who wrote the majority opinion in *Twombly* and the dissent in *Iqbal*) noted, there has long been an exception to the rule requiring that facts pleaded be taken as true in the narrow context of "allegations that are sufficiently fantastic to defy reality as we know it: claims about little green men, or the plaintiff's recent trip to Pluto, or experiences in time travel." If this case falls into the "little green men" category, then it was always permissible to dismiss such a claim despite the general requirement to take all pleaded facts as true.

Answer (B) is incorrect. Although in many cases courts will allow plaintiff an opportunity to amend, in order to provide additional factual allegations that will show potential entitlement to relief, such an opportunity is not required where the flaws in the complaint cannot be cured. It is probable that a court would not find that the problems with Lucy's complaint can be fixed by allowing the chance to provide further detail.

Answer (C) would be the correct answer in many cases, but not under these facts. Lucy's allegations, however, disclose that they are based on surmise rather than information and are inherently unbelievable, and so the court is unlikely to allow the opportunity for discovery.

Answer (D) is incorrect. As noted above, allegations of the "little green men" variety could be dismissed even before the Court's recent expansion of Rule 12(b)(6) dismissals.

TOPIC 2: PLEADINGS: DEFENDANT'S PLEADINGS

ANSWERS

9. **Answer (A) is correct.** Rule 12(b) provides certain defenses that a party may assert even before filing an answer, if it wishes, or that may be included in the party's answer. Rule 12(b)(6) is the one directed at legally insufficient allegations. It allows the determination, based on the pleadings alone, that all or part of a case should be dismissed because it fails "to state a claim upon which relief can be granted." The court, in ruling on such a motion, must assume that all the facts pleaded by the plaintiff are true, and should not consider matters outside the pleadings. In this case, Bert has alleged that Ernie's car has a bumper sticker containing a bad pun, that this bothered Bert when he read it, and that Bert therefore sues for damages based on his annoyance. The court should assume that those allegations are correct (Ernie has such a bumper sticker; Bert saw it; Bert was annoyed) but can still dismiss the allegation because there is no cause of action for "annoyance." This will eliminate the claim at the outset without further expenditures for discovery on these issues.

   Answer (B) is incorrect. Although an invalid claim could be disposed of by summary judgment, where, as here, it can be eliminated earlier through a Rule 12(b)(6) motion based on the plaintiff's allegations alone, the latter motion is the more efficient procedural vehicle.

   Answer (C) is incorrect. Ernie does not want more detail about the annoyance claim, he wants to get rid of it, and there is no likelihood that greater detail about the bumper sticker or Bert's reaction will be helpful to the court in disposing of this claim.

   Answer (D) is incorrect. The general demurrer was abolished for the federal courts by the Federal Rules of Civil Procedure.

10. **Answer (B) is correct.** Rule 11 is designed to require good faith in pleading, and a pleader must have a basis both in law and in fact for the contents of its pleadings, motions, and other papers filed with the court. Rule 11 has often been amended. Under the current version of the rule, there are four listed certifications that a party makes to the court when presenting a pleading, written motion, or other paper. Signing a complaint that does not live up to these certifications is a violation of Rule 11, and potentially subjects the violator to various types of sanctions. This question focuses on the requirements of Rule 11(b).

    Rule 11(b)(2) is aimed at pleadings that bring claims that are warranted neither by existing law nor by a nonfrivolous argument for its modification. Assuming that the annoyance claim does not exist under applicable substantive law, and that there is no indication Bert's lawyer can point to, not even a dissenting opinion or a law review article, advocating such a cause of action, the annoyance claim violates Rule 11(b)(2). Note that if Bert were actually advocating a change in the law (as opposed to just failing to research it), Rule 11 does not require him to identify it as such, but the Advisory Committee Notes to the 1993 amendments point out that "a contention that is so identified should be viewed with greater tolerance" under Rule

11.

Answer (A) is incorrect. Rule 11(b)(1) prohibits presenting the pleading for an improper purpose. Bert and his lawyer appear to fall more into the "empty head, warm heart" category: their conduct still violates Rule 11, but not because of their subjective motives.

Answer (C) is incorrect. This is not a pleading in which the problem is lack of factual basis. Bert knows and has alleged the facts surrounding the bumper sticker. Rule 11(b)(3) is aimed at parties who file claims without having evidentiary support for them.

Answer (D) is incorrect because there is no need for more factual investigation — more detail would not improve Bert's non-existent cause of action. (Note also that even if this were the case, the rule calls for contentions lacking evidentiary support to be "specifically so identified.")

11. Ernie should not file the Rule 11 motion immediately. The current version of Rule 11 contains so-called "safe harbor" provisions. A party who believes her opponent has violated Rule 11 may not go straight to the court for sanctions. She must first serve on the opposing party a motion describing the offending conduct, giving that party an opportunity to withdraw or correct the challenged claim. Only after this is done, and the pleading is *not* withdrawn, may a Rule 11 motion be filed with the court. The drafters hoped that this would encourage the parties to work out these disputes among themselves, reducing the number of hearings required. If the motion causes a party to drop the challenged contention, it also eliminates that contention from the lawsuit without further expenditure of attorney time. Ernie must therefore give that kind of advance notice to Bert before going to the court.

12. **Answer (D) is correct.** The flaw in Bert's pleading in this case is a legal one — the annoyance claim is legally frivolous. This is therefore a violation of Rule 11(b)(2), as you learned in question 9. When it comes time for sanctions, Rule 11(c)(5)(A) provides that monetary sanctions may not be awarded against a represented party for a violation of subsection (b)(2). Thus, any award in this case would have to be made against Bert's lawyer, not Bert himself. Rule 11(c)(1) provides that sanctions may be imposed on the attorneys, law firms, or parties that have violated Rule 11(b) or are responsible for the violation.

Answer (A) is not completely correct, and therefore not the best answer. Rule 11(c)(2) allows the court to award the party prevailing on the Rule 11 motion the reasonable expenses and attorney's fees incurred in presenting the Rule 11 motion, but that does not include any other fees incurred that were caused by the wrongful pleading itself.

Answer (B) is also not the best answer. Answer (B) is correct to point out that generally monetary penalties (beyond fees incurred in presenting or opposing the Rule 11 motion itself) are paid to the court rather than to the parties. *See* Rule 11(c)(4). The rule, however, allows the court to award monetary sanctions to the movant including "part or all of the reasonable attorney's fees and other expenses directly resulting from the violation." These are only proper "if imposed on motion and warranted for effective deterrence." The statement in Answer (B) that penalties *must* be paid to the court is therefore incorrect.

Answer (C) is incorrect. It correctly recognizes that the sanction can be paid to the moving party if warranted for effective deterrence. It likewise notes that the court may choose to award all or only part of the attorney's fees — Rule 11(c)(4) provides that a sanction "must be limited to what suffices to deter repetition of the conduct or comparable conduct by others similarly situated." In other words, it is deterrence rather than compensation that is to guide the court's decision about the amount or nature of any sanction. Answer (C), however, overlooks one point that makes it wrong and makes Answer (D) correct: when the Rule 11 violation stems from a frivolous legal position, the sanctions must be assessed against the attorney rather than against a represented client.

13. **Answer (B) is correct.** Ernie did not have to file a pre-answer motion, but once he did so he had to include certain defenses or waive them. Ernie filed a motion to dismiss for insufficiency of service of process under Rule 12(b)(5) but did not include in it a motion to dismiss for lack of personal jurisdiction under Rule 12(b)(2). The consequences of this sequence of events are governed by Rule 12(g) and (h). Rule 12(g) provides that a party who makes a motion under Rule 12 must not make another motion under Rule 12 raising a defense or objection that was available to the party but omitted from its earlier motion except as permitted in Rule 12(h)(2) or (3), which does not apply to Ernie's situation here. Rule 12(h)(1) provides that a defense of lack of jurisdiction over the person is waived by "omitting it from a motion in the circumstances described in Rule 12(g)(2)." Thus, Ernie has lost the right to complain about personal jurisdiction being asserted over him in Texas, even if his complaint would have been valid. Bert's case should therefore go forward.

Answer (A) is incorrect. Ernie waived the defense of lack of personal jurisdiction, as explained above.

Answer (C) is incorrect. Rule 8(b)(5) provides: "A party that lacks knowledge or information sufficient to form a belief about the truth of an allegation must so state, and the statement has the effect of a denial." It is quite likely that Ernie lacks information concerning the nature and extent of Bert's injuries, so his response to the damage allegations was proper.

Answer (D) is incorrect. When a defendant denies the allegations of the plaintiff's complaint, it shows that there is a factual dispute requiring that the case go forward. Defendants cannot achieve dismissal of the claims against them merely by denying those claims.

14. **Answer (D) is correct.** The defense of lack of personal jurisdiction is a disfavored one, subject to waiver if not raised in a timely way. However, Ernie has managed to hold on to his defense this time. Rule 12(h)(1) provides that a defense of lack of jurisdiction over the person is waived if it is neither made by motion under this rule (true in this case) nor included in a responsive pleading (also true — it was not in the answer) or *an amendment to the responsive pleading permitted by Rule 15(a) to be made as a matter of course*. This is the provision that saves Ernie. For pleadings to which no responsive pleading is required (like Ernie's Answer), Rule 15(a) allows a party to amend once as a matter of course "21 days after serving it." Because Ernie amended his answer only a week after serving it, he meets the requirements of Rule 15(a). Thus, Ernie's defense of lack of personal jurisdiction was included in an amendment to the answer permitted to be made as a matter of course and, therefore, was *not* waived under Rule 12(h).

Answer (A) is incorrect because pre-answer motions are optional. A party need not make one at all if it does not want to. If, however, Ernie had filed a pre-answer motion that omitted the personal jurisdiction defense, that defense would have been waived.

Answer (B) is incorrect because the timely amendment to the answer saved the defense. Had Ernie not amended his answer within 21 days of the time his original answer was served, (B) would be the correct answer.

Answer (C) is incorrect. While complaints about subject matter jurisdiction (the power of the court to hear the type of case involved) may be raised at any time under Rule 12(h)(3), Ernie's concern was jurisdiction of the court over him as a defendant. This kind of defense is indeed subject to waiver.

15. This question highlights the issue of affirmative defenses. Formerly called a "plea in confession and avoidance," an affirmative defense asserts some independent reason that the plaintiff cannot prevail. It is, thus, different from a denial. The most common affirmative defenses are listed in Rule 8(c). The defenses themselves are often governed by state law (*see* Topic 44). The *pleading* of the defenses, though, is governed by Rule 8. Here, Ernie is attempting to raise the affirmative defense of contributory negligence. In most states, this affirmative defense acts as a complete or partial bar to the plaintiff's recovery, even when the defendant is negligent. A defendant cannot raise this issue at trial unless he has pleaded it. The allegation that the plaintiff's own negligence is to blame for the accident in question is different from a mere denial that the defendant was negligent.

16. When a defendant wants to bring a claim for his own damage against the plaintiff, the pleading device that is used is called a "counterclaim." Counterclaims are governed by Rule 13 of the FRCP. Counterclaims are either "compulsory" or "permissive." A counterclaim is compulsory if it arises out of the same transaction or occurrence as the plaintiff's claim against the defendant. This may be considered under a test of whether there is a "logical relationship" between the complaint and counterclaim, or whether the two claims would involve the "same evidence." Under either test, Ernie's counterclaim against Bert would be a compulsory one.

17. **Answer (C) is correct.** Rule 7(a) provides for "an answer to a counterclaim designated as a counterclaim." This means that an answer containing Rule 8 defenses is required to join issue on the allegations of the counterclaim and to avoid them.

    Answer (A) is incorrect because denial defenses must be included in the reply. See Rule 8(b)(6), which provides that an "allegation . . . is admitted if a responsive pleading is required and the allegation is not denied."

    Answer (B) is incorrect because affirmative defenses to the counterclaim must be made to avoid waiver of the defenses.

    Answer (D) is incorrect because the reply is to the counterclaim, not the entire answer.

18. This is a tricky question and requires both an appreciation of contract law defenses and Rule 8(c). Under contract law, there is a contract based on mutual promises. There is no want of consideration. But because Ernie breached the contract, the consideration failed. Rule 8(c) lists *failure of consideration* as an affirmative defense, so it must be alleged by Bert specifically. Bert probably should allege that the consideration *failed* completely because the bargain required authentic long rifles. Out of an abundance of caution, Bert might also plead *want* of consideration alternatively. A weak argument can be made that there was no consideration, not merely that the consideration failed. In many jurisdictions, want of consideration is also considered an affirmative defense in cases involving written contracts because written contracts are presumed to be supported by consideration.

19. **Answer (B) is correct.** The drafters of the Federal Rules of Civil Procedure wanted to eliminate the prolonged "back and forth" of pleadings that characterized the common law pleading system. Therefore, Rule 7 put limits on the pleadings allowed. It does not normally allow a reply to an answer. Further, Rule 8(b)(6) provides the party with an automatic denial *and avoidance* of matters raised in a pleading to which no responsive pleading is required — which would include the answer. It therefore relieves Bert of the need to plead fraud in response to Ernie's pleading of release. Some state court systems would have a different rule, requiring the pleading of defenses that "avoid" affirmative defenses, in order to provide notice to the defendant that the plaintiff intends to raise this issue.

Answer (A) is incorrect. Fraud is an affirmative defense, and a defendant who wishes to raise a defense of fraud to the plaintiff's complaint would indeed have to plead it. However, when it appears in the context of an affirmative defense to an affirmative defense, Rule 8(b)(6) relieves the plaintiff of the need to plead it, as explained above. In fact, the plaintiff is not allowed to file a reply to the answer without the court's prior permission.

Answer (C) is incorrect. Rule 7 does not usually allow responsive pleadings to answers; it certainly does not require them.

Answer (D) is incorrect. The pleading of issues in avoidance — the essence of an affirmative defense — generally is required. A defendant who fails to plead an affirmative defense in response to the plaintiff's complaint may easily have waived that defense.

TOPIC 3: ANSWERS

PLEADINGS: HEIGHTENED SPECIFICITY

20. **Answer (A) is correct.** The basic requirements for the level of pleading specificity are set out in Rule 8(a). Rule 9 lists certain kinds of issues that must be alleged with a greater degree of detail, usually called "pleading with particularity" or "heightened pleading requirements." There are also certain statutes, such as the Private Securities Litigation Reform Act, that require more fact-specific pleadings before a plaintiff is allowed to proceed. Beyond that, however, the Supreme Court has repeatedly interpreted the rules to prevent individual judges from creating their own heightened pleading rules for categories of cases. *See, e.g., Leatherman v. Tarrant County Narcotics Intelligence & Coordination Unit*, 507 U.S. 163 (1993); *Swierkiewicz v. Sorema N.A.*, 534 U.S. 506 (2002). Note, however, that as interpreted in *Twombly* and *Iqbal*, Rule 8 may require a greater degree of detail than it was formerly thought to require even where Rule 9 does not apply.

    Answer (B) is not correct. It is probably true that judges have some amount of flexibility in individual cases in determining what constitutes a "short and plain statement of the claim showing that the pleader is entitled to relief." This does not, however, justify any kind of across-the-board rule like the one used by the judge in this question.

    Answer (C) is not correct either. In the particular circumstance of certain kinds of good faith immunity claims in civil rights cases, the Fifth Circuit has used the device of a Reply as a substitute source of particularized information from the plaintiffs. *See, e.g., Schultea v. Wood*, 47 F.3d 1427 (5th Cir. 1995) (en banc). The special policy concerns that apply in those cases do not apply in garden-variety tort claims, however, making it unlikely that the Supreme Court would approve of wholesale adoption of the Reply to get around the language of Rule 8(a).

    Answer (D) is also incorrect. *Leatherman* may have left a tiny hole for civil rights cases against individual government officials, but it did not give permission to require heightened pleadings generally.

21. **Answer (C) is correct.** Fraud claims must be alleged specifically because Rule 9(b) provides that in averments of fraud, a party must state with particularity the circumstances constituting fraud or mistake. This means that the plaintiff must plead who individually has done or said what, when, where, and why.

    Answer (A) is incorrect for the same reason that Answer (C) is correct.

    Answer (B) is incorrect because Rule 9(b) also provides that malice, intent, knowledge, and other conditions of a person's mind may be alleged generally. This contrasts with the PSLRA which requires factual support for scienter allegations.

    Answer (D) is incorrect. The liberal Rule 12(b)(6) standard is read in conjunction with the specific requirements of Rule 9.

22. At least in certain kinds of cases, a change that routinely requires pleading facts with

particularity would work to the disadvantage of plaintiffs. This would be particularly true if no discovery were allowed until a plaintiff satisfied the requirement of the pleading rule. There will be cases in which a plaintiff does not have access to the kind of information required for a fact-specific pleading, and while those cases can go forward under a notice pleading system, they would be dismissed under a heightened pleading standard. Also, because pleadings provide the outlines for development of the case through discovery, more specific pleadings would mean a narrower scope of discovery and less opportunity for a plaintiff to gain information with the help of the court. In cases in which both parties have fairly equal access to all relevant information before any litigation is filed, a change in the pleading rule would have less effect on the parties' comparative advantage.

TOPIC 4: AMENDED PLEADINGS — ANSWERS

23. **Answer (D) is the best answer, although Answer (A) is also correct.** Pretrial amendments to pleadings are governed by Rule 15(a). Once the period allowing amendments as a matter of course passes, amendments require permission from the court, but amendments are generally still favored: Rule 15(a)(2) says that the court "should freely give leave when justice so requires." Courts have interpreted this rule to mean that an amendment should be allowed unless the party opposing the amendment shows that it will be prejudiced in some way by the delay, as when relevant evidence has been lost, witnesses have become unavailable, or an amendment that makes a significant change in the nature of the lawsuit comes too late in the case. In the hypothetical, the defendant seeks to amend its answer only six weeks after it originally served its answer, and less than two months after suit was filed. It is unlikely that a change coming so early in the case would prejudice the plaintiff. Under other circumstances, the result could be different. Because of the pro-amendment attitude of the FRCP, Answers (D) and (A) are correct in that the amendment should be allowed. However, amended pleadings are subject to the requirements of Rule 11 as are other pleadings, and the defendant should not make this change unless the denial is "warranted on the evidence" as provided in Rule 11(b)(4). Because Answer (D) includes this caution, it is a better answer.

    Answer (B) is incorrect because January 15 is outside the time period in which pleadings can be amended without permission under Rule 15(a). For defendants, this time expires 21 days after its original answer is served, and in this question the request to amend came six weeks after the answer.

    Answer (C) is incorrect because parties are allowed to change their factual contentions as well as their legal theories. The FRCP's emphasis on using the entire pretrial process to develop the case assumes that as discovery and informal investigation progress the pleadings may need to be amended and that this is preferable to freezing the allegations to the parties' state of knowledge at the outset of the case.

24. Question 24 focuses only on whether Boxer's proposed amendments are proper as amendments; question 25 will add the problem of the statute of limitations. In this case, the court should allow the amendments. As in question 23, it is early in the lawsuit. Mastiff has not lost access to any kind of proof by virtue of the slight delay in correctly naming his business or in adding a claim for an additional type of damages. Thus, neither change would prejudice Mastiff, and both amendments should be allowed.

25. **Answer (B) is the best answer.** This question, based on the same facts, is more difficult. Now you are asked to assume that the original complaint was timely, but the amended complaint standing alone would be barred by the statute of limitations. Boxer's new damage claim and indeed any claim against Mastiff will be barred unless the amendments "relate back" to the filing of the original complaint. The answer, thus, depends on the application of Rule 15(c). In order to relate back, the new damage claim must arise out of the conduct,

transaction, or occurrence set forth in the original complaint. Here, Boxer's claim for consequential damages is alleged to be a consequence of the defect in the dog food, as was her original damage claim. Same "conduct, transaction, or occurrence" under Rule 15 is more concerned with notice to the defendant than with the evidence overlap and trial efficiency sought when a similar phrase is used in other rules. The different types of damages, although they will not involve the same evidence, will be considered part of the same transaction or occurrence and will be allowed to relate back. Boxer's amendment changing the naming of defendant from "BBD, Inc." to "Martin Mastiff, doing business as BBD Products" must meet additional tests. These tests are incorporated into Answer (B). Under Rule 15(c), this type of amendment also requires timely notice to the new defendant so that he will not be prejudiced in maintaining a defense on the merits. Notice of the institution of the action is timely if it is given "within the period provided by Rule 4(m) for serving the summons and complaint," i.e., within 120 days after the filing of the complaint. In this case, Mastiff himself was served with the original complaint before limitations ran and thus had notice of the allegations in the suit, avoiding prejudice due to late notification of the claim. Rule 15(c) also requires that within the same period the new defendant knew or should have known that, but for a mistake concerning the identity of the proper party, the action would have been brought against the new defendant. Here, Mastiff knew or should have known the name and legal status of his company, and therefore he should have known that but for Boxer's mistake he would have been sued individually. Answer (B) comes closest to including all of these requirements.

Answer (A) is incorrect. The consequential damage claim *does* arise out of the same conduct, transaction, or occurrence as Boxer's original claims. The original complaint puts the defendant on notice that he is being sued for the harm caused to Boxer by alleged defects in his dog food, and this new damage claim should not come as an unfair surprise to Mastiff.

Answer (C) is incorrect. This is exactly the kind of mistaken identity that Rule 15(c) was designed to rectify. A known defendant has been inadvertently misnamed.

Answer (D) is incorrect because it omits so much important information. While lack of prejudice is a factor to consider in whether to allow amendments, a number of other tests must be met, leaving this answer fatally incomplete.

26. Boxer needs for her amendment to relate back in order to defeat the bar of the statute of limitations. This is more difficult when the amendment changes the party against whom a claim is asserted. Here it would change from ABC Corporation to PoroCal Company. Even if PoroCal had timely notice of the suit, Boxer's claim only relates back if PoroCal knew that Boxer's failure to sue it was a "mistake" within the meaning of Rule 15(c). The Supreme Court, in *Krupski v. Costa Crociere S.p.A*, 560 U.S. 538 (2010), made clear that it is the new defendant's state of mind that is in issue. The question is not whether Boxer should have known that the company's name was PoroCal, but whether PoroCal knew or should have known during the Rule 4(m) period that it would have been named as a defendant but for an error. The Court has not yet addressed the question of whether the deliberate use of a pseudonym such as "John Doe" or "ABC Corporation," used because the plaintiff does not yet know the identity of the defendant, qualifies as a mistake.

27. The drafters of the Federal Rules of Civil Procedure tried to shift merits determinations of lawsuits from the initial pleadings to a later point in time, allowing an opportunity for

discovery, and resolving fact issues through trial. They envisioned a system in which the true issues in dispute between the parties would become clearer as the lawsuit progressed. Some issues would disappear, either because the plaintiff dropped them for lack of evidentiary support or because the defendant admitted the plaintiff's claims. Other issues would be added, as the plaintiff gathered evidentiary support for additional factual or legal theories. In order to facilitate this process, amendments to the pleadings are encouraged. These amendments, however, should not be allowed when they will prejudice one of the parties. This could happen when a significant amendment is allowed after evidence has been lost, or very shortly before trial. The trial court, therefore, has discretion to deny permission to amend to avoid prejudice to a party.

TOPIC 5: JOINDER OF CLAIMS — ANSWERS

28. **Answer (B) is correct.** With only one plaintiff and one defendant, this lawsuit involves joinder of claims but not joinder of parties. Rule 18 provides that a "party asserting a claim . . . may join, as independent or alternate claims, as many claims as it has against an opposing party." There is, therefore, no misjoinder under these circumstances.

    Answer (A) is incorrect. Because Rule 20 does not apply, the claims are not required to arise out of the same transaction or occurrence.

    Answer (C) is incorrect. Unlike some former procedural systems that put strict limits on joining claims, the Federal Rules of Civil Procedure do not impose this type of limitation. Instead, they encourage free joinder in order to dispose of issues efficiently.

    Answer (D) is incorrect. Not only is no "common question" required, if it were the statement in (D) is untrue — the mere fact that a claim is by the same person against the same person does not itself provide a common question of law or fact.

29. **Answer (D) is correct.** The trial judge has broad discretion to order separate trials for convenience, to avoid prejudice, or to expedite and economize. Rule 42(b). In addition, although the rule's language addresses "misjoinder" and these claims are not misjoined, courts have interpreted Rule 21 to allow judges to actually sever claims, even in cases involving one plaintiff and one defendant, to avoid prejudice. Severance results in separate lawsuits, while ordering separate trials results in different proceedings within a single case.

    Answer (A) is probably not correct. Although Rule 18(a) places no limit on joinder of claims, regardless of their type or relationship to one another (so that they cannot be "misjoined"), courts have concluded that severance orders may be issued under Rule 21 (entitled Misjoinder and Nonjoinder of Parties) as a matter of judicial discretion, to facilitate the administration of justice. It is true that dismissal is not a proper remedy, even if the claims were misjoined.

    Answer (B) is incorrect. Unlike Rule 20 (Permissive Joinder of Parties), which contains a nexus requirement. Rule 18(a) has no such requirement.

    Answer (C) is incorrect. It is correct that dismissal would be improper, but because there is no misjoinder of claims, severance is certainly not mandatory. Rather decisions about severance and separate trial are within the court's discretion to avoid prejudice, as noted in Answer (D).

TOPIC 6: PERMISSIVE JOINDER OF PARTIES — ANSWERS

30. **Answer (B) is the best answer.** The claims against Boris and Doris do not satisfy all three of the procedural requirements imposed by Rule 20 (1. claim asserted against defendants "jointly, severally, or in the alternative"; 2. with respect to or arising out of "the same transaction, occurrence or series of transactions or occurrences"; and 3. "any question of law or fact common to all defendants will arise in the action"). Because the claim against Boris is unrelated to the claim against Doris, it satisfies neither the second nor third requirements, and there is a misjoinder of parties. But misjoinder of parties is not a ground for dismissal of an action. It is a ground for a separate trial to prevent delay or prejudice (Rule 20(b)) or severance (Rule 21).

    Answer (A) is incorrect. Rule 21 expressly states that misjoinder of parties is not ground for dismissing an action.

    Answer (C) is incorrect for the reasons stated above.

    Answer (D) is also incorrect. Although trial judges have broad discretion in this context, it is not unlimited and it does not extend to permitting the joinder of completely unrelated claims.

31. **Answer (D) is correct.** Although the original version of Rule 18(a) contained a sentence that suggested that Rule 20 imposed limits on the joinder of claims in cases involving multiple parties, as amended in 1966 the sentence was deleted. The effect of the amendment is to permit joinder of unrelated claims in multiple party cases as long as the parties are properly joined, i.e., as long as one common claim links the defendants together. *See* Kaplan, *1966 Amendments of the Federal Rules of Civil Procedure*, 81 Harv. L. Rev. 591, 597 (1968). In this case, Rhona and Robin are properly joined as parties under the breach of contract claim. Although the claims are not therefore misjoined, Rule 20(b) allows the judge to enter orders designed to protect a party against "embarrassment, delay, expense, or other prejudice that arises from including a person against whom the party asserts no claim and who asserts no claim against the party." In a situation such as the one described here, the most common such protective measure would be an order that the libel claim be tried separately from the contract claim, or even severed pursuant to Rule 21.

    Answer (A) is incorrect. Rhona's remedy is severance or a separate trial, not a dismissal.

    Answer (B) is correct as explained above.

    Answer (C) is correct as explained above.

TOPIC 7:	**ANSWERS**
COMPULSORY JOINDER OF PARTIES	

32. **Answer (C) is the best answer.** The claims of Albert, Barbara, Clarence, and David satisfy the three procedural requirements of Rule 20, because they each claim liens on Edward's summer house. Because of the nature of their claims (all are asserting interests in the same piece of real property), they should be litigated in the same action if there are no jurisdictional impediments to doing so. The same reasoning applies to Foxworth. Rule 19(a) makes Foxworth a "person required to be joined if feasible" because he "claims an interest relating to the subject of the action" and disposing of the action in his absence may "impair or impede" his ability to protect the interest.

    Answer (A) is incorrect for the reasons stated above.

    Answer (B) is incorrect because Foxworth is a person who should be joined if feasible under Rule 19(a), even though Rule 19(b) might allow the action to proceed without him, particularly if none of the parties raised his nonjoinder in the trial court.

    Answer (D) is incorrect because Foxworth is not jurisdictionally "indispensable" to the adjudication of the claims of the other parties. If for some reason Foxworth is not or cannot be joined, the question will be whether the action should proceed in his absence, not whether the court has jurisdiction to do so.

33. **Answer (C) is correct.** Based on the Supreme Court's analysis and application of Rule 19(b) in *Provident Tradesmens Bank & Trust Co. v. Patterson*, 390 U.S. 102 (1968), Edward's attempt to obtain a windfall escape from his defeat at trial is foreclosed.

    Answer (A) is incorrect because under modern Rule 19, the issue is procedural, not substantive or jurisdictional.

    Answer (B) is incorrect because Foxworth did not need to be joined in order for the court of appeals to shape or frame relief to protect his lien interest, which probably can be enforced anyway.

    Answer (D) is incorrect. Even if Foxworth's lien is inferior, that is not an issue that the court of appeals would resolve *de novo*.

34. Because Foxworth was not a party to the first action, his lien was not extinguished and he is not bound by any judgment foreclosing the mechanics' and materialmen's liens on Edward's property. Assuming no jurisdictional problems exist, Foxworth can bring suit against Albert, Barbara, Clarence, and David to establish the priority of Foxworth's lien under applicable law. All of them can be joined under Rule 20 and each of them probably is a person to be joined, if feasible, under Rule 19. Edward should also be joined under Rules 19 and 20, along with any subsequent purchasers who acquired the summer home at the sale foreclosing the mechanics' and materialmen's liens. Of course, Foxworth may lose the case on the merits because his lien is inferior under applicable law, or because the subsequent purchasers can avoid the deed of trust lien under applicable property law.

TOPIC 8:	**ANSWERS**
INTERPLEADER	

35. **Answer (D) is probably the correct answer.** Rule interpleader is a device for joining rival claimants. Cookie and Dorothy are rival claimants to the same fund. Although the second phase of the case, after interpleader is permitted, will involve litigation between Cookie and Dorothy, who are both Texans, case law holds that there is no jurisdictional problem if diversity exists between the plaintiff bringing the interpleader action and the claimants. *See Aetna Life & Cas. Co. v. Spain*, 556 F.2d 747, 749 (5th Cir. 1977).

    Answer (A) is incorrect for the same reason.

    Answer (B) is correct as stated above.

    Answer (C) is correct as stated above.

36. **Answer (D) is the correct answer.** Statutory interpleader requires only minimal diversity between "[t]wo or more adverse claimants, of diverse citizenship" and money or property in the amount of $500 or more. 28 U.S.C. § 1335. Both of those requirements are met in this question. In addition, 28 U.S.C. § 2361 provides for nationwide service of process, so that Cookie's current lack of contacts with Texas is not a problem, and 28 U.S.C. § 1397 makes venue proper "in the judicial district in which one or more of the claimants reside."

    Answer (A) is correct as stated above.

    Answer (B) is correct as stated above.

    Answer (C) is correct as stated above.

37. Confederation Life probably can still interplead Dorothy and Cookie in either Texas or New Mexico and request injunctive relief against Cookie (and Dorothy) "restraining them from instituting or prosecuting any proceeding in any State or United States court affecting the property, instrument or obligation involved in the interpleader action." 28 U.S.C. § 2361. An interpleader claim might even be regarded as a compulsory counterclaim. Confederation Life probably could obtain interpleader by way of counterclaim in Connecticut, joining Dorothy as an additional party to the interpleader counterclaim, although venue would not ordinarily be proper there as to Dorothy. Some courts don't consider venue issues to be relevant to counterclaims. Still others recognize a concept of "ancillary" venue that might cover Dorothy.

TOPIC 9: INTERVENTION

ANSWERS

38. **Answer (C) is the best answer** because Albert "claims an interest" in the deed and his "ability to protect that interest" could be "impaired or impeded" by a delivery of the deed to Clarence. Thus, Albert is a person to be joined if feasible (Rule 19) and must be permitted to intervene in accordance with Rule 24(a).

    Answer (A) is incorrect. If a federal statute confers a right to intervene, intervention is appropriate, but it may also be appropriate in the absence of a statute.

    Answer (B) is incorrect. Permissive intervention requires only that an intervenor have "a claim or defense that shares with the main action a common question of law or fact." Because the standard is low (*cf.* Rule 20's more complex requirements), the trial judge has considerably more discretion to grant or deny permissive intervention.

    Answer (D) is incorrect. Although the trial court has some discretion to deny intervention to persons like Albert, the discretion is not broad.

TOPIC 10: JOINDER OF ADDITIONAL PARTIES

ANSWERS

39. **Answer (B) is the correct answer.** Third-party actions are derivative actions in the sense that they are brought to recover from third parties on the basis of the third party's derivative or secondary liability. Under Rule 14(a), a third-party complaint is appropriate only in cases where the third-party defendant would be secondarily liable to the original defendant in the event the latter is held liable to the plaintiff. Claims for contribution or indemnity are prototypical third-party claims.

    Answers (A), (C), and (D) are incorrect for the same reason that Answer (B) is correct.

40. **Answer (A) is the best answer** because the contribution claim is a proper basis for Nelson's third-party complaint. Nelson should be able to add any additional claims against Rios under Rule 18(a), which specifically references a "third-party claim."

    Answer (B) is plausible, but it is probably not necessary to engage in a two-step process before Nelson can add his personal injury claims.

    Answer (C) is incorrect for the same reason that Answer (A) is correct.

    Answer (D) is incorrect for the same reason that Answers (B) and (C) are incorrect.

TOPIC 11: COUNTERCLAIMS & CROSS-CLAIMS — ANSWERS

41. **Answer (D) is correct, because Answers (A), (B), and (C) are all correct.** As stated in **Answer (A)**, if the federal lawsuit proceeds to judgment first, the subsequent Connecticut action could be barred because Rule 13(a) probably makes Duds' counterclaim a compulsory claim in federal court. The preclusive effect of the federal judgment will be determined under federal common law, which in turn incorporates state preclusion law under most circumstances. *See Semtek Int'l Inc. v. Lockheed Martin Corp.*, 531 U.S. 497 (2001); *see generally* William M. Richman & William L. Reynolds, Understanding Conflict of Laws § 113(a) (3d ed. 2002).

    Answer (B) is correct, too. Nelson is an "opposing party" because Nelson sued Duds. This is significant because it invokes the compulsory counterclaim rule.

    Answer (C) is also correct, and it calls attention to an exception to the rule making counterclaims compulsory. *See* Rule 13(a)(2).

42. **Answer (A) is correct.** Under Rule 13(g), cross-claims against co-parties are not compulsory, they are permissive, even though they must arise out of the transaction or occurrence that is the subject matter of the original claim.

    Answer (B) is incorrect for the reasons stated above.

    Answer (C) is incorrect because although Nelson's claim against Big Motors is somewhat different from his claim against Duds and Rios, they are logically related and there would be significant evidence overlap in Nelson's claims against all three defendants.

    Answer (D) is incorrect because Answer (C) is not correct.

43. **Answer (C) is the best answer.** The answer is made more complicated by the fact that once Duds and Rios have made claims against Big Motors, its claims against them are both cross-claims and counterclaims. And the rules about asserting un-matured claims are different. Although counterclaims for contribution must be mature, cross-claims for contribution need not be mature at the time the cross-claim is filed. Hence, the unavailability of a counterclaim should not prohibit a cross-claim within the scope of Rule 13(a) merely because the co-party has already asserted a claim.

    Answers (A), (B), and (D) are incorrect for the same reason.

TOPIC 12:	**ANSWERS**
CLASS ACTIONS	

44. **Answer (A) is correct.** Of the four threshold requirements in Rule 23(a), it is probably true that the only one that is problematic here is "typicality." To be "typical" the class representative must "possess the same interest and suffer the same injury." *See East Texas Motor Freight v. Rodriguez*, 431 U.S. 395 (1977). This means that the claims must be based on the same legal theory and generally arise from the same event or course of conduct giving rise to the claims of other class members in a way that makes the class cohesive and ensures that by asserting her own claim, the named plaintiff also asserts the claims of class members. The typicality requirement thus seeks to eliminate potential conflicts of interest between the class representative and members of the class.

    Answer (B) is incorrect. Although there is no exact numerical threshold, clearly 1,000 purchasers, who live throughout the country, are too numerous to be joined as a practical matter.

    Answer (C) is incorrect. The qualifications of class representatives are not rigorous. A willingness to serve coupled with the retention of experienced counsel capable of handling the case and financing its prosecution should be sufficient.

    Answer (D) is probably incorrect. Rule 23(a)'s requirements of commonality and typicality tend to overlap somewhat in practice, both aiming to ensure the kind of cohesiveness that protects absent class members and makes class treatment effective. The commonality requirement looks at the relationship among the claims of members of the class, while typicality looks at the relationship between the named plaintiff and class members. Even under the Supreme Court's decision in *Wal-Mart Stores, Inc. v. Dukes*, 131 S. Ct. 2541 (2011), Andie's case should satisfy the commonality requirement. Although Andie and most class members are injured in slightly different ways, all challenge the same price-fixing behavior on the part of Panos and its supposed competitors, and litigation of their claims could generate a common answer as to the legality of those practices. Note that after *Wal-Mart* Andie would be required in a class certification hearing to offer evidence of the existence of these common questions (as well as all of the Rule 23(a) requirements), even if doing so overlaps proof of the merits of the class's claims.

45. **Answer (B) is correct.** This type of case would most likely be a Rule 23(b)(3) action requiring the trial court to find that there are common questions, that the common questions predominate in the sense that they will be the object of most of the effort of the litigants and the court, and that the classwide resolution of the issues is superior, both as a matter of judicial economy and fairness to the parties.

    Answer (A) is incorrect. Multiple money damage claims, even if trial results are inconsistent, do not subject the defendant to incompatible standards of conduct.

    Answer (C) is incorrect because the claimants are seeking money damages, not an injunction. The Supreme Court ruled in *Wal-Mart* that Rule 23(b)(2) is generally not available when the class seeks money damages, unless that kind of remedy is merely incidental to the type of court orders that section authorizes.

Answer (D) is incorrect. Individual cases would not have a preclusive or a practical effect on absent parties and so could not prejudice the interest of other class members.

46. **Answer (B) is correct.** The Supreme Court, in *Eisen v. Carlisle & Jacquelin*, 417 U.S. 156 (1974), held that regardless of the cost of providing notice to the class members, the plaintiff should bear the cost. Class action settlements often include an agreement by the defendant to bear the cost of notice, but in contested cases that cannot be ordered.

Answer (A) is incorrect. Unless the defendant would not incur any additional expense or the expense would be insubstantial because, for example, notices could be included in normal periodic mailings, as a general rule, the fact that a defendant can better afford notice costs does not matter.

Answers (C) and (D) are incorrect, as there is no authority to order these methods of allocating the costs of notice.

TOPIC 13:	ANSWERS
DISCOVERY: AUTOMATIC INITIAL DISCLOSURES	

47. **Answer (D) is correct.** Rule 26(a)(1) describes categories of information that must be disclosed at the outset of the case without the need for a discovery request. This includes, in Rule 26(a)(1)(A), the name and location information for "each individual likely to have discoverable information — along with the subjects of that information — that the disclosing party may use to support its claims or defenses, unless the use would be solely for impeachment."

    Answer (A) is incorrect. Disgruntled former clients are unlikely to support Nanny Nation's case, and so they need not be identified in initial disclosures.

    Answer (B) is incorrect. The rule does not require that witness e-mail addresses be provided, although it does specify that address and telephone numbers must be given if known.

    Answer (C) is incorrect. While some parts of Hibbins' file might come under the disclosure requirements of Rule 26(a)(1)(A)(ii), this rule also is confined to information that "the disclosing party [Nanny Nation] has in its possession, custody, or control and may use to support its claims or defenses." The troublesome evaluation from the former employer is not something Nanny Nation would use, and so automatic disclosure of this document is not required.

48. **Answer (B) is correct.** Rule 26(a)(1)(A)(iii) governs the disclosures required concerning the claim for damages. It requires "a computation of each category of damages claimed by the disclosing party — who must also make available for inspection and copying as under Rule 34 [requests for production of documents from parties] the documents or other evidentiary material, unless privileged or protected from disclosure, on which each computation is based, including materials bearing on the nature and extent of injuries suffered." Thus, although the pleading rules do not require an itemization of damages (*see* Topic 1), the automatic initial disclosure rules provide the defendant with that information.

    Answer (A) is incorrect. The requirements of this rule are not limited to economic harm.

    Answer (C) is incorrect. While the rule requires documents on which a computation of damages is based, it excludes material that is privileged. Correspondence with the attorney on this topic would be protected by the attorney-client privilege as well as work product protection.

    Answer (D) is not as good as Answer (B). While a computation of out-of-pocket expenses would be included in the required response, it omits a number of required types of damages.

49. August 23. Rule 26(a)(1)(C) requires the automatic initial disclosures to be made at or within 14 days after the Rule 26(f) conference. The Rule 26(f) conference must be held at least 21 days before a scheduling order is due under Rule 16(b). Thus, in this case, the Rule 26(f) conference must be held by August 9. The automatic initial disclosures, therefore, must be

made within 14 days after that, or by August 23. In cases in which each step is taken on the last possible day, the disclosures will be due 7 days before the scheduling order. However, note that the deadlines in Rules 26(a)(1)(C) and 26(f) run from when the scheduling order is actually due, or from when the Rule 26(f) conference is actually held, so that the exact timing will vary from case to case.

50. **Answer (A) is correct.** Rule 26(a) also governs automatic disclosures concerning testifying expert witnesses, although these disclosures take place at a later stage of the proceedings. The rule requires a report and other information relevant to examination and impeachment of the expert. Although Rule 26(a)(2)(D) encourages a case-specific court order, in the absence of an order the rule provides the timing and sequence of disclosure. Generally the disclosures are required "at least 90 days before the date set for trial or for the case to be ready for trial." Prynne's expert information is therefore due at this time. On the other hand, expert evidence "intended solely to contradict or rebut evidence on the same subject matter identified by another party" only needs to be made within 30 days after the other party's disclosure. Nanny Nation's expert testimony, which would be intended to rebut that of Prynne, probably falls under this category. As the Advisory Committee Notes indicate, in most cases the party with the burden of proof on an issue (usually the plaintiff) should disclose its expert testimony on that issue before other parties are required to make their disclosures with respect to that issue.

Answer (B) is incorrect. A defendant's disclosures, absent a counterclaim or an affirmative defense, generally do not need to be made simultaneously with the plaintiff's disclosures.

Answer (C) is incorrect. These disclosures are required in cases such as this and it requires a court order or stipulation to eliminate the requirement, not to impose it.

Answer (D) is incorrect. The disclosure requirement applies to all experts who are retained or specially employed to provide expert testimony, or whose duties as an employee of the party regularly involve giving expert testimony. The reference to "a witness" does not imply that the disclosures are limited to one person.

51. **Answer (C) is the correct answer.** While Rule 26(a)(2) requires significant disclosures from testifying experts, it does not cover employee-experts unless their duties regularly involve giving expert testimony.

Answer (A) is incorrect. Although a report from an employee-expert might indeed be helpful in providing the information needed to depose, and later cross-examine, the expert, the rules do not require it from an expert like Bobbins.

Answer (B) is incorrect. The degree of litigant control over the expert is not the criterion used by Rule 26.

Answer (D) is incorrect. Even though an employee, Bobbins has special training or expertise and will be testifying to her opinions, not to the facts surrounding the recruitment and training of Hibbins.

52. **Answer (B) is the best answer.** In cases involving voluminous document production, and especially cases involving extensive discovery of electronically stored information, parties sometimes agree on a procedure such as that described in (B) (which is sometimes referred to as a "claw back" or "snap back" process). This benefits the producing party, in that it can reduce the cost in time and attorney fees associated with pre-screening documents for

privilege, and can avoid the serious problem of privilege waiver. It can benefit the discovering party, in that it is likely to get access to the documents more quickly if it need not wait for a painstaking pre-production privilege review. On the other hand, in particular cases one party might prefer to leave the possibility of privilege waiver on the table. If an agreement is reached, asking the court to include it in a pretrial order has the advantage of greater clarity as to what exactly was agreed to, and is easier to enforce. (Rule 502 of the Federal Rules of Evidence may make such orders enforceable even in later state court proceedings.)

Answer (A) is not a probable choice. No party is likely to agree that any production of privilege, no matter how accidental, will automatically waive privilege.

Answer (C) is highly unrealistic. Even if the parties wanted their document production to be watched by a judge, they cannot agree between themselves as to what the judge will do, and it is extremely unlikely that a judge would be willing to spend his or her time in this way.

Answer (D) is close to the default rule in federal court in the absence of an agreement. Note that it makes the outcome of inadvertent production so unpredictable that it is unlikely that parties would negotiate for such a deal.

53. **Answer (D) is correct (and, therefore, so are (A) and (C)).** Rule 26(a)(3) sets out the requirements for disclosures to be made shortly before the trial begins. It includes both a listing of witnesses (except those to be used only for impeachment) and identification of documents and other exhibits. Unless the court orders otherwise, these disclosures must be made at least 30 days before trial.

Answer (B) is incorrect for two reasons. First, it gets the timing requirement wrong (it's 30 days, not 14), and second, it states that parties must reveal witnesses to be used only for the purpose of impeachment if their use can be anticipated in advance. While some state court rules do require the disclosure of such witnesses, the federal rules do not.

54. **Answer (B) is correct.** Rule 26(a)(3)(B) sets out the requirements for objecting to an opponent's pretrial disclosures, including the requirement that objections to admissibility (except for relevance) be made within 14 days of the disclosures.

Answer (A) is incorrect. While the pretrial disclosures do aid efficiency, their effect goes far beyond a mere list for the court's convenience. Absent good cause, the disclosure of exhibits both prevents the offering of additional exhibits and objections to the admissibility of those exhibits not made before trial. By doing so, they can streamline the trial by avoiding the time that would otherwise be consumed by examining the opposing party's exhibits and by making and ruling on objections.

Answer (C) is incorrect. As the Advisory Committee Notes explain, any witnesses, depositions, or exhibits not properly disclosed under Rule 26(a)(3) may be excluded from use at trial. *See also* Rule 37(c) ("If a party fails to provide information or identify a witness as required by Rule 26(a) . . . the party is not allowed to use that information or witness to supply evidence . . . at a trial, unless the failure was substantially justified or is harmless.").

Answer (D) is incorrect. Although parties may in fact list exhibits in the approximate order in which they plan to use them, the rules impose no such requirement.

TOPIC 14: ANSWERS
DISCOVERY: SCOPE OF DISCOVERY & DISCOVERY RELEVANCE

55. **Answer (C) is correct.** This answer tracks the language of Rule 26(b)(1), including the final sentence regarding information reasonably calculated to lead to the discovery of admissible evidence.

Under amended Rule 26(b)(1), which will become effective on December 1, 2015 (unless modified by the Supreme Court or Congress), the scope of discovery will be defined as "any nonprivileged matter that is relevant to any party's claim or defense and proportional to the needs of the case, considering the importance of the issues at stake in the action, the amount in controversy, the parties' resources, the importance of the discovery in resolving the issues, and whether the burden or expense of the proposed discovery outweighs its likely benefit. Information within this scope of discovery need not be admissible in evidence to be discoverable." The Advisory Committee Notes point out that moving the proportionality provisions to Rule 26(b)(1) "does not place on the party seeking discovery the burden of addressing all proportionality considerations. Nor is the change intended to permit the opposing party to refuse discovery simply by making a boilerplate objection that it is not proportional."

Answer (A) is incorrect. This was the test for relevance until the 2000 amendments to Rule 26(b), but it is no longer correct.

Answer (B) is incorrect. Information need not be admissible in evidence to be discoverable.

Answer (D) is incorrect. Information relevant to the parties' claims and defenses is discoverable without a showing of good cause.

56. **Answer (C) is correct.** Prynne's sexual history, however fascinating, is not related to the issues in the lawsuit. Relevance requires a relationship between the information to be discovered, the elements of claims and defenses, and the facts that tend to prove or disprove those claims or defenses. In this case the issues are whether Nanny Nation was negligent or grossly negligent in hiring and training Hibbins, whether it defrauded the plaintiffs, whether that conduct was the cause of the plaintiff's damages, and the extent of those damages. In order for the information about Prynne's sex life to be "relevant," it would have to make some fact of consequence to those issues more likely or less likely than it would be without the information about Prynne's sex life. Because that is not the case, the information is not relevant and therefore not discoverable.

Answer (A) is incorrect. Some information that bears on the credibility of a witness' testimony is relevant for discovery purposes. For example, information that might show a bias, or information that shows that a person is untruthful, might be relevant for purposes of impeachment. A person's sexual history is not, in a case unrelated to that history, apt to shed any light on the accuracy of the person's testimony and so is not discoverable for purposes of impeachment.

Answer (B) is incorrect. While a party waives certain privileges and privacy interests by bringing a lawsuit, the waiver extends only to things relevant to the issues in the action, not to any facet of her life.

Answer (D) is incorrect. If the possibility that a witness might answer any random question untruthfully made that question relevant, because the untruthfulness would be a basis for impeachment, then there would be no limits to discovery relevance.

57. **Answer (C) is correct.** Rule 26(b) requires that discoverable material be relevant to the claims and defenses of the parties. The plaintiffs' claims require proof of causation — that Nanny Nation's alleged wrongful acts were the cause of the harm to Pearl and to her parents. One part of causation is that Hibbins' behavior caused the traffic accident that harmed Pearl. Witnesses to the accident may have information relevant to whose behavior caused the accident. Access to these witnesses, whether by informal interview or by deposition, will allow Nanny Nation to ask questions concerning causation. Some or all of them may be called to testify at trial. This discovery request is, thus, relevant within the meaning of Rule 26(b)(1).

Answer (A) is incorrect. While the extent of Hibbins' intoxication may be relevant to the cause of the accident, and to the link between Nanny Nation's hiring and training practices and the accident, it is not the only relevant issue in the case.

Answer (B) is incorrect. The names themselves do not need to be admissible. *See* Fed. R. Civ. P. 26(b).

Answer (D) is incorrect. It overstates the scope of discovery. Prynne's lawyers may talk to people who end up knowing nothing of relevance to the case. In addition, a question phrased in terms of "whom did you interview while investigating this case" would be an improper request for attorney work product. (*See* Topic 15.)

58. Under Rule 26(a)(1), Prynne will have had to disclose the names and contact information for individuals who may be used to support Prynne's case. This might include witnesses to the car wreck, but only if those witnesses' version of events is helpful to Prynne. Only by sending an interrogatory asking for *all* persons with knowledge of this information can Nanny Nation be sure that Prynne has disclosed the identity of people of whom Prynne is aware with both favorable and unfavorable information.

59. **Answer (B) is correct.** Because Holgrave's claim for damages includes lost income from his law practice, documents that might tend to support or rebut that claim are relevant. This request, however, is not well tailored to discover those documents. Every piece of paper ever generated by Holgrave's law practice will not be relevant to income; most, in fact, will not. The request thus, on its face, requests documents that do not relate to any of the claims or defenses in the case.

Answer (A) is incorrect. While some of the requested documents will be relevant, most will not be.

Answer (C) is incorrect. Information relevant to damages is discoverable through the normal discovery devices.

Answer (D) is incorrect. All of the documents are not relevant. It is correct, however, that some of the documents called for by the request will take the form of communications between attorney and client and will thus be protected by attorney-client privilege. (*See* Topic 16.)

60. The definition of relevance for discovery purposes creates a direct tie to the pleadings. Discoverability requires relevance to the "claims and defenses" of the parties, and those claims and defenses will be contained in their pleadings. Discovery, however, is designed to provide the parties with further information to prepare their claims and defenses for trial, and to further refine the issues in dispute between the parties. This approach is consistent with the philosophy of the FRCP that cases should be disposed of on the merits and that all relevant information should be available to all of the parties.

TOPIC 15: ANSWERS
DISCOVERY: WORK PRODUCT

61. **Answer (B) is correct.** Rule 26(b)(3) protects such material from discovery absent a showing of substantial need for the information and the party's inability to secure the substantial equivalent of the information without undue hardship. The rule derives from the Supreme Court's landmark case, *Hickman v. Taylor*, 329 U.S. 495 (1947), which recognized protection for trial preparation materials. Rule 26(b)(3), however, is only a partial codification of *Hickman* because it does not cover intangible work product (such as the attorney's thoughts that have not been reduced to writing). *Hickman* itself continues to cover such information.

    Answer (A) is incorrect. Materials must have been prepared in anticipation of litigation to qualify as work product. Confidentiality alone is not enough.

    Answer (C) is incorrect. This answer describes attorney-client privilege. Some of this material may not qualify as work product. For example, work product protection would be lacking if the material is not prepared in anticipation of litigation.

    Answer (D) is incorrect. Although the list of persons who may prepare work product is broad ("prepared . . . by or for another party or its representative (including the other party's attorney, consultant, surety, indemnitor, insurer, or agent)"), material prepared by a person who is not the party's agent, prepared for his own purposes, would not meet the requirements of Rule 26(b)(3).

62. **Answer (C) is correct.** The material was prepared in anticipation of litigation by a party's agent, and so it is work product. Because the notes were prepared by the private investigator and appear to record only facts, they would be ordinary rather than opinion work product. Had they included opinions and strategies, they would instead qualify as opinion work product. Ordinary work product can be overcome by a showing of substantial need/undue hardship, and so it is also significant that Nanny Nation could itself interview or depose these neighbors and thereby get the substantial equivalent of the information in the notes. It does not matter that the neighbors might be more forthcoming to Prynne's representative than to Nanny Nation.

    Answer (A) is incorrect. Work product can be created by persons other than a party's lawyers.

    Answer (B) is incorrect. As set out above, unless these notes reflect mental impressions and opinions, they are ordinary rather than opinion work product.

    Answer (D) is incorrect. It is the time and purpose for making the notes, not the timing of the events they describe, that is important to whether the "anticipation of litigation" test is met.

63. This information is relevant and not privileged. While you might at first think this would be covered by the work product doctrine, work product protection shields "material" prepared

in anticipation of litigation. It also protects intangible thoughts and strategies a party or its agents may have. Work product does not protect underlying information from discovery. In *Hickman v. Taylor*, 329 U.S. 495 (1947), the original work product case, the Supreme Court noted that the doctrine did not shield relevant information from litigation because a party could ask "searching interrogatories" to get the needed information. Prynne could not ask "what did you learn from investigating our claims." But she can ask about the nature of Hibbins' training and her reaction to it.

64. **Answer (A) is correct.** Nanny Nation's recruiting policies are relevant to Prynne's claims of negligent screening of nannies. This review was done before Pearl's injury — clearly before Prynne anticipated a lawsuit. Sometimes an investigation done in anticipation of a particular type of litigation will qualify as work product, even though it was not done in anticipation of this particular plaintiff's claim. But nothing in this question suggests that the review was done for any purpose other than internal quality control, so it fails the "anticipation of litigation" test and is therefore not work product.

Answer (B) is incorrect. As noted above, it was not done in anticipation of litigation and so it is not work product.

Answer (C) is incorrect. If the report were work product, Prynne would not be able to satisfy the substantial need/undue hardship test to overcome the protection. The information about Nanny Nation's hiring practices is available to Prynne through other discovery devices, such as deposing people with knowledge and requesting documents that would reveal those practices. Prynne would therefore not be able to show that she was unable to get the substantial equivalent of the information without undue hardship.

Answer (D) is incorrect. It is unlikely that locating a single report made a little over a year ago would be so burdensome as to preclude discovery.

65. **Answer (C) is correct.** The investigator was hired to investigate Hibbins' background in anticipation of litigation, and therefore the tape of his interview with Pyncheon would qualify as work product. Because it is a verbatim transcript of a fact-based interview, it would most likely be ordinary rather than opinion work product. However, Pyncheon has become unavailable to provide this information to Prynne. This is the kind of case in which the discovering party may be able to meet the test for overcoming the protection normally provided to ordinary work product. Pyncheon can neither be interviewed nor deposed to get access to the information on the tape. Nor could other residents of the village be compelled to give evidence against their wishes. It is quite likely that the tape would be ordered produced.

Answer (A) is incorrect. It is protected as ordinary work product, but the substantial need/undue hardship override makes the "no" part of the answer incorrect.

Answer (B) is incorrect. Assuming that this tape does not reveal any mental impressions or strategies, it would be categorized as ordinary rather than opinion work product.

Answer (D) is incorrect. Relevant information is only discoverable if it is not protected by a privilege — the discovery privileges shield from discovery information that would otherwise be relevant and discoverable.

66. **Answer (B) is correct.** These interview notes, taken by the lawyer in anticipation of litigation, reveal his thoughts and strategies about the suit, so they are opinion work

product.

Answer (A) is incorrect. The evaluative comments make these notes opinion rather than ordinary work product.

Answer (C) is incorrect. Even if they were ordinary work product (and it might be possible to redact the evaluative comments, leaving a portion of the notes that do not disclose mental impressions), the substantial need/undue hardship test could not be met. Prynne could herself interview or depose Holgrave's former boss. If anything, this non-party witness is more available to Prynne than to Nanny Nation.

Answer (D) is incorrect. The fact that Holgrave's boss was not the client of the interviewer means that the notes are not protected by the attorney-client privilege. It does not prevent them from being protected as work product.

67. The Supreme Court in *Hickman v. Taylor*, 329 U.S. 495 (1947), gave several reasons for protecting work product. The Justices argued that if work product were discoverable, parties would engage in various kinds of undesirable behavior such as: (1) sharp practices like withholding documents or producing "red herrings"; (2) inadequately preparing cases for trial due to fear of discovery or lazy appropriation of opposing counsel's work; and (3) inadequate documentation of investigations. The court also feared that discovery of work product materials would have a demoralizing effect on lawyers, damaging the "welfare and tone" of the legal profession. The doctrine protects communications generated in anticipation of litigation and parties' litigation strategies. The existence of the doctrine, however, increases the cost of trial preparation for both sides, increases the cost to parties and the courts of disputing work product issues, and in some cases hides important information from discovering parties.

TOPIC 16: DISCOVERY: ATTORNEY-CLIENT PRIVILEGE

ANSWERS

68. **Answer (C) is correct.** While work product protection requires anticipation of litigation, communications between attorney and client can be privileged even when litigation is far from their minds if the communication is for the purpose of securing legal advice.

    Answer (A) is incorrect. Confidentiality *is* a requirement for attorney-client privilege to apply. The communication in question must be made in confidence, and it must remain in confidence or the privilege will be lost.

    Answer (B) is incorrect. In order to receive the protection of the attorney-client privilege, the communication must have been made in order to secure legal advice. So, for example, a communication with an attorney made in order to get business advice would not be protected by the privilege.

    Answer (D) is incorrect. Communications that were privileged when made can lose their privileged character if they are revealed to persons outside the attorney-client relationship. For example, if a client writes a memo to his attorney, asking for legal advice, and then later shows that memo to a friend to see the friend's reaction, the privilege has been waived.

69. **Answer (C) is correct.** When the "client" in question is a corporation rather than a human, it is sometimes difficult to identify which employees of the corporation can qualify as the "client" for purposes of the attorney-client privilege. Different states have adopted different tests. In a state-law based claim in federal court, the federal court will apply state privilege law; in federal question cases, it will apply a federal rule. Some states use a "control group" test: only employees who are high enough in the corporate hierarchy to seek legal advice and act on it qualify as "clients." Other states use a "subject matter" test. Lower level employees can also generate privileged communications as the "client" if these communications are necessary for the lawyer to get the information needed to properly advise the client. Matthew Maule, the Vice President for Human Resources, would probably qualify as a "client" under either test. He is probably high enough up in Nanny Nation's hierarchy to be a member of the control group, and his information about the recruitment and training of nannies makes him a person whose information is important to the lawyer in representing Nanny Nation. If this were a federal claim, it would be governed by *Upjohn Co. v. United States*, 449 U.S. 383 (1981), which did not specifically adopt either the control group or subject matter test, but it did extend the privilege to cover corporate communications involving lower level employees who have the information needed by the lawyer to advise the client.

    Answer (A) is incorrect, because it implies that Maule would not be a client under the control group test.

    Answer (B) is incorrect, because it implies that Maule would not be a client under the subject matter test.

    Answer (D) is incorrect, assuming that the questionnaire process meets the other requirements for attorney-client privilege, including confidentiality.

70. **Answer (D) is correct.** In a majority of jurisdictions, a communication between an attorney and the corporate client's *former* employee is not covered by the attorney-client privilege. The Supreme Court reserved this question in the *Upjohn* case, but most courts would hold that Chillingworth is not a "client." Because he is not a client, the communication is not protected by attorney-client privilege. Note that the questionnaire may be protected under the work product doctrine. (*See* Topic 15.)

Answers (A), (B), and (C) are incorrect because each one assumes that the Chillingworth questionnaire is protected by some version of the attorney-client privilege.

71. Because the direct question is ruled out by discovery privileges, Prynne must use ingenuity and determination to identify alternative sources of the information she wants. She will need to identify persons with knowledge of the hiring of Hibbins through automatic initial disclosures and interrogatories asking for this information. She will then need to depose some or all of them to see what they know, and to ask them who else might have relevant information. Prynne will need to request the production of documents that might relate to Hibbins' recruitment and hiring, and she will need to draft the request specifically enough to elicit the information she wants without being so specific that Nanny Nation can interpret the request not to include relevant documents. She may also try informal investigation (not using the power of the court to compel answers) about Hibbins, her background, and her hiring.

TOPIC 17: ANSWERS
DISCOVERY: EXPERT WITNESSES

72. Parties sometimes retain experts not to testify at trial but to assist them in preparation of their cases for trial. This type of witness is protected by a privilege contained in Rule 26(b)(4), and generally may not be deposed. Hawthorne is such an expert. However, the rule also recognizes that under certain unusual circumstances it may be unfair to protect a consulting expert witness from discovery. For example, a party may have retained all of the experts in a narrow field, or the consulting expert may have done destructive testing on an item at issue in the lawsuit. Under these kinds of "exceptional circumstances," discovery concerning the consulting expert is allowed. There is no indication that these exceptional circumstances apply here, however.

73. **Answer (A) is correct.** The protections from discovery provided by Rule 26(b)(4) only apply to experts retained in anticipation of litigation. Here, Bellingham has worked for Nanny Nation for a long time, and his information and opinions were not developed in anticipation of litigation but as part of the normal course of Nanny Nation's business.

    Answer (B) is incorrect. Although not the type of expert protected by Rule 26(b)(4), Bellingham is a person whose experience and training qualify him as an expert. Some of his testimony will be factual — for example, his knowledge of Nanny Nation's practices and the recommendations he made — but that does not negate his expert status. He would still be allowed to testify as to opinions, a privilege not generally accorded to lay witnesses.

    Answer (C) is incorrect. As noted above, because Bellingham was not retained in anticipation of litigation, his knowledge cannot be shielded from discovery by designating him as a consulting expert.

    Answer (D) is incorrect. While employees may sometimes, prospectively only, be designated as consulting experts for purposes of their work in assisting with the lawsuit, it is certainly not true that this may always be done. And even when such designation is allowed, pre-existing knowledge remains discoverable.

74. The answer to this question depends on the type of information shared. Rule 26(b)(4) protects certain information from discovery by treating it as trial-preparation material. This includes: (a) drafts of any report or disclosure required under Rule 26(a)(2), regardless of the form in which the draft is recorded; and (b) communications between the party's attorney and experts required to prepare a report, except to the extent that the communications relate to the expert's compensation, identify facts or data that the attorney provided and that the expert considered in forming the opinions to be expressed, or identify assumptions that the attorney provided and that the expert relied on in forming the opinions to be expressed. Therefore, Prynne/Holgrave could discover only communications in which Nanny Nation's attorney provided Bobbins with facts or data that Bobbins considered, or assumptions on which Bobbins will rely in giving her testimony.

75. Parties use experts for different reasons in the litigation process. Often the substantive law requires expert testimony in support of a cause of action, and even when it is not so required, it may aid the trier of fact. Parties therefore retain expert witnesses in order to testify on their behalf. It is important to maximize the reliability of this testimony. Opposing parties will therefore cross-examine the expert. In order to make this cross-examination meaningful, parties are allowed considerable discovery about the expert's opinion, the information underlying that opinion, and any biases that the expert might have. Other experts are used only to aid the parties in their preparation for trial. In technical areas, the expert may help the lawyer frame discovery requests and interpret information as it comes in. Because these experts will not testify, and therefore will not be cross-examined, their assistance falls within the zone of privacy provided for trial preparation.

TOPIC 18: DISCOVERY DEVICES — ANSWERS

76. **Answer (C) is the best answer.** The kind of information Prynne seeks can be effectively discovered by framing accurate questions and getting the answers under oath. Interrogatories can be sent to Nanny Nation, as it is a party to the lawsuit, and they are well suited to this type of specific background information.

Answer (A) is not the best answer because it suggests using a request for admission. This device would be less effective, because if Prynne is incorrect in the request Nanny Nation's only response will be "denied," not accurate substitute information.

Answer (B) is not the best answer because it suggests using a request for production of documents. While this might succeed in developing some of the desired information, it also might fail to do so. Parties are not required to create documents that did not exist in order to produce them. Nanny Nation, therefore, would only need to produce whatever it has in the way of corporate documents and organizational charts. They might be incomplete or outdated. Or they might not exist at all. So while such a request would be helpful, it would not be sufficient.

Answer (D) is not the best answer because it suggests deposing Nanny Nation's Director of Human Resources (DHR). Such a deposition might result in the information desired, if the DHR knows the information. He might or might not have accurate information about the company's official name and organizational status. He might or might not know the names and job titles of all relevant employees and contact information for them. An interrogatory, by contrast, can require an answer based on the collective knowledge of Nanny Nation's personnel. In addition, there are limits on the length of any one deposition, and Prynne might prefer to use her time with the DHR for narrative information more directly related to her claims. Finally, a deposition would be far more expensive than an interrogatory as a way to acquire this kind of specific information.

77. **Answer (D) is the best answer.** Sometimes a party's physical or mental condition is very important to the issues in the lawsuit. When it is, Rule 35 allows the court to order that person to submit to a medical examination tailored to the condition in question, by a doctor to be named in the order. An examination will only be ordered if the party's condition is "in controversy" and if the party desiring the examination can show "good cause" for the examination. In this case, Pearl's injuries and current condition are central to most of the plaintiffs' claims for damages. It is likely that a judge would order the examination to take place.

Answer (A) is not the best answer because it suggests a request for admission. This would not be as helpful. The most likely response — "denied" — leaves Nanny Nation without any further information about Pearl's condition.

Answer (B) is not the best answer because it suggests a request for production of Pearl's medical records. Such a request would be helpful. However, the reports are likely to record only the observations and opinions of Pearl's treating physician. If Nanny Nation wants an independent evaluation, it will want an examination in addition to the reports, so the Rule 35 examination will be necessary.

Answer (C) is not the best answer because it suggests interrogatories. Specific interrogatories might elicit specific information about Pearl's medical condition and treatment. However, the answers are likely to be brief (they are generally drafted with the aid of counsel) and will again be based on plaintiffs' perception of Pearl's injuries. Also keep in mind that the rules limit the number of interrogatories that can be sent to any one party.

78. Holgrave must produce these documents. The rules require parties to produce not only documents currently in their possession but also documents in the party's "control." This includes any documents that the party has the legal right to obtain on demand. Documents held by a party's attorney, expert, insurance company, accountant, or agent have been held to be within the party's control. In this case, Holgrave can get the documents from his accountant and, therefore, the request to Holgrave to produce the documents is proper.

79. **Answer (B) is the best answer.** When information is held by an entity rather than a human, it may be difficult for an outsider to know the identity of the persons within the organization who have the information they are seeking. Forcing an opposing party to repeatedly notice individuals for deposition, only to be told that that individual does not have the required information, would be extremely inefficient for all concerned. Therefore, Rule 30(b)(6) allows a party to "name as the deponent a public or private corporation, a partnership, an association, a governmental agency, or other entity" and describe with reasonable particularity the matters for examination. The named organization must then designate one or more persons who consent to testify on its behalf. The organization may set out the matters on which the person will testify. This allows Prynne to depose witnesses with knowledge of all the topics she names. The disadvantage of this procedure is that Nanny Nation is likely to name, insofar as possible, only individuals whose testimony will help Nanny Nation.

Answer (A) is less correct. Prynne could notice individual Nanny Nation employees by name. The danger, as noted above, is that she will waste time and money deposing people who do not have the needed information and will fail to depose people who do.

Answer (C) is incorrect. Prynne can depose the DHR. However, the DHR at his deposition will not be compelled to acquire information he does not have. He can instead answer that he does not know.

Answer (D) is less correct. Hibbins is not a party to the lawsuit. If Hibbins remains in England, Prynne cannot take her deposition without her consent. And even if Hibbins consents, she may not be aware of all of the individuals within Nanny Nation who know about her hiring and training, so her answer might be incomplete.

80. **Answer (B) is correct.** Poppins is not a party to the lawsuit, and so in order to depose its DHR a subpoena must be issued and served on the witness. Prynne could choose to subpoena "Poppins Ltd." and include a list of topics for the deposition, forcing Poppins to identify the relevant witnesses. Or Prynne could subpoena the DHR personally. In neither case would a notice of deposition suffice. The subpoena can also include a document list that, like a request for production of documents, must describe the desired documents with

"reasonable particularity." *See* Rule 34(b).

Answer (A) is incorrect. Because Poppins is not a party, a notice will not compel the attendance of a witness at a deposition.

Answer (C) is incorrect. Nanny Nation does not control Poppins, Poppins is not an employee of Nanny Nation, and so there is no way to compel Nanny Nation to produce another company's employee for deposition.

Answer (D) is incorrect. There are devices to secure information from non-parties before trial, and subpoenas for deposition (with or without documents) are the most common.

81. Rule 30(d)(1) provides that absent stipulation or court order a person's deposition is limited to a single day of seven hours.

82. Rule 33(a)(1) provides that a party may serve no more than 25 interrogatories, including discrete subparts, on any other party. Additional interrogatories can be served if allowed by stipulation or court order.

83. Prynne should begin by researching the substantive law to see what she will need to prove in order to prevail, both on liability and on damage claims. She should then consider what information will be needed to prove each element of each claim and each item of damages. Some of the information will be available to her outside the formal discovery process (e.g., information about her own actions and her own damages). Other information requires formal discovery. She will first receive automatic initial disclosures from Nanny Nation. She must then strategize, as to each type of information required, what discovery device(s) will best secure this information. In many cases, a party begins by sending interrogatories to identify persons with knowledge and relevant documents, as well as basic background information. The party then follows this with a request for production of the documents identified, and finally takes the depositions of the persons with the most crucial knowledge (depositions being expensive forms of discovery, and time being limited). During the process, Prynne should continue to compare the information she is getting with the information needed, in light of the proof requirements of the substantive law.

TOPIC 19: ANSWERS
DISCOVERY: ELECTRONICALLY STORED INFORMATION

84. It is likely that a company like Kliban, which does extensive business over the internet, maintains a number of its files in electronic form. In addition, a majority of modern businesses of any kind maintain significant amounts of digital information such as word processing documents, spreadsheets, data files, e-mail, text messages, voice mail, internet search records, and the like. To search only for hard copy documents would ignore significant sources of information. However, discovery of the electronically stored information raises logistical issues that are best dealt with early. Eliot's lawyer should therefore do his or her best to learn, before the discovery conference, what formats Eliot (or the firm) is best able to handle. Before and during the conference, the lawyer would want to learn what kind of records Kliban maintains, whether they are accessible in the everyday course of business, and the various formats that the data is kept in. Eliot will want Kliban to agree to produce the data in a searchable format. He will also want Kliban to agree to cease destruction of any data relevant to this case, whether routine or intentional. Given the allegations of dishonest behavior in this case, Eliot will likely want Kliban to produce records in a format that includes embedded data, including information about changes in documents and their authors, rather than a format that strips out such information.

85. **Answer (B) is the best answer.** While the rule allows the requesting party to ask for a format, and the producing party to suggest a format, neither is absolute and in the absence of agreement it is the judge rather than any particular party who makes the decision. Answer (B) states the default rule.

    Answers (A) and (C) are incorrect for the same reason. While the requesting party can specify a format that it prefers, the producing party may object to the requested format.

    Answer (D) is incorrect. There is no absolute right to convert documents to.pdf format. (It is correct, however, that conversion of documents to hard copy is objectionable since a non-searchable format is not reasonably usable.) As the Advisory Committee Notes point out, "If the responding party ordinarily maintains the information it is producing in a way that makes it searchable by electronic means, the information should not be produced in a form that removes or significantly degrades this feature."

86. **Answer (D) is the best answer.** Once Kliban knew that documents were likely to be relevant to the litigation, and certainly once the "litigation hold" was agreed to, it had a duty to preserve the data. This means that both tech support personnel and company employees generally need to be instructed to preserve information. The ignorance of badly-instructed technical employees is not a valid excuse. Here, where the plaintiff's complaint alleges that the stock sale was circumstantial evidence of the company's knowledge of tainted food, it should have been obvious that documents relating to the stock sale would be relevant to the litigation. Kliban may try to rely on the "safe harbor" provision of Rule 37(e): "Absent exceptional circumstances, a court may not impose sanctions under these rules on a party for failing to provide electronically stored information lost as a result of the routine, good-

faith operation of an electronic information system." However, Pound's deletion of his information is not the type of operation envisioned by this rule, and there is also a strong argument that his deletions were not done in good faith. The court may order Kliban to pay the cost of the more expensive production from the less accessible files, because its actions made that access necessary. Eliot's request is sufficiently targeted, is relevant to his claims, and its centrality to the dispute between the parties makes it appropriate for the court to order production at Kliban's expense.

Effective December 1, 2015 (unless modified by the Supreme Court or Congress), Rule 37(e) will be significantly changed. Retitled "Failure to Preserve Electronically Stored Information," the rule will state,

> If electronically stored information that should have been preserved in the anticipation or conduct of litigation is lost because a party failed to take reasonable steps to preserve it, and it cannot be restored or replaced through additional discovery, the court:
>
> (1) upon finding prejudice to another party from loss of the information, may order measures no greater than necessary to cure the prejudice; or
>
> (2) only upon finding that the party acted with the intent to deprive another party of the information's use in the litigation may:
>
> A. presume that the lost information was unfavorable to the party;
>
> B. instruct the jury that it may or must presume the information was unfavorable to the party; or
>
> C. dismiss the action or enter a default judgment.

Answer (A) is inapplicable for the reasons stated above. In addition, the Advisory Committee Notes point out that even routine, good faith deletion may still justify the court — not as a "sanction" but as a discovery management tool — in requiring the responding party to make greater efforts to provide relevant information.

Answer (B) is not as correct. It is true that the producing party normally pays the costs of production, but in situations involving ESI that is not reasonably accessible, courts have the discretion to allocate some of the costs of production to the discovering party, and may also order a preliminary sampling of information rather than a full search. Neither the scope of production nor the cost allocation is automatic.

Answer (C) is also less correct. Kliban will, undoubtedly, claim that the ESI is not reasonably accessible. However, its culpability in creating that situation means that it may be required to shoulder the cost of the more expensive search and production.

TOPIC 20: DISCOVERY SANCTIONS

ANSWERS

87. **Answer (A) is correct.** Nanny Nation has responded to Prynne's request but has not complied fully. Rule 37 controls the tools available to the court to encourage parties to comply with the discovery rules. Prynne must file a motion to compel production of the documents, but Rule 37(a)(1) requires the motion to contain "a certification that the movant has in good faith conferred or attempted to confer with the person or party failing to make disclosure or discovery in an effort to obtain it without court action." Prynne must begin by attempting in good faith to contact Nanny Nation and work out their disagreement. If no agreement can be reached, Rule 37(a)(3) provides for a motion to compel. Rule 37(a)(5) allows the successful party to recover the expenses of making the motion, including attorney's fees, unless Nanny Nation's opposition was substantially justified or other circumstances make the award of expenses unjust.

    Answer (B) is incorrect. Prynne must first at least attempt to confer with Nanny Nation or risk the wrath of the court and the loss of expenses even if she prevails.

    Answer (C) is incorrect. A serious sanction such as striking an answer (sometimes referred to as a "death penalty" sanction) is not allowed when a party has merely objected to making certain discovery. The more severe sanctions of Rule 37(b) do not become available until a party has failed to comply with a court order, or if a party completely fails to appear at a properly noticed deposition or completely fails to respond to interrogatories or document production requests. In addition, Supreme Court case law has placed limits on death penalty sanctions based on the Due Process Clause of the U.S. Constitution. *See, e.g., Societe Internationale Pour Participations Industrielles et Commerciales v. Rogers*, 357 U.S. 197 (1958). A party must be guilty of willfulness, bad faith, or other fault before the court may order litigation-ending sanctions.

    Answer (D) is incorrect both because it omits the required conference and because it goes too quickly to severe sanctions.

88. Rule 37(c) describes the sanctions available for failure to make required disclosures under Rule 26(a). Note first that these disclosures must be supplemented, as provided in Rule 26(e), if the party learns that the information disclosed was incomplete or incorrect. At some point, Nanny Nation must have realized that it had failed to disclose this "very important witness," making its previous answer incomplete. This will often be the case, as the automatic initial disclosures come very early in the litigation. By failing to include the witness' name initially or in a supplemental response, Nanny Nation has violated the disclosure rules. Unless such failure to disclose is harmless, which is unlikely in the case of a key witness, Rule 37(c) provides that the party is not permitted to use the witness not disclosed as evidence. The rule further provides that in addition (or instead), the court may impose other appropriate sanctions, and Rule 37(c) incorporates by reference the other sanctions in Rule 37, including both attorney's fees and the more severe sanctions of Rule 37(b)(2). Rule 37(c) also allows the court to inform the jury of the failure to make disclosures.

89. While courts have been split on this issue, the better rule has always been that objections should be specific and informative. Effective December 1, 2015, the language of Rule 34 will make this explicit. Amended Rule 34(b)(2)(C) will provide: "An objection must state whether any responsive materials are being withheld on the basis of that objection." As the Advisory Committee Notes explain,

> An objection may state that a request is overbroad, but if the objection recognizes that some part of the request is appropriate, the objection should state the scope that is not overbroad. Examples would be a statement that the responding party will limit the search to documents or electronically stored information created within a given period of time prior to the events in suit, or to specified sources. When there is such an objection, the statement of what has been withheld can properly identify as matter "withheld" anything beyond the scope of the search specified in the objection. . . . [Rule 34(b)(2)(C)] should end the confusion that frequently arises when a producing party states several objections and still produces information, leaving the requesting party uncertain whether any relevant and responsive information has been withheld on the basis of the objection.

TOPIC 21: ANSWERS
IINVOLUNTARY DISMISSALS AND DEFAULT JUDGMENTS

90. **Answer C is correct.** Rule 41(b) authorizes district judges to dismiss an action "[i]f the plaintiff fails to prosecute [the action] or to comply with these rules or a court order." Rule 41(b) itself envisions dismissals following a motion to dismiss, stating that under these circumstances, "a defendant may move to dismiss the action or any claim against it." Nevertheless, in *Link v. Wabash R. Co.*, 370 U.S. 626, 630-632 (1962), the Supreme Court held that the district court has "inherent power" to do so on its own initiative and without prior notice of the court's intention to dismiss the action. This power is justified by the need to prevent undue delays in the disposition of pending cases and to avoid congestion. Whether dismissal with prejudice is justified depends on all the circumstances of the case, but is authorized by Rule 41(b).

    Answer A is incorrect. Prior notice of the court's intent to dismiss based on the plaintiff's absence from the pretrial conference and the totality of the circumstances is not required. The availability of the remedy of reinstatement under the liberal standards provided by Rule 60(b)(1) renders the lack of prior notice and hearing of less consequence. *Link v. Wabash R. Co.*, 370 U.S. 626, 633-634 (1962).

    Answer B is incorrect. As explained in *Link v. Wabash R. Co.*, dismissal of a plaintiff's claim because of his counsel's unexcused conduct is not an unjust penalty because the plaintiff chose his attorney and the normal rule in civil litigation is that each party "is deemed bound by the acts of his lawyer-agent." *Link v. Wabash R. Co.*, 370 U.S. 626, 634-635 (1962).

    Answer (D) is incorrect because answers A and B are incorrect.

91. **Answer (D) is the correct answer.** Rule 55(a) provides that when a party against whom a judgment for affirmative relief is sought has failed to plead or otherwise defend, and that failure is shown by affidavit or otherwise, the clerk must enter the party's default. Fed. R. Civ. P. 55(a). Entry of default against the party who has failed to defend requires proof by "affidavit or otherwise" that the party was served as provided in Rule 4(l). Except for service by a United States marshal or deputy marshal, proof must be made by the server's affidavit. Fed. R. Civ. P. 4(l). Because the court clerk is not authorized to enter the default judgment unless the claim is "for a sum certain or a sum that can be made certain by computation," the plaintiff must apply to the court for a default judgment for the damages sought in the complaint. Fed. R. Civ. P. 55(b)(1)-(2).

    Answers (A) and (B) are incorrect. The court clerk must enter a party's default in the court's records, but may not enter a default judgment unless the claim is "for a sum certain or a sum that can be made certain by computation." Fed. R. Civ. P. 55(b)(1). Margie's tort claim against Jim Bob is for unliquidated damages, not for a sum certain. Hence, only the judge may enter judgment by default. Fed. R. Civ. P. 55(b). In such cases, the judge will need to determine the amount of damages at a prove-up hearing, which may be conducted by a master appointed by the court needed to perform an accounting or to resolve a difficult damages computation (*see* Fed. R. Civ. P. 53(a)(1)(B)) or by a magistrate judge. Fed. R. Civ.

P. 55(b)(2).

Answer (C) is incorrect because neither the clerk's entry of default nor the entry of a default judgment is automatic.

92. **Answer (B) is the best answer.** Rule 55(c) provides that the trial court may set aside an entry of default for "good cause." Fed. R. Civ. P. 5(c). Typically, courts are guided by three factors when determining good cause: (1) whether the default was willful or culpable; (2) whether granting relief from the default would prejudice the opposing party; and (3) whether the defaulted party has a meritorious defense. *See, e.g., Effjohn Int'l Cruise Holdings, Inc. v. A& L Sales, Inc.*, 346 F.3d 552, 563 (5th Cir. 2003). Rule 55(c) also provides that the court may relieve a party from a final judgment for "good cause" and it may set aside a default judgment under Rule 60(b) for "mistake, inadvertence, surprise, or excusable neglect" on motion made "within a reasonable time . . . no more than a year after entry of the judgment." *See* Fed. R. Civ. P. 60(b). The same factors that are used by trial courts to determine "good cause" for setting aside the clerk's entry of default are used by trial courts to determine whether sufficient grounds exist for setting aside default judgments under Rule 60(b). *See Rogers v. Hartford Life & Accident Ins. Co.*, 167 F.3d 933, 938 (5th Cir. 1999).

Under Rule 60(b), a court may impose "just terms" for granting the defaulted party relief from the default judgment. Fed. R. Civ. P. 60(b). The most commonly imposed term is that the defaulting party must reimburse the plaintiff for attorney's fees and costs incurred in securing entry of default and the default judgment and in defending the default.

In any case, most circuits follow the traditional policy that default judgments are disfavored because judgments should be based on the merits. *See Lacy v. Sitel Corp.*, 227 F.3d 290, 293 (5th Cir. 2000). Based on the foregoing, both the entry of default and any default judgment rendered against Jim Bob will probably be vulnerable to a direct attack in the trial court or on appeal.

Answer (A) is not a good answer because the trial court is not required to grant a default judgment and may consider any appropriate factors in refusing to do so, including the sufficiency of the complaint, the merits of the plaintiff's claim, the defendant's inadvertence or excusable neglect, and the sum of money at stake in the action, among others.

Answers (C) and (D) are not correct. Answer (C) is not correct because Jim Bob is not entitled to notice of the default prove-up hearing because he has not appeared in the action personally or by a representative. *See* Fed. R. Civ. P. 55(b)(2). This makes Answer (D) incorrect.

93. If Margie's claim is liquidated because it is "for a sum certain or a sum that can be made certain by computation the clerk — on the plaintiff's request, with an affidavit showing the amount due — must enter judgment for that amount and costs against a defendant who has been defaulted for not appearing and who is neither a minor nor an incompetent person." Fed. R. Civ. P. 55(b)(1).

TOPIC 22: ANSWERS
SUMMARY JUDGMENT: SUMMARY JUDGMENT BURDENS

94. **Answer (C) is correct.** A summary judgment ruling is a prediction. The court, by looking at discovery products plus affidavits, declarations, and other materials must predict whether, if the case were allowed to go to trial, there would be a genuine issue of material fact to be tried. At trial, on the other hand, the parties have actually presented live testimony, documents, and other physical evidence and the judge is deciding whether this evidence is sufficient for a reasonable jury to find in favor of the party with the burden of production.

Answer (A) is incorrect. The movant in either case must convince the court that there is or will be no legally sufficient evidence in favor of the non-movant.

Answer (B) is incorrect. The question in both cases is whether the party with the burden has produced a record on which a reasonable jury could find in its favor.

Answer (D) is incorrect. In both cases, the court is to view the evidence and take inferences in the light most favorable to the non-movant. In neither case is the court supposed to make decisions about credibility or to weigh the evidence.

95. **Answer (B) is correct.** For many years after the adoption of the FRCP, the summary judgment motion was disfavored. This attitude was reflected in the movant's burden. Although at trial the plaintiff will have the burden of production on every element of her cause of action, for summary judgment purposes that burden was flipped. In order to show that the defendant was entitled to summary judgment based on the weakness of the plaintiff's case, the defendant had to assume a burden he would not have at trial. He had to *disprove* some element of the plaintiff's claim before he would be entitled to summary judgment.

Answer (A) is incorrect. Demonstrating the existence of a fact issue on the plaintiff's cause of action merely demonstrates that the plaintiff is entitled to have her case decided by the jury.

Answer (C) is incorrect. Negating a single element sufficed. Because the plaintiff has to prove every element of her cause of action, eliminating one was enough to show that the plaintiff could not prevail and the defendant was entitled to summary judgment.

Answer (D) is incorrect. Merely pointing out the likely weaknesses in the plaintiff's case, while sufficient at trial, was not enough in the summary judgment context.

96. **Answer (A) is correct.** Referring to the movant's burden, Justice Harlan seemed to indicate that Kress had to negate the existence of a conspiracy to refuse service and to arrest Adickes. This could have been done by filing an affidavit that no police officer was in the store at the relevant time. Because Kress did not meet this burden, Adickes was not required to respond and provide evidence that the officer was in the store.

Answer (B) is incorrect. Justice Harlan's opinion does not focus on Kress' attack on

Adickes' evidence, but rather on Kress' own summary judgment evidence designed to show the lack of conspiracy. His opinion states, "[a]s the moving party, [Kress] had the burden of showing the absence of a genuine issue as to any material fact, and for these purposes the material lodged must be viewed in the light most favorable to the opposing party." Harlan goes on to examine Kress' support for its motion: the store manager's deposition; the officers' affidavits. He also noted that Kress did not submit any affidavits from the food counter supervisor or from the waitress who actually refused to serve Adickes. He therefore concludes that Kress "failed to fulfill its initial burden of demonstrating what is a critical element in this aspect of the case — that there was no policeman in the store. . . . Because [Kress] did not meet its initial burden . . . [Adickes] was not required to come forward with suitable opposing affidavits."

Answer (C) is incorrect. The opinion does not discuss whether there had been adequate time for discovery.

Answer (D) is incorrect. Justice Harlan's opinion recognizes that once the movant has properly made and supported a motion for summary judgment, the non-movant must do more than simply rely on the contrary allegation in her complaint. The purpose of the 1963 amendment to former FRCP 56(e) was to overcome case law to the contrary.

97. **Answer (B) is correct.** *Celotex* rejects an approach under which a summary judgment movant must assume a burden he would not shoulder at trial. Thus, a defendant moving for summary judgment based on the weakness of the plaintiff's case does *not* need to negate some element of the cause of action. Instead, Justice Rehnquist's opinion allows the movant to "point out" the absence of evidence in the pretrial record.

Answer (A) is incorrect. See above.

Answer (C) is incorrect. Producing evidence showing that there is a material fact issue demonstrates that summary judgment would be improper.

Answer (D) is incorrect. While Justice Rehnquist did note that the plaintiff had had two years to do discovery, he did not list this as a prerequisite to the motion. Rule 56(b) (Rule 56(a) at the time of the *Celotex* opinion) provides that a party may move for summary judgment "at any time."

98. **Answer (A) is correct.** Justice White's separate opinion emphasized that a naked motion with a conclusory statement that the plaintiff has no evidence would not meet the movant's burden.

Answer (B) is incorrect. Justice White's opinion does not require the moving party to negate anything.

Answer (C) is incorrect. Justice White specifically notes that a party need not depose witnesses to create a summary judgment record.

Answer (D) is incorrect. As noted above, simply moving for summary judgment does not require the non-movant to respond.

99. **Answer (D) is correct.** Once a motion for summary judgment has been properly made and supported, the non-movant must convince the court that it has some evidence to support its case, enough so a reasonable jury could find in its favor. This can be done by "(A) citing to particular parts of materials in the record, including depositions, documents, electronically

stored information, affidavits or declarations, stipulations (including those made for purposes of the motion only), admissions, interrogatory answers, or other materials; or (B) showing that the materials cited do not establish the absence or presence of a genuine dispute, or that an adverse party cannot produce admissible evidence to support the fact." Rule 56(c)(1). The summary judgment proof does not have to be in admissible form, but it does have to be evidence that can be put in admissible form. "A party may object that the material cited to support or dispute a fact cannot be presented in a form that would be admissible in evidence." Rule 56(c)(2). This is because evidence that will not be admissible will not be available to help the non-movant meet its burden of production at trial. The summary judgment proof does not need to be direct evidence, but it does have to support at least a reasonable inference in the non-movant's favor.

Answer (A) is incorrect. The evidence need not be in admissible form. (Note that some courts may have local rules to the contrary.)

Answer (B) is incorrect. Pointing to allegations in pleadings, even if they are sworn to, is not sufficient to demonstrate the existence of a fact issue. Former Rule 56(e) specifically addressed this issue, saying: "When a motion for summary judgment is made and supported as provided in this rule, an adverse party may not rest upon the mere allegations or denials of the adverse party's pleading, but the adverse party's response, by affidavits or as otherwise provided by this rule, must set forth specific facts showing that there is a genuine issue for trial." The current version of Rule 56, effective December 1, 2010, no longer contains this provision, but it is implicit in the Rule's requirement in subdivision (c) that a party "asserting that a fact cannot be or is genuinely disputed must support the assertion" with specified materials, which do not include the party's pleadings.

Answer (C) is only partly correct. The non-movant may point to evidence in the record at the time the summary judgment motion is filed, but it is not limited to such a response. It can also create new summary judgment evidence, such as affidavits and declarations, or provide the court with documents not formerly in the record, to demonstrate that a fact issue exists.

100. **Answer (B) is correct.** The court ruling on a motion for summary judgment must look at the evidence in the light most favorable to the non-movant. The court is not supposed to weigh evidence, or to decide which of competing reasonable inferences is the most probable.

Answer (A) is incorrect. It is the non-movant, not the movant, in whose favor inferences are to be drawn if reasonable.

Answer (C) is incorrect. The court is not supposed to weigh evidence, but only to decide whether there is some legally sufficient evidence in the non-movant's favor.

Answer (D) is incorrect. At one time some courts used the "any doubt" test: summary judgment was improper if there was any doubt. This approach is no longer used in federal courts. Just as plaintiffs must show the existence of more than a "scintilla" of evidence to avoid judgment as a matter of law, a plaintiff opposing summary judgment must show that an inference on its behalf would be a reasonable one.

101. The Supreme Court has made it easier for parties without the burden of proof at trial to achieve summary judgment in their favor, and has encouraged trial courts to grant summary judgment. Without having to make a significant showing of its own, and without producing any of its own evidence, a defendant can move for summary judgment. Even if the motion is

not granted, the defendant will get the benefit of a preview of the plaintiff's case and will force the plaintiff to spend time and money putting its evidence in proper summary judgment form. Systemically, it shifts power from juries to judges. The benefit of this approach is that it allows the court to dispose of non-meritorious claims more expeditiously, protecting defendants from the expense of litigation. The cost is that it creates a procedural disadvantage for plaintiffs, diminishes the role of the civil jury, and runs the risk that meritorious cases will be improperly eliminated. It also may increase the cost to the court system if it leads to the filing of numerous summary judgment motions that require court time but that are not granted.

TOPIC 23: SUMMARY JUDGMENT: THE BURDENS APPLIED — ANSWERS

102. **Answer (B) is correct.** It is not entirely clear whether this motion meets the requirements of Rule 56 and the *Celotex* trilogy. The motion was filed very early in the lawsuit, and it is fairly conclusory in nature. Pre-discovery summary judgment motions should be the exception rather than the rule, but the rule does permit early motions. The motion does cite a particular part of the record (Sarah's deposition testimony). This is very similar to the *Celotex* case, in which defendant Celotex pointed to the plaintiff's interrogatory answer to demonstrate the plaintiff's lack of evidence. *Celotex Corp. v. Catrett*, 477 U.S. 317 (1986). It would therefore be strategically dangerous for the plaintiffs to ignore this motion and risk the chance of losing their chance to respond. Because they have no evidence at this time, their best bet is to ask the court for more time to respond under Rule 56(d). This will require the plaintiffs to present affidavits or declarations explaining why they cannot at this time present facts essential to justify their opposition. The court has the power to defer considering the motion, deny it, allow more time to obtain affidavits or declarations or take discovery, or issue other appropriate orders. For example, the court may require the plaintiffs to describe the discovery they intend to seek, explain how that discovery would preclude the entry of summary judgment, and explain why that discovery could not have been done earlier. Having to reveal this is in itself a strategic disadvantage, but that damage may be outweighed by the danger that the court will consider and grant the motion for summary judgment.

    Answer (A) is incorrect. While it is probably true that the plaintiffs have not had enough time for discovery, ignoring the motion is a dangerous choice, as discussed above, especially given Sarah's deposition testimony.

    Answer (C) is incorrect. The problem states that the plaintiffs have no evidence. If they have some, it would be wise to consider whether they could put it in a form to present to the court. They might, for example, hire an expert witness who will study the situation and sign an affidavit opining that HH's negligence caused the chandelier to fall. The answer is incorrect, however, in stating that the evidence must be in admissible form. In *Celotex*, for example, the Court was willing to consider a letter written by the decedent's former employer which, although itself inadmissible as hearsay, demonstrated that the letter writer could be called as a witness to testify to relevant information within his personal knowledge. However, if the plaintiffs were to present material that could not be *put* into admissible form, the defendants could object and the information could not be used to avoid summary judgment.

    Answer (D) is incorrect. HH does not need to disprove the plaintiffs' claim in order to be entitled to summary judgment.

103. **Answer (C) is correct.** The parties' disagreement about the effect of the release centers on legal rather than factual issues. They agree that the release exists and that the plaintiffs signed it. They disagree about the legal effect of the release. HH argues that the release is

enforceable and covers the plaintiffs' claims. The plaintiffs argue that the release is unenforceable as applied to claims of the defendant's own negligence, and their legal argument is correct (for purposes of this question, anyway). Therefore, the court should deny the motion for summary judgment based on enforcement of the release. This denial is not based on the existence of a fact issue. Because the release is unenforceable even if signed, the question of whether or not the plaintiffs signed it is not a "material" fact.

Answers (A) and (D) are incorrect. Because the release is not enforceable as a matter of substantive law, it does not matter if the plaintiffs signed it, so they have no need to try to demonstrate that they did not.

Answer (B) is incorrect. Neither Rule 56 nor case law implementing it prohibit successive summary judgment motions. Recall that in *Celotex* itself the Court was considering a second motion for summary judgment. Successive motions might annoy the trial court, but they are not improper. Note, though, that some courts' local rules may prohibit multiple summary judgment motions.

104. **Answer (C) is correct.** With this motion, HH is attempting to disprove an element of the plaintiffs' claim. While not required, this would certainly suffice to show that the plaintiffs cannot succeed. The affidavit testimony of the expert witness appears to cover the relevant issues and to be within the appropriate area of expertise. The plaintiffs could have responded in a way to defeat summary judgment, as by questioning the factual basis of the expert's opinion or by countering with an expert of their own, but given the plaintiffs' failure to respond, the court could properly grant summary judgment to the defendant.

Answer (A) is incorrect. Canvassing the discovery record and pointing out the lack of evidence to support the plaintiff is one way to show entitlement to summary judgment, but it is not the only way.

Answer (B) is incorrect. Expert testimony can form the basis of a motion for summary judgment. In certain cases, trial courts have the authority under *Daubert v. Merrell Dow Pharms., Inc.*, 509 U.S. 579 (1993), to exclude expert testimony as unreliable. In such a case, the expert's affidavit could be used neither to support summary judgment nor to oppose it. Absent such a situation, however, expert deposition testimony or affidavits can be considered in summary judgment proceedings when live expert testimony would be proper at trial.

Answer (D) is incorrect. The non-movant's failure to respond may create a situation in which the court may grant summary judgment, but this is not inevitable. If the movant has failed to meet its initial burden, summary judgment would be improper despite the lack of a response. Even if the movant has made a strong argument that there is no genuine dispute as to a material fact, the trial court has some discretion to deny summary judgment and allow further factual development of the case. Behind the word "shall" in Rule 56(a) lies a heated debate between those who think that the court "must" grant summary judgment if the movant meets its burden and those who think that the court should retain at least a degree of discretion to deny summary judgment if, for example, the record is very thin, easily available evidence has not been presented to the court, or for other reasons (and that the rule means that the judge "may" grant summary judgment). In order to help guide appellate courts, Rule 56(a) now requires the court to "state on the record the reason for granting or denying the motion."

105. **Answer (D) is correct.** While the defendant's expert's affidavit in isolation might have

justified summary judgment (see the previous question), the situation here is different. There are now two expert witnesses, each having examined the available evidence, who have reached different conclusions about the cause of the chandelier accident. In the absence of a *Daubert* problem with one of the experts, this merely demonstrates the existence of a genuine issue of material fact. That fact issue makes summary judgment improper. The judge is not to compare the testimony of the two experts and decide which one he finds more convincing; that is the jury's job.

Answers (A) and (B) are incorrect. As noted above, the judge's role in considering a motion for summary judgment is not to weigh or compare evidence, but merely to decide the threshold issue of whether there is a genuine issue of material fact to go to the jury.

Answer (C) is incorrect. The defendant's motion on its own was adequately supported (see the preceding question). The plaintiff's motion on its own might at least have justified a partial summary judgment (it would not be sufficient to prove the plaintiffs' damages as a matter of law). It is the conflict demonstrated by the two expert affidavits that leads to the need to deny the motion rather than the defects in either motion standing alone.

106. The court should deny the defendant's motion for summary judgment. The plaintiffs' response was sufficient to avoid summary judgment. The letter from the insurance adjuster is not itself admissible. Even if properly authenticated, it would constitute hearsay. If the insurance adjuster were to testify at trial, however, and his opinion were based on his observations and established expertise, his testimony would constitute some evidence of breach and causation. The plaintiffs would improve their response by making clear that they intend to call the adjuster as a witness at trial.

The deposition of Rhea Max will not be as helpful. It was taken in another proceeding in which HH was not a party, and the former testimony exception to the hearsay rule will not make this deposition testimony admissible. Because Max is dead, she cannot be called as a witness in this case.

If the court believes that more information about the installation of the chandelier is required, the plaintiffs have pointed to crucial evidence (the carpenter's testimony) that has been unavailable to them. Their position would be stronger if they explain the efforts they have made to show that they have been diligent and explain to the court reason they think the carpenter's testimony will help them. By coming up with a plausible plan to get access to the carpenter's testimony they could ask the court to delay its ruling until this evidence is available.

TOPIC 24:	**ANSWERS**
RIGHT TO JURY TRIAL	

107. **Answer (D) is correct.** The Supreme Court's decisions in *Beacon Theatres, Inc. v. Westover*, 359 U.S. 500 (1959), and *Dairy Queen, Inc. v. Wood*, 369 U.S. 469 (1962), hold that where both legal claims and equitable claims are presented in a single case, the right to a jury trial exists for factual questions, regardless of whether the case would previously have been categorized as basically equitable or basically legal. Hence, because the money damages claim presents legal issues, all factual questions involving those issues (i.e., the elements of the trespass claim, including damages) must be tried to a jury, assuming a timely and proper demand is made for a jury trial.

    Answer (A) is probably incorrect. If the issues are entirely equitable, there is no right to a jury trial. It is possible that one or more of the issues in Fred's trespass case for injunctive relief could be classified as legal under the Court's celebrated footnote in *Ross v. Bernhard*, 396 U.S. 531, 538 n.10 (1970) — "As our cases indicate, the 'legal' nature of an issue is determined by considering, first, the pre-merger custom with reference to such questions; second, the remedy sought; and, third, the practical abilities and limitations of juries." But based on the factors identified, that classification is unlikely.

    Answer (B) is incorrect. This action for damages is entirely legal.

    Answer (C) is incorrect. The incidental character of the money damages claim does not matter. The equitable "clean up" doctrine has been eliminated by *Beacon Theatres* and *Dairy Queen*.

108. **Answer (C) is correct.** The Supreme Court has held that the constitutional guarantee of a jury trial is applicable to antitrust damage suits, whether or not equitable (non-jury) claims are joined with the legal claim. *Beacon Theatres, Inc. v. Westover*, 359 U.S. 500 (1959).

    Answer (A) is not correct. The "gist" or principal thrust of the action does not matter. That is not the test.

    Answer (B) is not correct. Although the Sherman and Robinson Patman Acts are federal statutes enacted after 1791, the Seventh Amendment is not confined to causes of action recognized by English common law in 1791. The Seventh Amendment guarantee applies to actions for damages, particularly if there is an analogous common law cause of action that was triable to an English jury in 1791.

    Answer (D) is not correct for the same reason that Answer (C) is correct.

109. Although the Third Circuit has recognized a complex case exception grounded on the Due Process Clause of the Fifth Amendment for antitrust suits that are so complicated that a jury is unable to decide in a rational manner (*see In re Japanese Elec. Prods. Antitrust Litig.*, 631 F.2d 1069 (3d Cir. 1980)), there is probably no complex case exception. *See In re U.S. Fin. Sec. Litig.*, 609 F.2d 411 (9th Cir. 1979). Similarly, the celebrated footnote in *Ross*

v. Bernhard, 396 U.S. 531, 538 n.10 (1970), cannot be stretched to make complex cases equitable.

TOPIC 25: SELECTION AND COMPOSITION OF JURIES	ANSWERS

110. **Answer (B) is correct.** This question has both a constitutional and rule-based dimension. For many years, it was believed that because the Seventh Amendment preserves the right to jury trial that existed at common law, it also required twelve-member juries. However, in *Colgrove v. Battin*, 413 U.S. 149 (1973), the Supreme Court upheld a local rule providing for six-member juries, arguing that the Constitution defines the type of case for which juries are guaranteed, not the "incidents" of trial by jury such as the number of jurors. Today, Rule 48 provides that a jury "must begin with at least 6 and no more than 12 members, and each juror must participate in the verdict unless excused under Rule 47(c)." Rule 47(c), in turn, allows the court to excuse a sitting juror for "good cause." In theory, this would even allow a jury of less than six to render a verdict, but at least in criminal cases, the Supreme Court has found a number less than six to be constitutionally deficient, and Rule 48(b) allows a verdict of less than six only on the parties' agreement. For that reason, courts often choose more than six jurors to begin with, so that even if a juror needs to be excused for a personal emergency, six jurors will remain to render a verdict and a mistrial will be avoided.

Answer (A) is incorrect, although a jury of twelve is the historic requirement, and empirical research supports the argument that larger juries deliberate more thoroughly and effectively than smaller ones.

Answer (C) is incorrect as a general rule. Some districts, however, have adopted Local Rules that supplement Rule 48's provisions and choose a specific number between six and twelve. Some choose eight. Others instead list various factors that the court should consider in choosing a number. *See, e.g.*, Idaho Local Civil Rule 47.1.

Answer (D) is incorrect. While the court has a great deal of leeway in the 6-12 juror range, it could not go below six nor above twelve jurors without violating Rule 48. As noted above, it is also possible that a jury of less than six would be constitutionally impermissible.

111. **Answer (A) is correct.** Unless the parties agree otherwise, the verdict must be unanimous. Rule 48(b).

Answers (B), (C), and (D) are incorrect because they all envision non-unanimous verdicts. Note, however, that many state court systems allow for a non-unanimous (although often a super-majority) verdict in civil cases.

112. **Answer (D) is correct.** Peremptory challenges are those for which a party needs no explanation and do not require that the potential juror be disqualified by relationship, bias, or other problem. Given the availability of challenges for cause, and the potential of peremptory challenges to be improperly used in a discriminatory fashion (*see* 113 below), their numbers are limited. As 28 U.S.C. § 1870 provides, "[i]n civil cases, each party shall be entitled to three peremptory challenges. Several defendants or several plaintiffs may be considered as a single party for the purposes of making challenges." The statute actually provides the court with even a bit more leeway to allocate peremptory strikes to allow a full

and fair jury selection process, providing that "the court may allow additional peremptory challenges and permit them to be exercised separately or jointly." Rule 47(b) incorporates the statute by reference.

Answer (A) is incorrect. Rule 47(a) allows the court to permit the parties or their attorneys to examine prospective jurors. Although it also allows the court to be the only questioner, the judge must ask any of the additional questions requested by the parties that he or she considers proper. (Note, though, that it is extremely unusual for a trial court to be reversed for refusing to allow a question.)

Answer (B) is incorrect. A challenge for cause removes from the jury panel a person who is disqualified for reasons such as relationship to a party, financial interest in the case, or a pre-existing bias that would make it impossible for the juror to fairly judge the particular case. Because challenges for cause are designed to eliminate potential jurors whose service would be inappropriate for this case, there is no limit on the number of challenges for cause.

Answer (C) is incorrect. Litigants do not actually "choose" a jury (as one would choose a playground sports team) but rather de-select those potential jurors who they believe would be least sympathetic to their position. The goal of jury selection is to arrive at an impartial jury, through the process of allowing each party to eliminate a small number of people who, though not sufficiently biased to be challenged for cause, are likely to be more favorably disposed to the opponent's case.

113. **Answer (D) is the best answer.** Although peremptory challenges are a long-established part of the jury selection process, the Supreme Court has recognized that they have been used for invidious purposes and has carved out an exception. Beginning in the criminal case of *Batson v. Kentucky*, 476 U.S. 79 (1986), the Court has held that it violates the equal protection rights of both the litigant and the potential juror for a peremptory challenge to be exercised on the basis of race, national origin, or sex. This line of cases has also been recognized as applying in civil cases. In attempting to protect the continued use of peremptory strikes while disallowing discrimination, a *Batson* motion involves a three-step process. Step one requires the person challenging an opponent's use of peremptory challenges to make a *prima facie* case of discrimination — in other words, to provide enough evidence of possible discrimination to the judge to support an inference of discrimination. In this case, a showing that all three strikes were used to eliminate minority jurors likely meets this requirement.

If step one is successfully accomplished, step two requires the lawyer who exercised the challenged strikes to articulate a neutral, permissible reason for the strike. The reason can be silly or superstitious or even inaccurate — it just can't be based on an impermissible categorization. So, for example, Drayton's lawyer could not successfully defend the strike by saying, "I think African-American jurors will be unsympathetic to my client." On the other hand, "I struck Juror No. 3 because she is a teacher" would be a permissible, race-neutral explanation.

Once the race-neutral explanation has been made, it remains for the party challenging the strike to convince the court that it was done for a discriminatory purpose. Part of that process is often a demonstration that the race neutral reason is pretextual, which in turn is often done by showing that other jurors sharing the same characteristic were not challenged. In this example, Prentice might show that Drayton did not use peremptory challenges on Anglo teachers.

Batson has heightened our collective consciousness of discrimination in jury selection, and has changed the way we talk about the use of strikes, but has not been gigantically successful at rooting out subtle discrimination, because it is relatively easy to articulate a non-discriminatory reason for peremptory challenges. *See, e.g.*, *People v. Randall*, 671 N.E.2d 60, 65 (1996) (referring to "the charade that has become the *Batson* process" and giving examples of explanations that have been accepted as race-neutral). *See also* Jeffrey Bellin & Junichi P. Semitsu, *Widening* Batson's *Net to Ensnare More Than the Unapologetically Bigoted or Painfully Unimaginative Attorney*, 96 Cornell L. Rev. 1075 (2011).

Answers (A), (B), and (C) are not the best answers for the reasons stated above. [Answer (A) is inaccurate, and both (B) and (C) are true, making (D) the best answer.]

TOPIC 26: JURY INSTRUCTIONS: FORM AND OBJECTIONS

ANSWERS

114. **Answer (B) is the best answer.** Verdict formats are governed by Rule 49. Interestingly, the rule does not mention the most common format: the general verdict. That method of informing and questioning the jury was assumed; the methods mentioned in Rules 49(a) & (b) were recent innovations at the time the Federal Rules of Civil Procedure were adopted. Black's Law Dictionary defines a "general verdict" as "a verdict by which the jury finds in favor of one party or the other, as opposed to resolving specific fact questions." Although at one point in U.S. history, the jury was empowered to find both law and facts, today the judge must instruct the jury on relevant legal standards for liability and damages. In this case, Judge Haller might instruct the jury on the burden of proof, the definitions of negligence and causation, and the proper way to calculate damages. For the liability question, he would tell the jury that if they found that defendant Billy's Carwash was negligent, they should find for plaintiff Mona Vito and if not, they should find for defendant, and the jury's answer form might say something like "We, the jury, find for ________."

    Answer (A) is incorrect. As explained above, even with general verdicts, the judge is supposed to explain the law to the jury.

    Answer (C) is incorrect. Rule 49(a)(3) does give the judge discretion to use the special verdict, and that discretion is broad. The rule provides that the special verdict should request a finding on "*each* issue of fact." Use of the special verdict gives the judge more influence on the shape of the jury's deliberations, but the jury still exercises a constitutional power as fact finder. It would be improper for the judge to allow the jury to decide only issues about which he personally felt uncertain. (It is true, though, that if the special verdict inadvertently omits some necessary issues without objection, the parties are said to have waived the right to have the jury decide them.)

    Answer (D) is incorrect. Rule 49(b) provides the third verdict format option, the "general verdict with answers to written questions." Unlike the special verdict, in which the jury is to be asked each issue of fact, and unlike the general verdict, where the jury broadly decides the whole case, this option combines that broad general decision with a few focused questions — "*one or more issues of fact* that the jury must decide. The court must give the instructions and explanations necessary to enable the jury to render a general verdict and answer the questions in writing, and must direct the jury to do both." The written questions may be used to draw the jury's attention to specific sub-issues or to be sure that the general verdict is consistent with those specific findings.

115. **Answer (D) is correct.** Rule 51(a) allows parties to file requests for the jury instructions it wants the court to give before or at the close of the evidence (or at any earlier reasonable time that the court orders). After this point, requests are timely on issues that could not have been reasonably anticipated by an earlier deadline, and the court has the discretion to

consider untimely requests. Note that the requests should be furnished to every other party.

Answer (A) is incorrect. While the final pretrial conference is intended to result in a trial plan, Rule 16(e) does not require that jury instructions be part of the pretrial conference or order.

Answers (B) and (C) are incorrect because they are inconsistent with Rule 51(a).

116. **Answer (C) is correct.** Until Rule 51 was amended in 1987, judges were instructed to read the instructions to the jury at the conclusion of trial, after closing arguments. Since that amendment, however, the trial judge may choose to instruct the jury at either time: before or after the lawyers make their arguments. Proponents of instructing the jury prior to closing arguments note that it allows the lawyers to structure their arguments more clearly within the framework of the instructions, and thus focuses the jury very effectively on the decisions they will be asked to make.

Answers (A) and (B) are incorrect for the reason explained above; the judge has the discretion to read the charge at either time.

Answer (D) is incorrect. The instructions must be read in open court. Further (though this may surprise you) many judges do not provide juries with written copies of the instructions, even voluminous ones, despite empirical data showing that having a copy of the instructions improves juror performance.

117. **Answer (D) is correct and Answer (C) is incorrect.** Rule 51(b)(2) provides that the judge "must give the parties an opportunity to object on the record and out of the jury's hearing before the instructions and arguments are delivered" and that is what Judge Haller is doing. Further, Rule 51(c)(2) makes that objection timely if it is made at the hearing provided, unless the attorney is not informed of the instruction before the opportunity to object. Those rules mean that "object now" is the correct response. Answer (D) is preferable to Answer (C), because the court has some slight leeway to consider unpreserved plain error if it affects substantial rights. Rule 51(d)(2).

Answer (A) is incorrect because, except in the case of plain error, a timely trial objection is required.

Answer (B) is incorrect because Rule 51(c)(1) requires that objections be specific, "stating distinctly the matter objected to and the grounds for the objection."

118. **Answer (C) is correct.** Rule 49(a)(3) provides: "A party waives the right to a jury trial on any issue of fact raised by the pleadings or evidence but not submitted to the jury unless, before the jury retires, the party demands its submission to the jury. If the party does not demand submission, the court may make a finding on the issue. If the court makes no finding, it is considered to have made a finding consistent with its judgment on the special verdict." The issue of causation was not submitted to the jury, Billy's Carwash waived the right to that submission, the trial court made no finding, and so it is deemed made in a way that supports the trial court's judgment.

Answer (A) is incorrect. Because Billy's Carwash did not object to the omission of the causation element (or request a question on causation), it waived the right to have the jury decide that issue.

Answer (B) is incorrect. While the trial court could have made such a finding if the omission had been discovered before judgment was entered, the appellate court is instructed by Rule 49 to assume that the trial court has made a finding consistent with its judgment, and here the court's judgment for Mona Vito implies a finding that the negligence of the carwash was the proximate cause of the damage to Mona's car.

Answer (D) is incorrect. Courts are instructed to read the jury's answers as consistent when that is possible. Here we have no inconsistency. The jury found that the carwash was negligent and that Mona suffered damages, and both of those answers can be simultaneously factually and legally true. Conflicts are more common when the court submits a general verdict accompanied by interrogatories. It would likely be inconsistent in this case, for example, if the jury answered the general question "we find for the plaintiff" but also answered an interrogatory "no" that asked, "was Billy's Carwash negligent?"

TOPIC 27: ANSWERS

BURDENS OF PROOF AT TRIAL; PRIMA FACIE CASE AND PRESUMPTIONS

119. **Answer (A) is correct.** Ordinarily, the plaintiff has the burden both of production and persuasion on all of the elements of each cause of action. The burden of production can shift during trial (if, for example, Kate introduced such convincing evidence during her case in chief that no reasonable jury could fail to find for her, the burden of production would shift to Dave), but normally the burden of production for the plaintiff's own case is on the plaintiff, and the burden of persuasion stays with the plaintiff to prove her cause of action by a "preponderance of the evidence."

    Answer (B) is incorrect. The burden of production only shifts to Dave if Kate introduces evidence that is so conclusive that, in the absence of a rebuttal, it proves her claim as a matter of law. If Kate merely introduces enough evidence to meet her burden of production (i.e., to raise questions of fact for the jury on the elements of her claim), no burden of production shifts to Dave to introduce evidence to contest Kate's case-in-chief. Dave will have the opportunity to introduce rebuttal evidence, but he does not have the technical burden to do so to avoid judgment as a matter of law. This answer is correct in that the burden of persuasion remains on Kate.

    Answer (C) is incorrect. As noted above, the burden of production would only shift to Dave under limited circumstances, and the burden of persuasion would not shift to him.

    Answer (D) is incorrect. Dave has the burden of production and persuasion on his affirmative defense of contributory negligence (i.e., that Kate was negligent and that her negligence was the cause of the occurrence in question), but that does not give him either burden with regard to Kate's claim that Dave was negligent.

120. **Answer (B) is correct.** If Kate fails to produce evidence on which a reasonable jury could find for her, she has failed to meet her burden of production. This would entitle Dave to move for judgment as a matter of law and the judge could properly grant the motion rather than sending the case to the jury.

    Answer (A) is incorrect. If Kate meets her burden of production, producing enough evidence that a reasonable jury could find in her favor, it is the jury and not the judge who decides whether Kate has met her burden of persuasion. It would therefore be improper for the judge to take the case from the jury.

    Answer (C) is incorrect. While the Seventh Amendment does provide an important right to jury trial in civil cases, if there is no fact issue to decide there is no constitutional right to have a jury decide the case. Therefore, if Kate fails to meet her burden of production, the judge can properly take the case from the jury.

    Answer (D) is incorrect. As the plaintiff, Kate will go first in presenting her evidence. At the end of this phase of the trial, when Kate rests, Dave has had the opportunity to cross examine Kate's witnesses but has not yet had the opportunity to put on evidence of his own.

Although her case might appear very strong in isolation, Dave might be able to show its weaknesses with his own evidence. It is not at all irrelevant what evidence he might have. Only if the evidence for Kate remains conclusive after *both* Kate and Dave have rested and closed their cases may the judge grant judgment as a matter of law for Kate without sending the case to the jury.

121. **Answer (A) is correct.** The defendants have the burden of production and persuasion on almost all affirmative defenses; they must plead them, they must provide evidence to support them, and they must prove them by a preponderance of the evidence. The burden of persuasion on this issue will not shift but will stay on Dave throughout the case.

Answer (B) is incorrect. Dave has both the burden of persuasion and the burden of production on all the elements of his affirmative defense.

Answer (C) is incorrect. It would not be enough for Dave to carry the burdens on one element of contributory negligence. Unless there is enough evidence on *all* elements that a reasonable jury could find for Dave, evidence on one element will not be enough. Similarly, Dave must prove all the elements by a preponderance of the evidence.

Answer (D) is incorrect. As noted above, Dave has both burdens.

122. **Answer (C) is the best answer.** Federal Evidence Rule 302 provides that a presumption respecting a fact that is an element of a claim or defense as to which state law supplies the rule of decision is determined in accordance with state law. Fed. R. Evid. 302. This rule conforms the federal evidence rules to the requirements of the *Erie* doctrine. *See Cities Service Oil Co. v. Dunlap*, 308 U.S. 208, 212 (1939); *Palmer v. Hoffman*, 318 U.S. 109, 116-120 (1943).

Under Texas law (and probably the majority rule) as applied in automobile accident cases, when it is established that the driver of the vehicle is an employee of the owner of the vehicle, a rebuttable presumption arises that the employee was acting in the course and scope of employment at the time of the incident in question. *See Mitchell v. Ellis*, 374 S.W.2d 333, 335 (Tex. Civ. App.—Fort Worth 1963, writ ref'd) (regular employee driving employer's truck at time of accident). This presumption is based on the premise that the employer has better access to the facts than the claimant. *Salmon v. Hinojosa*, 538 S.W.2d 22, 24 (Tex. Civ. App.—San Antonio 1976, no writ).

Answers (A) and (D) are both incorrect. The mere fact of the defendant's ownership of the vehicle in question and employment of the driver is insufficient to prove the course and scope of employment element as a matter of law or as a matter of fact as a permissive inference. *See Robertson Tank Lines, Inc. v. Van Cleve*, 468 S.W.2d 354, 358 (Tex. 1971).

Answer (B) is also not correct. The presumption is not evidence. The presumption's only function is to shift the burden of production to the defendant. If the presumption is not rebutted by evidence that the employee was not within the course and scope of employment at the time of the incident in question, the course and scope element is established by it. But if the presumption is rebutted by the introduction of contrary evidence, the presumption "vanishes." *See Bell v. VPSI, Inc.*, 205 S.W.3d 706, 715-716 (Tex. App.—Fort Worth 2006, no pet.) (presumption rebutted by evidence driver was on personal business before accident).

123. **Answer (D) is correct.** This problem is meant to illustrate special rules for burden shifting that are applicable to employment discrimination cases under federal law. In order to ease

the burden on discrimination plaintiffs, the Supreme Court created a burden-shifting method of proof, when there is no direct evidence of an employer's discriminatory intent. *See Texas Dep't of Community Affairs v. Burdine*, 450 U.S. 248, 254 (1981); *McDonnell Douglas Corp. v. Green*, 411 U.S. 792, 793 (1973).

Under this approach, the plaintiff must make a prima facie case, which is done in age discrimination cases by showing the plaintiff: (1) suffered some adverse employment action, (2) was qualified for the position in question, (3) is a member of the protected class of persons older than 40 years of age, and (4) was replaced by someone outside the protected class, by someone younger or was otherwise discriminated against because of her age. *Reeves v. Sanderson Plumbing Prods, Inc.*, 530 U.S. 133, 142 (2000) ("[P]etitioner satisfied this burden here: (1) at the time he was fired, he was a member of the protected class (individuals who are at least 40 years of age, 29 U.S.C. § 631(c)), (ii) he was otherwise qualified for the position of . . . supervisor, (iii) he was discharged by respondent, and (iv) respondent successively hired three persons in their thirties to fill petitioner's position"). If this showing is made at trial or in response to a motion for summary judgment, by producing evidence of a prima facie case, the plaintiff is entitled to a rebuttable presumption of purposeful discrimination.

Once the plaintiff makes a prima facie showing, the burden shifts to the defendant to produce legally sufficient evidence of a legitimate nondiscriminatory purpose for the employment action. *McDonnell Douglas Corp.*, 411 U.S. at 802-803. In this context, the term "prima facie case" means the establishment of a rebuttable presumption of employment discrimination, but not necessarily enough evidence to permit the trier of fact to infer discrimination. *Texas Dept of Community Affairs v. Burdine*, 450 U.S. 248, 254 n.7 (1981). If the defendant does not meet its burden of production, the plaintiff is entitled to judgment as a matter of law based on the presumption. *Burdine*, *supra* at 254. But if the defendant meets this burden of production, the presumption bursts and the plaintiff must prove that the employer's legitimate nondiscriminatory reason for the adverse employment action was merely pretext for its discriminatory purpose. *See Reeves* at 142-143. Even though the presumption vanishes, ". . . the trier of fact may still consider the evidence establishing the plaintiff's prima facie case 'and the [reasonable] inferences properly drawn therefrom' . . . on the issue of whether the defendant's explanation is pretrextual."

For the foregoing reasons, **Answers (A), (B), and (C) are all correct answers**, but Answer (D) is the best answer, because it includes the entire process.

TOPIC 28: ANSWERS

MOTIONS FOR JUDGMENT AS A MATTER OF LAW: STANDARD AND SCOPE OF REVIEW

124. The court should grant the motion because although the Seventh Amendment affords McPherson the right to a trial by jury on all factual issues, expert testimony was necessary on the professional standard of care applicable to Dr. House and on the cause of McPherson's injuries. The right to a jury trial of factual issues (i.e., the right to have a jury determine factual questions concerning the elements of legal claims) depends on the production of legally probative evidence concerning the factual issues. Because the substantive law requires expert testimony in medical negligence cases to set the professional standard of care and, in most cases, to provide evidence of the cause-in-fact of the claimant's injuries, McPherson presented no legally sufficient evidence for a reasonable jury to find in her favor on the issues of negligence and causation.

125. **Answer (B) is probably correct.** One of the most important aspects of the right to jury trial under the Seventh Amendment to the Constitution is the jury's ability to draw inferences from circumstantial evidence. Because juries typically decide mixed questions of law and fact and because most cases do not involve clashes between direct evidence presented by eyeball (percipient) witnesses, the power to choose between opposing reasonable inferences is extremely significant. Neither the trial judge nor a reviewing court is at liberty to substitute its view for the jury's decision, as long as the inference drawn by the jury is reasonable. If reasonable minds can differ, the fact finder's choice is sustainable in the sense that it is supported by a legally sufficient evidentiary basis. Although News Ltd.'s evidence is probably sufficient to support the reasonable inference of Maurice's *de facto* membership in Creedlove, based on the totality of the evidence viewed in the light that is most favorable to the jury's finding, reasonable minds could differ. *See Reeves v. Sanderson Plumbing Prods., Inc.*, 530 U.S. 133, 150-151 (2000) (courts "must disregard all evidence favorable to the moving party that the jury is not required to believe"). Hence, News Ltd. is not entitled to judgment as a matter of law. The same would be true for Maurice.

Answer (A) is incorrect. Maurice's testimony may be unconvincing, but it is not incredible and lacking any probative value, such as if he had testified contrary to the laws of physics.

Answer (C) is probably incorrect. Maurice's so-called direct evidence about Creedlove does not negate the evidentiary value of any reasonable inference that could be drawn from the circumstantial evidence.

Answer (D) is incorrect. It is for the jury to decide the credibility of witnesses.

126. The trial court may grant the motion if the trial judge concludes that Maurice's testimony is unconvincing. In contrast to a jury trial, in a bench trial Rule 52(c) authorizes a trial judge to render judgment against a claimant on a claim or defense if the claimant "has been fully heard on an issue" and the court "finds against the party on that issue." This means that the trial judge can render judgment against a claimant after the claimant rests, if the judge does

not credit the claimant's evidence and finds that Maurice was a member of Creedlove.

127. Rule 50(b) treats a post-verdict motion as a renewed motion for a delayed directed verdict to avoid a direct clash with the Reexamination Clause of the Seventh Amendment, which states that "no fact tried by a jury, shall be otherwise re-examined in any Court of the United States, than according to the rules of the common law." Although the Supreme Court long ago determined that certain common law practices, somewhat different in form from directed verdict motions, were analogous to directed verdict motions such that the use of a directed verdict motion did not offend the Reexamination Clause, no common law analogs exist for post-verdict motions for judgment contrary to the verdict. Accordingly, to comply with the Seventh Amendment, the post-verdict motion, which actually is filed after judgment, must be characterized as a renewed motion leading to a delayed, but constitutionally valid, directed verdict. State constitutions (which govern trial practice in state courts) that do not contain Reexamination Clauses do not require renewed motions.

128. **Answer (D) is the best answer, because Answer (A) is clearly correct and Answer (C) is also correct.** In 2006, the Supreme Court resolved a split of authority between the circuits by holding that an appellant must renew a pre-verdict Rule 50(a) motion as specified in Rule 50(b) in order to make a sufficiency of the evidence challenge in the court of appeals. *Unitherm Food Systems, Inc. v. Swift-Eckrich, Inc.*, 546 U.S. 394 (2006); *see also Johnson v. New York, N.H. & H.R. Co.*, 344 U.S. 48 (1952). In other words, a denial of a pre-verdict Rule 50(a) motion is not reviewable on appeal unless a Rule 50(b) motion renews the Rule 50(a) motion after judgment. The Rule 50(a) motion is a prerequisite to a Rule 50(b) motion, but is not sufficient to preserve a legal insufficiency complaint. The *Unitherm* opinion also explains that the denial of a post-judgment motion for new trial can be a basis for appellate complaint concerning the sufficiency of the evidence. In this situation, the movant/appellant is entitled only to a new trial, not to a judgment in its favor. In *Unitherm*, the appellant did not request a new trial under Rule 59.

Answer (B) is incorrect for the same reasons.

129. No, denial of a summary judgment motion is not reviewable after full trial on the merits. The full record developed in court at trial supersedes the record existing at the time of the summary judgment motion, and the appeal should be taken from the trial. *Ortiz v. Jordan*, 562 U.S. 180 (2011). News Ltd. must use the motion for judgment as a matter of law under Rule 50 to preserve its right to make a "matter of law" challenge to the jury's verdict at trial and seek rendition of judgment in its favor.

TOPIC 29: ANSWERS
BENCH TRIALS; FINDINGS OF FACT AND CONCLUSIONS OF LAW

130. No. Although various appellate courts, including the Supreme Court, have criticized courts for rubber-stamping proposed findings of fact prepared by prevailing parties, it is now well established that even when the trial judge adopts proposed findings verbatim, the findings are regarded as those of the trial court and may be reversed only if clearly erroneous. *See Anderson v. Bessemer City*, 470 U.S. 564, 673 (1985).

131. **Answer (D) is the best answer because Answers (A) and (C) are both correct. Answer (A) is correct** because Rule 52(a)(6) states that "[f]indings of fact, whether based on oral or other evidence, must not be set aside unless clearly erroneous, and the reviewing court must give due regard to the trial court's opportunity to judge the witnesses' credibility." Under this standard, a fact finding is not "clearly erroneous" unless there is no probative evidence to support it or "although there is evidence to support it, the reviewing court on the entire evidence is left with the definite and firm conviction that a mistake has been committed." *Anderson v. Bessemer City*, 470 U.S. 564, 575 (1985). **Answer (C) is also correct** because the trial judge's conclusions of law are subject to de novo review on appeal. *See Bose Corp. v. Consumers Union of U.S., Inc.*, 466 U.S. 485, 500-501 (1984). This approach is followed because a judgment that rests on errors of law or a "misunderstanding of the governing rule" is entitled to no deference by a reviewing court.

Answer (B) is not correct. Rule 52(a)(5) states: "a party may later question the sufficiency of the evidence supporting the findings [for the first time on appeal], whether or not the party requested findings, objected to them, moved to amend them or moved for partial findings." *See* Fed. R. Civ. P. 52(a)(5).

132. Yes. Federal Rule 52(c) provides that a trial judge may issue a judgment against a party who "has been fully heard on an issue" when the trial "court finds against the party on the issue" with respect to a "claim or defense that, under the controlling law, can be maintained or defeated only with a favorable finding on the issue." Fed. R. Civ. P. 52(c); *see also* Fed. R. Civ. P. 52 Advisory Committee Notes, 2007 amendment ("The standards that govern judgment as a matter of law in a jury case have no bearing on a decision under Rule 52(c).").

TOPIC 30: ANSWERS

MOTIONS FOR NEW TRIAL & RULE 60(B) MOTIONS

133. **Answer (D) is correct.** Motions for new trial may be made and granted "for any reason for which a new trial has heretofore been granted in an action at law in federal court." Rule 59(a). This includes a lot of territory, including any error that occurred during the pretrial phase of the litigation or that occurred during trial. Significantly, however, the motion also may be used to challenge the verdict or a particular jury finding that is not supported by factually sufficient evidence, i.e., a verdict that is supported by some legally sufficient evidence but that is manifestly against the weight of the evidence.

Answer (A) is incorrect. Judge-made findings are generally inappropriate in a case tried to a jury.

Answer (B) is incorrect. Because the erroneous instructions actually favored Sunderland and Sunderland still lost, the problem lies elsewhere. However, it may be the case that the assessment of the sufficiency of the evidence would be affected by the erroneous charge.

Answer (C) is probably incorrect because the admission of improper evidence in a civil case normally does not entitle a complaining party to a new trial unless the entire case turned on the inadmissible evidence.

134. It is now clear that complaints concerning both the legal and the factual sufficiency of the evidence must be made in the trial court in order to challenge the sufficiency of the evidence on appeal. Legal sufficiency complaints are preserved by Rule 50(a) motions "renewed" as Rule 50(b) motions after judgments. Factual sufficiency complaints are preserved by Rule 59 motions for new trial. *Unitherm Food Systems, Inc. v. Swift-Eckrich, Inc.*, 546 U.S. 394 (2006).

135. **Answer (C) is correct.** Rule 50(b) provides expressly for alternative motions for new trial coupled with renewed motions for judgment.

Answer (A) is incorrect. Clark can move for judgment as a matter of law even if he had the burden of proof on the whole case, assuming compliance with Rule 50(b).

Answer (B) is incorrect. If the verdict is against the weight of the evidence, the remedy is a new trial, not a judgment contrary to the verdict.

Answer (D) is incorrect for the reasons stated above.

136. If the trial judge concludes that the jury's damage award is excessive as against the manifest weight of the evidence, the trial judge may grant a new trial. It is conceivable that the new trial could be granted on the issue of damages alone. A partial new trial is possible on an issue or issues that are separable without unfairness to the parties. Additionally, in cases of excessive verdicts, the trial judge can suggest a remittitur of the excess and condition the denial of a new trial on the acceptance by the plaintiff of the trial court's suggestion. On appeal, an abuse of discretion standard will be applied to the appellate issue of the factual

sufficiency of the evidence to support the finding.

137. **Answer (D) is correct because (A) and (B) are correct.** Duke has 28 days after entry of judgment to move for a new trial on legal or equitable grounds. However, Rule 60(b) provides additional time. A Rule 60(b) motion based on "mistake, inadvertence, surprise, or excusable neglect" may be made not more than one year after the entry of the judgment. Rule 60(c)(1).

Answer (A) is correct because the clerk is not authorized to enter a default judgment for unliquidated damages under Rule 55(b).

Answer (B) is correct for the reasons stated above.

Answer (C) is not correct. Judgments based on false testimony are not void, although they are subject to attack under Rule 60(b).

138. Duke can attack the judgment if Ace's affidavit was false or fraudulent. A Rule 60(b) motion based on fraud (whether previously called intrinsic or extrinsic), misrepresentation, or misconduct by an opposing party may be made "within a reasonable time" and no more than one year after the entry of the judgment. Rule 60(c)(1).

139. Rule 60(d) provides that an independent action may be brought to relieve a party from a judgment, and notes that Rule 60 does not limit a court's power to set aside a judgment for "fraud on the court."

TOPIC 31: ANSWERS
SUBJECT MATTER JURISDICTION: DIVERSITY OF CITIZENSHIP

140. **Answer (D) is correct.** The statute creating jurisdiction in cases involving citizens of different states (28 U.S.C. § 1332) has been interpreted to require complete diversity. In other words, no plaintiff can be a citizen of the same state as any defendant. In this case, the plaintiff is a citizen of Texas. One defendant, Mark, is a citizen of Mississippi, creating minimal diversity. However, defendant Acme is a corporation, and corporations are citizens both of their state of incorporation and of their principal place of business. Acme is therefore a citizen both of Alabama and of Texas. Therefore, both Tom and Acme are Texas citizens, destroying complete diversity.

    Answer (A) is incorrect. Diversity does exist between Tom and Mark, but this is not sufficient for federal court jurisdiction.

    Answer (B) is incorrect. It is the citizenship of plaintiffs vs. defendants that matters for purposes of diversity jurisdiction, not the citizenship of co-defendants. In fact, if the plaintiffs were from Texas and both defendants were from Mississippi, diversity jurisdiction would exist.

    Answer (C) is incorrect. As explained above, Tom and Acme are citizens of the same state because of the way corporate citizenship is determined.

141. Yes. Multiple parties on the same side of the lawsuit may be citizens of the same state, as long as all plaintiffs are diverse in citizenship from all defendants. Therefore, the fact that Clara and Carl are both from California, and that Ida and Irene are both from Illinois, does not destroy diversity.

142. **Answer (D) is correct.** A person when born acquires a domicile of origin (the parents' domicile). In order to change to a new domicile (a domicile of choice) one must intend to make the new place home for an indefinite period of time and must be physically present there at least briefly. Here, Pam has changed her domicile to Texas because she is a resident there and intends to make it her home. The fact that she has not yet secured a permanent job does not prevent Texas from being her domicile.

    Answer (A) is incorrect. Pennsylvania is her domicile of origin. It is also true that students, especially undergraduates, often have not changed domicile by going off to school. They tend to lack the necessary intent to make the location of the school a permanent home. Pam's return during the summers to her parents' home reinforces this belief here. But it is not true that students can never acquire a new domicile of choice.

    Answer (B) is incorrect. Under different circumstances, Pam might have changed her domicile to Massachusetts. She was physically present there. But her practice of returning home to Pennsylvania during the summers, her continuing financial dependence on her parents, and her apparent intention to leave Massachusetts upon graduation are indications that she did not change her domicile.

Answer (C) is incorrect. It is not clear whether Pam's domicile changed briefly to Virginia. If she considered it to be home, and had no intention of leaving at a fixed time, that might be true. It seems more likely, though, that Pam had already planned to leave Virginia to move to Texas to attend law school. In either case, her subsequent move to Texas with intent to stay there means that Virginia is not her domicile at this time.

143. **Answer (A) is correct.** The statement that Karen has always lived in Kansas indicates that Kansas is her domicile of origin. She has the required intent to make New York her home. However, she lacks the second requirement for acquiring a domicile of choice: presence at the new domicile. A person keeps her old domicile until she acquires a new one, and because she did not yet reach New York, she is still domiciled in Kansas.

Answer (B) is incorrect. Karen is present in Ohio, but she lacks the necessary intent to make it her home. If a person intends to leave at some fixed point in time, for example graduation from school or, as here, recovery from her injuries, she does not have the intent required to acquire a domicile of choice.

Answer (C) is incorrect. As explained above, intent alone is not enough for a change of domicile.

Answer (D) is incorrect. Everyone has a domicile at all times (it's just a rule — while there may be a "man without a country" there is no such thing as a "man without a domicile"). Traditionally, people had a single domicile for all purposes, although the more modern approach might recognize different domiciles for different purposes.

144. **Answer (B) is correct.** This question focuses on the timing of the domicile issue for purposes of diversity jurisdiction. At the time Mike's cause of action accrued, he was domiciled in (and hence a citizen of) Maine. However, he successfully changed his domicile to New Hampshire by moving there with the correct intent. It is his domicile at the time he files the lawsuit that determines his citizenship for purposes of diversity jurisdiction. While there is a statute forbidding improper or collusive joinder of parties to achieve diversity jurisdiction (28 U.S.C. § 1359), it does not apply to a bona fide change of domicile by a party to the suit.

Answer (A) is incorrect. It is his domicile at the time of commencement of the action, not at the time the cause of action arose, that counts.

Answer (C) is incorrect. Mike's change of citizenship does affect the existence of diversity jurisdiction.

Answer (D) is incorrect. The ownership of property is a factor that courts may consider in determining a person's domicile, but it is not determinative. For example, a person domiciled in New Jersey might own a summer home on Cape Cod and go there for a few weeks each summer, but the person's domicile would remain in New Jersey.

145. **Answer (C) is correct.** This claim could properly be brought in federal court based on diversity jurisdiction, because the parties are from different states and the amount in controversy is sufficient. Diversity jurisdiction, however, is just an option for the parties. The federal courts have concurrent jurisdiction with the state courts in diversity cases, and so these lawsuits can also be filed in state court. (Under certain circumstances, defendant sued

in state court may choose to "remove" the case to federal court. *See* Topic 31.)

Answer (A) is incorrect. There is complete diversity between Greg and Frank and the amount in controversy requirement is satisfied, but federal jurisdiction is not exclusive.

Answer (B) is incorrect. Although the purpose of diversity jurisdiction includes the protection of out-of-state defendants from local prejudice, that makes diversity jurisdiction available, not mandatory. And the facts of this question do not tell us whether Frank is being sued in Georgia or at home in Florida.

Answer (D) is incorrect. Neither diversity jurisdiction nor generic federal question jurisdiction is exclusive in the federal courts. There are a few federal statutes requiring certain kinds of federal claims to be brought in federal rather than state court, but this is the exception rather than the rule. In general, both diversity and federal question jurisdiction are concurrent with the state courts.

146. **Answer (D) is correct.** The Supreme Court has held that an unincorporated association is a citizen of the states of domicile of each member. *See, e.g., United Steelworkers of America v. R.H. Bouligny, Inc.*, 382 U.S. 145 (1965). Therefore, the Brotherhood of Bison is a citizen of Wisconsin, Illinois, and all the other states in which members are domiciled, including Minnesota. Because Marilyn, the plaintiff, is from Minnesota, this case lacks complete diversity and cannot be brought in federal court on that basis.

Answer (A) is incorrect. Although the principal place of business is significant in determining the citizenship of a corporation, the same is not true for an unincorporated association.

Answer (B) is incorrect. The domicile of a majority of members is not the only citizenship of an unincorporated association.

Answer (C) is incorrect. It can be difficult to get diversity jurisdiction when a party is an unincorporated association, because it may be a citizen of so many states. But it is not true that its citizenship can never form the basis of diversity jurisdiction.

147. **Answer (A) is correct.** For purposes of diversity jurisdiction, a class takes the citizenship of its named plaintiff(s). Here the only named plaintiff is Terry, a citizen of Tennessee. There are class members from every state, but their domiciles are not considered for purposes of diversity jurisdiction. Because defendant Cheap Computers is a citizen of Montana, the diversity requirement is satisfied.

Answer (B) is incorrect. It is true that some members of the class will be citizens of Montana, but their citizenship does not count unless they become named plaintiffs.

Answer (C) is incorrect. The diversity of citizenship requirement does indeed apply to class actions.

Answer (D) is incorrect. Because the citizenship of class members is not counted, Terry need not exclude citizens of Montana from the class in order to achieve complete diversity.

148. **Answer (C) is correct.** Although under traditional principles of diversity jurisdiction this case could not be maintained in federal court, the Multiparty, Multiforum Jurisdiction Act, 28 U.S.C. § 1369, creates jurisdiction for cases such as this. Because at least some of the plaintiffs are not citizens of either Utah or Delaware, there is minimal diversity. More than 75 people died in the accident, and UA "resides" in places in addition to Idaho, where a

substantial part of the accident took place. Note that under § 1369(c)(2), a corporation resides in "any State in which it is incorporated or licensed to do business or is doing business."

Answer (A) is incorrect because complete diversity is not required under § 1369.

Answer (B) is incorrect because UA is a citizen of both Delaware and Utah.

Answer (D) is incorrect because "substantial parts of the accident" taking place in multiple states is only one of the possible situations under which § 1369 creates jurisdiction.

149. **Answer (D) is correct.** In 2010, the U.S. Supreme Court resolved a split in the circuits regarding the proper test for determining a corporation's "principal place of business" under § 1332. After examining statutory language, legislative history, and based on the policy of making subject matter jurisdiction more easily predictable, the Court held that a corporation's principal place of business is its "nerve center" — "the place where a corporation's officers direct, control, and coordinate the corporation's activities. . . . [I]n practice it should normally be the place where the corporation maintains its headquarters — provided that the headquarters is the actual center of direction, control, and coordination, *i.e.*, the 'nerve center,' and not simply an office where the corporation holds its board meetings (for example, attended by directors and officers who have traveled there for the occasion)." *Hertz Corp. v. Friend*, 559 U.S. 77, 93 (2010).

Answers (A) and (B) are incorrect. Although prior to *Hertz* some circuits used those tests for principal place of business, they were rejected by the Court in its *Hertz* opinion.

Answer (C) is also incorrect. This is the test for corporate residence for purposes of venue, not citizenship for purposes of diversity jurisdiction.

150. **Answer (D) is the best answer, because answers (B) and (C) are both correct.** Answer (B) is correct because alienage jurisdiction is proper under § 1332(a)(2) in actions between a United States citizen and a corporation that is a citizen or subject of a foreign state. *See* 28 U.S.C. § 1332(a)(2) and (c). Answer (C) is correct because there is diversity of citizenship between Mark and Big Star Cycle Corporation, and § 1332(a)(3) makes jurisdiction proper even though Rhine Ludwig AG is joined as an additional party.

Answer (A) is incorrect. Corporations qualify as citizens or subjects of foreign states for the purpose of 28 U.S.C. § 1332. *See* 28 U.S.C. § 1352(c).

151. **Answer (A) is the best answer.** Because Jason is a permanent resident of the United States who is domiciled in California, he is not able to use alienage jurisdiction under Subsection 1332(a)(2) as amended in 2011.

Answer (B) is incorrect. Jurisdiction is not proper under § 1332(a)(3), which provides for original jurisdiction in cases between "citizens of different States and in which citizens or subjects of a foreign state are additional parties," because the case between Barbara and Pacific American Airlines is not between "citizens of different States," it is between a citizen of Canada and a corporate citizen of California and of Texas. Section 1332(a)(3) only helps when there is complete diversity between US citizens on both sides of the lawsuit. In those cases, the statute permits aliens on one or both sides of the dispute as additional parties.

Answer (C) is also incorrect for the same reason that Answer (A) is correct. Jason's permanent residence status means that he is not treated as a citizen of a foreign state, despite his actual Canadian citizenship.

TOPIC 32: ANSWERS
SUBJECT MATTER JURISDICTION: AMOUNT IN CONTROVERSY

152. **Answer (C) is correct.** In order for diversity jurisdiction to be proper, the amount in controversy must exceed $75,000, exclusive of interest and costs (28 U.S.C. § 1332). There are various rules regarding the circumstances under which multiple claims can be aggregated (added together) to reach the $75,000 threshold. All claims asserted by one plaintiff against the same defendant may be aggregated (although the same damages may not be counted twice). Here, Nick can add the two distinct claims to reach a total of $80,000.

    Answers (A) and (B) are incorrect. The claims will be added, as noted above.

    Answer (D) is incorrect. Even if Nick is due interest on this breach of contract claim, interest is not counted in computing the amount in controversy.

153. No. You cannot aggregate the claims of multiple plaintiffs even against a single defendant. This question is governed by a different aggregation rule. Claims asserted by multiple plaintiffs against the same defendant, or claims asserted by the same plaintiff against multiple defendants, cannot be aggregated. There is a small exception to this rule for a historical category of "common and undivided interest," but that exception would not apply here.

154. **Answer (A) is correct.** Although the general rule is that the claims of multiple plaintiffs cannot be aggregated, there is an exception for claims that are jointly held by multiple claimants. The exception is based on the concept that joint claims are brought by the joint claimants collectively.

    Answers (B), (C), and (D) are incorrect. There is only one claim made under the circumstances of the problem, so the amount is $100,000.

155. **Answer (B) is the correct answer.** Because the defendants are not jointly and severally liable for the entire amount owed to Alice under the two separate contracts, there is no aggregation.

    Answer (A) is incorrect for the same reason that (B) is correct.

    Answer (C) is incorrect because diversity is complete between Alice and each defendant. Co-defendants may be citizens of the same state without destroying diversity of citizenship.

    Answer (D) is incorrect because (C) is incorrect.

156. **Answer (B) is correct.** Under traditional principles of tort law, joint tortfeasors are each liable for the entire loss under circumstances making the injury indivisible. Although modern tort reform legislation has frequently modified this approach, if joint and several liability is a possible outcome under the law and the evidence, the claims can be aggregated.

    Answer (A) is incorrect for the same reason, i.e., joint and several liability is an exception to the normal nonaggregation rule.

Answer (C) is incorrect for the reasons stated in (B), i.e., either defendant could be liable for the entire loss.

Answer (D) is incorrect. Jurisdiction cannot depend on what is established at trial.

157. **Answer (B) is correct.** This question requires you to think about the difficulties in computing amount in controversy when the plaintiff seeks injunctive relief rather than money damages. The controversy must be quantified in some way. Case law is not entirely consistent in this area, but many courts measure the amount in controversy by the value of the claim to the plaintiff. One influential treatise advocates upholding jurisdiction if the amount exceeds the jurisdictional minimum from either plaintiff's or defendant's viewpoint. *See* 14 AA Wright, Miller & Cooper, Federal Practice and Procedure § 3703 (2011). Here, that means that the value of the claim is the difference in value of Susan's property with and without the shack. So although the cost to Nate of complying with the injunction would be only $300, it is most likely that the amount in controversy is $100,000.

Answer (A) is incorrect. Susan's land is not worthless even with the shack, and so the full value of the land is not the best measure of the amount in controversy.

Answer (C) is incorrect. Most courts will not measure the amount in controversy by the cost to the defendant. A minority of courts might do so. Some academics have advocated using the smaller number, on the theory that the parties could bargain for a resolution at that amount, but this is not the majority view.

Answer (D) is incorrect. Even though the plaintiff is not seeking monetary relief, an amount in controversy must be calculated if jurisdiction is based on diversity of citizenship.

158. **Answer (A) is correct.** Although the courts are not entirely consistent on this issue, the majority ignores the value of the counterclaim when computing the amount in controversy. *See* 14 AA Wright, Miller & Cooper, Federal Practice and Procedure § 3706 (2011). The plaintiff must establish a basis for jurisdiction without adding the counterclaim to reach $75,000.

Answer (B) is incorrect. Counterclaims are not aggregated with the primary claim even when they are compulsory.

Answer (C) is incorrect. Counterclaims are also not compared with the plaintiff's claim to determine how much money might ultimately change hands.

Answer (D) is incorrect. As noted above, counterclaims are not aggregated with the plaintiff's claim to compute the amount in controversy.

159. **Answer (A) is correct.** The court generally looks at the face of the plaintiff's complaint to determine the amount in controversy. However, if the plaintiff has requested damages that are legally unavailable, they will not be counted because they cannot be recovered whatever the facts of the case might turn out to be. Here, under the applicable law, the punitive damages are unavailable, so they may not be counted in computing the amount in controversy. The only remaining claim is for $15,000, well short of the required $75,000.

Answer (B) is incorrect. Courts will not try to predict whether the plaintiffs will really recover as much money as they have prayed for in computing the amount in controversy. Unless it appears to a legal certainty that the amount requested cannot be recovered, the plaintiff's complaint will determine the amount. This answer is therefore wrong because it indicates that it is the jury's probable reaction rather than the legal unavailability of the punitive damage claim that would defeat jurisdiction.

Answer (C) is incorrect. It is true that damages based on contract and tort theories can be aggregated (if they are different damages). That does not rescue the punitive damages in this case.

Answer (D) is incorrect. The problem is not whether Naomi's two types of damages can be added together, but that the $100,000 claim is legally invalid.

160. **Answer (D) is correct.** Even cases that otherwise meet the requirements for diversity jurisdiction based on their citizenship and the amount in controversy may fall outside of federal jurisdiction if they fall within an exception created by the courts. One such exception, applicable here, is the domestic relations exception. This exception was carved out by the Supreme Court long ago, based on a belief that such cases are better left to the state courts. See *Ankenbrandt v. Richards*, 504 U.S. 689 (1992), for a discussion of the doctrine. The other such exception is for probate proceedings.

Answer (A) is incorrect. Romeo has apparently changed his domicile to Rhode Island. But this still does not confer diversity jurisdiction over a divorce case.

Answers (B) and (C) are incorrect. The size of the marital estate is immaterial.

161. The court should deny the motion to dismiss. Plaintiffs, in their complaints, must plead the basis for federal jurisdiction. In diversity cases, this includes an allegation that the amount in controversy exceeds $75,000. If the existence of subject matter jurisdiction were to depend on the amount a plaintiff ultimately recovers, a number of cases could go through lengthy discovery and trial only to end up being thrown out of court when the plaintiff recovered less than the jurisdictional minimum. This inefficient result is avoided by the "legal certainty" rule. Only if the defendant can prove to a legal certainty that the plaintiff cannot recover the amount requested should it dismiss the case for insufficiency of the amount in controversy. The measure of damages is determined by the applicable substantive law. In a breach of contract case such as this, Heather may be entitled to recover lost profits if they were contemplated by the parties at the time of contracting. It is more difficult for new businesses to prove lost profits, because damages must be supported by evidence and cannot be completely speculative. It may be difficult for Heather, as a business without a track record, to prove lost profits, but you cannot say to a legal certainty that her damages would be less than $75,000.

TOPIC 33: ANSWERS
SUBJECT MATTER JURISDICTION: FEDERAL QUESTIONS

162. **Answer (D) is correct.** Tony's claim that excessive force used during his arrest violated his constitutional rights states a claim for relief under a cause of action created by federal law. It, therefore, can form the basis for federal question jurisdiction under 28 U.S.C. § 1331. Where federal question jurisdiction exists, the parties' citizenship and the amount in controversy are not relevant. *See also* 42 U.S.C. § 1983.

    Answers (A), (B), and (C) are incorrect. When a federal question exists, there is no minimum amount in controversy requirement, nor do the parties need to be from different states.

163. **Answer (C) is correct.** In most cases, the state and federal courts have concurrent jurisdiction over federal question cases. In a few situations, federal statutes make federal jurisdiction exclusive over particular claims. In most situations, including a civil rights claim such as this one, the plaintiff can choose to file the case either in state or federal court. (Under certain circumstances, the defendant may choose to remove a case filed in state court to federal court. *See* Topic 31.)

    Answers (A) and (B) are incorrect. Federal jurisdiction is not exclusive over federal questions generally or federal questions based on constitutional rights.

    Answer (D) is incorrect. Tony need not have a state law based claim to authorize state court jurisdiction.

164. **Answer (C) is probably correct.** In a case called *Louisville & Nashville R.R. v. Mottley*, 211 U.S. 149 (1908), the Supreme Court established the "well-pleaded complaint rule." Under this principle, the federal issue must constitute part of the plaintiff's claim and appear on the face of the complaint. The existence of a federal defense, even if that defense will be the primary issue litigated, does not confer federal question jurisdiction. Therefore, the existence of a First Amendment defense to this libel claim does not create federal question jurisdiction; it is still just a state law tort claim. An argument can be made that malice has become a federal "ingredient" of the common law defamation claim, turning the plaintiff's claim into one arising under the Constitution. This argument is not likely to be successful because it would turn too many common law defamation claims into federal question claims.

    Answer (A) is incorrect. The federal courts' interest in consistent interpretation of the Constitution would make a strong policy argument that federal defenses *should* confer federal question jurisdiction. Nevertheless, they do not.

    Answer (B) is incorrect. An issue of federal law is highly likely to be determined in the case. It is nevertheless a defense and not a basis for federal question jurisdiction under *Mottley*.

    Answer (D) is incorrect. Plaintiffs cannot get around this rule by anticipating the federal defense in the complaint. Nor can it be avoided by filing a declaratory judgment action for what would otherwise be a federal defense.

165. **Answer (A) is the correct answer.** In *Merrell Dow Pharm., Inc. v. Thompson*, 478 U.S. 804 (1986), the Supreme Court ruled that in cases like this one the claim does not arise under federal law because no private federal cause of action exists for FDCA violations. The Court reasoned that "the mere presence of a federal issue in a state cause of action does not automatically confer federal question jurisdiction," thereby casting the "ingredient" theory of federal question jurisdiction in doubt. However, in *Grable & Sons Metal Prods., Inc. v. Darue Eng'g & Mfg.*, 545 U.S. 308 (2005), the "ingredient" theory made a substantial comeback. *Grable* rejected the claim that a private right of action under federal law is essential to federal question jurisdiction, but re-affirmed the result in *Merrell Dow* based on a balancing of state and federal interests.

    Answer (B) is incorrect for the same reasons that Answer (A) is correct.

    Answer (C) is incorrect because it is sufficient but not always necessary for the federal law to create the claim.

    Answer (D) is incorrect. Even though an issue may be the most important one in the case, the issue needs to be part of the plaintiff's case under the "well pleaded complaint" rule.

166. **Answer (D) is probably the best answer.** A number of federal courts have considered this issue, and the majority has concluded that the issue of the meaning and application of the federal regulations, embedded in the mortgage contract, mean that there is a disputed federal issue necessary to the decision in the case. Further, that issue is "substantial" in the sense that uniformity is important and the federal courts have greater expertise regarding the federal regulations involved. However, since there is no private right of action under these regulations (that would make the case an easy federal question, as the plaintiffs would be suing directly under federal law), courts have expressed concern that recognizing this as a federal question would open a floodgate of essentially state law claims in the federal court, especially given the huge number of federally-insured mortgage loans currently in default. In other words, the lower courts have found that this situation is more like *Merrell Dow* than like *Grable*. For an example of one of these cases, see *Buis v. Wells Fargo Bank*, 401 F. Supp. 2d 612 (N.D. Tex. 2005).

    Answer (A) is incorrect. Although it is true that Gale's cause of action is based on state law and that Gale may not sue directly for a violation of the HUD rules, under some circumstances a federal issue that forms an essential ingredient of a state claim may create a federal question.

    Answer (B) is incorrect because it is incomplete, as explained above.

    Answer (C) is also incorrect. The importance of the federal issue is only one part of the balancing of state and federal interests required in analyzing this type of federal question jurisdiction.

167. **Answer (C) is correct.** As a general rule, the ultimate outcome of a case on the merits is not the determining factor in whether federal question jurisdiction exists. As with questions of amount in controversy, it would be extremely wasteful if losing a case resulted in the court losing jurisdiction. There is, however, a small exception to this rule. The Supreme Court has indicated that if the federal claim is "wholly insubstantial and frivolous" it cannot provide the basis for federal question jurisdiction. The line between a weak case and a frivolous one is

not always easy to draw. Hamlet's claim for a constitutional right to an A, however appealing, is so totally unsupported that it would likely be considered frivolous.

Answer (A) is incorrect. In most cases, if the plaintiff pleads a federal claim, it will support federal jurisdiction. This one, however, crosses the line and could not support federal question jurisdiction. (It might also subject Hamlet to Rule 11 sanctions. *See* Topic 2.)

Answer (B) is incorrect. Normally, decisions about subject matter jurisdiction are not based on the ultimate merits of the federal claim. This is the exception.

Answer (D) is incorrect. This case can be dismissed from the outset. Losing a facially valid federal claim on the merits, however, does not demonstrate lack of subject matter jurisdiction.

TOPIC 34: ANSWERS
SUBJECT MATTER JURISDICTION: SUPPLEMENTAL JURISDICTION

168. **Answer (D) is correct.** When dealing with the addition of claims and parties, we tend to jump immediately to thinking about supplemental jurisdiction. But these added claims sometimes have their own independent bases for federal jurisdiction, making use of the supplemental jurisdiction statute unnecessary. Here, Dorothy's claim against the Clinic provides the initial basis for the case to be in federal court. She is a citizen of Texas, and the Clinic is a citizen of Minnesota, providing diversity. Her claim exceeds the $75,000 minimum. The Clinic has used Rule 14 to add Dr. Houston as a third-party defendant. Dr. Houston is a citizen of Texas. As between the Clinic and Dr. Houston, the requirements of diversity of citizenship are also met. Because the Clinic seeks indemnification for the entire $5 million claim, the third-party claim also satisfies the amount in controversy test.

    Answer (A) is incorrect. The answer correctly notes jurisdiction over Dorothy's claim against the Clinic. However, because this third-party claim is (at this point) solely between the Clinic and Houston, and they are diverse, the fact that Dorothy and Houston are both Texans does not destroy diversity.

    Answer (B) is incorrect. The answer correctly notes jurisdiction over Dorothy's claim against the Clinic. It is also correct that the third-party claim arises out of a common nucleus of operative fact with Dorothy's claim against the Clinic. If supplemental jurisdiction were needed, this would be a crucial determination. However, because there is independent federal jurisdiction over the third-party claim, supplemental jurisdiction is unnecessary and this is not the determining issue.

    Answer (C) is incorrect. The specific claims involved are supported by diversity jurisdiction. (And even if they were not, e.g., if the Clinic and Houston were from the same state, supplemental jurisdiction would, in fact, allow a claim by a defendant/third-party plaintiff against a third-party defendant that arose out of the same constitutional case as the original claim.)

169. **Answer (C) is probably the best answer. Answer (D) also could be argued to be correct.** This question involves a counterclaim by the Clinic against Dorothy. We know that their citizenship is diverse. But this claim is only for $50,000, and, therefore, taken alone it could not be brought in federal court. We therefore need to examine whether supplemental jurisdiction will allow the claim. The answer can be found by working through 28 U.S.C. § 1367. First, in order for there to be constitutional and statutory power to hear this counterclaim, it needs to be part of the same constitutional case as the claim that originally justified federal jurisdiction (here, Dorothy's claim against the Clinic). The test here comes from a Supreme Court case called *United Mine Workers v. Gibbs*, 383 U.S. 715 (1966): we must look to see whether the claims share a "common nucleus of operative fact." Imagine that the claims went to trial. Would there be a significant overlap of facts necessary to support both claims? Dorothy's claim is for malpractice. It will require the court to look at the nature of the medical care provided to her and whether that care meets the applicable

standard of care. The Clinic's counterclaim is for an alleged libel, based on statements that were made after Dorothy was no longer its patient. In order to prevail, the Clinic would have to prove that Dorothy made or was otherwise responsible for the statements, and that they were untrue. Some of Dorothy's statements had to do with her own experience. It, therefore, appears that the Clinic's defamation claim will also include examination of the nature and quality of Dorothy's medical treatment. This will provide some overlap in the claims. Is this enough to make it the same constitutional case? Probably. If it is, then Answer (D) is incorrect. The § 1367 analysis proceeds to section (b), which prohibits certain kinds of claims that are inconsistent with the requirements of the diversity statute. The Clinic, although it is the party seeking to bring a claim for affirmative relief, is not a "plaintiff" within the meaning of § 1367(b). Therefore, the statute allows supplemental jurisdiction over the counterclaim. This makes Answer (C) the best one. If, instead, you believe that the claims are not sufficiently related to form the same constitutional case, then Answer (D) is correct. This would make Answer (C) incorrect, because if it is not the same "case" then it does not matter that the Clinic is not a "plaintiff" — supplemental jurisdiction would still be improper.

Answer (A) is incorrect. Permissive counterclaims, which do not arise out of the same transaction or occurrence as the plaintiff's claim, would not satisfy the same constitutional case requirement of § 1367(a) and, therefore, the counterclaims would not be granted supplemental jurisdiction.

Answer (B) is incorrect. The insufficiency of the amount in controversy is what set us on our quest for supplemental jurisdiction. A claim over $75,000 would have an independent basis for federal jurisdiction. The smaller claim does not preclude supplemental jurisdiction, it just makes it necessary.

170. **Answer (A) is correct.** Based on the "common nucleus of operative fact" test in *Gibbs v. United Mine Workers*, § 1367(a) is satisfied and none of the exceptions in § 1367(b) applies.

Answer (B) is not correct because Cyrus appears clearly to fit within the exception to supplemental jurisdiction precluding persons from intervening as plaintiffs under Rule 24. *See* 28 U.S.C. § 1367(b).

Answer (C) is incorrect because Answer (A) is correct and because a co-plaintiff making his own distinct claim in a tort case is not a Rule 19 person needed for just adjudication.

Answer (D) is incorrect because Answer (A) is correct.

171. If Cyrus had established a new domicile in Minnesota, he obviously would not be of diverse citizenship from National Clinic or Dr. Heart. So the first question would be whether § 1367(a) would allow his claim either as an original plaintiff or as an intervenor. It does not. As explained in *Exxon Mobil Corp. v. Allapattah Servs. Inc.*, 545 U.S. 546 (2005), "[I]n order for a federal court to invoke supplemental jurisdiction under *Gibbs*, it must first have original jurisdiction over at least one claim in the action. Incomplete diversity destroys original jurisdiction with respect to all claims, so there is nothing to which supplemental jurisdiction can adhere." Even if this logic cannot be applied easily if Cyrus intervenes (see last sentence of § 1367(a)), § 1367(b)'s hostility to intervention in diversity cases also slams the door on Cyrus.

172. **Answer (C) is the correct answer.** A contribution claim is surely part of the same case as

the main claim against the original defendant because it arises from the same facts. In addition, although the exceptions in § 1367(b) are hard to understand, the best reading of the first exception in § 1367(b) does not prohibit third-party claims by defendants (third-party plaintiffs) against third-party defendants in diversity cases. Defendants are not *plaintiffs*, even when they are third-party plaintiffs under Rule 14, so contribution claims are not "claims by plaintiffs against persons made parties under Rule 14."

Answer (A) is not correct for the same reason that Answer (C) is correct.

Answer (B) is not correct for the same reason. A contribution claim is part of the same case or controversy under Article III.

Answer (D) is not correct because the main case (*Woodman v. National Clinic*) provides a basis for federal jurisdiction and the "contamination" theory does not apply to third party.

173. **Answer (C) is correct.** Although the "common nucleus of operative fact" test is satisfied, the first exception in § 1367(b) applies to prohibit supplemental jurisdiction in diversity cases "over claims by plaintiffs against persons made parties under Rule 14, 19, *20* or 24 of the Federal Rules of Civil Procedure."

Answers (A) and (B) are incorrect primarily because the satisfaction of § 1367(a) does not override the prohibitions contained in § 1367(b).

Answer (D) is incorrect because compliance with the Federal Rules of Civil Procedure does not excuse noncompliance with statutes governing the existence of subject matter jurisdiction.

174. **Answer (D) is probably the best answer. Answer (C) could be argued to be correct.** Again the outcome turns on the relationship between the desired supplemental claim and the claim that provided the federal court with jurisdiction. The claim creating diversity jurisdiction was Dorothy's malpractice claim against the Clinic. The Clinic's third-party claim against Houston also has a basis for federal jurisdiction. The claim in question here is brought by a third-party defendant (Houston) against the original plaintiff (Dorothy). It must be proper under the joinder rules and must have some basis for federal jurisdiction. This claim does not have an independent basis for federal jurisdiction, because it is based on state contract law and the parties are from the same state. Rule 14 allows such claims if they arise out of the same transaction or occurrence as the original plaintiff's claim (Dorothy's claim) against the defendant/third-party plaintiff (Clinic). The supplemental jurisdiction statute supports jurisdiction if the new claim and the original claim share a common nucleus of operative fact. (These tests tend to be very similar in application.) Is the relationship sufficient? Dorothy's claim will involve evidence about her treatment by the Clinic and the relevant standard of care. The Clinic's third-party claim will involve disputes about whether Houston's treatment of Dorothy was negligent, and about what caused Dorothy's post-operative complications. Houston's proposed claim will involve evidence of her treatment of Dorothy and the proper charges for this treatment. Is that enough overlap for either Rule 14 or for § 1367(a)? If not, Answer (D) is correct. Although Answer (C) is correct, it would be irrelevant. On the other hand, if the overlap is sufficient to meet both tests, so that the claim is procedurally and constitutionally proper, then § 1367(b) would not bar supplemental jurisdiction. Houston's claim is one brought by a person made a party under Rule 14, not a claim by a plaintiff.

Answer (C) would be the correct answer.

Answer (A) is not the best answer. Rule 14 does sometimes allow third-party defendants to bring claims against plaintiffs. It does not always do so. And it does not provide federal jurisdiction over those claims.

Answer (B) is incorrect. The parties' common citizenship and the size of the claim do create the need for supplemental jurisdiction. It does not, however, mean that those tests cannot be met.

175. This question deals with an unsettled issue in applying § 1367(b). This question assumes that the following claims are in the case: (1) *Dorothy v. Clinic*; (2) *Clinic v. Houston*; and (3) *Houston v. Dorothy* for fees. The issue is whether Dorothy can add a claim against Houston for malpractice. There is no independent basis for such a claim — both Dorothy and Houston are Texans, so diversity is lacking. It seems likely that the same constitutional case requirement of § 1367(a) is met. Dorothy's claim against Houston will overlap substantially with her claim against the Clinic and the Clinic's claim against Houston.

The problem is § 1367(b). Dorothy's claim against Houston is inconsistent with the requirements of the diversity statute. And Houston is a person made a party under Rule 14. Thus, supplemental jurisdiction will be improper if Dorothy is a "plaintiff." This is where the disagreement comes in. Some argue that Dorothy is of course a plaintiff. She brought this lawsuit and is making affirmative claims for relief. She chose a federal forum and should not be allowed an end run around the complete diversity requirement by waiting for the Clinic to implead Houston. Others argue that in this context Dorothy is not a "plaintiff." She is responding with a counterclaim, probably what would generally be a compulsory counterclaim, to a claim that Houston made against her and so in this context is acting as a defendant. From the standpoint of judicial efficiency, these authorities argue, it would be far better to hear all of these claims in a single forum rather than to force a separate trial of Dorothy's malpractice claim against Houston. The Supreme Court has not yet had occasion to tell us which argument is correct.

TOPIC 35: ANSWERS

SUBJECT MATTER JURISDICTION: COMPARING SUPPLEMENTAL JURISDICTION & THE CLASS ACTION FAIRNESS ACT

176. **Answer (A) is correct.** There is complete diversity between Sleep Hotels/Alice on the one side and Mall Mart on the other. Sleep Hotels' claim exceeds $75,000. The supplemental jurisdiction statute, 28 U.S.C. § 1367, provides jurisdiction over Alice's claim. It meets the requirements of § 1367(a) because the claims of Alice and Sleep Hotels share a common nucleus of operative fact — both will revolve around evidence of the method for calculating thread count and the failure of the sheets to truthfully represent the count (although evidence of damages and the specific sheets involved will differ). Since this is a diversity case and Alice is a plaintiff, we must also look to § 1367(b) to see if the claim is excluded. As the *Exxon/Ortega* case held, § 1367(b) does not exclude claims brought by plaintiffs joined under Rule 20. *See Exxon Mobil Corp. v. Allapattah Servs. Inc.*, 545 U.S. 546 (2005).

    Answers (B) and (C) are incorrect for the reasons stated above.

    Answer (D) is incorrect because the claims of multiple plaintiffs are not aggregated to determine the amount in controversy.

177. **Answer (B) is correct.** Barbara's claim destroys jurisdiction. Like Alice's, it is part of the same case or controversy, but *Exxon* also noted that when the parties are not completely diverse, jurisdiction is destroyed and so there is no "good" claim on which supplemental jurisdiction can be based. The presence of the non-diverse plaintiff "contaminates" the entire case, leaving no proper basis for federal jurisdiction. There is no need to go on to § 1367(b).

    Answer (A) is incorrect for the reasons stated above.

    Answer (C) is incorrect because § 1367(b) is not the problem. As noted above, Barbara's citizenship means that the case structured this way does not even meet the requirements of § 1367(a), so § 1367(b) is irrelevant. (In addition, Barbara's claim — a claim by a plaintiff joined under Rule 20 — is not on the § 1367(b) list.)

    Answer (D) is incorrect. While Article III can be satisfied, under some circumstances, by minimal diversity, jurisdiction also requires statutory authorization, and the general diversity of citizenship statute has consistently been interpreted to require complete diversity. Since § 1367 does not provide for supplemental jurisdiction under these facts, Article III's broader possible scope for jurisdiction does not create jurisdiction.

178. No. The Court in *Exxon* found that § 1367(b), as drafted, does not prohibit supplemental jurisdiction over a claim by a plaintiff made a party under Rule 20 — and that's what Sleep Hotels and Alice are. However, § 1367(b) *does* prohibit supplemental jurisdiction over claims *against persons made parties under Rule 20*. In this version of the case, Mall Mart and SheetSheet, as co-defendants, were made parties under Rule 20. Therefore, § 1367(b) does withdraw jurisdiction here. Sleep Hotels and Alice might try bringing separate lawsuits (*SH & A v. MM*; *SH & A v. SS*) in the same district and hope for consolidation, but filed as one

suit there is no subject matter jurisdiction.

179. **Answer (D) is correct.** Claire's claim, if filed alone, would be sufficient for jurisdiction. She is of diverse citizenship from defendant BBB and her claim exceeds $75,000. In class actions, it is only the citizenship of the named plaintiff that counts, and so it doesn't matter that some class members are citizens of the same state as the defendant. Their claims are too small to have supported jurisdiction if filed separately, but under *Exxon* the federal court has supplemental jurisdiction over those claims. They arise out of the same "case or controversy" as Claire's claims, they satisfy § 1367(a), and § 1367(b) does not prohibit supplemental jurisdiction over the claims of persons made parties under Rule 23.

Answer (A) is incorrect for the reason explained above — it doesn't matter that the class members' claims are too small.

Answer (B) is incorrect. In class actions, it is only the named plaintiff(s) who must be diverse from the defendants.

Answer (C) is incorrect. The Class Action Fairness Act would not provide jurisdiction over this case, because the aggregate class claims do not exceed $5 million.

180. **Answer (D) is correct.** At first it appears that the Class Action Fairness Act would provide jurisdiction over this case. There is at least minimal diversity between a class member and the defendant. The class claims exceed $5 million (100,000 × $55). There are more than 100 class members. However, this case falls into the category in which the federal court "shall" decline jurisdiction: more than two thirds of class members are from the forum state, as are all primary defendants (even if non-Connecticut defendants were added, the damage occurred in Connecticut, where the sheets were purchased, and Connecticut law will probably apply).

Answer (A) is incorrect. Under CAFA, the minimal diversity can be between a class member and the defendant — unlike under the normal rule, the citizenship of the named plaintiff is not the only relevant question.

Answer (B) is incorrect because the case is concentrated in one state and the statute contemplates trying such disputes in the relevant state court. Otherwise, however, it meets the requirements of CAFA as noted above.

Answer (C) is incorrect. This class action would not be proper under supplemental jurisdiction. Dana does not satisfy the requirements for diversity jurisdiction (her claim is too small), and so there is no independently adequate claim for the others to supplement.

TOPIC 36: SUBJECT MATTER JURISDICTION: REMOVAL — ANSWERS

181. **Answer (C) is correct.** The removal statute (28 U.S.C. § 1446) provides that the notice of removal shall be filed "within thirty days after the receipt by the defendant, through service or otherwise, of a copy of the initial pleading . . . or within thirty days after the service of summons upon the defendant if such initial pleading has then been filed in court and is not required to be served on the defendant, whichever period is shorter." For a while, some courts interpreted this statute so that the receipt of a courtesy copy of a complaint, even if before the lawsuit was filed, started the running of the 30 days. The Supreme Court has held that this interpretation is incorrect. *Murphy Bros., Inc. v. Michetti Pipe Stringing, Inc.*, 526 U.S. 344 (1999). The time limit is triggered by simultaneous service of the summons and complaint, "through service or otherwise," after and apart from service of the summons, but not by mere receipt of the complaint unattended by any formal service of the summons. Applying this rule, it is service of the summons and complaint on July 15 that starts the clock running; the summons functions as the *sina qua non* directing a defendant to participate in a civil action. Thus, if the summons and complaint are served together, the 30-day period for removal runs from the date of service. Second, if the defendant is served with the summons but the complaint is furnished to the defendant sometime later, the period for removal runs from the defendant's receipt of the complaint. Third, if the defendant is served with the summons and the complaint is filed in court, but under local rules, service of the complaint is not required, the removal period runs from the date the complaint is made available through filing. Finally, if the complaint is filed in court prior to any service, the removal period runs from the service of the summons.

    Answer (A) is incorrect. The deadline does not run from the drafting of the complaint.

    Answer (B) is incorrect. As explained above, the pre-filing courtesy copy does not start the running of the 30 days.

    Answer (D) is incorrect. There is indeed a deadline for removal.

182. **Answer (D) is correct.** This case meets the requirement for diversity jurisdiction. Martin is a citizen of Michigan, and Blue Hat is a citizen of Delaware and Oregon. The amount in controversy is sufficient. Martin could have filed his suit in federal court. However, under these facts (filing in state court in Oregon), Blue Hat may not remove. The removal statute (28 U.S.C. § 1441(b)) does not allow a defendant sued in its home state to remove a case based on diversity jurisdiction. The fear of local court prejudice against a non-resident defendant does not apply when the defendant is a citizen of the forum state. Blue Hat is a citizen of Oregon and the case was filed there.

    Answers (A) and (C) are incorrect. It is not true that cases can be removed at any time, and timing aside, this one cannot be removed at all.

    Answer (B) is incorrect. Although Martin could have filed the case in federal court, because he chose state court, Blue Hat cannot remove it.

183. **Answer (C) is correct.** This time Martin has added a claim created by a federal statute, clearly meeting the requirements for federal question jurisdiction. This makes it removable despite the lack of diverse citizenship and despite the fact that Blue Hat is a citizen of the forum state. *Exxon Mobil Corp. v. Allapattah Service, Inc.*, 545 U.S. 546, 563-564 (2005) ("[A] district court has original jurisdiction of a civil action for purposes of § 1441(a) as long as it has original jurisdiction over a subset of the claims constituting the action.").

Answer (A) is incorrect. The prohibition on removal by resident defendants applies only to cases in which jurisdiction is based on diversity.

Answer (B) is incorrect. Federal question jurisdiction does not require diversity of citizenship.

Answer (D) is incorrect. If this were a situation in which the defendant's citizenship mattered (and it is not), § 1441(b) prohibits removal if any of the "parties in interest properly joined and served as defendants is a citizen of the State in which such action is brought." A corporation is a "citizen" of both its state of incorporation and its principal place of business.

184. **Answer (D) is correct.** As amended in 2011, § 1441(c) permits removal of the case but requires that a federal district court sever the federal and state law claims and remand the state law claims. "This sever-and-remand approach is intended to cure any constitutional problems while preserving the defendant's right to remove claims arising under Federal law." Report by Committee on the Judiciary on Federal Courts Jurisdiction and Venue Clarification Act of 2011, at p. 11.

Answers (A) and (C) are incorrect. Although § 1445(c) provides that "[a] civil action in any state court arising under the workmen's compensation law of such state may not be removed to any district court of the United States," the new sever-and-remand procedure contained in § 1441(c) is not incompatible with § 1445(c).

Answer (B) is not correct for the reasons explained above.

185. **Answer (A) is correct.** The removal statute (28 U.S.C. § 1441(a)) provides that cases are removed "to the district court of the United States for the district and division embracing the place where such action is pending." In this case, that means that removal will be to the Eastern District of Michigan.

Answer (B) is incorrect. When a state has more than one federal judicial district, the case must be removed to the district in which the state court sits. The Western District of Michigan would be incorrect.

Answers (C) and (D) are incorrect. The defendant does not get to choose some other federal court, even if the plaintiff could properly have filed the lawsuit there originally.

186. **Answer (C) is correct.** As discussed above, the defendant normally has only 30 days from being initially served with process to remove a case to federal court. There are special rules, however, for cases that were not originally removable but which become removable later. One such situation involves the addition for the first time of a federal claim that would create federal question jurisdiction. That is what has happened here. The removal statute (28 U.S.C. § 1446(b)(3)) provides:

> Except as provided in subsection (c), if the case stated by the initial pleading is not removable, a notice of removal may be filed within thirty days after receipt by the defendant, through service or otherwise, of a copy of an amended pleading, motion, order, or other paper from which it may first be ascertained that the case is one which is or has become removable.

In this case, when Blue Hat received a copy of the amended complaint containing the ADEA claim, it had 30 days to remove the case, despite the fact that more than 30 days had passed since it was served with the original complaint.

Answers (A) and (B) are incorrect for reasons set forth above.

Answer (D) is incorrect. The one-year limit applies to diversity cases, not federal questions.

187. **Answer (D) is correct.** This situation calls into play the exception to the rule in the previous question. In most cases, when an amendment makes a case removable for the first time, the defendant may still remove the case. This is not true in diversity cases. The remainder of § 1446(c) creates an exception: "a case may not be removed . . . on the basis of jurisdiction conferred by § 1332 of this title [diversity jurisdiction] more than 1 year after commencement of the action unless the district court finds that the plaintiff has acted in bad faith in order to prevent a defendant from removing the action." Because Martin's case has been pending for 18 months, dropping the non-diverse in-state defendant at this time does not allow removal.

Answer (A) is incorrect. Had Martin been dropped in time for Blue Hat to remove less than a year after the action was filed, this answer would be correct. After 18 months, it is incorrect.

Answer (B) is incorrect. As discussed above, it is too late.

Answer (C) is incorrect. Subsequent changes to the lawsuit can create the potential for removal, but again, it is too late.

188. **Answer (A) is correct.** A party who believes that a case was improperly removed to federal court can file a "motion to remand." A motion to remand based on any defect other than lack of subject matter jurisdiction must be made within 30 days after the filing of the notice of removal (28 U.S.C. § 1447(c)). Here, Martin's motion to remand is based on technical errors in the removal papers, and so he must make it within this deadline.

Answer (B) is incorrect. The deadline runs from the filing of the notice of removal, not from when the plaintiff receives it.

Answer (C) is incorrect. This motion to remand is not based on a lack of subject matter jurisdiction.

Answer (D) is incorrect. Cases may be remanded based on procedural defects in the removal process.

189. Martin is trying to add a non-diverse defendant in order to destroy complete diversity. When this happens after removal, the judge has a choice. She can deny joinder and allow the case to proceed in federal court without the new defendant. She can also permit joinder and remand the action to the state court. *See* 28 U.S.C. § 1447(e).

TOPIC 37: TERRITORIAL JURISDICTION: VOCABULARY — ANSWERS

190. **Answer (B) is correct.** When a court has personal jurisdiction over a defendant, it is empowered to enter a judgment that fully adjudicates the dispute between the parties. The judgment makes all of the defendant's non-exempt assets available to satisfy the judgment, and a judgment awarding an injunction can be enforced through the court's contempt power.

Answer (A) is incorrect. While the presence of property belonging to a defendant in the forum state might be relevant to the constitutionality of jurisdiction, it is neither necessary nor sufficient in all cases.

Answer (C) is incorrect. Presence of the defendant in the forum state at the time of service, assuming service was not procured by fraud, is sufficient, but not required. Even before the development of the "minimum contacts doctrine," which generally controls the exercise of jurisdiction over non-residents of the forum state, a domiciliary of the forum state could be served with process and compelled to defend while absent from the state.

Answer (D) is incorrect. When the court has *in personam* jurisdiction, its power is over the defendant, not just over some property in the state. The judgment is, therefore, not limited to some piece of property over which the court has jurisdiction.

191. **Answer (A) is correct.** A court acquires *in rem* jurisdiction by getting power over some thing, often real property, within its borders. Technically and formally the action is against the thing rather than against particular persons. And jurisdiction of this kind can result in a judgment affecting the interests of *all* persons in the thing (in Latin, the "*res*") whether they have been served with process or not. The most well-known examples are jurisdiction in admiralty cases brought "against the ship" and in probate litigation determining ownership interests in decedents' estates.

Answer (B) is incorrect. *In rem* jurisdiction gives the court power only over the disputed property, and not jurisdiction to adjudicate the plaintiff's rights generally.

Answer (C) is incorrect. As noted above, *in rem* jurisdiction allows the court to enter a judgment that is not limited to parties before the court.

Answer (D) is incorrect. When jurisdiction is *in rem*, it is the presence of the disputed thing rather than power over people that gives the court the authority to act.

192. **Answer (D) is the best answer.** (This means that **Answers (A) and (B) are also correct**, but not the best answer because each omits the other.) One type of *quasi in rem* jurisdiction involves a plaintiff seeking to apply the defendant's property to the satisfaction of a claim against the defendant that is unrelated to that property. It is, again, the court's power over the thing within its borders that allows it to act. However, the Supreme Court held in 1977 in *Shaffer v. Heitner* that *quasi in rem* jurisdiction must also satisfy the requirements of due process. *Shaffer v. Heitner*, 433 U.S. 186 (1977). This requirement removed a lot of the special appeal of *quasi in rem* jurisdiction, and it is now used most often to enforce a

judgment already rendered for the plaintiff in another state.

Answer (C) is incorrect. Where still proper, *quasi in rem* jurisdiction gives the court the power to adjudicate the rights of named parties in the property before the court, not the right to adjudicate the interests of anyone anywhere who might have some interest in the property.

TOPIC 38:	ANSWERS
CONSENT, STATUS, DOMICILE & TRANSIENT JURISDICTION	

193. **Answer (C) is correct.** Defendants can consent to a court's personal jurisdiction before suit. If in a valid and enforceable contract a party agrees that suit may be filed in a given court, that contractual provision will be enforced. Sometimes the court will declare the provision to be unenforceable under applicable contract law, but absent such a finding the federal courts have tended to enforce such clauses, even when they purport to bar litigation in any other courts, and even when they are part of a contract of adhesion. For examples, see *Nat'l Equip. Rental v. Szukhent*, 375 U.S. 311 (1964) (Michigan defendants agreed to be sued in New York), and *Carnival Cruise Lines, Inc. v. Shute*, 499 U.S. 585 (1991) (enforcing choice of forum clause found on back of the plaintiffs' cruise tickets).

Answer (A) is incorrect. Defendants can be sued in states other than their domiciles if the requirements of due process are otherwise met.

Answer (B) is incorrect. The cases that allow suit to determine a person's status, even in the absence of personal jurisdiction over the defendant, concern issues such as the termination of a family relationship. The "status" exception does not permit the court to establish parties' rights under a contract under the guise of adjudicating their status under the contract. The status exception is extremely limited. For example, in a divorce case the court could assume jurisdiction to grant the divorce itself but could not divide marital property or order support payments in the absence of personal jurisdiction over the defendant.

Answer (D) is incorrect. Even assuming Goneril and Regan lack sufficient purposeful contacts with the state of New York, the contractual clause consenting to jurisdiction allows the New York courts to assert jurisdiction over them.

194. **Answer (A) is correct.** This is a correct use of the status exception, unlike the misuse in Answer (B) in the previous question. Goneril would not be able to get an enforceable order for spousal support, but because all she wants is the divorce itself the court will have the power to give her one even without jurisdiction over Albany.

Answer (B) is incorrect. The state that was once a person's home does not permanently retain sufficient contacts to provide a basis for personal jurisdiction.

Answer (C) is incorrect. It may be true that after five years Albany's contacts with Michigan are too attenuated to satisfy the minimum contacts test. But in this case that is immaterial. The fact that Goneril seeks only a declaration of divorce means that the court does not need to have personal jurisdiction over Albany.

Answer (D) is incorrect because it misconceives the issue involved. The issue of whether Michigan has jurisdiction to issue a divorce is not a question of whether Albany has consented, and so his lack of consent is irrelevant.

195. **Answer (D) is correct.** Courts of a defendant's home state traditionally have personal

jurisdiction over her whether or not the claim is otherwise tied to that state. The Supreme Court has long held that "domicile in the state is alone sufficient to bring an absent defendant within the reach of the state's jurisdiction." *Milliken v. Meyer*, 311 U.S. 457 (1940). The benefits of citizenship are said to justify reciprocal duties. As a practical matter, it is efficient for plaintiffs to know there is one place where a defendant is certainly amenable to jurisdiction, and those defendants will not usually be unduly inconvenienced by being sued at home.

Answer (A) is incorrect. Service of process out of state (generally permitted by virtue of a state "long-arm statute") is constitutional if the defendant has the required contacts with the forum state.

Answer (B) is incorrect. When a human defendant is sued in her domicile, the cause of action need not have arisen out of contacts with the forum state.

Answer (C) is incorrect. Although Cordelia does have enough contacts with Iowa to justify specific personal jurisdiction over some claims, that is not the reason that jurisdiction would be correct in this case. That lower level of contacts, if that were all that existed, would not justify jurisdiction over Cordelia in Iowa with regard to a cause of action that arose in Delaware.

196. **Answer (B) is correct.** This question highlights what is known as "transient jurisdiction" or "tag" jurisdiction. Dating back to the time when a court's jurisdiction was based on asserting power over a person within the state's boundaries, transient jurisdiction is based on service of process on the defendant within the state. Serving Kent with process in Colorado, even though Colorado is not his home, meets the requirements of transient jurisdiction. In *Burnham v. Superior Court*, 495 U.S. 604 (1990), the Supreme Court upheld transient jurisdiction in a very split opinion. Some Justices believe that transient jurisdiction, because it was traditionally accepted, is *per se* constitutional. Others believe that it must be subjected to a due process test, but nevertheless approved the service in *Burnham* based on service on a defendant who was in California on business and to visit his children. This opinion, joined by Justices Brennan, Marshall, Blackmun, and O'Connor found no due process problem when the defendant served in the state had even briefly taken advantage of "significant benefits provided by the State." It left open the possibility of a different result when the defendant's presence in the state is "involuntary or unknowing." Kent's regular visits to Colorado and the service of process on him there should meet the requirements for transient jurisdiction.

Answer (A) is incorrect. While coming to Colorado every summer, coupled with service in Colorado, met the requirements for transient jurisdiction, coming to Colorado every summer is not sufficient alone. The cause of action asserted by the plaintiff in this case is not related to Kent's activities in Colorado, and so for this cause of action the repeated summer contacts are insufficient. The result would be different if the cause of action arose out of a tort Kent committed while in Colorado that injured Colorado residents.

Answer (C) is incorrect. Transient jurisdiction includes jurisdiction over claims unrelated to the reasons the defendant was present in the state when served.

Answer (D) is incorrect. Transient jurisdiction, under most circumstances, remains constitutional, as noted above. In the international arena, however, a judgment based only on transient jurisdiction is generally considered to be improper. It could be difficult to enforce such a judgment abroad if the defendant does not have non-exempt assets in the U.S.

TOPIC 39: ANSWERS
IN PERSONAM JURISDICTION: OVERVIEW

197. **Answer (D) is the best answer.** The reasons are set forth for each of the correct options below. Answers (A) through (C) are all correct.

Answer (C) is correct. In cases such as *Pennoyer v. Neff*, 95 U.S. 714 (1878), the Supreme Court explained the traditional requirement for territorial jurisdiction. For *in personam* jurisdiction, the court needed power over a defendant, demonstrated by the presence of the defendant within the state's borders.

Answer (A) is correct. Defendant's domicile in the state has always been sufficient to establish personal jurisdiction, regardless of where the defendant was served with process. *See Milliken v. Meyer*, 311 U.S. 457 (1940) ("domicile in the state is alone sufficient to bring an absent defendant within the reach of the state's jurisdiction.").

Answer (B) is correct. Defendants who owned property could still be subject to personal jurisdiction under *in rem* or *quasi in rem* jurisdiction, which had to be asserted by the attachment of the property by some form of legal process at the commencement of the action. *See Pennoyer v. Neff*, 95 U.S. 714 (1878).

198. **Answer (D) is the best answer.** The reasons are explained for each of the correct options below. **Answers (A) through (C) are all correct.**

Answer (A) is correct. Because a corporation is not an actual physical entity but a collection of assets and employees, a legal fiction, it was more difficult to determine when a corporation was "present" in a state under the old formulation. Courts made this decision based on an analysis of the company's level of activity in the forum state, and the results were somewhat arbitrary and unpredictable. Were regular purchases from the state enough? Regular sales? Low level employees? In making these decisions about "presence," the courts were also considering whether the level of activity was sufficient for it to be "fair" for the company to be required to defend in the forum. The "presence" or "transacting business" approach came to be extremely unsatisfactory.

Answer (B) is correct. States wanted to be allowed to regulate conduct within their borders. Within the framework of traditional personal jurisdiction analysis, they began to legislate consent-based exceptions to the "presence" requirement. For example, states would require out-of-state corporations to register for a license to do business in the state, and that license would be said to include an actual or implied consent to service in the state. Similarly, states passed statutes providing that if a person did certain kinds of harm in the state (for example, caused an automobile accident), that person consented to be served in the state. These statutes either require the designation of a registered agent for service of process, or appoint some state official such as the secretary of state to accept service on the defendant's behalf. Either resulted in service of process on the defendant within the state, and personal jurisdiction. This created a kind of jurisprudential doublethink, with some defendants unreachable under *Pennoyer* and some subject to jurisdiction based on this type of legal fiction. Most states still have statutes requiring businesses who engage in a high level of intrastate business to get a license to do business, and such statutes may provide that the business consents to the jurisdiction of the state's courts.

Answer (C) is correct. The increasing mobility of the population (accelerated by the proliferation of the automobile), and the increasing likelihood that companies would engage in business in a number of states, meant that these issues of personal jurisdiction were arising more and more often. The unworkable old rule finally had to go.

199. **Answer (A) is correct.** In specific jurisdiction cases, there must be some kind of relationship between the defendant's contacts with the forum and the plaintiff's cause of action. Courts often describe this by saying that the cause of action "arises out of" the contacts. For example, assume the defendant comes to the forum state and drives negligently, causing harm to the resident plaintiff. The contacts are coming to the forum and driving. The cause of action arises directly from those contacts. Sometimes the required relationship is described as requiring that the cause of action "relate to" the contacts. The meaning of this test is a little fuzzier. What is clear, though, is that this lower level of contacts does not provide the basis for jurisdiction over the defendant when the claim is unrelated to its contacts with the forum.

Answer (B) is incorrect. While "general jurisdiction" allows the assertion of claims against the defendant that did not arise out of its contacts with the forum state, specific jurisdiction does not.

Answer (C) is incorrect. While the similarity of names might be confusing ("specific jurisdiction" and pleading with "specificity"), the concepts are unrelated. The distinction between specific and general jurisdiction turns on the relationship between the forum and the cause of action, not on the level of detail in the complaint.

Answer (D) is incorrect. The existence of proper jurisdiction over the defendant on one claim does not confer proper jurisdiction over the defendant on all claims. When the defendant's contacts with the forum are only sufficient for claims arising out of those contacts (specific jurisdiction), those contacts do not also authorize the court to take jurisdiction over additional claims that do *not* arise out of the defendant's contacts with the forum (general jurisdiction).

200. **Answer (B) is correct.** The Supreme Court has interpreted the Due Process Clause of the Fourteenth Amendment to require that before a state may exercise jurisdiction over a defendant, that defendant must have sufficient contacts, undertaken purposefully by the defendant, with the forum state, and it must be fair to subject the defendant to suit there. This standard has been applied in a long line of cases beginning with *Int'l Shoe v. Washington*, 326 U.S. 310 (1945). It is often described as a two-step test. The first step involves showing a sufficient level of purposeful contacts with the forum. The second step involves analyzing whether the exercise of jurisdiction would be fair, taking into consideration a list of factors. You should also be aware, however, that the two steps may interact. Justice Brennan's opinion in *Burger King* indicates that the fairness factors may bolster a comparatively weak showing of purposeful contacts. *Burger King v. Rudzewicz*, 471 U.S. 462 (1985). It can also work the other way: even a defendant who has enough contacts to meet the contact requirements of step one may not be subject to jurisdiction, because such jurisdiction would be unfair under step two. An example of the latter situation is found

in *Asahi Metal Indus. Co. v. Superior Court*, 480 U.S. 102 (1987).

Answer (A) is incorrect. States are permitted to exercise jurisdiction over non-residents if the requirements of due process are met.

Answer (C) is incorrect. When a defendant's contacts with the forum are "so continuous and systematic" that the defendant is "essentially at home in the forum state . . ., i.e. comparable to a domestic enterprise in that state," *Daimler AG v. Bauman*, 134 S. Ct. 746, 751, 758 n. 11 (2014), the defendant is subject to general jurisdiction. This is a much higher level of contacts than is required for specific jurisdiction. For individuals, this means where the defendant is domiciled and probably not elsewhere. *See Goodyear Dunlop Tires Operations, S.A. v. Brown*, 131 S. Ct. 2846 (2011). For corporations and business entities, the Supreme Court has explained that "[g]eneral jurisdiction calls for the appraisal of a corporation's activities in their entirety, nationwide and worldwide. A corporation that operates in many places can scarcely be deemed at home in all of them. Otherwise, 'at home' would be synonymous with 'doing business' tests framed before specific jurisdiction evolved in the United States." *Daimler AG v. Bauman*, 134 S. Ct. at 762 n. 20.

Answer (D) is incorrect. "Presence" was the test before the Court's decision in *International Shoe*. It is no longer the test, however. All states have "long-arm statutes" that allow service on persons outside the state as long as certain statutory requirements are met. The application of the long-arm statutes to the defendant must also satisfy the constitutional requirements of due process.

201. **Answer (C) is correct.** In order to be subjected to general jurisdiction, a defendant's contacts with the forum must be so extensive that it is fair to compel it to defend a claim that arose elsewhere. The term of art that the Supreme Court first used to describe this level of activity was "continuous and systematic." It comes from the old pre-*Shoe* cases trying to decide whether a defendant was "present" in the forum. For many years, there was not much Supreme Court case law to flesh out the meaning of "continuous and systematic" — one case in which the company's activities were found to be sufficient, and two in which they were not. *Compare Perkins v. Benguet Consol. Mining Co.*, 342 U.S. 437 (1952) (Philippine mining company had its headquarters in Ohio and so subject to general jurisdiction), *with Helicopteros Nacionales de Colombia, S.A. v. Hall*, 466 U.S. 408 (1984) ("mere purchases" of millions of dollars' worth of helicopters and parts insufficient to confer general jurisdiction over Columbian corporation). In *Goodyear Dunlop Tires Operations, S.A. v. Brown*, 131 S. Ct. 2846 (2011), the Supreme Court unanimously held that foreign subsidiaries of Goodyear USA were not subject to general jurisdiction in North Carolina simply because thousands of tires similar to those that defendants manufactured, and that injured the plaintiffs' sons in France, had somehow made their way to North Carolina.

More recently, in *Daimler AG v. Bauman*, 134 S. Ct. 746 (2014), the Supreme Court held that Daimler AG, a German corporation with its home office in Stuttgart, Germany was not subject to general, all-purpose jurisdiction in California, even though the German corporation had as an "indirect subsidiary" (MBUSA), a Delaware limited liability company that served as Daimler AG's "exclusive importer and distributor in the United States, purchasing Mercedes-Benz automobiles from Daimler in Germany, then importing those vehicles, and ultimately distributing them to independent dealerships throughout the Nation." MBUSA had multiple California-based facilities and was the largest supplier of luxury vehicles in California, accounting for 2.4% of Daimler AG's worldwide sales, but

MBUSA's principal place of business was in New Jersey. Simply stated, "Daimler's slim contacts with [California] hardly render it at home there," even if MBUSA is at home in California and even if MBUSA's contacts are attributed to Daimler AG. Both *Goodyear* and *Daimler* identify a corporation's place of incorporation and principal place of business as "paradigm . . . bases for general jurisdiction." The possibility of another basis for general, all-purpose jurisdiction is not foreclosed in *Daimler*, but the Court does not do more than speculate about its existence.

Answer (A) is incorrect. The fact that a defendant conducts some business in the forum will not subject it to general jurisdiction. The level of business activity needs to be substantial and of the right kind. For example, in *Helicopteros*, the Court ruled that purchases of goods and services were not sufficient for general jurisdiction and in *Goodyear* the Court rejected a steady but comparatively small stream of sales. In contrast, the operation of a principal place of business in a particular forum would be sufficient. *Perkins, supra.*

Answer (B) is incorrect. This is the test for specific jurisdiction. This level of contacts may not be sufficient to support general jurisdiction.

Answer (D) is incorrect. The *plaintiff's* residence is not relevant to the existence of general jurisdiction over the defendant. It is the defendant's contacts with the forum that determine whether the court has jurisdiction. The Court also noted in *Goodyear* that the interest of North Carolina parents in suing Goodyear's foreign subsidiaries at the parents' home in North Carolina was not relevant to general jurisdiction analysis.

202. **Answer (B) is correct.** Once a defendant is subject to general jurisdiction in the forum state, a plaintiff may sue it there for claims that did not arise out of those contacts. A defendant with such a high level of contacts with the state is thought to have benefited significantly from its constant and pervasive affiliations there. Such a defendant is also not generally placed at a disadvantage to defend itself there.

Answer (A) is incorrect. General jurisdiction does allow adjudication of claims that arise out of the defendant's contacts with the forum, but it is not limited to such claims.

Answer (C) is incorrect. The *Perkins* case, the only case in which the Supreme Court has found sufficient contacts for general jurisdiction, involved a situation such as this. *Perkins v. Benguet Consol. Mining*, 343 U.S. 917 (1952). The Court has not held that general jurisdiction is limited to a temporary crisis headquarters, and although it has referred to *Perkins* as the "textbook case of general jurisdiction appropriately exercised," it has more generally talked about where the foreign corporation is essentially "at home." *Daimler AG v. Bauman*, 134 S. Ct. 746, 758 n. 11 (2014).

Answer (D) is incorrect. Jurisdiction must be established over each defendant. Jurisdiction over one defendant, whether specific or general, does not by itself confer jurisdiction over co-defendants.

TOPIC 40: SPECIFIC JURISDICTION — ANSWERS

203. **Answer (C) is correct.** The Texas store may have wronged Carton, but it did so at its home in Texas. It does not have sufficient contacts with Virginia to be sued there. Nor did the store take any purposeful act aimed at Virginia or seek to serve the Virginia market. The fact that a Virginian was allowed to enter the store does not provide the kind of contact with Virginia that the courts look for to establish personal jurisdiction. The facts do not even indicate that the store was aware that Carton was from Virginia during its encounter with him.

Answer (A) is incorrect. The tort of wrongful imprisonment is an intentional one. But it was not committed in Virginia or directed toward injuring a Virginia citizen in Virginia. The intentional nature of the tort does not change the result under these facts.

Answer (B) is incorrect. While it will often be true that plaintiffs can sue at home, that is not invariably true. The jurisdictional analysis is based on the defendant's relationship with the forum, not the plaintiff's relationship with it.

Answer (D) is incorrect. The defendant did not initiate its contacts with Carton; Carton came to it. The constitutional test requires that the defendant take some purposeful act directed at the forum state, and selling a small item to a customer who has come to the defendant's home base is not sufficient to provide jurisdiction in the customer's home state over the customer's wrongful imprisonment claim.

204. **Answer (C) is correct.** The store's contacts with Virginia are still insufficient. And Virginia's claim to personal jurisdiction is still weak. This is still a fairly low level of activity, and it was initiated by the Virginians. First, the sale of books is unrelated to Carton's cause of action and therefore cannot be used to support jurisdiction over the store on his wrongful imprisonment claim. Second, the Virginians initiated the purchase transaction.

Answer (A) is incorrect. As was true in the previous question, the fact that the cause of action is an intentional tort does not improve the jurisdictional claim when neither the tortious act nor its consequences took place in the forum state.

Answer (B) is incorrect. These minimal contacts certainly would not justify the exercise of general jurisdiction. Therefore, because they are not related to Carton's cause of action, they do not "count" when assessing the store's amenability to Carton's cause of action. Some commentators argue that courts should be allowed to consider both related and unrelated contacts in determining the appropriateness of jurisdiction in a kind of "hybrid" jurisdictional analysis, but the Supreme Court continues to discuss them as two separate types of jurisdiction, including in the two 2011 cases, *Nicastro* and *Goodyear*, and the two 2014 cases, *Daimler* and *Walden*.

Answer (D) is incorrect. The mere existence of some amount of profits generated by sales to residents of the forum state does not guarantee the existence of personal jurisdiction, particularly when the cause of action is unrelated to those profits.

205. **Answer (A) is probably correct.** This situation has the kind of contacts that Carton's case lacked. Here DeFarge regularly and purposefully made a large volume of direct sales to the forum state. Lucie's claim arises out of DeFarge's contacts with California: it sold knitting needles there, and her claim is that one of those needles was defective and injured her. This defendant has benefited from the California market, and it is fair to require it to defend itself in a California court in a suit involving the products voluntarily sold there.

Answer (B) is incorrect. DeFarge has done a sufficient volume of voluntary business with California to provide sufficient contacts for the state to constitutionally assert jurisdiction over it. That does not, however, mean that it has actually consented to jurisdiction. Although Justice Kennedy's plurality opinion in *J. McIntyre Machinery Ltd. v. Nicastro*, 180 L. Ed. 2d 765 (2011), says that a defendant's contacts with a forum means that it "submits to the judicial power" of the forum, his reasoning is joined only by three other Justices, and even Justice Kennedy distinguishes this concept of "submission" from actual consent.

Answer (C) is incorrect. Continuous and systematic contacts are not required for specific jurisdiction, and Lucie's cause of action (defective knitting needle) arises out of DeFarge's contacts with California (selling knitting needles).

Answer (D) is probably incorrect. An isolated sale of goods initiated by a consumer might not be sufficient to justify jurisdiction. However, a large volume of voluntary sales over some period of time will be sufficient for jurisdiction, even if the contracts are structured so that the "offers" come from the customers. Be aware, however, that some courts defer to defendants' attempts to structure their businesses to avoid jurisdiction, and so if DeFarge did nothing to solicit the business of California consumers and all of DeFarge's contacts with California were initiated by the customers, many courts might find that California lacked jurisdiction over DeFarge on Lucie's claim, especially if the quantity of sales was small or sporadic.

206. **Answer (D) is probably correct.** DeFarge has deliberately marketed its product in the state of Maine. This was done partly through a national publication that is available in Maine. Note, though, that in *J. McIntyre Machinery Ltd. v. Nicastro*, Justice Kennedy's plurality opinion treated a foreign corporation's marketing to the entire United States as not targeting any particular state. Untargeted national media, therefore, may not "count" even for domestic defendants. But the fact that DeFarge sent an employee to Maine to sell the Super Chopper is the kind of "purposeful availment" that was missing in *Nicastro*. Further, this is a large, expensive machine, so that a single sale is more significant than the sale of a single pair of knitting needles. (That argument, though, was more persuasive to *Nicastro*'s dissenters than to the plurality, which still treated that sale of one large machine as a single, isolated transaction.) That same machine is now said to have injured the plaintiff in Maine. That combination of facts may be sufficient to support a conclusion that DeFarge has sought to serve the Maine market, and that its contacts are sufficient to support personal jurisdiction. Although there is only a single sale, it was purposeful, it was initiated by the defendant's seeking to sell in Maine, and it is precisely this contact that is alleged to have caused damage to the plaintiff.

Answer (A) is probably incorrect, but it might be held to be correct by some courts. The "stream of commerce" metaphor is so beguiling that it can be overused. Cases involving purposeful direct sales to the forum can show more "purposeful availment" and the kind of desire to serve the market that is absent in cases in which a product reaches the forum state through a less direct means. The stream of commerce cases involve situations in which the defendant did not make a sale directly into the forum state (e.g., component part manufacturers as in *Asahi*; sales through independent distributors, as in *Nicastro*; consumers bringing products to the forum as in *World-Wide Volkswagen*). There is nevertheless a tendency in some courts to use "isolated sales" to label both types of cases, and to deny jurisdiction. The concurring Justices in *Nicastro* (Justices Breyer and Alito) also remarked that "[n]one of our precedents finds that a single isolated sale, even if accompanied by the kind of sales effort indicated here, is sufficient" (citing *World-Wide Volkswagen* and Justice O'Connor's opinion in *Asahi*).

Answer (B) is incorrect because it is incomplete. If DeFarge's only contact with Maine had been one ad in a nationally-circulated publication, that would not be a sufficient level of contact to support jurisdiction. As noted above, some Supreme Court Justices treat national-level solicitations as not targeting any individual state, as with the defendant's appearances at national trade conventions in *Nicastro*. A similar situation exists when a defendant advertises on a fairly passive website that is available in the forum. These contacts can be considered along with others, but they do not alone constitute the kind of targeted contacts that the courts require.

Answer (C) is incorrect. There may be substantive tort law issues concerning when a person who did not purchase a defective product may sue for injuries caused by the defect. But from a personal jurisdiction standpoint, DeFarge has still purposefully created sufficient contacts with Maine by marketing and selling the machine there, and Lorry's personal injury claim arises out of those contacts. A contractual relationship with Lorry is not required.

207. **Answer (C) is correct.** Catherine was the consumer of the ladder and saw, and she purchased both in Kentucky from a local business. There is no indication that Hindley's attempted to market its products in Tennessee. When Hindley's sold the ladder, Catherine was a Kentucky resident. When Hindley's sold Catherine the saw, the salesman was aware that Catherine lived in Tennessee, but that awareness of a single sale to a known resident of Tennessee will not be sufficient to support an argument that Hindley's sought to serve the Tennessee market. The potentially defective products were brought into Tennessee by the consumer, not by the seller. They are not even inherently mobile products like the car in *World-Wide Volkswagen Corp. v. Woodson*, 444 U.S. 286 (1980), and the Supreme Court rejected a claim of jurisdiction there. At the risk of being repetitious, it is the defendant's voluntary acts directed at the forum, and not the plaintiff's ties to the forum, that provide the basis for jurisdiction over the defendant. The plaintiff's "unilateral acts" cannot fill in the gap.

Answer (A) is incorrect. Foreseeability, in the sense that Hindley's could imagine that its products might end up in Tennessee, is not the proper inquiry for personal jurisdiction. Instead, the Court has looked for situations in which the defendant could "reasonably anticipate being haled into court" there. The plurality in *Nicastro* has rejected any kind of foreseeability as the proper inquiry, arguing instead the defendant's forum activities are a way of submitting to the power of the forum state. "[I]t is the defendant's actions, not his expectations, that empower a State's courts to subject him to judgment."

Answer (B) is incorrect. Hindley's knowledge that its customer was from Tennessee is not sufficient to say that it sought to serve the Tennessee market. Hindley's wanted to sell the saw, and was probably indifferent regarding where Catherine would use it.

Answer (D) is incorrect. The problem with jurisdiction here is not that it involved inexpensive, low-profit products. The problem is that it was the consumer rather than Hindley's who took the products to Tennessee.

208. In this question, the subject of an allegedly libelous story wants to sue the reporter who wrote it. It is possible, but most unlikely, that in this situation a court would find jurisdiction over Nelly in Tennessee. This is very similar to *Calder v. Jones*, 465 U.S. 783 (1984), in which Shirley Jones was allowed to sue not only the *National Enquirer* but also the writer and the editor of a story about her, even though the story was written, edited, and printed in Florida, and even though the reporter did not control the distribution of the newspaper. The Supreme Court noted that the individual defendants aimed their tortious actions at California: they knew that the article would have an impact on Jones and that the impact would be felt in California. In *Calder* the story concerned a California resident, was drawn from California sources, was about an alleged California incident, and most of the injury Jones suffered would be felt in California where she lived and worked. The *National Enquirer* also had its largest circulation in California.

More recently, in *Walden v. Fiore*, 134 S. Ct. 1115 (2014), the Supreme Court concluded that the "crux of *Calder* was that the reputation-based 'effects' of the alleged libel connected the defendants to California, not just to the plaintiff . . . who happened to live there. That connection, combined with the facts that gave the article a California focus, sufficed to authorize the California court's exercise of jurisdiction." 134 S. Ct. at 1123-1124.

In Catherine's case, some but not all of those facts are present: the publication had *much* more limited circulation in Tennessee; Nelly knew that the article would have an impact on Catherine that she would feel at her home in Tennessee; some of the sources were likely from Tennessee, although more were probably from Kentucky; and Nelly sent a photographer to Tennessee to try to get a photo to accompany the story. It's unclear whether the target audience for the story was in Georgia (more likely, given the paper's circulation) or in Tennessee. Similarly, the level of sales of the *Journal* (12/issue) in Tennessee are not sufficient to justify jurisdiction under *Keeton v. Hustler Magazine*, 465 U.S. 770 (1984). In that case, the Court relied on sales of 10,000 to 15,000 copies of the magazine in the forum state to find sufficient contacts to justify personal jurisdiction over Hustler.

It is doubtful that Nelly's telephone conversations with sources in Tennessee or sending a photographer there in an effort to get a picture of Catherine to accompany the story would be sufficient to support the exercise of specific jurisdiction in Tennessee. Assuming that these actions by Nelly count as contacts with Tennessee, as is likely, they are not likely to meet the purposeful availment standard in *Walden* that the nonresident defendant's activities must be directed at the forum state itself, not one or a few of its residents.

209. The issue of interstate defamation has now spread to the Internet. Here there are no physical sales of the publication to bolster the finding of jurisdiction. Instead, there is a website which produces images that can be viewed anywhere in the world, but those images are not physically distributed in Tennessee in the same way that the *Journal* was in the previous question. The law in this area is still developing, but there is an argument for jurisdiction over "TheDirt.com" just as there was an argument for jurisdiction over Nelly; just as in Nelly's case, these are not the strongest facts for jurisdiction. Courts seem to be

looking to see whether the publication "targeted" the forum state. One factor relevant to the existence of targeting is the publication's knowledge that the plaintiff lives in the forum. However, more indications that the publication aimed its story at the forum are required. Here, "TheDirt.com" knew that Catherine lived in Tennessee and that its story would affect her there. It did not do the original research, but it did add some items with ties to Tennessee, hinting at an interest in a Tennessee audience for a story about one of its current residents. The tort alleged is once again intentional rather than negligent, but after *Walden*, this probably no longer matters. *See Walden v. Fiore*, 134 S. Ct. 1115, 1123 (2014). It is quite likely that internet journals and their reporters may find themselves the subject of lawsuits in the domiciles of the persons about whom they write; whether personal jurisdiction will be upheld is still unpredictable at this time.

210. **Answer (B) is probably correct.** Jurisdiction arising out of internet-based contractual relationships is also still evolving. At the present time, some courts trying to evaluate virtual contacts look at the nature of the web page on a kind of sliding scale. *Zippo Co. v. Zippo Dot Com*, 952 F. Supp. 1119 (W.D. Pa. 1997), is often cited as the source of this test. A purely passive web page (just pictures and text, with little or no interactivity and no way to purchase a product online) will not provide the contacts needed for personal jurisdiction. The customer generally will be regarded as having come to the website, rather than the website being regarded as having sought to sell to the forum residents. At the other end of the scale, a commercial website through which the merchant conducts business over the Internet with forum residents will often support jurisdiction. Goggles.com may fall into this category, particularly if it has a high volume of sales to forum residents. While online merchants whose products are delivered through cyberspace sometimes claim not to know where their customers are located, technology has developed that can identify the location of the customers in many cases. Websites with an intermediate level of interactivity are judged on a case-by-case basis, considering the level of interactivity and the commercial nature of the website. Because most websites fall into that middle category, courts citing *Zippo* often go through the motions of explaining the sliding scale, but then decide the case using more conventional personal jurisdiction analysis.

This case could also be analyzed as other cases would be analyzed: has Goggles.com purposely sought to serve the Massachusetts market by promoting its products and benefitting from a high level of sales there? Has it knowingly entered into contracts with residents of Massachusetts? The *Zippo* sliding scale is increasingly unsatisfactory as a way to make jurisdictional decisions about web-based contacts. Some courts have even specifically rejected *Zippo* as flawed and unhelpful. *See, e.g., Caiazzo v. Am. Royal Arts Corp.*, 2011 Fla. App. LEXIS 8078 (June 1, 2011). You can expect that during your practice lifetimes this area of the law will continue to develop; you can hope that it will become more predictable. Thus far, however, the Supreme Court has avoided this subject in its four most recent opinions decided in 2011 and 2014.

Answer (A) is incorrect. A purely passive website will not alone support jurisdiction.

Answer (C) is incorrect. Even though in a technical sense a website is perpetually available, in another sense it is not located anywhere at all in physical space. Courts have rejected the argument that the always-on quality of the Internet results in continuous and systematic contacts of the kind required for general jurisdiction (which would make it possible to sue the defendant in that state even for claims having no relationship to the forum whatsoever).

Answer (D) is incorrect. Internet contacts, whether contractual as in this question, or tort-based as in the previous question, can sometimes provide the basis for personal jurisdiction. Some internet contacts solicit business, some provide the means of contract formation, and some (as in defamation cases) communicate the allegedly wrongful message or violate the plaintiff's intellectual property rights. Because website and e-mail based transactions interact with and predictably affect real world people and entities, they will continue to be part of a jurisdictional analysis, even as the technology enabling the contacts and the courts' method for analyzing these contacts become more sophisticated.

211. **Answer (B) is probably correct.** This case involves a component part manufacturer's amenability to suit when the "stream of commerce" takes the finished product to a state in which the parts manufacturer does not reside. The Supreme Court case law on this subject is inconclusive. In *Asahi Metal Indus. Co. v. Superior Court*, 480 U.S. 102 (1987), Justice O'Connor's plurality opinion argued that the component part manufacturer's knowledge that the finished product (containing its part) would end up in the forum, and its profits from those sales, were not enough to support jurisdiction. The O'Connor group (which also included Chief Justice Rehnquist and Justices Powell and Scalia) wanted to see more evidence that the defendant was seeking to serve the forum state. It noted possible ways a company might do that: advertise; appoint a sales agent in the state; create a consumer advice mechanism; customize the product for the forum state (all actions that seem fairly unlikely for most component part manufacturers).

Twenty-four years later, in *J. McIntyre Machinery Ltd. v. Nicastro*, 180 L. Ed. 2d 765 (2011), the Court again split badly in a stream of commerce case involving a foreign manufacturer. Justice Kennedy (writing for himself and Justices Roberts, Scalia, and Thomas) required targeting of the forum state specifically, and knowledge that a product (even a large, expensive one) was sold there, even when the defendant had participated in marketing the product throughout the United States, was not enough to justify jurisdiction. Keep in mind, though, that this view did not command a majority of the Court. The "no jurisdiction" result won only with the support of the concurring opinion of Justices Breyer and Alito, which rejected this limiting interpretation and ruled based on the evidence in the record and specific facts of the case. The concurrence did, however, reject a rule that would provide for jurisdiction wherever a product is known to be sold, because it would "permit every State to assert jurisdiction in a products-liability suit against any domestic manufacturer who sells its products (made anywhere in the United States) to a national distributor, no matter how large or small the manufacturer, no matter how distant the forum, and no matter how few the number of items that end up in the particular forum at issue."

Answer (A) is incorrect. The knowledge of a large volume of sales (and profits) over a long number of years would probably satisfy Justices Ginsburg, Sotomayor, and Kagan (the dissenters), but it is unlikely to have satisfied Justice Kennedy. He certainly did not so state in his opinion. The position he would take, however, is not entirely clear, because the long history of sales in HairCo's case may be distinguishable from the single sale in *Nicastro*. Sales through a distributor might be distinguishable from the sales of a component part, controlled by the seller of the finished good. Justice Kennedy's opinion did seem to be influenced by the defendant's lack of actual control over the marketing of the product, so that knowledge of sales, and actual profits from sales, might easily still be insufficient for the

Justices who joined this opinion.

Answer (C) is incorrect. It is true that the defendant in *Nicastro* was a British company, marketing through an independent distributor to the entire U.S. without targeting any particular state. The case preceding *Nicastro*, *Asahi* was even more problematic as precedent because it involved only non-U.S. parties (a Taiwanese tire manufacturer and a Japanese tire valve manufacturer). The original U.S. plaintiff, who was injured in a motorcycle accident, had sued the Taiwanese company, which had impleaded the Japanese company. All of the plaintiff's claims settled, leaving only the indemnity claim between the two component part manufacturers. All of this made it difficult to directly apply *Asahi*, particularly its analysis of the fairness of subjecting the component part manufacturer to jurisdiction. Nevertheless, both cases discuss the requirements of due process generally — and *Nicastro* explicitly mentions domestic defendants. It is *not* true that the cases are irrelevant to cases involving U.S. defendants.

Answer (D) is incorrect. In fact, it is backwards. Justice Breyer's opinion, joined by Justice Alito, expressed considerable concern about the possible plight of small businesses, foreign or domestic, if sales through distributors or over the Internet would subject them to jurisdiction wherever the goods end up being sold. It suggested that fairness might vary depending on the defendant's size, distance from the forum, and volume of sales, and expressed hope that a later case will provide the Court with a better vehicle to rethink personal jurisdiction doctrine, possibly with some guidance from the Solicitor General.

212. **Answer (D) is correct.** When analyzing specific jurisdiction, the question of the nature and sufficiency of the defendant's contacts with the forum is only the first step. In *Burger King v. Rudzewicz*, 471 U.S. 462 (1985), the Court articulated a two-step analysis. The question of minimum contacts/purposeful availment is step one. Step two considers fairness. Remember the old *International Shoe* formulation: "certain minimum contacts . . . such that the maintenance of the suit does not offend 'traditional notions of fair play and substantial justice.'" Step two is where the fair play and substantial justice come in. The Court has listed factors that should be considered: (1) the burden on the defendant; (2) the forum state's interest in adjudicating the dispute; (3) the plaintiff's interest in obtaining convenient and effective relief; (4) the interstate judicial system's interest in obtaining the most efficient resolution of controversies; and (5) the shared interest of the several states in furthering fundamental substantive social policies. Answer (D) corresponds with the first factor. *See also Int'l Shoe v. Washington*, 326 U.S. 310 (1945). Justice Brennan suggested in *Burger King* that under some circumstances, a balance that tips strongly in favor of the plaintiff's need for this forum, and the forum state's interest in the dispute, might bolster a weak case of purposeful availment; under this view the analysis is more holistic and less two separate steps. The plurality opinion in *Nicastro*, however, suggests that Chief Justice Roberts, Justice Scalia, Justice Kennedy and Justice Thomas would be concerned with the defendant's submission to the forum court's lawful authority by purposefully establishing minimum contacts with it rather than general fairness considerations. *See J. McIntyre Mach. Ltd. v. Nicastro*, 131 S. Ct. 2780, 2788 (2011). The five other members of the Supreme Court reject the plurality's seemingly new paradigm. *See also Nicastro*, 131 S. Ct. at 2792, 2803 (concurring and dissenting opinions).

Answer (A) is incorrect. The details of the forum's procedural rules (which could be the FRCP, or state rules very similar to the FRCP, or state rules that are not as similar) are not one of the issues that the court is to consider. Note, though, that in considering the burden on the defendant in *Asahi*, the Court did point out that the geographic inconvenience was heightened by the foreign nature of the legal system (California's) to the defendant, which would have been more familiar with the Japanese system.

Answer (B) is incorrect. The trial judge (who would be ruling initially on a motion to dismiss for lack of personal jurisdiction) does not consider whether he considers himself to be a good judge, nor do the appellate courts consider this issue as part of the fairness analysis.

Answer (C) is incorrect. The plaintiff's interest in obtaining convenient and effective relief *is* a factor. This could include considerations such as whether the plaintiff is a resident of the forum and whether the forum allows jurisdiction over all necessary parties. It does not, however, measure the fervency with which the plaintiff prays to keep the case in the forum state.

TOPIC 41: GENERAL JURISDICTION

ANSWERS

213. **Answer (B) is correct.** The facts of this problem are similar to those of *Perkins v. Benguet Consol. Mining Co.*, 343 U.S. 917 (1952), the only case in which the Supreme Court has upheld jurisdiction based on contacts unrelated to the forum. Benguet was a Philippine corporation whose operations there were disrupted by World War II. During that time period, the company's president moved its operations to his home in Ohio. The court noted that the president kept office files in Ohio, carried on correspondence from Ohio, drew and distributed salary checks drawn on an Ohio bank, and maintained two active bank accounts carrying substantial balances of company funds. He generally supervised the company's rehabilitation efforts back in the Philippines from the Ohio office. In addition, several directors' meetings were held in Ohio. The Supreme Court found that these contacts permitted Ohio to exert jurisdiction over Benguet even though the plaintiff's claim "arose from activities entirely distinct from" the activities in Ohio. The Court recently reaffirmed this analysis in *Goodyear Dunlop Tires Operations v. Brown*, 180 L. Ed. 2d 796 (2011), and in *Daimler AG v. Bauman*, 134 S. Ct. 746 (2014). Both cases allow and possibly restrict general jurisdiction to situations in which the defendant corporation's affiliations with the forum state are "so continuous and systematic" as to render it "essentially at home in the forum state," i.e. comparable to a domestic enterprise in that state. *Daimler AG v. Bauman*, 134 S. Ct. 746 (2014) ("With respect to a corporation, the place of incorporation and principal place of business are 'paradig[m] . . . bases for general jurisdiction.'"). MMC's move to Vermont and its activities there appears to make Vermont the corporation's principal place of business, even though it may not be permanent. Even the Court's opinion in *Daimler AG v. Bauman* does not overrule and seems to affirm the Court's earlier opinion in the *Perkins* case.

    Answer (A) is incorrect. Because Mrs. Morgan's claim does not arise out of MMC's Vermont activities, a level of contacts that would suffice for specific jurisdiction would not be sufficient to support jurisdiction.

    Answers (C) and (D) are incorrect. Because MMC's level of involvement in Vermont is continuous and systematic, it can be sued there on causes of action arising elsewhere, whether they involve mining or not. Commentators disagree about the extent to which the Court's opinion in *Perkins* can be extended beyond its facts. The situation described in this question, however, would meet even the stricter interpretation of *Perkins*.

214. **Answer (C) is correct.** Dave's claim against Coaster Country is unrelated to its contacts with Texas, so his suit would depend on the existence of general jurisdiction. Coaster Country does have a longstanding relationship with Texas, and that would be the basis of a claim that it has "continuous and systematic" contacts with the state, justifying such general jurisdiction. However, these kinds of contacts, although of some substance and of long duration, will not suffice. In *Helicopteros Nacionales de Colombia v. Hall*, 466 U.S. 408 (1984), the Supreme Court's second general jurisdiction case, the Court stated that "mere

purchases, even if occurring at regular intervals, are not enough to warrant a State's assertion of *in personam* jurisdiction over a nonresident corporation in a cause of action not related to those purchase transactions." It thus rejected a claim of general jurisdiction in Texas over a company that had purchased 80% of its helicopter fleet, over a number of years, and at a cost of more than $4 million from a Texas company. Coaster Country's longstanding purchases of food from Texas will likewise fail to provide a source of general jurisdiction. The Court's decision in *Goodyear Dunlop Tires Operations, S.A. v. Brown* also rejected a general jurisdiction claim based on the sale within the forum state of thousands (out of tens of millions) of defendants' tires, sent there by related but distinct Goodyear subsidiaries and unrelated to the plaintiff's cause of action. Although Justice Ginsburg's majority opinion in *Goodyear* did not explicitly say so, its treatment of a corporation's state of incorporation and principal place of business as the "paradigms" of proper general jurisdiction seem to indicate that the Court wants to restrict general jurisdiction to a very limited number of situations.

The Court's subsequent opinion in *Daimler* confirms and expands this attitude. *See Daimler AG v. Bauman*, 134 S. Ct. 746, 751, 762 n. 20 (2014) ("General jurisdiction instead calls for an appraisal of a corporation's activities in their entirety, nationwide and worldwide. A corporation that operates in many places can scarcely be deemed at home in all of them. Otherwise 'at home' would be synonymous with 'doing business' tests framed before specific jurisdiction evolved in the United States.").

Answer (A) is incorrect for the reasons set forth above.

Answer (B) is incorrect. Dave's claim about the flaws in the roller coaster operation and design is not related to the purchase of food.

Answer (D) is probably incorrect. Dave could certainly sue in North Dakota. The park is located there, its allegedly wrongful acts occurred there, and that is where he was injured. It is unlikely, however, that he could sue the park in New Mexico. Although he is from New Mexico, he chose to go to the park's home in North Dakota and his contacts with Coaster Country occurred there. Unless the park aggressively advertised for New Mexico residents to come (which is possible, but not included in the question), it is unlikely that it has sufficient contacts with New Mexico to be sued there. In *Goodyear*, the Court rejected the argument that the plaintiff's convenience or need for a forum has any relevance whatsoever to general jurisdiction analysis.

215. **Answer (C) is correct.** This question involves a suit against a corporation in the state of its main office when that suit involves a cause of action that arose elsewhere. In this case, RBE has its principal place of business in Illinois, but Little's claim arose in California. There is considerable controversy about the level of activity necessary for general jurisdiction over corporations. This, however, is a clearer case. The defendant corporation is sued at the location of its principal place of business (comparable to suing a human in his home state), and the cause of action is similar to one which could have arisen from its Illinois business (all involve fast food sales). Both the holding in *Perkins* and dictum in *Goodyear* support this conclusion. Traditional analysis also recognizes general jurisdiction over a corporation in its state of incorporation.

The more difficult corporate general jurisdiction cases involve national businesses that regularly conduct some business in the forum, but which are not headquartered there. For example, should a person who fell in a Wal-Mart store in California be able to sue Wal-Mart in Texas because Wal-Mart has a very large number of stores (but not its headquarters) there? Courts and commentators are split on this issue, and *Goodyear* and *Daimler* did not resolve it. Both cases did, however, define general jurisdiction as applying only when a corporation's "affiliation with the State are so 'continuous and systematic' *as to render them essentially at home in the forum State.*" (Emphasis added.)

In the case of large national corporations, the issue may not often arise. Justice Ginsburg's opinion also suggests in dictum that companies that are "registered to do business" in a state may be subject to general jurisdiction there — as Goodyear USA was in this case. If that is correct (and lower courts have split on the issue), many corporations will be subject to jurisdiction based on their compliance with state law requiring that non-resident corporations engaging in intra-state business register to do business there.

If it is not correct, a complete personal jurisdictional analysis will be required even if the corporation has registered to transact business on the forum state and appointed a registered agent to accept service of process. *See, e.g., Conner v. ContiCarriers & Terminals, Inc.*, 944 S.W.2d 405, 416 (Tex. App.—Houston [14th Dist.] 1997, writ ref'd) ("By registering to do business, a foreign corporation only potentially subject itself to jurisdiction"); *see also Siemer v. Learjet Acquisition Corp.*, 966 F.2d 179, 181-182 (5th Cir. 1992).

Answer (A) is incorrect. It is true that the contacts and cause of action are not directly related, but if general jurisdiction exists that is not important. In addition, the case for jurisdiction here is strengthened by the similarity between the contacts that are the basis for Little's claim and RBE's contacts with Illinois.

Answer (B) is incorrect. While the level of activity required is not clear, some type of general jurisdiction over corporations does exist, even if it is not as extensive as some lower court cases have held it to be. In *Perkins* the Court upheld what we now call general jurisdiction, and in *Helicopteros* and *Goodyear*, the Court recognized the existence of the concept, while finding it inapplicable to the facts before it in those particular cases.

Answer (D) is incorrect. Even the most expansive notion of general jurisdiction does not contend that a "huge" corporation (whatever that would mean) can be sued anywhere, regardless of the extent of its contacts with that forum.

TOPIC 42: ANSWERS
PERSONAL JURISDICTION: PROCEDURAL ISSUES

216. **Answer (B) is correct.** Dan has properly raised the issue of personal jurisdiction under Rule 12, and if the court agrees that it lacks jurisdiction over him it should dismiss the case. Such a dismissal does not adjudicate the merits, however, so Peter may refile it in a jurisdiction that does have jurisdiction over Dan.

Answer (A) is incorrect. The correct remedy for a case lacking personal jurisdiction over the defendant is dismissal. In some cases, when a defendant moves for change of venue within the federal system in addition to attacking personal jurisdiction, the court is allowed to transfer the case to a district in which venue (and personal jurisdiction) are proper under 28 U.S.C. § 1406 instead of dismissing the case. Even under these circumstances, however, the plaintiff, who has filed in the wrong place, has lost the right to absolute choice among proper forums.

Answer (C) is incorrect. A dismissal for lack of personal jurisdiction should not be a dismissal with prejudice. The court has held that the defendant may not be sued there, not that the plaintiff has no claim on the merits.

Answer (D) is incorrect. Rule 12 allows the defendant to ask the court to dismiss the case for lack of personal jurisdiction without generally appearing, if it raises the issue at the proper time under Rule 12(g) and (h).

217. **Answer (D) is correct.** Unlike the previous question, in which the defendant raised the issue of personal jurisdiction before answering, Dick has filed an answer first, and that answer did not raise the defense of lack of personal jurisdiction. It is now too late to amend this answer as a matter of course under Rule 15(a). Dick has therefore waived his right to raise the issue of personal jurisdiction. Even if Dick has no contacts with the forum, his appearance means that the court may not grant his late-filed motion and (absent some other reason for dismissal or transfer) the case will stay in Wyoming.

Answer (A) is incorrect. The case will not be transferred, as noted above.

Answer (B) is incorrect. Dick has waived his objection to the court's lack of jurisdiction over his person.

Answer (C) is incorrect. The court should not dismiss the case at all.

218. **Answer (B) is correct.** Because she did not participate in the Wisconsin case, Donna retains the right to raise the issue of personal jurisdiction as a defense to enforcement of the judgment against her. If she is correct, and the Wisconsin court lacked personal jurisdiction over her, then the judgment is not enforceable. Had she appeared in Wisconsin and challenged personal jurisdiction, she would not be allowed to re-raise this issue when enforcement was sought in Pennsylvania.

Answer (A) is incorrect. Donna has not yet litigated the issue of personal jurisdiction, and the lack of personal jurisdiction is a defense to the enforcement of a sister state judgment.

Answer (C) is incorrect. It is correct that Donna may complain about the Wisconsin court's lack of jurisdiction over her. However, if she is wrong about that (the court did have jurisdiction), then she has lost the ability to defend on the merits. This makes the route that Donna has chosen (ignoring the case rather than fighting jurisdiction in Wisconsin) a risky one. If she has guessed wrong about the personal jurisdiction issue, she has lost any defenses that she might have had to the case.

Answer (D) is incorrect. (In fact, it is exactly backward.) See the explanations above.

TOPIC 43:	**ANSWERS**
SERVICE OF PROCESS	

219. **Answer (C) is correct.** "Federal courts ordinarily follow state law in determining the bounds of their jurisdiction over persons." *Daimler AG v. Bauman*, 134 S. Ct. 746, 753 (2014). This is true because a federal district court's authority to assert personal jurisdiction in most cases is linked to service of process on a defendant "who is subject to the jurisdiction of a court of general jurisdiction in the state where the district is located." Fed. R. Civ. P. 4(k)(1)(A). Rule 4(e) and (h) authorize federal plaintiffs to use state law procedures in effecting service. *See* Fed. R. Civ. P. 4(e)(1) and (h)(l)(A).

    Answer (A) is incorrect for the same reason that Answer (C) is correct.

    Answer (B) is also incorrect. Although Rule 4(h) authorizes service on a corporation "by delivering a copy of the summons and complaint to a corporate officer or another agent authorized by appointment or by law . . . ," federal plaintiffs have a choice between federal law and state law. In either case, substantial compliance with state or federal law is sufficient.

    Answer (D) is incorrect. Despite recent developments, RobCo is probably subject to personal jurisdiction in Texas courts in this situation. RobCo purposefully contacted Sally in Texas and entered into a contract to be performed in Texas.

220. **Answer (D) is correct.** Rule 4 allows for service of process (summons and complaint) to be conducted pursuant to the law of the state where service is sought to be effected or pursuant to the law of the forum state where the action will be adjudicated. Thus, both answers (B) and (C) are correct. *See* Fed. R. Civ. P. 4(e)(1); *see also Deininger v. Deininger*, 677 F. Supp. 48, 490 (N.D. Tex. 1988) (jurisdiction proper over defendant when served pursuant to Texas long-arm statute). Further, "dismissal of a complaint is inappropriate when there exists a reasonable prospect that service may yet be obtained. In such instances, the district court should at most, quash service, leaving the plaintiff free to effect proper service." *Umbenhauer v. Woog*, 969 F.2d 25, 30 (3d Cir. 1992).

    Answer (A) is incorrect for the same reason that Answers (B) (C) and (D) are correct. *See* Fed. R. Civ. P. 4(e)(1).

221. Although American courts have accepted citation by publication in the form of a brief notice published in the classified section of a local newspaper for more than a century, when a defendant's identity is known, service by publication is generally inadequate. *See, e.g.*, Restatement (Second) of Judgments § 2, cmt. a (1982) ("The critical distinction is between notice to known claimants and notice to persons unknown. Notice by publication meets the requirement of adequate notice to the latter but not as to the former."); *Mullane v. Cent. Hanover Bank & Trust Co.*, 339 U.S. 306, 313-319 (1950); *Mennonite Board of Missions v. Adams*, 462 U.S. 791, 798-800 (1983) ("Notice by mail or other means as certain to ensure actual notice is a minimum constitutional precondition to a proceeding which will adversely

affect the liberty or property interests of any party . . . if its name and address are reasonably ascertainable.").

TOPIC 44: VENUE GENERALLY

ANSWERS

222. **Answer (D) is correct.** Proper venue for Woolf's suit against Austen is governed by 28 U.S.C. § 1391(b). Section (b)(1) provides that venue is proper in a judicial district in which any defendant resides, if all defendants reside in the same state. As there is only one defendant, the judicial district of her residence, W.D. La., is proper. Section 1391(b)(2) also provides that venue is proper in a judicial district in which a substantial part of the events or omissions giving rise to the claim occurred. In this case, the negligence and its consequences occurred in E.D. Okla., making venue proper there as well. Because both Sections 1 and 2 make U.S. venue available, Section 3 does not apply.

   Answer (A) is incorrect. The plaintiff's residence is not for that reason a district of proper venue.

   Answers (B) and (C) are incorrect because they are incomplete. The various venue options listed in § 1391 are all available, and the plaintiff may choose among the districts in which venue is proper.

223. **Answer (D) is correct.** Venue is proper under § 1391(b)(1) in a judicial district in which any defendant resides, if all defendants reside in the same state. Here both defendants reside in Louisiana, so both E.D. La. and W.D. La. would be proper. Venue is also proper in a judicial district in which a substantial part of the events or omissions giving rise to the claim occurred, making E.D. Okla. proper as well. Because both Sections 1 and 2 make U.S. venue available, Section 3 does not apply.

   Answer (A) is incorrect. When multiple defendants reside in the same state, any of their districts of residence provide proper venue, but other districts in the state do not. The M.D. La. is therefore improper.

   Answer (B) is incorrect because it is incomplete. It omits the districts in which the defendants reside, as both reside in Louisiana.

   Answer (C) is incorrect, as it includes a district in which no defendant resides and in which no part of the events or omissions giving rise to the claim occurred.

224. **Answer (D) is correct.** This question examines the problem of what constitutes a "substantial part" of the events or omissions giving rise to the claim. The legislative history makes clear that more than one district can qualify — the statute does not require the identification of a single district that has the most events or omissions. In this case, it is likely that a district in which trade secrets were stolen and a district in which they were wrongfully used would both qualify as places where a "substantial part" of the events or omissions occurred. Again, Section 3 is not applicable.

   Answers (A) and (B) are incorrect because they omit districts in which venue would be correct for the reasons set forth above.

Answer (C) is incorrect. The statute does not make the district of the plaintiff's residence a place of proper venue.

225. **Answer (D) is correct.** The defendants do not live in the same state, making Section (b)(1) unavailable. That leaves Section (b)(2), a district in which a substantial part of the acts or omissions occurred. Here the trespass alleged occurred in D. Mass., making it a district where venue is proper. Because Section 2 produced a district in which venue is available, Section 3 is not applicable.

Answers (A), (B), and (C) are incorrect. Because the defendants do not reside in the same state, none of their districts of residence can form the basis of proper venue.

226. **Answer (D) is the best answer.** Absent enough contacts for general jurisdiction in some other district, the only district in which Fast Ride has sufficient contacts to subject it to personal jurisdiction *in this case* is the Central District of California, the district in which the events or omissions giving rise to Lance's claim occurred.

Answer (A) is incorrect because California has more than one district and Fast Ride is not subject to personal jurisdiction in all of them. Section 1391(d) requires a district-by-district analysis. (And it is unlikely that Fast Ride is subject to general jurisdiction in any of them.)

Answer (B) is incorrect because Lance's residence is immaterial under current law.

Answer (C) is incorrect for the same reason that Answer (D) is correct. Fast Ride does not "reside" in any of the districts in which Lance's claim did not arise under § 1391(d) because its contacts are not sufficiently continuous and systematic so that Fast Ride is "at home" in those districts. It is likely that the company is subject to general jurisdiction only in Delaware, where it is incorporated, and in Pennsylvania, where it has its principal place of business. *See Daimler A.G. v. Bauman*, 134 S. Ct. 746, 758 n.11 (2014) (general jurisdiction requires affiliations "so continuous and systematic" as to render a foreign corporation "essentially at home in the forum state . . ., i.e., comparable to a domestic enterprise in that state").

227. The question of venue in *Dawson v. Wow Chemicals* will be determined under §§ 1391(b) and (d). Starting with Section 1, one option will be a district in which the defendant resides. This time the defendant is a corporation rather than a human, so the question of where it "resides" is governed by § 1391(d). It provides that "a defendant that is a corporation shall be deemed to reside in any judicial district in which it is subject to personal jurisdiction at the time the action is commenced." In states having one judicial district, then, the defendant "resides" in a state if it is subject to personal jurisdiction there. In states having more than one judicial district, if the defendant is subject to personal jurisdiction in the state, it "resides" in "any district in that State within which its contacts would be sufficient to subject it to personal jurisdiction if that district were a separate State." In this case, it appears that Wow "resides" in the Southern District of Texas because it is subject to general jurisdiction there, but not in the other Districts because it is probably not "at home" and not subject to general jurisdiction there. But regardless of where Wow Chemicals resides, it would be subject to *specific* personal jurisdiction in the Northern District because the chemical that injured Jack was manufactured there. Section 1391(b)(2) also applies, making venue proper in the Northern District where a substantial part of the events or omissions giving rise to

Jack's claim occurred.

228. **Answer (C) is correct.** This question illustrates the unusual case in which the fallback venue provision found in Section 3 of 1391(b) comes into play. Section 1 will not result in a district of proper venue, because the defendants reside in different states. Section 2 will not result in a district of proper venue, because the events giving rise to the claim occurred wholly outside the United States. Section 3 permits venue in a judicial district "in which any defendant is subject to the court's personal jurisdiction with respect to such action." Section 3 would permit venue in either N.D. Okla. or D. Neb., but Kathy would also have to get personal jurisdiction over the non-resident defendant and that might not be possible.

Answers (A), (B), and (D) are incorrect for reasons explained above.

TOPIC 45: CHANGE OF VENUE	ANSWERS

229. Bloomer has filed her suit in a district in which venue is improper. This case could have been filed in D. Utah (Pankhurst's residence) or D. Colorado (where the "omission" of delivery of the widgets occurred), but no provision of § 1391(b) makes venue proper in Wyoming. Pankhurst can file a motion to dismiss, or, in the alternative, transfer the case for improper venue under 28 U.S.C. § 1406(a). (She must be careful to file this Rule 12 defense at the proper time or it will be waived. *See* Topic 2.) The court may either dismiss the action, or transfer it to any district or division in which it could have been brought. The trial court in D. Wyoming will most likely transfer the case either to D. Utah or D. Colorado.

230. **Answer (C) is the correct answer.** Section 1404(a) of Title 28, authorizes a convenience transfer to Missouri "in the interest of justice" and for "the convenience of parties and witnesses." 28 U.S.C. § 1404. The case could be transferred to any district or division where it might have been brought, which would include the Eastern District of Missouri. In ruling on a motion under § 1404, the court will consider whether party and forum convenience override the plaintiff's choice of forum, which is given considerable weight. Party considerations include relative ease of access to witnesses and evidence, the cost of obtaining the attendance of witnesses, the ability to compel the attendance of key witnesses and, where applicable, the jury's ability to view the scene of the accident. Forum considerations include the effect on the courts' dockets, the burden of jury duty on the possible fora, local interest in the case, and the substantive law that will apply to the issues in the case. Under the rule of *Van Dusen v. Barrack*, 376 U.S. 612 (1961), if the case is transferred, the transferee court must follow the law that would be applied by the transferor court; to avoid gamesmanship, the transfer should result in the change of courtrooms, not a change in the governing law.

Answer A is incorrect. Venue is proper in Iowa because the plane crash occurred in Iowa. 28 U.S.C. § 1391(b)(2) ("a judicial district in which a substantial part of the events or omissions giving rise to the claim occurred").

Answers (B) and (D) are incorrect for the same reason that Answer (C) is correct.

231. Under both the general venue statute (28 U.S.C. § 1391(b)(2)) and the patent and copyright venue statute (29 U.S.C. § 1408(b)), the Northern District of Texas is a place of proper venue for Edison's action against Franklin. This means that transfer of the action to another judicial district in the United States must be based on 28 U.S.C. § 1404, which is applicable when venue of the action to be transferred is proper under federal venue statutes, rather than 28 U.S.C. § 1406(a), which applies when the case has been filed "in the wrong district or division." *See* 28 U.S.C. § 1406(a).

In *Hoffman v. Blaski*, 363 U.S. 335 (1960), § 1404(a)'s "might have been brought" language was interpreted to allow "transfer only to places where venue and personal jurisdiction would have been proper as defined by law at the time the action was originally filed." Thus, because venue of the action in Nevada would not have been proper under the pertinent venue statutes, a convenience transfer under 28 U.S.C. § 1404 would not have been.

More than 60 years after *Hoffman v. Blaski* was decided, Congress passed the Jurisdiction and Venue Clarification Act of 2011, adding language to 28 U.S.C. § 1404(a) allowing transfer to "any district or division to which the parties consented." This provision appears to apply if the plaintiff files the action in one venue and then agrees with the defendant to transfer the action to another venue. Under this analysis, the new provision probably does not change the result in *Hoffman v. Blaski*, in which the plaintiff did not consent to the transfer. Should Edison agree to venue in Nevada (it is, after all, his home), then the 2011 amendment probably would make the transfer proper.

TOPIC 46: ANSWERS
VENUE, FORUM NON CONVENIENS, AND PROCEDURAL ISSUES

232. **Answer (C) is the correct answer.** The Supreme Court has determined that when a party to a contract containing a forum selection clause files suit for breach of the contract in a federal court in accordance with the situational requirements of 28 U.S.C. § 1391, but in violation of the clause, the proper procedural vehicle to use in enforcing the clause is a motion to transfer under 28 U.S.C. § 1404(a), which requires that such a clause selecting venue in another federal district court must be given controlling weight in most cases. *Atlantic Marine Constr. Co. v. United States Dist. Court*, 134 S. Ct. 568, 578 (2013) ("proper application of § 1404(a) requires that forum-selection clause be given controlling weight in all but the most exceptional cases"). By contrast, the appropriate way to enforce a forum selection clause selecting a state court or a foreign forum is through the doctrine of forum non conveniens. *Id.* at 580. Unlike other venue transfers made pursuant to 28 U.S.C. § 1404, the usual *Van Dusen* rule (*see Van Dusen v. Barrack*, 376 U.S. 612, 635 (1964) (law that transferor court would have applied must be applied by transferee court)) is not applicable when the defendant's motion is premised on the enforcement of a valid forum selection clause. *Atlantic Marine Constr. Co. v. United States Dist. Court*, 134 S. Ct. 568, 583 n. 8 (2013) ("same standards should apply to motions to dismiss for forum non conveniens in cases involving valid forum selection clauses pointing to state or federal forums").

Answers (A) and (B) are not correct. Because the requirements of 28 U.S.C. § 1391(b) were satisfied ("A civil action may be brought in . . . a judicial district in which a substantial part of the events giving rise to the claim occurred"), neither 28 U.S.C. § 1406(a) nor Rule 12(b)(3) are available procedural mechanisms. These provisions allow dismissal only when venue is "wrong" or "improper" under the requirements of federal venue laws, which "say nothing about a forum selection clause." *Atlantic Marine Constr. Co. v. United States Dist. Court*, 134 S. Ct. 568, 576-578 (2013).

Answer (D) is incorrect. The doctrine of forum non conveniens only applies when the forum selection clause points to a state or foreign forum.

233. **Answer (C) is correct.** A court, even though it has jurisdiction over the case and the defendant, may choose to dismiss a lawsuit under certain circumstances under the doctrine of forum non conveniens. The leading cases are *Gulf Oil Corp. v. Gilbert*, 330 U.S. 501 (1947), and *Piper Aircraft v. Reyno*, 454 U.S. 235 (1981). A party moving for a transfer under the doctrine must show that considerations of party and forum convenience override the plaintiff's choice of forum and justify dismissal. Party considerations (sometimes called "private considerations") include things like comparative ease of access to proof, the ability to compel the attendance of witnesses, and, where applicable, the jury's ability to view the scene of the accident. Sometimes, especially when the plaintiff resides in the forum state, this will act as a strong private factor in favor of keeping the case in the forum; the plaintiff's choice of forum is given great weight. Considerations of forum convenience (sometimes called "public factors") include a comparison of the burdens and benefits of locating the

litigation in the two fora. Courts may consider the case backlog of the two systems, local interest in the dispute, and the burden that jury service would impose. Public factors also include considerations of choice of law — litigation is thought to be simpler in the forum whose substantive law will govern the case.

Answer (A) is incorrect. The defendant's residence in the forum is not (at least formally) a factor in forum non conveniens analysis. A defendant may do business in the forum and nevertheless succeed in urging dismissal, as, for example, when all the events relevant to the suit and all the evidence related to the dispute are located elsewhere.

Answer (B) is incorrect. The location where the cause of action accrued is also not formally a part of forum non conveniens analysis. It may be that the location where a claim arose is also the place where the bulk of the witnesses and other evidence are located, in which case a motion to dismiss based on forum non conveniens would be unlikely to succeed. It may also be true that the law of a place where a cause of action accrued will govern the dispute. However, it is these convenience-based factors, rather than a search for the birth of the cause of action, that are relevant to the forum non conveniens analysis.

Answer (D) is incorrect. A party seeking dismissal must show that an adequate alternative forum is available. This does not require, however, that the alternative forum be procedurally identical to the American forum, or even that the relief available in the alternative forum would be the same as that available under U.S. law.

234. Most (but not all) judges in cases parallel to the problem case have dismissed them. Although some evidence (in the form of Wow Chemical documents and employees) will be available in the Southern District of Texas, the plaintiffs themselves, the plaintiffs' employers, and the evidence regarding the application of the chemicals and the plaintiffs' damages are located in Costa Rica. The plaintiffs' lack of a tie to the forum is also generally seen as weakening the deference ordinarily due to the plaintiffs' choice of forum. Product liability claims such as these can be time consuming to the courts, and so the public factors are often seen to militate in favor of the Costa Rican forum — the citizens of Texas are seen as having little stake in whether the Costa Rican plaintiffs were wronged or whether they will be compensated. It is also possible that Costa Rican rather than Texas law would be applied to the case, making it more convenient for the Costa Rican court system than for the Texas court system. The judges that have retained these cases have emphasized the plaintiffs' willingness to make themselves available for discovery and trial, the defendant's access to evidence about its chemical, and the forum state's interest in the behavior of its corporate citizens, even when that behavior is alleged to have caused injury outside of the United States.

TOPIC 47:	**ANSWERS**
CLAIM PRECLUSION	

235. **Answer (A) is correct.** The judgment in Paul's first lawsuit satisfies all of the requirements for claim preclusion. It was final, on the merits, involved the same parties, and concerns the same claim as Paul's proposed second suit. A majority of states use the Restatement (Second) of Judgments' definition of "same claim," which adopts a transactional approach to defining a claim, making "same claim" for preclusion purposes much like "same transaction or occurrence" in the joinder rules. Some states use older approaches that look for things like "same right" or "same evidence." Because Paul's proposed second suit is identical to the first one, it would qualify as the same cause of action under any of these definitions. From the standpoint of vocabulary, when a party loses the claim he is now trying to reassert, we say that the claim is "barred" by the first judgment.

    Answer (B) is incorrect. It is correct that Paul may not properly bring the second suit, but the language here is wrong. It is only when the party succeeds the first time, getting a judgment in his favor, that we say that all of the claims that are part of the same claim are "merged" into the judgment. In essence, the claim is extinguished and replaced by the judgment.

    Answer (C) is incorrect for the reasons above — and hiring a new lawyer does nothing to restore a claim. It is the parties who are subject to preclusion rules, not the attorneys.

    Answer (D) is incorrect for the same reasons. It doesn't matter whether the statute of limitations has run or not; the second suit is barred by preclusion even if it is not time-barred.

236. **Answer (C) is correct.** Claim preclusion does not merely bar litigation of issues that were actually raised. It includes other issues that could have been brought that are part of the same "claim." As noted in the previous answer, in a majority of states the question is whether the issue raised in the second suit is part of the same transaction as the first. Here, Paul's negligence claim and battery claim are both based on the events of the car wreck. Switching theories of relief will not make it a new "claim" for preclusion purposes.

    Answer (A) is incorrect. Although negligence and battery are different legal theories, in the context of Paul's lawsuits they are part of the same "claim."

    Answer (B) is incorrect. Claim preclusion does not require actual litigation of the claim to be barred. (Contrast this with issue preclusion, discussed in the next Topic.)

    Answer (D) is incorrect because neither (A) nor (B) is correct.

237. **Answer (B) is correct.** Here, Paul successfully obtained a judgment in his first suit. That judgment constitutes his relief for his entire "claim," which includes additional remedies that he could have sought but did not. While under earlier views of claim preclusion a party could bring separate suits for personal injuries and property damage, the majority approach today

requires all damages from a single incident to be included in a single suit.

Answer (A) is incorrect. Because Paul got a judgment in his favor in the first suit, his second is "merged" into that judgment rather than "barred."

Answer (C) is incorrect. A minority of jurisdictions might still use a "same right" definition of "same claim" that would allow separate suits for different kinds of damages, but most states would not. It would be extremely inefficient to allow independent lawsuits for each category of damages.

Answer (D) is incorrect for the reasons discussed above.

238. **Answer (D) is correct because Answers (B) and (C) are correct.** Even under a transactional approach to "same claim," one person's claim is not the same claim as a different person's claim. Looking only at principles of preclusion, the defendant's failure to file a counterclaim based on the same transaction does not usually preclude a later suit based on the counterclaim. (There are exceptions for cases in which "the relationship between the counterclaim and the plaintiff's claim is such that successful prosecution of the second action would nullify the initial judgment or would impair rights established in the initial action." But that's not applicable here.) *See* RESTATEMENT (SECOND) OF JUDGMENTS § 22. Therefore, although both Paul and Doug have claims arising out of the car wreck and involving much of the same evidence, Doug's claim is not the same as Paul's claim. The doctrine of claim preclusion does not bar Doug's claim. (It is, however, possible that a later claim that involves the same issues, actually litigated, decided, and necessary, may be subject to issue preclusion. *See* Topic 42.) However, in most jurisdictions a counterclaim that arises out of the same transaction or occurrence as the plaintiff's claim is compulsory — it must be brought them or lost forever. Since Doug's claim for damages in the car wreck arises out of the same transaction of occurrence as Paul's claim for damages from the same wreck, it would have been a compulsory counterclaim. Since Doug did not bring it in *Paul v. Doug*, it's gone.

Answer (A) is incorrect. As explained above, Doug's claim is not the same as Paul's claim, and so the requirements of claim preclusion are not met.

Answers (B) and (C) are correct, as explained above.

TOPIC 48: ISSUE PRECLUSION — ANSWERS

239. **Answer (D) is correct.** Even though the claim for negligent installation of the chandelier is probably not the same "claim" as the claim for negligent installation of the kitchen cabinets, the issue of whether Handy was acting as an independent contractor is the same in both cases. It also meets the other requirements for issue preclusion: it was actually litigated and decided in the first case (note that the jury made a finding on the issue). It was necessary to the judgment, because if Handy had not been acting as HH's agent, HH would not have been liable for his negligence. And both cases involve the same parties: Brandon and HH.

Answer (A) is incorrect. It doesn't matter whether the installation of the chandelier and the cabinets were part of the same "claim" — that's the test for claim preclusion, not issue preclusion. Fact issues that are actually litigated (and meet all the other requirements of issue preclusion) can bar relitigation even when they are relevant to different causes of action. (Contrast this with claim preclusion, where litigation of a "claim" can bar relitigation even of issues that were not actually raised.)

Answer (B) is incorrect. As noted above, the question of Handy's status — independent contractor or employee — was crucial to the result in the first case.

Answer (C) is incorrect. It doesn't matter whether Handy was a party to the first suit, as he is not the party that Brandon is trying to estop.

240. **Answer (B) is the best answer.** Issues can only form the basis of issue preclusion if they were necessary to the judgment in the first case. Here, the finding that led to the judgment for HH was that Handy was not negligent; HH would have won whether or not the contract was enforceable. Because the finding that the exculpatory contract was unenforceable did not affect the judgment, it was not "necessary" and does not bind HH.

Answer (A) is incorrect. While it's true that the judge's conclusion meets those other requirements, that is not enough to base preclusion on a finding that was not necessary.

Answer (C) is incorrect. Issue preclusion can be based on decisions both by judges and juries when the other requirements of the doctrine are met.

Answer (D) is incorrect. The treatment of alternative grounds is complicated. In this case, where an issue is not necessary because it was decided in favor of the losing party, the result is as explained above. The question is more difficult when a litigant prevails on two independent and equally sufficient grounds. Suppose that the jury found both that Handy was not negligent and that he was not acting as HH's employee on the renovation project. Either finding would be sufficient to support a judgment for HH. The RESTATEMENT (SECOND) OF JUDGMENTS § 27, comment i, would deny preclusive effect to both decisions (in other words, Brandon would be allowed to relitigate both), because it is impossible to tell which was necessary to the judgment. The ALI argues that alternate grounds may not have been as fully litigated, and the losing party may have insufficient incentive to appeal one ground when he will lose on the other. Note, though, that if the judgment is actually appealed the result could be different. If the court of appeals "upholds both of these determinations as sufficient, and accordingly affirms the judgment, the judgment is conclusive as to both determinations [because] the losing party has here obtained an appellate decision on the issue, and thus the balance weighs in favor of preclusion." A number of jurisdictions have declined to follow the Restatement approach and either give preclusive effect to *both* issues or examine the record and give preclusive effect only to holdings that were given full consideration in the first suit.

241. **Answer (D) is correct.** One of the requirements for issue preclusion is that the party to be estopped has litigated the issue and lost. Here, although HH litigated the issue of Handy's negligence, Handy has not. Sometimes a party may be bound if he is in "privity" with a party to the first case. Although privity is an elusive concept, the privity that can lead to issue preclusion is a relationship between two parties that is sufficiently close so as to bind them both to an initial determination, at which only one of them was present. Generally, that only applies to a nonparty who has succeeded to a party's interest in property or a nonparty who controlled the original suit. Under this approach, an employee is not in privity with his employer despite the existence of a contractual agency relationship between them. The relationship between HH and Handy is not sufficient for HH's loss to bind Handy.

Answers (A) and (C) are incorrect. The issue was litigated, but that does not justify estopping a person who was not a party and thus never had his day in court. Efficiency concerns are not enough to overcome the unfairness of binding a party who never had a chance to defend himself.

Answer (B) is incorrect for two reasons. First, the issue of Handy's negligence was in fact necessary to the judgment against HH. Second, even though necessary, it still cannot bind Handy, who was not a party. As you will see in the next Topic, modern courts are relaxing the "same party" rules in some ways, allowing a person who was *not* a party to try to *benefit* from issue preclusion by using it against someone who *was* a party. However, the party to be bound (i.e., the person *against* whom issue preclusion is being asserted) must have been a party to the first suit, or issue preclusion will not apply.

TOPIC 49: NON-MUTUAL ISSUE PRECLUSION — ANSWERS

242. **Answer (B) is correct.** Although traditionally courts required "mutuality of estoppel" — that both the party asserting collateral estoppel and the party to be estopped were parties to the first suit — under the modern approach mutuality is not required. Because Kelly was a party to the first suit, and because the issue of his heart attack is the same issue, was actually litigated and decided, and was necessary to the result in the first case, Dr. MacMahon may assert issue estoppel against him under the Restatement (Second) approach. Because MacMahon is using the heart attack issue in his defense, this is referred to as defensive non-mutual issue preclusion.

    Answer (A) is not the correct answer. While it is true that mutuality of estoppel is lacking, persons who were not parties to the first suit are now allowed to rely on issue preclusion when asserting it as a defense against someone who *was* a party.

    Answer (C) is not the correct answer. While it is true that WWF and MacMahon are not in privity, privity is not required in order for issue preclusion to apply here.

    Answer (D) is incorrect, because (A) and (C) are not the correct answers.

243. **Answer (C) is the best answer.** Wings-Are-Up's liability was actually litigated and the judgment in favor of Henrietta and Polly clearly rests on the findings of defect, unreasonable danger, and causation. Since the Restatement (Second) does not require mutuality, the question becomes whether the findings can be used "offensively" by Larry's parents. Unlike the question above, when the nonparty was using the findings only in defense, here Larry's parents seek to use them to establish elements of their cause of action. This is a very controversial issue, and while the Supreme Court has allowed offensive, non-mutual collateral estoppel, it has warned that under certain conditions a court might not choose to allow it. *Parklane Hosiery v. Shore*, 439 U.S. 322 (1979). As the Restatement (Second) puts it, issue preclusion is unavailable if the party who would be bound "lacked full and fair opportunity to litigate the issue in the first action or other circumstances justify affording him an opportunity to relitigate the issue." The circumstances that might lead to a refusal to use issue preclusion are: (1) the new plaintiff's purposeful choice to await the outcome of the first suit, hoping to get the benefit of estoppel without risking losing; (2) small stakes in the first suit, so that the defendant lacked adequate incentive to litigate the issue fully; (3) restrictive procedural rules in the first suit so that the defendant could not litigate effectively; and (4) multiple inconsistent judgments, indicating that it would be unfair to give conclusive effect to any one of them. In this case, however, it appears to be fair to allow Larry's parents to take advantage of issue preclusion. They had no duty to intervene in Henrietta's case and there is no indication they were hedging their bets by failing to do so; the stakes in Henrietta's case were very large, so that Wings-Are-Up had every incentive to litigate vigorously; Henrietta's suit was litigated in a conventional U.S. court, so the procedural differences would have been insignificant; and there are no other inconsistent

judgments.

Answers (A) and (B) are not correct for states that have abandoned the mutuality requirement and allow offensive non-mutual use of issue preclusion. There are, however, some states that would decline to allow Larry's parents to rely on a finding in Henrietta's case.

Answer (D) is incorrect. Larry's parents could not be bound or barred by Henrietta's judgment because neither Larry nor his parents were parties to the first action. While the failure of Larry's parents to intervene in Henrietta's case is a factor that courts might consider in deciding whether to allow them to make affirmative use of that case's liability findings, failure to intervene will *not* bar them from bringing their own suit.

TOPIC 50: THE LAW OF THE CASE DOCTRINE

ANSWERS

244. **Answer (C) is correct.** The law of the case doctrine is not inexorable. It is typically regarded as a discretionary doctrine that gives way if a change in the law or the facts requires reconsideration of the earlier decision.

Answer (A) is not correct for the reasons stated above.

Answer (B) is incorrect because the law of the case doctrine does have vitality as a preclusion doctrine, despite its discretionary character. A *de novo* standard would ignore the effect of the earlier order.

Answer (D) is not correct. It is a classic red herring. The rejected intervenors are likely to lose their appeal on the merits, but an argument does not lose jurisdiction because it is weak.

TOPIC 51: STATE LAW IN FEDERAL COURT: OVERVIEW

ANSWERS

245. **Answer (A) is correct.** It includes the correct language from the Rules of Decision Act.

Answer (B) is incorrect. The statute does not refer to the common law, and state statute law is one thing that the Court has consistently included in the part of state law that federal courts must apply.

Answer (C) is incorrect. The RDA provides for state law to apply where federal law does not, and even under *Swift v. Tyson*, 41 U.S. 1 (1842), the courts applied state statutes and local law.

Answer (D) is incorrect. This answer understates the application of federal law, as the RDA directs the courts to apply state law where federal law does not otherwise supply the rule of decision.

246. **Answer (C) is correct, because answers (A) and (B) are correct.** The language in those choices mirrors the current language of the Rules Enabling Act, 28 U.S.C. § 2072(a) (choice (A)) and § 2072(b) (choice (B)). Although it could be argued that the Court has never put much teeth into (b), and that Justice Scalia's plurality opinion in *Shady Grove Orthopedic Assocs., P.A. v. Allstate Ins.*, 130 S. Ct. 1431 (2010), reads § 2072(b) to mean essentially the same thing as § 2072(a), it is nevertheless a separate test, and statutorily required, so that Answer (A) alone would not be the best answer.

Answer (D) is incorrect. The Court has noted that the extensive process leading to the adoption of a federal rule gives the rules a sort of presumption of validity. *See Hanna*, 380 U.S. at 471. However, it is not true that a rule that was adopted in a procedurally proper way is automatically valid.

247. **Answer (A) is correct.** The Court in *Swift* viewed the common law as having a kind of independent existence, so that the "laws of the several states" embodied that law, and federal courts could discern that law for themselves. State statutes, on the other hand, were seen to be the enactment of a legal rule by the government of the state, whatever the common law rule might be, and the RDA required the federal courts to apply that in the absence of a federal statutory provision. Similarly, the kind of "local" law that dealt with title to real property was historically seen as governed by the specific law of the place where the property was located. With those exceptions, the federal courts were free to make their own decisions about the content of the common law.

Answer (B) is incorrect. Under *Swift* the federal courts did not have to follow the common law decisions of state courts, even a state supreme court, except in that narrow band of subjects that were considered "local."

Answer (C) is incorrect. The Court's conception of the law under *Swift* did not count noses to see which rules had the most votes. Not only did federal courts not have to follow state law if it was consistent with the majority rule, they did not even have to follow the "majority" of other federal courts. The judge's job was to reason logically from basic principles to determine the content of the law — the "true rule."

Answer (D) is incorrect. While the principles of the common law that U.S. states received from England were influential, they were also not binding on the federal courts, whether or not adopted by state courts.

248. Under *Swift v. Tyson*, federal courts were not bound by the case law of any particular state when deciding tort law claims. Unless the state law was embodied in a statute, in which case it constituted part of the "law of the several states" under the RDA, the federal judge would make federal general common law. This might be quite different from the law that would be applied in state courts in the state in which the federal court sat. Historians have noted that this federal general common law tended to be more favorable to business interests than was state common law. *See, e.g.*, Edward Purcell, *The Story of Erie, in* Civil Procedure Stories (Kevin Clermont ed., 2d ed. 2008). It was this kind of difference that set up the kind of "discrimination" between in-state and out-of-state parties that came to trouble the Court, ultimately leading to the rejection of *Swift*'s approach in *Erie*.

249. **Answer (B) is the best answer.** By the time *Erie* was decided, courts were operating under a different conception of "law," in which even common law decisions were perceived to be the creation of government officials with the authority to make law. Once state law was viewed in this way, it became problematic for the federal courts to supplant that law with their own views of what the law should be. Thus Justice Brandeis's opinion in *Erie* holds that in applying *Swift*'s interpretation of the RDA, "this Court and the lower courts have invaded rights which in our opinion are reserved by the Constitution to the several states."

Answer (A) is incorrect. The Court did *not* hold that the RDA itself was unconstitutional, but rather that the application of *Swift*'s interpretation of "laws of the several states," which ignored state common law, was unconstitutional.

Answer (C) is incorrect. *Erie* does speak of "discrimination," and even mentions "equal protection," but it is not talking about *discrimination* in the modern sense of race or gender discrimination in violation of the equal protection clause of the Fourteenth Amendment. Nor does its holding seem to rest on the discrimination issue. The Court here is obliquely referring to the ability of an out-of-state defendant to remove cases against it to federal court, to take advantage of more favorable federal law. Because in-state defendants cannot remove diversity cases (*see* Topic 31, Removal), the existence of the general law created by the federal courts gave those non-citizen defendants different rights than a citizen defendant would have.

Answer (D) is incorrect. *Erie* was not a question of the content of federal premises liability law, but a question of federal vs. state law. In a reversal of the normal pattern, federal law was more favorable to persons such as Mr. Tompkins; Pennsylvania common law recognized an extremely minimal duty. Once the Court decided that the common law of Pennsylvania must apply, as "there is no federal general common law," it remanded the case to the court of appeals to determine and apply Pennsylvania law. (Mr. Tompkins, who had earlier lost his arm, now lost his judgment as well.)

TOPIC 52: ANSWERS
STATE LAW IN FEDERAL COURT (THE *ERIE* DOCTRINE)

250. **Answer (D) is probably the best answer.** (This means that **Answers (B) and (C) are also correct.**) Under both the "outcome determinative" test developed in *Guaranty Trust Co. v. York*, 326 U.S. 806 (1945), as recast in *Hanna v. Plumer*, 380 U.S. 460 (1965) ("The 'outcome determinative' test . . . cannot be read without reference to the twin aims of the *Erie* rule: discouragement of forum-shopping and avoidance of inequitable administration of the laws."), and the interest balancing approach developed in *Byrd v. Blue Ridge Rural Elec. Coop., Inc.*, 356 U.S. 525 (1958), the application of Kansas state law is required. This question is very similar to *Walker v. Armco Steel Corp.*, 446 U.S. 740 (1980), which concluded that Rule 3 was not meant to "affect states' statutes of limitation." Under this reasoning, the federal rule did not govern the issue, making the choice one between an informal federal practice and a state law, and making the outcome governed by the RDA.

    Answer (A) is incorrect because Rule 3 has been specifically held to be a procedural rule that "governs the date from which various timing requirements of the federal rules begin to run, . . . not [to] affect state statutes of limitation." *Walker v. Armco Steel Corp., supra.*

251. **Answer (D) is probably the best answer.** Determining the correct answer to questions such as these requires examination of the differences in the Court's opinions in *Gasperini v. Center for Humanities*, 518 U.S. 415 (1996) (federal rule must be interpreted sensitively so as to avoid conflict with important state interests; state rule regarding excessiveness of damages applied), and *Shady Grove Orthopedic Associates, P.A. v. Allstate Insurance Co.*, 130 S. Ct. 1431 (2010) (plurality holds that federal rule covers issue, really regulates procedure, and availability of class action in federal court when individual claims would be required in state court does not enlarge, abridge, or modify substantive rights). Because the Court's 4-4 split in *Shady Grove* reveals significant disagreement about the proper analysis for cases like this, and because the deciding fifth vote belonged to Justice Stevens, whose concurring opinion agreed with the result that Justice Scalia reached, but for reasons that sometimes looked more like the dissent's analysis. Since Justice Stevens is no longer on the Court, only time will tell how the Court will handle clashes between procedural federal rules and "procedural" state rules adopted to accomplish the somewhat substantive purpose of encouraging or discouraging particular types of claims. Thus the last clause of (D) is correct: absent other changes on the Court, Justice Kagan may have the important deciding vote on the proper method of analyzing *Erie* issues.

    More specifically, **Answer (A) is correct** because it highlights the huge importance of whether a state/federal difference is analyzed under the Rules Enabling Act or under the Rules of Decision Act. The former results in a high probability that the federal rule will be held to be properly procedural and to govern; the latter will subject the federal practice to the "outcome determinative" test. Because much "tort reform" legislation takes a procedural form but is designed to affect substantive outcomes, the difference between state and federal rules may often be the sort that would lead to forum shopping and hence be labeled outcome determinative. This in turn means that the state law is likely to apply, although occasionally — as with the federal standard of review in *Gasperini* and the jury function in *Byrd* — the importance of the federal interest may be so high that the federal rule will nevertheless apply.

Answer (B) is also correct. It appears that Justices Scalia, Roberts, Thomas, and Sotomayor look at the language of the federal rule and its normal function in the federal system in deciding whether it covers the issue. Then, following, *Sibbach v. Wilson*, 312 U.S. 1 (1941), they examine the federal provision to see if it "really regulates procedure," and incidental impact on substantive rights is permissible, even expected. Justice Scalia's opinion in *Shady Grove* explicitly rejects the argument that state law is relevant to this question. ("In sum, it is not the substantive or procedural nature or purpose of the affected state law that matters, but the substantive or procedural nature of the Federal Rule.")

Answer (C) is also correct. Justices Ginsburg, Kennedy, Breyer, and Alito take a different approach, insisting that the question of whether the federal rule applies to an issue must be determined in context, by looking at it with an "awareness of, and sensitivity to, important state regulatory policies." These Justices point to earlier decisions such as *Gasperini*, *Walker v. Armco*, and numerous others as examples of narrower readings of federal rules designed to avoid unnecessary conflict with state law. This approach might easily lead these justices to consider the Texas expert report requirement as wholly separate from the rules governing pleadings themselves.

How would a case like this come out? Even before *Shady Grove*, courts were reaching different conclusions. *See Chamberlain v. Giampapa*, 210 F.3d 154 (3d Cir. 2000) (federal rules not broad enough to cover; state law applies); *Cruz v. Chang*, 400 F. Supp. 2d 906 (W.D. Tex. 2005) (same result). *But see Poindexter v. Bonsukan*, 145 F. Supp. 2d 800 (E.D. Tex. 2001) (federal rules regarding expert reports and sanctions broad enough to cover; state law does not apply). *See generally* Dace A. Caldwell, Comment, *Medical Malpractice Gets Eerie: The* Erie *Implications of a Heightened Pleading Burden in Oklahoma*, 57 OKLA. L. REV. 977 (2004).

252. MM will argue that Rule 68, although it does not explicitly address the issues of plaintiff's recovery or attorney's fees, rejects them by implication by not allowing them and is therefore broad enough to cover the issue of the proper treatment of offers of judgment. As in *Shady Grove*, the federal and state provisions do not have to directly contradict each other for the federal provision to be broad enough. Sleep Hotels will argue that Rule 68 does not cover the issue because it does not deal with offers made by plaintiff or with the recoverability of attorney fees, just defendant-made offers and costs. The federal rule is therefore inapplicable. Sleep Hotels could also argue that if Rule 68 did cover the issue it would run afoul of part (b) of the Rules Enabling Act because it would abridge the plaintiff's right to recover attorney fees under state law. Therefore, the scope of Rule 68 should be read "sensitively" and narrowly in order to avoid undermining the important state policies that led Texoma to encourage settlement by empowering both parties to make an offer of judgment, and by providing that the sanction for refusing an offer includes payment of the opponent's attorney fees.

253. Sleep Hotels wants state law to apply, and so will argue that the difference between state and federal law is outcome determinative. While the result of applying the state and federal rules will not be win/lose, *Gasperini* made it clear that a difference need only be "outcome

affective." *Hanna* defined "outcome determinative" as implicating the "twin aims of *Erie*": (1) avoiding incentives for forum shopping; and (2) avoiding inequitable administration of the law. The possibility of forum shopping is analyzed prospectively, from the point in time before the lawsuit is filed. Although one could imagine a situation where an offer of judgment is central, it seems unlikely generally that a party would choose a forum because IF it made an offer of judgment and IF it is turned down and IF plaintiff recovers more than the offer plaintiff could recover post-offer fees. The plaintiff here did not choose state court, for example. The time frame for analyzing inequitable administration of the law is less clear, because cases have gone both ways. In *Walker v. Armco*, the Supreme Court looked at it retrospectively. Viewed from that perspective, the fee award makes a large difference in Sleep Hotels' recovery and the difference could be argued to be inequitable. Even if the test should be examined prospectively as *Hanna* indicates, Sleep Hotels could argue that the existence (or not) of offer of judgment sanctions significantly changes the settlement bargaining position of the parties and thus reflects a substantial difference between state and federal courts that would be inequitable.

TOPIC 53: FEDERAL COMMON LAW

ANSWERS

254. Yes, federal common law exists. Despite the fact that the Rules of Decision Act provides that the "laws of the several states" provide the rules of decision "except where the constitution, treaties or statutes of the United States" provide otherwise (28 U.S.C. § 1652), the Supreme Court has developed specialized federal common law in a number of areas, including some cases involving foreign relations and the law of nations, *Sosa v. Alvarez-Muchain*, 542 U.S. 692, 724-732 (2004), admiralty and general maritime law, *see Panama R. Co. v. Johnson*, 264 U.S. 375, 386 (1924), certain cases in which the United States is a party, *Clearfield Trust Co. v. United States*, 318 U.S. 363 (1943), and certain interstate disputes involving state boundaries and equitable apportionment of interstate water resources. In fact, on the same day that *Erie* was decided, the Supreme Court applied federal common law to an interstate dispute concerning the equitable allocation of water from interstate streams because this subject is an area of national concern. *See Hinderlider v. La Plata River & Cherry Creek Ditch Co.*, 304 U.S. 92, 110 (1938) ("[W]hether the water of an interstate stream must be apportioned between the two States is a question of 'federal common law' upon which neither the statutes nor the decisions of either state can be conclusive.").

Federal common law is also sometimes inferred or derived from federal statutory provisions or constitutional provisions that cannot fairly be read to provide for it. *See, e.g.*, *Bivens v. Six Unknown Federal Narcotics Agents*, 403 U.S. 388 (1971) (private cause of action inferred from Fourth Amendment). Other less well known examples of this type of federal common law include *Semtek International Inc. v. Lockheed Martin Corp.*, 521 U.S. 457 (2001) (prescribing claim preclusive effects of federal judgments), and *Del Costello v. International Brotherhood of Teamsters*, 462 U.S. 151, 170-172 (1983) (prescribing federal statute of limitations for breach of collective bargaining agreement).

Regardless of the type of federal common law, it is within the coverage of the Supremacy Clause and supersedes any state law on the subjects covered by it.

TOPIC 54:	**ANSWERS**
APPELLATE JURISDICTION	

255. **Answer (A) is the correct answer.** The dismissal of both health care claims with prejudice disposed of all issues and parties in the case and is a final judgment as provided in 28 U.S.C. § 1291.

Answer (B) is incorrect. Rule 54(b)'s method of finalizing separate claims was not used or needed to dispose of any of the health care claims.

Answer (C) is incorrect. The dismissal with prejudice is a merits dismissal because it precludes refiling even though it is grounded on the plaintiff's failure to file expert reports during the pretrial phase of the litigation.

Answer (D) is incorrect. The collateral order doctrine is inapplicable. To come within the small class of cases covered by the doctrine, the order must conclusively determine the disputed question, resolve an important issue completely separate from the merits, and be effectively unreviewable on appeal from a final judgment. *Cohen v. Beneficial Indus. Loan Corp.*, 337 U.S. 541, 546 (1949); *Coopers & Lybrand v. Livesay*, 437, U.S. 463, 468 (1978). In this problem, the issues to be covered by the expert reports are not "completely separate" from the merits and the propriety of the dismissal order is reviewable on appeal.

256. **Answer (B) is correct.** Rule 54(b) deals with cases that involve "more than one claim for relief . . . [or] multiple parties" and allows a trial judge to "direct entry of a final judgment as to one or more, but fewer than all, claims or parties." To do so, however, the judge must "expressly determine[] that there is no just reason for delay." Although Rule 54(b) is applicable to the facts presented in the problem, which involves an order that adjudicates the rights and liabilities of fewer than all of the parties, the dismissal order must be drafted in compliance with the requirements of Rule 54(b) to finalize the order dismissing HCH.

Another somewhat disfavored method for finalizing the HCH order would be by a severance of Payne's claim against HCH from Payne's claim against Dr. Practer. *See* Fed. R. Civ. P. 21. However, this was not done here.

Answer (A) is incorrect. Neither the dismissal order involving HCH nor the denial of Dr. Practer's motion disposes of the entire case. A final judgment "ends the litigation on the merits." *See Catlin v. United States*, 324 U.S. 229, 233 (1945).

Answer (C) is incorrect because the dismissal with prejudice is an adjudication of the merits of Payne's malpractice claim against HCH. The problem is that the order is not a final judgment because it does not end the case or comply with Rule 54(b).

Answer (D) is incorrect. To come within the small class of cases covered by the doctrine the order must conclusively determine the disputed question, resolve an important issue completely separate from the merits, and be effectively unreviewable on appeal from a final judgment. *Cohen v. Beneficial Indus. Loan Corp.*, 337 U.S. 541, 546 (1949); *Coopers &*

Lybrand v. Livesay, 437 U.S. 463, 468 (1978). The collateral order doctrine probably does not apply to a dismissal in this situation both because the order is not completely separate from the merits or unreviewable on appeal of the ultimate final judgment.

257. **Answer (D) is the best answer.** (Thus, **Answer (B) or Answer (C) is correct**). **Answer (B) is correct** because the Supreme Court has ruled that a denial of a motion to dismiss on the basis of qualified immunity from suit is a collateral order if the denial of the officers' summary judgment rests on a question of law, rather than the existence of a disputed factual question. *See Mitchell v. Forsyth*, 472 U.S. 511, 526 (1985) ("The entitlement [to summary judgment] is an *immunity from suit* rather than a mere defense to liability; and like an absolute immunity, it is effectively lost if a case is erroneously permitted to go to trial."); *see also Behrens v. Pelletier*, 516 U.S. 299, 313 (1996) (case is appealable when it involves "a dispute concerning an 'abstract issu[e] of law' relating to qualified immunity," such as whether the law proscribed the actions the plaintiff claims the officer took). But if the collateral order doctrine does not apply under the circumstances of the case, **Answer (C) is probably correct** because a permissive appeal of an interlocutory order under 28 U.S.C. § 1292(b) can be sought if the district court certifies that (1) the order raises a controlling law question, (2) there is substantial ground for difference of opinion on the question, and (3) an interlocutory appeal may materially advance the ultimate termination of the litigation. 28 U.S.C. § 1292(b). If such a certification is obtained, the appropriate court of appeals may permit an appeal to be taken from the order if application is made to the court of appeals within 10 days after entry of the order. *See* 28 U.S.C. § 1292(b); *see also* Fed. R. App. P. 5.

Answer (A) is incorrect for the same reasons that Answers (B) and (C) are correct. In addition, a collateral order is regarded as a final judgment.

TOPIC 55:	**ANSWERS**
APPELLATE PROCEDURE	

258. **Answer (D) is the best answer.** The second dismissal order's entry in the civil docket disposed of the remaining issues in the case. But it did not satisfy the requirement of Rule 58 (or Appellate Rule 4) that a "separate document" must be used for entry of a final judgment. *See* Fed. R. Civ. P. 58. Rule 58 requires that there must be a self-contained document distinct from any opinion and any other orders that don't dispose of the entire case. *Bankers Trust Co. v. Mallis*, 435 U.S. 381, 385 (1978). So the order did not start the appellate clock contained in Appellate Rule 4. As provided in Rule 58 and Appellate Rule 4, the judgment was "entered" by law when 150 days ran from entry of the second dismissal order. Fed. R. Civ. P. 58(c); Fed. R. App. P. 4(a)(7). As the following excerpt from the Supreme Court's *Mallis* opinion shows, the appellant may waive the separate document requirement over the objection of the appellee as long as the order in question clearly evidences the trial court's intent that the order is a "final decision" for the purposes of 28 U.S.C. § 1291:

> The separate-document requirement was . . . intended to avoid the inequities that were inherent when a party appealed from a document or docket entry that appeared to be a final judgment of the district court only to have the appellate court announce later that an earlier document or entry had been the judgment and dismiss the appeal as untimely. The 1963 amendment to Rule 58 made clear that a party need not file a notice of appeal until a separate judgment has been filed and entered. *See United States v. Indrelunas*, 411 U.S. 216, 220-22 (1973). Certainty as to timeliness, however, is not advanced by holding that appellate jurisdiction does not exist absent a separate judgment. If, by error, a separate judgment is not filed before a party appeals, nothing but delay would flow from requiring the court of appeals to dismiss the appeal. Upon dismissal, the district court would simply file and enter the separate judgment, from which a timely appeal would then be taken. Wheels would spin for no practical purpose.

Bankers Trust Co. v. Mallis, 435 U.S. 381, 385 (1978). *See also* Fed. R. App. P. 4(a)(7)(B) (codifying *Mallis*).

Answers (A), (B), and (C) are incorrect. Fed. R. App. P. 4 authorizes the filing of a premature notice of appeal. Fed. R. App. P. 4(a)(2). But neither of the two dismissal orders disposes of the entire case. Hence, another "separate document" is needed to finalize the case before expiration of 150 days.

259. **Answer (C) is correct.** If a motion for new trial is filed, the time for giving notice of appeal runs from the entry of the order denying a new trial. Fed. R. App. P. 4(a)(4)(A). Moreover, another "separate document" is (sensibly) not required. The entry of the order denying the last postjudgment motion finalizes things and starts the appellate clock. *See* Fed. R. Civ. P. 58(a)(4).

Answers (A) and (B) are incorrect for the same reason. The dates of the earlier orders don't matter.

Answer (D) is incorrect because only 30 days are allowed for the filing of notices of appeal unless the United States or its officer or agency is a party. Fed. R. App. P. 4(a).

260. **Answer (C) is the best answer.** Appellate Rule 4 allows for reopening the appeal for a period of 14 days after the date when the court's order to reopen is entered under the following conditions: (A) the moving party did not receive notice under Rule 77(d) of the entry of the order to be appealed within 21 days after entry; (B) the motion to reopen is filed within 180 days after the judgment or order is entered or within 14 days after the movant receives a Rule 77(d) notice, whichever is earlier; and (C) no party would be prejudiced. Fed. R. App. P. 4(a)(6).

Answer (A) is incorrect because Appellate Rule 4 does provide a safe harbor under the circumstances stated in (C). *See* Fed. R. App. P. 4(a).

Answer (B) is incorrect because a motion for extension must be filed within 30 days after entry of the order denying Payne a new trial.

Answer (D) is probably incorrect because the detailed requirements of Appellate Rule 4 probably preclude using Rule 60(b) to avoid them.

261. In addition to the notice of appeal, an appellant in a civil case may be required to file a cost bond (Fed. R. App. P. 7), will need to file the record (Fed. R. App. P. 10, 11), and file an appellant's brief and an appendix (Fed. R. App. P. 28, 30–32).

Unless another time is designated by the court, the attorney who filed the notice of appeal must, within 14 days after filing notice of appeal, file a statement with the circuit court clerk naming the parties the attorney represents on appeal. Fed. R. App. P. 12(b).

To obtain preparation of the record, the appellant must first order from the court reporter a transcript of the parts of the proceedings that the appellant needs to prosecute the appeal. The order must be made in writing within 14 days after filing the notice of appeal or entry of the order disposing of the last timely postjudgment motion specified in Rule 4(a)(4)(A), whichever is later. Within the same period, a copy of the order must be filed with the district clerk. Fed. R. App. P. 10(b)(1). At the time of ordering, the appellant must make satisfactory arrangements with the reporter for paying the cost of the transcript. Fed. R. App. P. 10(b)(4).

The appellant must do whatever else is necessary to enable the clerk to assemble and forward the record. *See* Fed. R. App. P. 11.

The appellant must serve and file a brief within 40 days after the record is filed. The appellee must serve and file a brief within 30 days after the appellant's brief is served. The appellant must serve and file a reply brief within 14 days after service of the appellee's brief, but at least 7 days before argument, unless the court allows a later filing. Fed. R. App. P. 31(a).

The circuit court clerk is required to advise all parties whether oral argument will be scheduled and, if so, the date, time, and place for it, and the time allowed for each side. Fed. R. App. P. 34(b).

PRACTICE FINAL EXAM: ANSWERS

ANSWERS

PRACTICE FINAL EXAM

262. One vehicle would be to file a counterclaim and to add Mark as an additional party. Rule 13(h) notes that Rule 20 governs "the addition of a person as a party to a counterclaim." (This language replaces, without an intended change in meaning, the prior rule language allowing defendants to make "persons other than those made parties to the original action" parties to a counterclaim.) If the claim against Mark satisfies Rule 20's "same transaction or occurrence/common question of law or fact" requirements, then this method would work. Another option is to use Rule 14 to bring a derivative claim against Mark. He could be alleging that if he is liable to plaintiff, Mark is liable to him. The Rule 14 process, also known as impleader, is often used to assert contribution and indemnity claims when those claims are authorized under the applicable state law.

263. **Answer (B) is correct.** Once a party has brought a claim for relief as an original claim, counterclaim, cross-claim, or third-party claim against another party that meets the requirements of the joinder rules, Rule 18 allows the addition of as many other claims as the party has against the opposing party. Here Donald has brought the contribution claim against Mark and can use Rule 18 to add the negligence claim. Incidentally, the negligence claim would also satisfy the requirements of Rule 20 as it arises out of the same transaction or occurrence as the contribution claim and raises common questions of law and fact.

     Answer (A) is incorrect. Rule 13 governs counterclaims and cross-claims, and it does not address when a party can add claims against a third-party defendant (which is what Mark is here).

     Answer (C) is incorrect. Donald was required to use a derivative claim to bring Mark into the lawsuit under Rule 14 — the contribution and indemnity claim is a derivative one. However, additional claims may be added that are not derivative in nature, as explained above.

     Answer (D) is incorrect. Because Donald has a proper claim against Mark already (the contribution and indemnity claim), Rule 18 permits the addition of other claims even if they do not arise out of the same transaction or occurrence as the others. (Whether the federal court has jurisdiction over these claims is another issue, which later questions address.)

264. **Answer (B) is correct.** Rule 18 permits the addition of other claims whether or not they arise out of the same transaction or occurrence. The court is not required to try unrelated claims together. It may, for example, order separate trials under Rule 42. But the claims are not misjoined.

     Answer (A) is incorrect. Rule 20 would require the claims to arise out of the same transaction, occurrence, or series of transactions or occurrences and to share a common question of law or fact. It is unlikely that the breach of contract claim and negligence claims meet this test. They did occur close together in time, and anger regarding the negotiations may have contributed to some party's negligence, but that is not apt to be a close enough logical tie or a sufficient overlap of evidence to be considered part of the same transaction or occurrence.

Answer (C) is incorrect. As explained above, the defendant/third-party plaintiff is allowed to add non-derivative claims to the claim that supports impleader under Rule 14.

Answer (D) is incorrect. Because Donald has a proper claim against Mark already (the contribution and indemnity claim), Rule 18 permits the addition of other claims even if they do not arise out of the same transaction or occurrence as the others.

265. **Answer (D) is correct.** Rule 14(a) allows third-party defendants such as Mark to bring claims against the original plaintiff (Charley), but only if those claims arise out of the same transaction or occurrence that is the subject matter of the plaintiff's claim against the defendant/third-party plaintiff. This would allow Mark to bring a negligence claim against Charley, but not a contract claim on its own. Once a proper negligence claim is filed, however, Rule 18 would allow Mark to add the contract claim against Charley.

Answer (A) is incorrect because Rule 18 does not help Mark until after he has filed a proper Rule 14 claim against Charley.

Answer (B) is incorrect. The answer correctly states the requirements for the claims that Rule 14 allows, but it ignores the additional claims that Rule 18 makes possible.

Answer (C) is incorrect. Rule 14 does allow some claims by the third-party defendant against the plaintiff, but they must arise out of the same transaction or occurrence as the plaintiff's claim against the original defendant.

266. **Answer (A) is correct.** As explained above, Rule 13(h) cross references Rule 20, and permits the addition of parties to a counterclaim. This means that Donald's claim against Mark would have to arise out of the same transaction or occurrence as Donald's claim against Charley. A claim for negligence would meet this requirement. Once that negligence claim has been brought, Rule 18 allows the addition of the unrelated contract claim. The contract claim alone, however, would not be proper.

Answer (B) is incorrect. Rules 13(h) and Rule 20 allow the addition of new parties to counterclaims, but only if the requirements of Rule 20 are met.

Answer (C) is incorrect. Impleader under Rule 14 is one method (probably the most common one) by which defendants can add parties to the lawsuit. But it is not the only method, as new parties may also be added to a counterclaim or cross-claim.

Answer (D) is incorrect. As long as Donald brings a related claim against Mark (here, the negligence claim), he can also add an unrelated claim (the contract claim).

267. **Answer (D) is correct.** Charley's claim against Donald provides a basis for federal jurisdiction: the parties are of diverse citizenship and the amount in controversy exceeds $75,000. The counterclaim, however, does not meet these requirements because it is too small. Donald must look to supplemental jurisdiction to justify the presence of his counterclaim in federal court. Under 28 U.S.C. § 1367(a), district courts have supplemental jurisdiction over claims "that are so related to claims in the action within such original jurisdiction that they form part of the same case or controversy under Article III of the United States Constitution." Donald's counterclaim for negligence, involving claims about

the same accident, will meet this requirement. In addition, jurisdiction must not be negated by § 1367(b). This would be true if the case were in federal court based solely on diversity jurisdiction, and the claim in question were a claim by a plaintiff against a person made a party under Rule 14, 19, 20, or 24, and when exercising supplemental jurisdiction would be inconsistent with the requirements of the diversity statute. Here, although Donald is asserting a claim for relief, he is not a "plaintiff" within the meaning of the statute. Donald's counterclaim will be eligible for supplemental jurisdiction.

Answer (A) is incorrect. Although the parties are from different states, this is not sufficient to provide diversity jurisdiction when the amount in controversy does not exceed $75,000.

Answer (B) is incorrect. The amount in controversy is too low to provide an independent basis for federal jurisdiction, but supplemental jurisdiction is available as explained above.

Answer (C) is incorrect. Allowing jurisdiction over the *Donald v. Charley* claim, if it stood alone, would be inconsistent with the requirements of § 1332. However, because it is a counterclaim, it can be supported by supplemental jurisdiction. Because it is not a claim by a plaintiff, it is not booted out by § 1367(b)'s requirement that exercising jurisdiction not be inconsistent with § 1332.

268. **Answer (B) is correct.** The contribution and indemnity claim, which would request that Mark pay any sums that Donald is ordered to pay Charley, is large enough to have an independent basis for federal jurisdiction. The negligence claim by Donald against Mark is part of the same constitutional case and is not a claim by a plaintiff under § 1367(b), so the court would have supplemental jurisdiction over the negligence claim. The contract claim, however, is only for $50,000, and so it does not have an independent basis for federal jurisdiction. Nor is it related to Charley's negligence claim against Donald or Donald's indemnity claim against Mark. The court may not exercise supplemental jurisdiction over the contract claim under § 1367(a).

Answers (A) and (C) are incorrect, because the court has jurisdiction over two of the three claims, as set forth above.

Answer (D) is incorrect. The supplemental jurisdiction statute may provide jurisdiction over claims that are too small. In addition, the amount in controversy requirement is computed according to the plaintiff's good faith claim for relief, and not by the amount the plaintiff eventually recovers.

269. **Answer (A) is correct.** Mark and Charley are from different states, and the amount in controversy exceeds $75,000. There is, therefore, no need to rely on the supplemental jurisdiction statute to allow this claim. (The joinder rules probably make it improper, depending on all the various claims by the parties, but this question asked only about subject matter jurisdiction.)

Answer (B) is incorrect. Since Mark's claim has an independent basis for federal jurisdiction, it does not matter whether it shares a common nucleus of operative fact with Charley's claim against Donald. If Mark's claim did not exceed $75,000, supplemental jurisdiction would be necessary, and "common nucleus of operative fact" is the test for whether the claims are part of the same constitutional case.

Answer (C) is incorrect. It is a claim by a person made a party under Rule 14. But this is not relevant to the issue of subject matter jurisdiction here.

Answer (D) is incorrect. It is true that Mark is not a plaintiff under § 1367(b) — but as supplemental jurisdiction is not required here, that fact is irrelevant.

270. **Answer (C) is correct.** This question is governed by the rules of *res judicata*, or claim preclusion. The judgment in the original case was a final decision, on the merits, between the same parties (here, Donald and Mark), on the same cause of action. Under modern rules of preclusion, a person's claim for personal injuries is part of the same cause of action as that person's claim for property damage arising out of the same occurrence. Since Donald got a judgment against Mark in the original case, his claim for personal injuries is said to be "merged" into the original judgment. Had Donald lost the first case, his claims would be said to be "barred."

Answer (A) is incorrect. The fact that the personal injury claim was not actually litigated prevents it from being subject to collateral estoppel, or issue preclusion. However, claims that are part of the same cause of action cannot be the subject of a later suit even if they were not actually litigated the first time around.

Answer (B) is incorrect. As noted above, when a party has won a claim, and then seeks to recover additional damages from the same cause of action, the omitted damage claims are properly referred to as having been "merged" into the judgment, not barred by it.

Answer (D) is incorrect. The Restatement (Second) of Judgments § 24 uses a "transaction" test and defines the claim precluded by the judgment to include "all rights of the plaintiff to remedies against the defendant with respect to all or any part of the transaction, or series of connected transactions, out of which the [original] action arose." The test for "transaction, or series of . . . transactions":

> is to be determined pragmatically, giving weight to such considerations as whether the facts are related in time, space, origin, or motivation, whether they form a convenient trial unit, and whether their treatment as a unit conforms to the parties' expectations or business understanding or usage.

While each state determines its own preclusion rules, the Second Restatement approach is the most common test today.

271. **Answer (A) is correct.** Donald did not actually bring a contract claim against Charley in the original suit, so issue preclusion will not bar it. Claim preclusion does not bar it either. Donald did bring a negligence claim against Charley, but the breach of contract claim is not part of that "transaction" and so not part of the same cause of action. Charley did not bring a breach of contract claim against Donald, and so it was not a compulsory counterclaim. Donald was free to wait and bring that claim later, subject only to the statute of limitations.

Answer (B) is incorrect. Charley only sued Donald for negligence. Any counterclaim, including the contract claim, arose out of a different transaction or occurrence and was permissive rather than compulsory.

Answer (C) is incorrect. Donald's claim against Mark does not involve the same parties as Donald's claim against Charley, and this is a requirement for claim preclusion.

Answer (D) is incorrect. State law varies as to when a judgment is "final" for preclusion purposes. One of the most common differences has to do with whether a judgment that is on appeal is "final" while the appeal is still pending. A final trial court judgment that has not been appealed, however, will be final for purposes of preclusion.

272. **Answer (D) is correct.** The issue of Donald's negligence was actually litigated in the original suit. However, preclusion does not operate against a person who was not a party (or in privity with a party) to that original case. This rule grows out of considerations of fairness: Ed has not yet had a chance to litigate this issue, and he should not be bound by the results of a case in which he was not involved. He will therefore be allowed to bring his case and to attempt to prove Donald's negligence. (Whether he would be better advised to sue Mark is a separate issue.)

Answer (A) is incorrect. The finding of Donald's lack of negligence was necessary to the first case. Had he been negligent to some degree, he might have been ineligible to recover damages from Mark, or his recovery might have been decreased, and he might have been liable to Charley. Even had it not been necessary, however, Ed would not have been estopped by the finding because he was not a party to the original case, as explained above.

Answer (B) is incorrect because Ed was not a party to the original case.

Answer (C) is incorrect. Even jurisdictions that allow non-mutual collateral estoppel apply estoppel principles *only against* a person who *was* a party to the first suit. The element that varies is whether a stranger to the first action may estop someone who was a party or whether identity of all parties is required.

273. This pleading is probably insufficiently specific. Claims for fraud are governed by a more exacting standard of pleading than claims generally. Rule 9(b) requires that "[i]n alleging fraud . . . a party must state with particularity the circumstances constituting fraud . . . . Malice, intent, knowledge, and other conditions of a person's mind may be alleged generally." Here, Steven's complaint has referred to the allegedly fraudulent statements only generally — "guaranteed law review membership." Most courts would require Steven to plead more precisely the statements that constituted the fraud and the facts that make the statement false. Some would even require more detail in the pleading of DTPA Press' knowledge of the falsehood, despite the language of Rule 9. This is especially true since the Supreme Court's decisions in *Twombly* and *Iqbal*, which required specific allegations of the ways in which defendants conspired (*Twombly*) and defendants' knowledge and intent (*Iqbal*) as part of the general Rule 8 pleading requirements.

274. **Answer (C) is correct.** Interrogatories may only be sent to parties under Rule 33.

Answer (A) is incorrect. The question may, in fact, be one in which the burden of answering exceeds the likely materiality of the answer, but even if that were not true the interrogatory need not be answered. Steven has used the wrong device to try to get this information.

Answer (B) is incorrect. It is a correct statement about discovery relevance, and the names of the book's purchasers might indeed lead to the discovery of admissible evidence — the fates of others who bought and relied on The Ultimate Study Guide. However, that does not overcome the impropriety of sending interrogatories to non-parties.

Answer (D) is incorrect. Had the bookstore been a party to the case, the burden imposed by the question might lead the court to refuse to compel an answer, as in Answer (A), or to reduce the scope of the question, as in Answer (D). Again, however, an interrogatory will not work here at all.

275. **Answer (B) is probably correct.** Trade secrets are sometimes hard to define. In discussing trade secrets, the Restatement of Torts describes it as:

> any formula, pattern, device or compilation of information which is used in one's business, and which gives him an opportunity to obtain an advantage over competitors who do not know or use it. It may be a formula for a chemical compound, a process of manufacturing, treating or preserving materials, a pattern for a machine or other device, or a list of customers. A trade secret is a process or device for continuous use in the operation of the business. Generally it relates to the production of goods as, for example, a machine or formula for the production of an article.

Restatement of Torts § 757, comment b. DTPA Press would have to show that its research meets these requirements and that it was kept confidential. It seems unlikely to be the kind of information that constitutes a trade secret. Even if it did, however, trade secrets are entitled to only a conditional privilege. When the information is extremely important to the lawsuit, the information may be ordered produced, although it may be accompanied by a protective order requiring the discovering party to use the information only in the suit and to keep it confidential. Here, Steven must prove that DTPA Press' claims were false, and that it knew they were false. The information on which DTPA relied in making these claims is central to this determination, and it is probable that a court would order the documents produced.

Answer (A) is incorrect. The factual basis, if any, for the statements that The Ultimate Study Guide would guarantee law review status is relevant both to Steven's claim that the statement was false and to his claim that DTPA Press knew it was false.

Answer (C) is incorrect. Although this may vary by jurisdiction, the trade secret privilege is generally a conditional one, meaning that it can be overcome under the right circumstances. (The protection for ordinary work product, for example, is also conditional in that it can be overridden with a showing of substantial need and undue hardship.)

Answer (D) is incorrect. Trade secrets are generally protected, and more than ordinary relevance is required to overcome that protection.

276. **Answer (C) is correct.** Consulting experts (experts retained for litigation who will not testify) are generally protected from discovery. There is an exception if the discovering party can show exceptional circumstances. This might be true if the consulting expert had done destructive testing on some object in issue in the suit, or if the number of experts in the field were very small and all had been hired by the other party. In this case, there are likely to be a number of educational experts who can provide information and expertise about the benefits of student study aides, so Blackstone will be protected from deposition.

Answer (A) is incorrect. Blackstone's information undoubtedly is relevant, but relevant information is not discoverable if protected by a privilege.

Answer (B) is incorrect. While consulting experts can rarely be deposed, it is not true that it can never be allowed.

Answer (D) is incorrect. As explained above, exceptional circumstances are such that the consulting expert has information otherwise unavailable, or that no other expert is available. Just because a party has hired the best known expert to consult does not satisfy the requirement of exceptional circumstances.

277. **Answer (B) is correct.** This question is controlled by Rule 26(a)(2)(B). In the absence of agreement or court order, parties must identify testifying expert witnesses and provide a report prepared and signed by the witness. Among other things, this report must include "a list of all other cases in which, during the previous 4 years, the witness testified as an expert at trial or by deposition."

Answer (A) is incorrect. The rule is limited as to time and does not include cases in which the expert did not testify.

Answer (C) is incorrect. The report also needs to disclose cases in which the expert's only testimony was by deposition.

Answer (D) is incorrect. Information about the expert's testimony in other cases may be relevant in discerning the basis for the expert's opinion, and it may also be relevant for purposes of impeachment. Imagine, for example, that the witness has testified in a prior case in a way that is inconsistent with her testimony in this case.

278. **Answer (A) is correct.** Steven needs to prove that his failure to make law review was caused by the flaws in The Ultimate Study Guide. Defendants will want to challenge that assertion, and one way to do that is to explore other possible causes of Steven's law school grades. The way he spent his time, and his mental and physical health, may be relevant to the issue of causation. Since Steven is claiming damages based on mental anguish, his mental state may also be relevant to the issue of damages. The identity of his friends and health care providers is not itself admissible, but those identities may lead to the discovery of admissible evidence when DTPA follows up by deposing or interviewing these people. This kind of information is generally considered private, and some of it may be privileged. Nevertheless, by bringing a lawsuit that makes this information relevant, Steven will be held to have waived his rights to keep this information secret.

Answer (B) is incorrect for the reasons explained above.

Answer (C) is incorrect. The privacy rights of parties and others are often protected in discovery. This privacy interest, however, can be waived as noted above.

Answer (D) is incorrect. Lawsuits may make information about non-parties relevant and therefore generally discoverable. Absent a statute or rule providing otherwise, these non-parties are not entitled to advance notification before they are named or discussed during the discovery process.

279. **Answer (C) is correct.** The work product doctrine protects communications made in anticipation of litigation or for trial. The question here is whether casual conversations with friends are "in anticipation of litigation" just because the friends are law students. The answer is "no." The protection from discovery is intended to protect trial preparation materials, and to allow parties a zone of privacy in which to prepare their cases. It is not intended to protect all conversations a party might have about his case.

Answer (A) is incorrect. Conversations do not become work product merely because their subject is litigation.

Answer (B) is incorrect. Steven cannot convert non-privileged communications into privileged ones by repeating them to his attorney. However, the defendant would not be able to ask "What did you tell your attorney about what you told your friends?" The communication between attorney and client *is* privileged. But it does not prevent a question like "What did you tell your friends about your lawsuit?"

Answer (D) is incorrect. DTPA Press will not need to show substantial need/undue hardship because the communications are not protected. If they did need to make such a showing, this would not be sufficient. Because DTPA Press can do its own interviews or depose Steven's friends, the likelihood that the friends will be less cooperative than they were for Steven does not constitute substantial need.

280. **Answer (D) is correct.** Conversations between attorney and client are only privileged if they were made for the purpose of obtaining legal advice. Here, it appears that the President was asking for business rather than legal advice, and so the communication is not privileged just because one of the parties to it was the company lawyer.

Answer (A) is incorrect. The President would be the "client" under either test, but this is the wrong kind of conversation.

Answer (B) is incorrect. The President was asking for advice, but it was not legal advice.

Answer (C) is incorrect. The attorney-client privilege does not require that the communication be made in anticipation of litigation.

281. **Answer (C) is correct.** The requirement that the party opposing the class has acted or refused to act on grounds generally applicable to the class applies only to class actions certified under Rule 23(b)(2), not to all class actions. Steven's class action is for damages for fraud and breach of warranty, and it would be certified, if at all, under Rule 23(b)(3). All class actions must show that the class is so numerous that joinder is impracticable and that the named plaintiff's claim is typical of the claims of class members (Rule 23(a)). And damages class actions under Rule 23(b)(3) must also be superior to other methods of adjudicating the controversy.

Answers (A), (B), and (D) are incorrect (i.e., Steven *must* demonstrate them in order to secure class certification) for the reasons explained above.

282. The judge probably should not certify this class. The requirements of Rule 23(a) are probably met. This class seems large enough that joining all purchasers in a single suit would not be practicable. There are questions of law and fact common to the class — what representations did DTPA Press make, were they false, do they constitute a breach of warranty, etc. This situation can be distinguished from the *Wal-Mart* case in that involves claims arising out of identical written representations rather than individual decisions about hiring, pay, and promotion. Steven's claims are typical of those of the class members, and it appears that he and his lawyers will adequately represent the class. The bigger obstacles are the additional requirements of Rule 23(b)(3). The court would have to find that the common questions predominate over questions affecting only individual members. The differences in the substantive law applicable to class members in various states will tend to work against a finding that common questions predominate, as will the need of each class member to individually prove reliance, and to prove his or her own damages. Also, Steven has alleged that each class member (all of whom are law students or lawyers) has at least $75,000 in damages, a stake which may give the class members an interest in individually controlling their claims, which would work against class certification. On the other hand, the alleged

fraud was made as identical printed representations to book purchasers, and it is possible that the kinds and degrees of reliance will be very similar. Some courts might certify this case as a class action, or at least as an "issues class" — treating only the question of violation as a class claim and leaving the rest to individual litigation — but nationwide damage classes based on varying state law are unusual.

283. **Answer (A) is probably correct.** Since its decision in *Hanna v. Plumer*, 380 U.S. 460 (1965), the Supreme Court has used two different methods of analysis in considering whether the federal court must apply state law. One track is followed when the normal federal rule comes from a Federal Rule adopted pursuant to the Rules Enabling Act, or a federal statute regulating procedure. In such cases, the court is supposed to begin the analysis by asking whether the federal rule involved is broad enough to cover the issue raised by the state law. This test is sometimes phrased as asking whether the two rules collide, or whether they are inconsistent with each other. In this case, Rule 11(a) states, "[u]nless a rule or statute specifically states otherwise, a pleading need not be verified or accompanied by an affidavit." The court would begin by deciding whether Rule 11 thereby covers the issue of whether a complaint seeking punitive damages must be made under oath.

Answers (B) and (D) are incorrect. Only if Rule 11 does not cover the issue should the court apply the "outcome determinative test," and that test turns on a comparison of the state and federal rules rather than one rule alone.

Answer (C) is incorrect. The source of the state rule is not relevant.

284. **Answer (A) is correct.** If Rule 11 does cover the issue, the court must ascertain whether the rule really regulates procedure and does not modify or abridge any substantive right. These requirements come from the Rules Enabling Act. Assuming these tests are met, the federal court should apply the federal rule.

Answer (B) is incorrect. The outcome determinative test does not apply when the rule adopted under the Rules Enabling Act covers the issue.

Answer (C) is incorrect. This option restates the outcome determinative test.

Answer (D) is probably incorrect. When the court is using the Rules Enabling Act analysis, a state interest does not come into play unless the Federal Rule of Civil Procedure in question goes so far as to modify or abridge a substantive right (in which case the Rule is invalid). Note, though, that both Justice Ginsburg's majority opinion in *Gasperini v. Center for Humanities, Inc.*, 518 U.S. 415 (1996), and her dissenting opinion (joined by three other Justices) in *Shady Grove*, argue that the court should consider the state regulatory interest when deciding whether the federal rule covers the issue in question.

285. **Answer (D) is probably correct.** Even under the more lenient *Celotex* standard, and under the current text of Rule 56, the summary judgment movant needs to identify for the court the parts of the record that demonstrate that the non-movant will have no evidence to prove some element of its claim or defense. *Celotex Corp. v. Catrett*, 477 U.S. 317 (1986). Justice White's opinion, needed for the fifth vote in *Celotex*, noted that a naked motion is insufficient. Here, Alpha Omega has done nothing more than file a motion. The suit has only been pending for a month, there has been no discovery, and so there is nothing in the record except Rodriguez's complaint (and possibly Alpha Omega's answer) on which to base the motion. Unless the movant needs to do nothing more than file the motion, this one is

insufficient.

Answer (A) is probably incorrect. As noted above, the *Celotex* plurality plus Justice White require more than a conclusory motion, and Rule 56(c) discusses the ways in which a party asserting that a fact "cannot be or is genuinely disputed" must "support" that assertion. Identifying the issue in question, without more, is probably insufficient.

Answer (B) is incorrect. Alpha Omega does not have to disprove an element of Rodriguez's claim in order to be entitled to summary judgment.

Answer (C) is incorrect. Although waiting until the parties have had an opportunity for discovery is preferable, Rule 56 allows a party to move for summary judgment "at any time."

286. **Answer (C) is correct.** Parties who "admit away" their cases at deposition are not always allowed to create a fact issue by contradicting those admissions in an affidavit. However, when there is a reasonable explanation for the change, as when the admission was equivocal or the questions were unclear, a witness may be permitted to clarify that testimony through an affidavit. Here, the affidavit is not directly contrary to the deposition testimony in any case — the deposition questions concerned the particular carts that injured Rodriguez. Her affidavit concerns the condition of carts generally at the Alpha Omega store where she fell. The fact that the questions were couched in legal jargon and that English is Rodriguez's second language also make the need for clarification understandable. Looking at the affidavit, Rodriguez has provided circumstantial evidence that grocery carts at this store are often bent and in bad condition. She has also described her fall, including a claim that the carts stuck together and pushed her over. In ruling on Alpha Omega's motion for summary judgment, the court must give credence only to evidence in Rodriguez's favor and consider reasonable inferences in her favor. While her evidence is circumstantial rather than direct, it is still some evidence of dangerous baskets and of Alpha Omega's knowledge, so the court should deny the motion for summary judgment.

Answer (A) is incorrect. First, Rodriguez admitted only that she lacked direct knowledge that any employee knew about the particular baskets that caused her fall. This may not be necessary. Second, given the nature of the questions and Rodriguez's statement that she had a hard time understanding those questions, the court may consider her affidavit.

Answer (B) is incorrect. Parties do not need direct evidence in order to prevail at trial or to avoid summary judgment. They do need circumstantial evidence from which a reasonable inference can be drawn.

Answer (D) is incorrect. A "mere scintilla" of evidence is not enough to avoid summary judgment. The party with the burden of proof must produce at least enough evidence to support a reasonable inference in its favor.

287. **Answer (C) is correct.** In ruling on a motion for judgment as a matter of law, the court will first review the whole record in order to identify the direct and circumstantial evidence favoring the non-movant (Rodriguez). Based on the evidence and reasonable inferences favorable to the non-movant, the court tests the sufficiency of the evidence by "giving credence" only to the evidence that supports a finding in the non-movant's favor. (The court may also consider uncontradicted, unimpeached evidence in favor of the movant, but there is no indication in this hypothetical that there is any such evidence in the record.)

Answer (A) is incorrect. In moving for judgment as a matter of law at this point, Alpha

Omega is arguing that Rodriguez has produced legally insufficient evidence on a crucial element of her cause of action. It is Rodriguez's evidence that is in issue and Rodriguez's evidence that the court should examine. The court is not acting as a finder of fact here, and it is generally not allowed to consider evidence in favor of the party who moved for judgment as a matter of law.

Answer (B) is incorrect. The motion is not premature. Rodriguez has rested her case. Rule 50 allows the motion to be filed once "a party has been fully heard on an issue."

Answer (D) is incorrect. The judge is not supposed to weigh the evidence in ruling on a motion for judgment as a matter of law. The question is not which evidence the judge finds most convincing, but whether the party with the burden of proof has produced sufficient evidence that a reasonable jury could find in her favor.

288. Alpha Omega has re-urged its motion for judgment as a matter of law before the case is submitted to the jury. The judge must consider the evidence in favor of Rodriguez and the reasonable inferences in favor of Rodriguez. The judge may also consider evidence for Alpha Omega *if* that evidence is uncontradicted and unimpeached. Under these principles, the court may consider the testimony of Rodriguez and the witnesses in her favor. This testimony supports at least an inference that baskets at this Alpha Omega store are often bent and stick together, and that Alpha Omega is aware of this problem. It supports an inference that the baskets that injured Rodriguez were defective in this way. The cross-examination of Kay Rett supports Rodriguez's claim and so it, too, may be considered. It provides more circumstantial evidence that the baskets at the Alpha Omega store in question were in poor condition and that the company knew about the condition of the carts. The court should not consider the testimony of Hugh Cumber. It does not favor the non-movant (Rodriguez), nor is it the type of evidence that the jury would be required to believe, as his testimony has been impeached by evidence of his recent promotion. Unless the substantive law requires proof that the defendant knew about these particular carts on the day that Rodriguez fell, the court will likely deny the motion.

289. **Answer (D) is correct.** The right to jury trial is protected by the Constitution, and the jury's function is central to our court system. It is the jury, and not the judge, that holds the power to decide disputed fact issues. The jury's decision is, therefore, entitled to great deference. In order to protect the jury's role, the judge who is ruling on a motion for new trial does not sit as a "thirteenth juror." The question is not whether the judge would have ruled the same way had this been a bench trial. The question is whether the jury's verdict is so far out of line with the evidence that the trial should be done over. In federal court, this is often expressed as a question of whether the verdict was "clearly erroneous" or "against the clear weight of the evidence." In making this decision, the judge is allowed to consider all of the evidence.

Answer (A) is incorrect. See above.

Answer (B) is incorrect. The question of whether a reasonable jury could have found for Rodriguez is relevant to the motion for judgment as a matter of law. If a reasonable jury could have found for Rodriguez, it was correct to submit the case to the jury for decision. A party can avoid a judgment as a matter of law, but the state of the evidence can still be such that a grant of a new trial would be proper.

Answer (C) is incorrect. The judge is not permitted to quiz the jurors about their reasoning process in order to decide whether to grant a new trial. In fact, the rules of evidence prohibit most inquiry into the jury's deliberations.

290. **Answer (A) is correct.** The long-arm statute allows service here, since Pilchard entered into a contract with Builder, an Ohio resident. However, long-arm statutes must also be constitutional before personal jurisdiction is proper. Here, Builder solicited the contract, it was to be performed wholly outside of Ohio, and Pilchard's only "contacts" consisted of Pilchard in Pennsylvania talking on the phone to Builder while he was in Ohio. This is not a strong case for personal jurisdiction over Pilchard in Ohio. In addition, venue is probably also improper. Under 28 U.S.C. § 1391(b), venue would be proper either where Pilchard resides (and if there is no personal jurisdiction over Pilchard in the relevant judicial district in Ohio it does not "reside" there for venue purposes under § 1391(d)) or where a substantial part of the events or omissions giving rise to the claim occurred. It is unlikely that the phone calls with Ohio negotiating the deal or the fact that a resident of Ohio suffered financial losses would be sufficient to meet this test. Although more than one location may be proper under this test, in this case it is more likely that West Virginia (where the materials were to be delivered) or Pennsylvania (where the contract was made and where the defendant was going to perform the contract in part) would be the places where the events or omissions were "substantial."

Answers (B), (C), and (D) are incorrect. See above.

291. **Answer (B) is correct.** The court, after deciding that personal jurisdiction and venue were both improper, could dismiss the case. But such a dismissal would at least allow Builder to refile in West Virginia, his second choice for a forum. The court can instead choose to transfer the case to another federal court in which venue would be proper and where there would be personal jurisdiction over the defendant. Pennsylvania meets these requirements. And this type of transfer would result in the new forum's applying its own choice of law rules (and, under the assumptions for this question, its own substantive law). This would leave Builder in a jurisdiction in which he would be entitled only to recover about $100,000 even if he prevailed on the merits. Even if he could convince the E.D. Pa. to again transfer the case, this time from Pennsylvania to N.D.W. Va. under 28 U.S.C. § 1404, the transfer would not bring a choice of law change, and the court would still apply Pennsylvania law. This would leave Builder unhappy indeed.

Answer (A) is less correct. Dismissing the case would not make Builder happy, but it would be less disastrous than the transfer to Pennsylvania.

Answer (C) is incorrect. Lack of personal jurisdiction and incorrect federal venue are not a basis for sending a case to state court. And as this case was originally filed in federal court and not removed to there, "remand" is not an option.

Answer (D) is incorrect. The court could choose to transfer the case to West Virginia. While Builder's first choice of forum is Ohio, if Ohio is improper, West Virginia is actually his next best option.

292. Yes, a federal court in Pennsylvania would have jurisdiction over Pilchard and proper venue in Builder's case. Pennsylvania may easily have general jurisdiction over Pilchard Supplies, which is headquartered and therefore "at home" there. Even if it does not, in this case Pilchard negotiated the contract from Pennsylvania, entered into the contract there, and probably would have performed its obligations there, at least in part. This would be sufficient for specific personal jurisdiction. (Nor would Pilchard be likely to object to being sued at

home where the law is favorable, and it could waive an objection to personal jurisdiction if it had one.) Venue is also proper in the district of Pennsylvania in which Pilchard has its headquarters, as it "resides" there, and it is also likely to be a district in which a substantial part of the acts or omissions giving rise to Builder's claim occurred.

293. **Answer (D) is correct.** That means that **Answers (B) and (C) are both correct.** Answer (B) is correct because "residence" of a corporation for venue purposes is determined according to whether the corporation is subject to personal jurisdiction. *See* § 1391(d). It is likely that Pilchard would be subject to personal jurisdiction here in the district of West Virginia (N.D.W. Va.) in which it had contracted to deliver materials to Builder's job site. This would make venue proper under § 1391(b)(1). Answer (C) is correct because Pilchard "omitted" to deliver the building materials to N.D.W. Va. as promised.

Answer (A) is incorrect for the reasons stated above. "Residence" for venue purposes is a different issue from corporate citizenship for purposes of diversity jurisdiction.

294. Pilchard could choose to file in Ohio, hope that it can convince the judge that Ohio has personal jurisdiction, and go for the best of the available laws. However, unless there are facts strengthening the argument that Pilchard is subject to personal jurisdiction in Ohio that the problem does not mention, I would recommend that Builder file his lawsuit in West Virginia. Going for the long-shot Ohio forum creates a substantial risk that the case will end up in Pennsylvania and be governed by Pennsylvania law, and this would cost Builder $900,000.

295. **Answer (A) is correct.** Ohio does not have personal jurisdiction over Pilchard here, so the court must dismiss the case. A state court does not have the option of transferring a case to a court in another state — this option only exists in the federal court system. The dismissal would be without prejudice, so Builder could refile the case.

Answer (B) is incorrect. A dismissal for lack of personal jurisdiction is not a dismissal on the merits, and so Builder will be allowed to refile it.

Answer (C) is incorrect. An Ohio court does not have the power or mechanism to transfer a case to a state court in Pennsylvania (or any other state).

Answer (D) is incorrect. Because it is unlikely that Ohio has personal jurisdiction over this claim against Pilchard, it should dismiss the case.

296. Yes, if Builder filed the case in state court in Ohio, Pilchard could properly remove it. There is complete diversity of citizenship (Builder/Ohio vs. Pilchard/Pa.) and the amount in controversy exceeds $75,000. This is a diversity case, and Pilchard is not a resident of the forum state (Ohio). The time for removal has not run out.

297. **Answer (C) is correct.** As discussed above, the Ohio court lacks personal jurisdiction over Builder's claim against Pilchard. Venue is correct, however, because cases are removed to the district "embracing the place where such action [the state case] is pending." 28 U.S.C. § 1441(a). Normal venue analysis does not apply in removed cases. *See* § 139(c) and 17 MOORE'S FEDERAL PRACTICE § 110.08 (3d ed. 2000 & Supp. 2011). The case would therefore be removed to the district in Ohio in which the state court sits, and this would be correct venue. The motion to transfer for the convenience of parties and witnesses and in the interests of justice under § 1404, however, would likely succeed. Although the plaintiff's choice of forum

is given great weight, it seems probable that in this case most of the witnesses and evidence except the plaintiff himself will be in Pennsylvania. There could be facts beyond those in the problem that change this result, but from what we know at this point transfer seems likely. Since the Ohio forum lacks personal jurisdiction over Pilchard, this time the transfer would achieve a change in choice of law rules, and Pilchard would have secured both a transfer and a change to more favorable substantive law. (The court could also choose to dismiss the case, but this was not one of the multiple choice options.)

Answer (A) is incorrect. Filing a removal petition does not waive the right to complain about personal jurisdiction and venue if the defendant raises them properly as soon as the case lands in federal court.

Answer (B) is incorrect. Venue is proper in this removed case as explained above.

Answer (D) is incorrect. While venue is correct, personal jurisdiction is not and so the court may not keep the case.

298. Pilchard could argue that the case should be dismissed under the doctrine of forum non conveniens. Its argument would be that the case has very little connection with Ohio, because the contract was made in Pennsylvania, and was to be performed in Pennsylvania and West Virginia. It would have to convince the court that the private and public factors outweigh Builder's choice of an Ohio forum. This would include pointing out that other than Builder himself, all witnesses are in other states, and they might not be subject to compulsory process in Ohio. Also, Pilchard should point out whatever he can about the comparative dockets of the courts and the burden on Ohio juries of hearing a case with little connection to Ohio. Pilchard's argument will be weakened by the fact that Builder is an Ohio resident and that Ohio law would be applied by the Ohio court. But if Pilchard's argument succeeds, the court would dismiss the case because there is no mechanism for one state court to transfer to another.

299. Pilchard would like the case to end up in Pennsylvania and with Pennsylvania law applying. While not a guaranteed result, removing the case to federal court and moving to transfer to Pennsylvania provides Pilchard's best chance at achieving this goal. If the case stays in state court it would merely be dismissed, and we can imagine that Builder would refile in West Virginia, where Pilchard might still be liable for $1 million. The federal court, however, might choose to transfer to Pennsylvania rather than dismissing the case, and so the removal/motion to transfer option provides Pilchard with more control over the destination of the case than does the state court dismissal motion.

300. **Answer (C) is correct.** A ruling on personal jurisdiction is not a final judgment and is not on the merits, so claim preclusion is not applicable here. However, a decision that Pilchard had sufficient contacts with Ohio might lead to issue preclusion under some facts. This is not true here, as it is not the same issue. The earlier case decided that the contacts arising out of that plaintiff's cause of action were sufficient to justify specific personal jurisdiction. That is not the same issue as whether Pilchard has sufficient contacts with Ohio out of which Builder's claim arises. Pilchard is, therefore, not estopped from challenging the sufficiency of its contacts in this case.

Answer (A) is incorrect. Offensive non-mutual collateral estoppel is not recognized in every jurisdiction, but it is not considered improper everywhere.

Answer (B) is incorrect. Pilchard did litigate a personal jurisdiction issue, but it was not the same issue and so issue preclusion does not apply here.

Answer (D) is incorrect. The first case's decision about personal jurisdiction was necessary to its decision — absent personal jurisdiction it would not have been justified in keeping the case. However, as before, the issue litigated there was a different one from the issue in Builder's case

301. There are several limits on the plaintiff's choice of forum. First, the plaintiff can only choose a federal rather than state court if there is either a federal question or diversity of citizenship. Second, the plaintiff's choice of a state rather than federal forum is subject to the defendant's right to remove the case where allowed by statute. In terms of geography, the plaintiff must choose a state with which the defendant has sufficient contacts to justify personal jurisdiction. The plaintiff must also choose a location in which venue is correct. In federal court this will mean a state tied either to defendant's residence or to the events leading to the cause of action. State court systems will have their own venue rules that must be satisfied.

302. **Answer (C) is correct.** The Class Action Fairness Act would provide jurisdiction over this case because there is minimal diversity between a class member and the defendant (*see* 28 U.S.C. § 1332(d)(2)(A)); the class claims exceed $5 million (60,000 × $100) (*see* 28 U.S.C. § 1332(d)(2)); there are more than 100 class members (28 U.S.C. § 1332(d)(5)(B)); and less than one-third of the class members are from California, where the action was filed. (28 U.S.C. § 1332(d)(3), (4)).

Answer (A) is incorrect. Under CAFA, the minimal diversity can be between one class member and the defendant. Whether there is diversity of citizenship between the class representative and the defendant is not the only relevant question. Prior to CAFA, federal jurisdiction of class action lawsuits required complete diversity of citizenship between the class representative and the defendant without regard to the citizenship of the class members. *See, e.g., Supreme Tribe of Ben-Hur v. Cauble*, 255 U.S. 356, 365–366 (1921).

Answer (B) is incorrect. This class action would not be proper under supplemental jurisdiction because Amy is a citizen of California and her claim is too small. Thus, Amy has no independently adequate claim for the others to supplement. *See Exxon Mobil Corp. v. Allapattah Servcs. Inc.*, 545 U.S. 546 (2005).

Answer (D) is incorrect. Although Answer (C) is correct, Answer (B) is incorrect.

303. **Answer (D) is the best answer.** Although Rule 34 allows the requesting party to specify its preferred format, and the producing party to suggest a format, neither is absolute. Rule 34(b) explains that absent agreement between the parties or court order specifying a format for the production of electronically stored information ("ESI"), documents shall be produced "as they are kept in the usual course of business or must [be organized and labeled] to correspond to the categories in the request." Fed. R. Civ. P. 34(b)(2)(E)(i). Rule 34 also states that the information must be produced "in a form or forms in which it is ordinarily maintained or in a reasonably usable form or forms" if the requesting party did not specify a form for production. Fed. R. Civ. P. 34(b)(2)(E)(ii).

Answer (A) is incorrect. A responding party may indicate the format it intends to use for production if it objects to the format specified by the requesting party or if the requesting party did not specify a format. Fed. R. Civ. P. 34(b)(2)(D). But the responding party does not have the right to choose the format in which it will produce the ESI.

Answer (B) is incorrect. Although the requesting party can specify a format that it prefers, the producing party may object to the requested format. Fed. R. Civ. P. 34(b)(2)(D).

Answer (C) is incorrect. According to Rule 34, a party is not required to produce the same ESI in multiple forms, unless the parties so agree or the court orders production of the information in more than one form. Fed. R. Civ. P. 34(b)(2)(E)(iii).

304. **Answer (C) is probably correct.** In *Zubulake*, the court explained that "it would be wholly inappropriate to even consider cost-shifting" when the producing party "maintains the data in an accessible and usable format, and can respond to [the] request cheaply and quickly." *Zubulake v. UBS Warburg LLC*, 217 F.R.D. 309, 320 (S.D.N.Y. 2003). The *Zubulake* court, however, differentiated between the information stored in an easily accessible format and information stored on backup tapes, because the information stored on backup tapes is not easily accessible. Under Rule 26, the court can order discovery of information that is not reasonably accessible for good cause and with conditions, including cost-shifting. *See* Fed. R. Civ. P. 26(b)(2)(B).

Answer (A) is incorrect. According to the Advisory Committee Note to Rule 26(b)(2), the rule requires that "reasonably accessible" ESI must be produced. *See* Fed. R. Civ. P. 26. *Zubulake* explains that the producing party should bear the cost of production for reasonably accessible ESI. *Zubulake v. UBS Warburg LLC*, 217 F.R.D. 309, 320 (S.D.N.Y. 2003). The e-mails currently stored on the company's computers are reasonably accessible; therefore, Hayden Corp. will bear the cost of producing those documents.

Answer (B) is probably incorrect because depending on the circumstances, a trial court can limit discovery of the e-mails that are difficult to retrieve, shift the cost of some or all of the expense to the requesting party, or deny discovery of those e-mails altogether. *See* Fed. R. Civ. P. 26(b)(2)(B), (C).

Answer (D) is incorrect because the court will weigh several factors in order to decide whether to limit discovery. Even if Hayden Corp. demonstrates that the ESI is not reasonably accessible, the court will likely order discovery if Smith "shows good cause," but the court may also limit discovery to make it less burdensome on Hayden Corp. Under Rule 26(b)(2)(B), the scope of discovery of ESI that is not reasonably accessible is in the court's discretion.

305. **Answer (D) is correct. Answer (B) is correct** because the summary judgment obtained by Anderson did not dispose of the entire case. A final judgment "ends litigation on the merits." *See Catlin v. United States*, 324 U.S. 229, 253 (1945). **Answer (C) is also correct.** Rule 54(b) allows a trial judge to finalize an order that adjudicates fewer than all the claims or parties involved in the case only if the court "expressly determines that there is no just reason for delay" and "directs entry of a final judgment." Fed. R. Civ. P. 54(b). Although Rule 54(b) is applicable to the facts presented in the problem, which involve an order that adjudicates the rights and liabilities of fewer than all of the claims made against the parties, the dismissal order must be drafted in compliance with the requirements of Rule 54(b) to finalize the summary judgment in favor of Anderson.

Answer (A) is incorrect. To come within the small class of cases covered by the doctrine, the order must conclusively determine the disputed question, resolve an important issue completely separate from the merits, and be effectively unreviewable on appeal from a final judgment. *Cohen v. Beneficial Indus. Loan Corp.*, 337 U.S. 541, 546 (1949); *Coopers & Lybrand v. Livesay*, 437 U.S. 463, 468 (1978). The collateral order doctrine does not apply to the problem both because the summary judgment is not separate from the merits or unreviewable on appeal of the ultimate final judgment.

306. **Answer (C) is correct.** Entry of the second dismissal order in the civil docket disposed of the remaining issues in the case. However, Rule 58 (or Appellate Rule 4) states that a "separate document" must be used for entry of a final judgment. *See* Fed. R. Civ. P. 58. Rule 58 requires a self-contained document distinct from any other orders in the case. *Bankers Trust Co. v. Mallis*, 435 U.S. 381, 385 (1978). Thus, neither dismissal order started the appellate clock, as neither meets the "separate document" requirement. Therefore, as provided in Rule 58 and Appellate Rule 4, the judgment was "entered" by law when 150 days ran from entry of the second dismissal order. The Advisory Committee Notes to Rule 58 indicate that the 150-day rule was only "intended to apply to cases in which the court intended its order to be final," but due to mere oversight, the court fails to enter a separate document. *See Utah v. Norton*, 396 F.3d 1281, 1287 (10th Cir. 2005).

Answers (A), (B), and (D) are incorrect because neither the July 24 summary judgment order nor the July 26 summary judgment order is considered a final judgment.

307. **Answer (D) is correct.** Appellate Rule 4 allows for reopening the appeal for a period of 14 days after the date when the court's order to reopen is entered under the following conditions: (A) the moving party did not receive notice under Rule 77(d) of the entry of the order to be appealed within 21 days after entry; (B) the motion to reopen is filed within 180 days after the judgment or order is entered or within 14 days after the movant receives a Rule 77(d) notice, whichever is earlier; and (C) no party would be prejudiced. Fed. R. App. P. 4(a)(6).

Answer (A) is incorrect because Appellate Rule 4 does allow for reopening the appeal under the circumstances explained above. *See* Fed. R. App. P. 4(a).

Answer (B) is incorrect because a motion for extension must be filed within 30 days after entry of the order denying Kent a new trial.

Answer (C) is incorrect because Appellate Rule 4 probably precludes the use of Rule 60(b) to vacate and reenter the order denying a new trial in order to restart the appellate clock.

308. **Answer (D) is correct.** Based on the Supreme Court's analysis and application of Rule 19(b) in *Provident Tradesmens Bank & Trust Co. v. Patterson*, 390 U.S. 102 (1968), Pickles' attempt to obtain a windfall escape from his defeat at trial is foreclosed.

Answer (A) is incorrect because Travis Bank is not a party whose absence would require the action to be dismissed under Rule 19(b) because the trial court could grant relief to the plaintiffs that protects Travis Bank's lien interest without its joinder as a party to the case.

Answer (B) is incorrect. Under modern Rule 19, the issue is procedural, not jurisdictional.

Answer (C) is incorrect. Even if Pickles' lien is inferior, that is not an issue that the court of appeals would resolve in deciding joinder issues.

309. **Answer (C) is correct.** Hybrid Cars can file a cross-claim for contribution, as the

contribution claim need not be mature when the cross-claim is filed. *See* Fed. R. Civ. P. 13(g). It should not matter that the contribution claim is also a counterclaim, and that contribution counterclaims must be mature. Otherwise, ASAP could cross-claim against Hybrid Cars and not be subject to a responsive claim.

Answers (A), (B), and (D) are incorrect for the same reason Answer (C) is correct.

310. The Supreme Court distinguishes between specific jurisdiction and general jurisdiction by explaining that for specific jurisdiction the plaintiff's cause of action arises out of or relates to the defendant's contacts with the forum (while for general jurisdiction it does not). It has not, however, provided much guidance about where to draw the line, particularly as to the question of whether the contacts "relate to" the cause of action. In Justice Brennan's dissent in *Helicopteros*, for example, he suggested that if that case had been pleaded differently — if, for example, the plaintiffs claimed that the helicopter crash in Peru was caused by poor training in Texas — it would have been a specific rather than general jurisdiction case. And footnote 10 of the majority opinion made clear what they were *not* deciding: "Absent any briefing on the issue, we decline to reach the questions (1) whether the terms 'arising out of' and 'related to' describe different connections between a cause of action and a defendant's contacts with a forum, and (2) what sort of tie between a cause of action and a defendant's contacts with a forum is necessary to a determination that either connection exists. Nor do we reach the question whether, if the two types of relationship differ, a forum's exercise of personal jurisdiction in a situation where the cause of action 'relates to,' but does not 'arise out of,' the defendant's contacts with the forum should be analyzed as an assertion of specific jurisdiction." *Helicopteros Nacionales de Colombia, S. A. v. Hall*, 466 U.S. 408, 416 n.10 (1984)

Absent Supreme Court precedent, the lower courts have devised different tests to put cases in one category or the other. Some courts use a "but for" test: if the plaintiff's claim would not have arisen "but for" the contacts, then a specific jurisdiction test is proper. Plaintiffs prefer this test, because it means that more situations will be treated as specific jurisdiction, and that requires a lesser showing of contacts with the forum state. Under this test, Brad could argue that "but for" the Americana's solicitation of his business, he never would have gone to Montana and therefore never fallen in the spa. This would put his lawsuit in the specific jurisdiction category. Other courts use a "substantive relevance" test. Under this test, specific-jurisdiction contacts with the forum state must be elements of the plaintiff's claim for liability; contacts are only relevant for specific jurisdiction if they would be relevant in a case where everything happened in the same state. In a jurisdiction using this test, Brad's claim would be treated as one for general jurisdiction. His claim is for negligence in the spa — oily feet, no mats, insufficient supervision, and the like. The fact that the Americana solicited business in Texas is not included as one of the facts underlying his actual claim. In such a jurisdiction, Brad's claim would be in the general jurisdiction category, and he could only sue the Americana in Texas if its contacts there are so substantial, continuous, and systematic that it is "at home" there, and these facts show that the Americana's "home" is Montana. For a discussion of the various approaches, see *Moki Mac River Expeditions v. Drugg*, 221 S.W.3d 569 (Tex. 2007).

311. **Answer (C) is correct.** The "private factors" in § 1404 (and forum non conveniens) analysis are factors that relate to the convenience and interests of the parties themselves. Therefore,

the availability of witnesses and sources of proof are treated as private factors.

Answers (A) and (B) are incorrect. While they would be relevant to the decision regarding whether the case should be transferred, they are considered "public" factors — factors that relate to the interests of the court systems and the general public.

Answer (D) is also incorrect. The comparative pleasantness of climates is not a factor in § 1404 transfers.

312. **Answer (D) is probably the best answer.** The counterclaim does not have an independent basis for federal jurisdiction, because it is below the amount in controversy floor even though there is diversity of citizenship. However, it probably meets the requirements for supplemental jurisdiction. Under § 1367(a), the counterclaim would have to be part of the same constitutional "case" as Brad's claim. This is the hard part — do the two claims share a common nucleus of operative fact? Viewed narrowly, Brad's claim is about what happened to him in the spa, and the hotel's claim is about an unpaid bill. There would be little overlap. However, because the claim for the bill will include a description of the services rendered by the hotel, and Brad's defense to the counterclaim appears to include his injury in the spa, there may be sufficient overlap to satisfy Article III and § 1367. If that hurdle is cleared, supplemental jurisdiction will be proper because the remaining requirements are met. This case is in federal court based on diversity jurisdiction, so we must examine § 1367(b). But this counterclaim by the Americana is not a claim by a "plaintiff," nor is it a type of claim prohibited by section (b), and so supplemental jurisdiction would be proper.

Answer (A) is incorrect. While it is true that because of the amount in controversy there is no independent basis for federal jurisdiction, this option ignores the availability of supplemental jurisdiction.

Answer (B) is incorrect. What it says about compulsory counterclaims may be true. But the question is not whether the claim is proper under the joinder rules but whether there is jurisdiction over the claim. And while it is often said that "there is supplemental jurisdiction over compulsory counterclaims," that is a shorthand for the way cases normally come out, not a statement of the way they should be analyzed.

Answer (C) is incorrect. The fact that the claim is inconsistent with the requirements of § 1332 is one thing to consider in determining whether § 1367(b) takes away the jurisdiction granted by § 1367(a) — but it is only one part of the equation, and ignores more crucial elements, as explained above.

313. **Answer (D) is probably the best answer.** First, the claim is proper under the joinder rules. Rule 14(b) provides that when "a claim is asserted against a plaintiff, the plaintiff may bring in a third party if this rule would allow a defendant to do so." Here, the Americana has asserted a claim against Brad. Brad's claim against Angelina is a derivative one: "if I have to pay the Americana, you have to pay me." It is therefore the proper kind of claim to form the basis of impleader. Second, if there is supplemental jurisdiction over the Americana's counterclaim (see above), there should also be supplemental jurisdiction over this claim. It is based on the same facts regarding the unpaid hotel bill — with only the possible addition of information about the liability of both parties for the contract, or the liability of one spouse for another's debts.

Answer (A) is probably incorrect. It is correct that this is a proper impleader claim. But if the explanation above is correct, then Answer (A) is wrong in concluding that there is no subject matter jurisdiction over Brad's claim.

Answer (B) is incorrect. As explained above, plaintiffs may use Rule 14 to add new parties under the circumstances here.

Answer (C) is incorrect. While the question of jurisdiction is a close one, impleader is proper.

314. **Answer (B) is the best answer.** This question illustrates the complexity of lawsuit structure, and the difficulty of categorization when multiple parties are allied on some issues and opponents on others. Angelina was not a party to the original *Brad v. Americana & Vince* lawsuit, nor was she made a party to the Americana's counterclaim against Brad. Rather, she was brought into the lawsuit by Brad, who asserted a derivative claim against her under Rule 14(b). This is a mirror image of the kind of impleader that you are more used to seeing. Angelina, as a third-party defendant, may "assert against the plaintiff any claim arising out of the transaction or occurrence that is the subject matter of the plaintiff's claim against the third-party plaintiff." Fed. R. Civ. P. 14(a)(2)(D). As applied to this lawsuit, that means that Angelina may assert against Americana (the "plaintiff" in its claim against Brad) any claim arising out of the transaction or occurrence that is the subject matter of the Americana's claim against Brad. Courts occasionally describe a claim asserted by a third-party defendant against the original plaintiff as a "cross-action," but this terminology reflects historical or state practice; Rule 14 merely calls them "claims." They are not cross-claims or counterclaims within the meaning of the Federal Rules of Civil Procedure.

Answer (A) is incorrect. Angelina *could* have joined with Brad as a co-plaintiff in the beginning, but she did not. (And had she done so, the court would have had supplemental jurisdiction over her claim under the reasoning of the Supreme Court in *Exxon/Allapatah.*) Angelina could have intervened as a plaintiff after he filed the suit, although in that case she would have had a problem with subject matter jurisdiction, given the prohibitions of § 1367(b) ("claims by persons seeking to intervene as plaintiffs"). But she did not enter the lawsuit in that way, and so is not a conventional co-plaintiff.

Answer (C) is incorrect. Although Brad has asserted claims against them both, Angelina and the Americana are not on the same "side" of the lawsuit, so they are not "coparties" and a claim between them is not a cross-claim.

Answer (D) is incorrect. While it is a claim made by a third-party defendant, it is not a "third party claim."

315. **Answer (C) is correct.** Angelina's claim does not have an independent basis for federal jurisdiction, because it is for less than $75,000. Once again we must analyze the supplemental jurisdiction statute. In order to satisfy part (a), her claim needs to share a common nucleus of operative fact with the claims that provide the court with jurisdiction — here Brad's claim against the Americana. Her claim for her own damages arising from seeing Brad's injury will share many facts with Brad's own claim, and therefore it meets that requirement. Next, we must check to make sure that part (b) does not take away that supplemental jurisdiction. This is a case based on diversity. Is Angelina's claim the claim of a "plaintiff"? She is seeking to recover damages for her own injuries, yet procedurally she was brought into the lawsuit as a defendant to Brad's Rule 14 claim. Just as courts have not treated defendant's making counterclaims as "plaintiffs," they should not treat Angelina as a plaintiff. However, one can imagine courts being concerned that Angelina could have been a

plaintiff from the beginning and deciding to categorize her accordingly. We should therefore go on to consider the nature of Angelina's claim, to be sure it is not prohibited by (b). It is not a claim against a person made a party under Rule 14, 19, 20, or 24 (none of those rules explain how the Americana came to be in the lawsuit or the nature of Angelina's claim against the Americana), nor is it a claim by a person to be joined as a plaintiff under Rule 19 or 24. Therefore, § 1367(a) grants supplemental jurisdiction over Angelina's claim, and § 1367(b) does not take that jurisdiction away.

Answer (A) is incorrect. It's true that the amount in controversy is too small for independent federal jurisdiction, but that does not answer the question.

Answer (B) is incorrect. (B) is a correct description of the claim's procedural posture, but it does not answer the question of subject matter jurisdiction.

Answer (D) is incorrect because Answer (B) is incorrect.

316. **Answer (D) is correct.** Rule 13(g) governs cross-claims, and it requires that the cross-claim arise out of the same transaction or occurrence "that is the subject matter of the original action or of a counter-claim." Vince's OSHA claim arose at a different time, and for different reasons, than any of the other claims in this lawsuit. Nor does Vince have some other proper cross-claim that he can use as the basis for adding his OSHA claim through Rule 18.

Answer (A) is incorrect. While some claims between co-parties are proper, unrelated ones like this are not.

Answer (B) is incorrect. The fact that all of the claims arise out of events that occurred in the same place gives them a bit of commonality, but all events that happen to occur in the same location over time are not part of the same transaction or occurrence if there is no other tie between them.

Answer (C) is incorrect. While the kind of contribution or indemnity claim described in (C) is one type of proper cross-claim, it is not the only kind that is allowed. The quoted language, from Rule 13(g), actually functions to allow un-matured contribution claims to be filed.

317. **Answer (D) is correct, because Answers (A) and (C) are correct.** Answer (A) is correct because it highlights the lack of diversity of citizenship between Vince, a human domiciled in Montana and therefore a citizen of Montana, and the Americana, a corporation that is a citizen of Montana because its principal place of business is there. Answer (C) is correct because it highlights the obstacle to supplemental jurisdiction. Both Article III of the Constitution and § 1367(a) require that the claim that provides jurisdiction and the would-be supplemental claim are part of the same "case." As defined in *United Mineworkers v. Gibbs*, that means they must share a "common nucleus of operative fact." Here, there are almost no commonalities between Brad's claims against the Americana and Vince (their alleged negligence leading to his fall in the spa) and Vince's claim against the Americana for firing him for complaining about the storage of toxic chemicals. There would therefore be no supplemental jurisdiction over Vince's claim.

Answer (B) is incorrect for the reasons explained above.

318. **Answer (C) is correct.** Federal question jurisdiction can be based on a federal issue embedded in a state law claim, but only if certain requirements are met. The Supreme Court's opinion in *Grable & Sons Metal Products, Inc. v. Darue Engineering &*

Manufacturing, 545 U.S. 308 (2005), explained that the federal issue must be actually disputed, necessary, substantial, and nondisruptive. Vince's claim does include a federal issue — whether he was fired for complaining about OSHA violations — but all of the *Grable* requirements are not met. It is actually disputed in the sense that the Americana denies that they fired Vince for complaining about OSHA violations, but there does not appear to be a dispute about the requirements themselves. It may not be necessary to decide anything about the federal issue if the court were to find that Vince was fired for fighting with a hotel guest rather than for anything to do with OSHA. Similarly, the OSHA issue may not be considered substantial — because this is not a dispute about the meaning of the regulations, federal expertise would not be helpful, nor is uniform interpretation of the rules an issue. Finally, if every employee's claim that he or she has been fired for pointing out OSHA violations is recognized as a federal question, a large number of cases that had been state law wrongful termination cases might become federal questions, disrupting the balance between state and federal caseloads. *See also Gunn v. Minton*, 133 S. Ct. 1059 (2013).

Answer (A) is incorrect. Even claims based on state law may sometimes form the basis for federal question jurisdiction when they have the right kind of embedded federal issue.

Answers (B) and (D) are incorrect for the reasons explained above.

319. **Answer (B) is correct.** Rule 15(a)(2) provides that the court should "freely give leave [to amend] when justice so requires." Generous allowance of amendments is part of the philosophy behind the federal system of pleading and discovery — as parties learn more through discovery, they are encouraged to drop claims without support and add claims that have come to light — and so amendments are favored unless they prejudice the opposing party. Amendments that come this early in the case, before discovery has even been done, are generally allowed. There is no indication that the two-month gap has caused any harm to Brad either through lost opportunity or delay in the case.

Answer (A) is incorrect. While it's too late to amend as a matter of course (without needing the court's permission) under Rule 15(a)(1), that does not mean that it is too late to amend at all.

Answer (C) is incorrect. The kind of "prejudice" that might preclude an amendment is not that an added claim or defense will make a party's position less favorable. It is instead prejudice growing out of the time gap between the original filing and the proposed amendment — was evidence available at the beginning that has now been lost? would allowing an amendment now require re-opening of discovery, or require that the trial be postponed? The need to counter the affirmative defense of contributory negligence, which will likely involve almost exactly the same evidence as Brad's own claim, does not create the kind of prejudice that would justify denying leave to amend.

Answer (D) is incorrect. This is not an amendment to a right to recover that is limited by a statute of limitations, it is an affirmative defense. Limitations are not even relevant here. In addition, even when parties seeking affirmative relief request amendments to add claims on which limitations have run, Rule 15(c) may allow those claims to "relate back" to the time of the original filing. Answer (D) is thus wrong for two reasons.

320. **Answer (B) is correct.** Sections (g) and (h) of Rule 12 govern the filing of Rule 12 defenses, and waiver of those defenses when they are not timely filed. Rule 12(g) provides that (except as provided in Rule 12(h)(2) or (3), which we'll get to in a minute) "a party that makes a

motion under this rule must not make another motion under this rule raising a defense that was available to the party but omitted from its earlier motion." Here, the defense of insufficient service of process (12(b)(5)) was available to CC at the time it served its original Rule 12 motion to dismiss. Is it saved by 12(h)? No. Rule 12(h)(1) provides that a party "waives any defense listed in Rule 12(b)(2) to (5) by . . . omitting it from a motion in the circumstances described in Rule 12(g)(2)." Nor do sections (2) or (3) save CC, because they do not include insufficient service of process in their list of defenses that may still be raised. Does the fact that CC attempted to use an "amended motion" rather than a second motion save it? Not here. While some judges have found discretion to allow a quick amended motion that asserts otherwise-waived defenses, a motion that has already been ruled on may not be amended. CC's motion is really a second motion, and so it's too late.

Answer (A) is incorrect. It appears to be looking to Rule 15(a), about amending pleadings as a matter of course, and suggesting that that somehow is relevant to CC's attempt to amend its motion to dismiss. However, a motion is not a "pleading" (see Rule 7 for a list of pleadings), so this rule is inapplicable.

Answer (C) is incorrect. Rule 12(h)(1)(B) does mention the option to "include [the Rule 12 defense] in a responsive pleading," and an answer is a responsive pleading. But this part of the rule does not provide a reprieve when a party has filed a pre-answer motion but omitted a defense listed in Rule 12(b)(2)–(5). If *no* pre-answer motion is filed, these defenses may be included in the answer, or even in an amendment to the answer allowed as a matter of course under Rule 15(a), but that is not the situation here.

Answer (D) is incorrect. While notice is a component of due process, technical deficiencies in the manner of service can be waived, as explained above.

321. **Answer (D) is correct, because Answers (B) and (C) are correct.** When a party seeks leave to amend its complaint after the statute of limitations has run, two issues must be addressed: (1) whether to allow the amendment at all; and (2) whether the amended allegations will "relate back" to the original filing. As to the first issue, Rule 15(a) provides that the court "should freely give leave when justice so requires." Although the Flaxes' requested amendment does add a new claim, it comes very early in the lawsuit and does not require new evidence that is unavailable to Sprint. It should therefore be allowed. Thus Answer (B) is correct. As to the second issue, Rule 15(c)(B) allows amendments to relate back (in other words, we will act as though they were filed when the original complaint was filed) if it "asserts a claim or defense that arose out of the conduct, transaction, or occurrence set out — or attempted to be set out — in the original pleading." Here, the allegation that Susan Sprint was talking on her cell phone when she rear-ended the Flaxes' van and the allegation that she was speeding when she rear-ended the van clearly arise out of the same transaction — the collision between Sprint's car and the Flax family van. The purpose of the "same transaction" requirement for purposes of relation back is to assure that the defendant had adequate notice of the claim, and Sprint was on notice that she was accused of negligent driving — additional factual theories underlying the negligence claim will not unfairly surprise her. Thus Answer (C) is also correct.

Answer (A) is incorrect. Although the cell phone claim would be barred by limitations if it were filed by itself for the first time, it will be treated as relating back, as explained above.

322. **Answer (C) is correct.** Here the issue is whether the claims against the two defendants are properly joined under Rule 20, which requires that a right to relief is "asserted against them

jointly, severally, or in the alternative with respect to or arising out of the same transaction, occurrence, or series of transactions or occurrences; and any question of law or fact common to all defendants will arise in the action." Fed. R. Civ. P. 20(a)(2). In this context, the purpose of the "same transaction" requirement is to achieve an efficient trial package — the efficiency of trying the claims together should exceed any prejudice that might arise from the combination. Some courts articulate this as a requirement that there be a "logical relationship" between the claims; others talk about whether they involve enough of the "same evidence." Either way, the claim against CC and the claim against Flax share enough common facts, law, and evidence that joinder is proper. Indeed, even if separate cases were brought against CC and Flax, you could expect them to bring up the other's actions in arguing that their own conduct was not the cause of the plaintiffs' injuries. The motion to sever should be denied.

Answer (A) is incorrect. While it identifies some of the correct test ("same transaction or occurrence"), its conclusion is wrong. The legal and factual claims need not be identical to satisfy Rule 20, and it would be less efficient to have two separate lawsuits arising out of this accident than to hear it all together.

Answer (B) is incorrect. First, it is possible that both Sprint's driving and CC's design contributed to the plaintiffs' injuries. Second, even if the claims were inconsistent, Rule 8(d)(3) allows a party to state "as many claims . . . as it has, regardless of consistency." Pleading in the alternative is proper so long as it can be done without violating Rule 11. And third, none of these questions govern joinder of parties under the Federal Rules.

Answer (D) is incorrect. Rule 12 only provides for the waiver of Rule 12 defenses ("under this Rule"). Motions to sever are not lost if not made at the outset. Indeed, in some cases the desirability of such a motion may not become clear until after some discovery has taken place and the claims and positions of the parties have become more clear.

323. **Answer (D) is probably the best answer.** The first lawsuit was *Sheridan v. CC* (wrongful termination) with a counterclaim of *CC v. Sheridan* (wrongful disclosure of trade secrets). While Sheridan's right to reveal certain CC information does appear to have been part of the "claim" in that case, the Flaxes were not parties to it (in fact, they had not yet even been injured). By attempting to use that judgment to bind the Flaxes, CC is attempting to use the judgment against a non-party, and this is not proper under either claim or issue preclusion. The proper way to try to enforce the injunction against Sheridan would be to go back to the original court and ask that judge to hold Sheridan in contempt of court for violating the agreed injunction (contempt is the vehicle for enforcing injunctive relief). In addition, even if the Flaxes had been parties to that first suit, its recitations that certain CC information was protected as a trade secret or by attorney-client privilege cannot be used for purposes of issue preclusion. Issue preclusion requires that the issues have actually been litigated and decided, so agreed judgments do not have issue preclusive effect. All of this does not leave CC without a remedy — it may still assert objections based on privilege or trade secret at Sheridan's deposition.

Answers (A), (B), and (C) are incorrect for the reasons explained above.

324. **Answer (D) is correct, because Answers (B) and (C) are correct.** It may be true that the material on the backup tapes is not reasonably accessible (although under Rule 26(b)(2)(B), CC would have to show that undue burden or cost makes it not reasonably accessible). However, the court has the discretion to order production of such information if the

requesting party shows good cause. The factors involved in a finding of good cause often involve the centrality of the information, the specificity of the discovery request, the comparative resources of the parties, and the circumstances leading to destruction of more easily accessible versions of the information. Here, what CC knew about the alleged defects in the minivan is central to the issues in the case. The need to resort to the backup tapes is also the result of CC's decision to shred the original materials and report. In addition, it is possible that CC's decision to shred the original documents might be considered spoliation, if litigation about this issue was reasonably foreseeable, in which case paying the cost of producing information from the backup tapes might be justified as a sanction. In situations such as this, judges often order that a sample be made in order to make a more informed decision about what kind of discovery to order and how to allocate the costs of production. Based on the factors discussed above and the results of the sampling, Judge Prius might also order the Flaxes to pay part of the cost of production.

Answer (A) is incorrect. Although it is relevant that these materials are not readily accessible, that is not an automatic bar to discovery.

325. **Answer (A) is probably correct.** Complaints by other consumers about the same product are often considered relevant, because they can lead to the discovery of admissible evidence. They may disclose a pattern of defects or incidents; they may identify other people with knowledge of relevant facts; if they show the manufacturer's knowledge of the defect, that information may be relevant to a duty to warn, or to a claim for punitive damages. Settlement agreements are a bit different — they may reveal some or all of the same information, but they also include information about the disposition of those claims, including the amounts paid to particular claimants. A court might choose to permit discovery of the settlements but redact information (such as the amounts) either because it is not relevant or in order to protect the privacy interest of the settling parties.

Answer (B) is probably incorrect. First, settlement agreements often recite the parties' allegations, and so provide more than just a name and a number. Second, information can be relevant in the discovery sense even if the agreements themselves do not meet the test for relevant trial evidence.

Answer (C) is incorrect. As noted above, documents need not be admissible to be discoverable. *See* Rule 26(b)(1).

Answer (D) is incorrect. In most jurisdictions, settlement agreements need not be made public. Settlements may be entered into before any lawsuit is filed, and even if the settlement ends litigation, the settlement agreement itself is often a confidential contract between the parties, and the court record will contain merely an agreed order of dismissal.

326. **Answer (C) is correct.** A central issue in the case, and the factual basis for the Flaxes' negligence per se claim, is whether Sprint was talking on her cell phone at the time of the accident. She has denied doing so. Her cell phone billing records should show the times during which she made or received calls, and those times can be compared to the time of the accident. They are therefore relevant and discoverable. On the other hand, cell phone records, even for a month, would reveal a lot more information about who Sprint called and when, and this private information is not relevant to the Flaxes' claims. Judge Prius might therefore choose to allow discovery of those portions of the bill that show the relevant time

period but deny discovery of the entire bill.

Answer (A) is incorrect. While Sprint does have some privacy interest in her phone bill, that interest is not a complete bar to the discovery of relevant information.

Answer (B) is incorrect. As discussed above, while Sprint's "habits" generally may not be relevant, the issue of whether she was using the phone at the time of the accident is relevant, and her cell phone bill would shed light on that issue.

Answer (D) is incorrect. First, information about the times of Sprint's calls is itself relevant, not merely relevant for purposes of impeachment. Second, the Advisory Committee Notes to the 2000 amendments to Rule 26 (which changed the scope of discovery from "subject matter" to "claims and defenses") noted that information needed for purposes of impeachment might be considered relevant to the claims and defenses of the parties. "[I]nformation that could be used to impeach a likely witness, although not otherwise relevant to the claims or defenses, might be properly discoverable. . . . [T]he determination whether such information is discoverable because it is relevant to the claims or defenses depends on the circumstances of the pending action."

The amendments to Rule 26 that will become effective on December 1, 2015, also leave open the possibility that impeachment materials will satisfy the definition of relevance.

327. **Answer (B) is correct.** The 2010 amendments to Rule 26 specifically deal with the discoverability of drafts of expert reports. An earlier version of the rule made information provided to a testifying expert and communications with that testifying expert discoverable, leading parties to seek discovery of the drafts of their opponents' testifying experts' reports. Arguing that such discovery was intrusive and expensive but rarely yielded helpful information, the Advisory Committee amended the rule. Rule 26(b)(4)(B) now provides that "Rules 26(b)(3)(A) and (B) [trial preparation materials] protect drafts of any report or disclosure required under Rule 26(a)(2), regardless of the form in which the draft is recorded."

Answer (A) is incorrect. While communications that identify "facts or data" that the party's attorney provided to the expert and that the expert considered in forming the opinions to be expressed are discoverable, Rule 26 specifically excepts draft reports, as noted above.

Answer (C) is incorrect for the reasons noted above.

Answer (D) is incorrect. Draft reports may be relevant, but they are made privileged by Rule 26(b)(4).

328. **Answer (C) is correct.** *See* Rule 26(b)(4)(C)(iii).

Answer (A) is incorrect. While generally those communications are protected as work product (since the 2010 amendments), there is an exception for assumptions that the attorney provided and the expert relied on in forming the opinions to be presented.

Answer (B) is incorrect. While some communications between attorney and testifying expert might otherwise be privileged, the need to effectively cross-examine the testifying expert has led the rulemakers to lift the privilege to some degree. (The applicable privilege is more often identified as work product, since many jurisdictions would not recognize an expert as an agent of the attorney for purposes of attorney-client privilege, and in diversity cases attorney-client privilege is defined by state law.) While communications revealing strategy are now protected, it is important to know where the facts or data on which the expert relies came from, and what it is, and so Rule 26(b)(4) makes facts, data, and assumptions provided by the attorney discoverable.

Answer (D) is incorrect because both (A) and (B) are incorrect.

329. **Answer (B) is correct.** Rule 37(c) provides that when a party fails to identify a witness (either through automatic disclosures or by failing to supplement a discovery response), a variety of sanctions are available. CC should have identified Dave Disgruntled in response to the Flaxes' interrogatory, and the failure to list him made it incomplete or incorrect and it should have been supplemented pursuant to Rule 26(e). Although one possible sanction is that the party is not allowed to use the witness, that sanction is not meaningful when a party has failed to disclose a witness whose testimony would be harmful to it. That is the case here. Rule 37(c)(1)(B) provides that the court "may inform the jury of the party's failure" to properly disclose or supplement. A sanction would be improper if the failure was substantially justified or harmless, but it appears that Dave had crucial and unique information, so concealing his identity was not harmless. Nor is "we don't want our opponent to know about this person" an acceptable justification ("substantial justification" often involves situations in which a witness has only just been located despite diligent efforts). Answer (B)'s option is therefore correct.

Answer (A) is incorrect. While prohibiting a witness from testifying is one of the possible sanctions for failure to disclose or supplement, it is not the only possibility.

Answer (C) is probably incorrect. It is true that Rule 37(c) makes the sanctions listed in Rule 37(b)(2)(A)(i)–(vi) available for failure to disclose, and rendering a default judgment is one of those options. However, extremely severe sanctions such as that (often called "death penalty" sanctions) are reserved for extremely serious and willful violations of the discovery rules. There are also due process limits on the imposition of such sanctions, including a requirement that the disobedience justify an inference that the party's case lacks merit. While CC's decision not to include Dave in its interrogatory answer was deliberate, if this was their only discovery rule violation and the Flaxes had access to similar information from other sources (such as Sheridan, other witnesses, or document production), it is less likely that the court would choose default judgment as a sanction.

Answer (D) is incorrect. As noted above, dislike of sharing harmful information does not constitute "substantial justification."

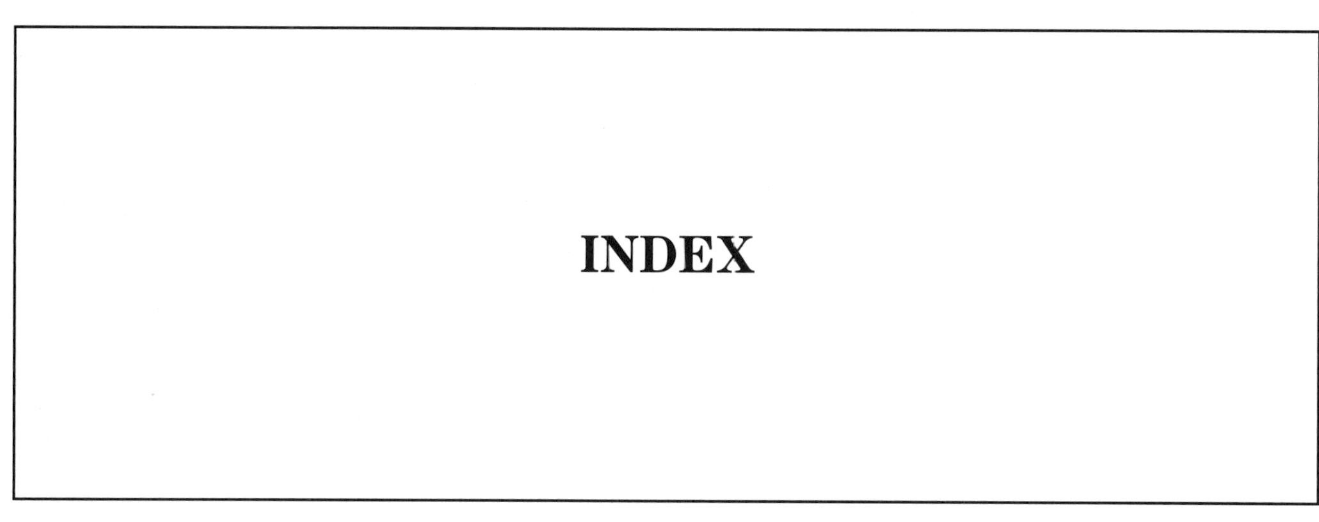

INDEX

INDEX